Punished
by
Rewards

The Trouble With Gold Stars, Incentive Plans, A's, Praise, and Other Bribes

ALFIE KOHN

REPLICA BOOKS

A DIVISION OF BAKER & TAYLOR
BRIDGEWATER, NJ

FIRST REPLICA BOOKS EDITION, MAY 1999

Published by Replica Books, a division of Baker & Taylor,
1200 Route 22 East, Bridgewater, NJ 08807

Replica Books is a trademark of Baker & Taylor

Biographical Note

This Replica books edition, first published in 1999, is an
unabridged republication of the work first published by
Houghton Mifflin, Boston in 1993
Reprinted by special arrangement with
Houghton Mifflin Company

Baker & Taylor Cataloging-in-Publication Data

Kohn, Alfie.
Punished by rewards : the trouble with gold stars,
incentive plans, A's, praise, and other bribes / Alfie
Kohn. —1st Replica Books ed.
p. cm.
ISBN 0735101388
Originally published: Boston : Houghton Mifflin, 1993.
Includes bibliographical references and index.
1. Reward (Psychology) 2. Motivation (Psychology) 3.
Behaviorism (Psychology) I. Title.
BF505.R48 K65 1999
153.8'5—dc 21

Manufactured in the United States of America

"Once again, Alfie Kohn destroys a universal myth — this time convincingly exposing the destructive effects of using rewards to control children and adults. Every parent, teacher, and manager should read this book — and hurry."

— Thomas Gordon, Founder of
Parent Effectiveness Training (P.E.T.)

"Unorthodox, occasionally utopian, revolutionary in its implications, this eye-opening critique of behaviorist reward-and-punishment psychology will challenge and enlighten."

— *Publishers Weekly*

"Alfie Kohn opens a new world of living, helping the reader to clarify the heavy losses from reward — and to replace costly practices with better ones."

— W. Edwards Deming,
Management Consultant

"A clear and compelling challenge to some of our most cherished assumptions about what makes people tick. *Punished by Rewards* will be relevant to managers, teachers, and parents — and unnerving to those who rely on the carrot and stick."

— Richard M. Ryan, Professor of Psychology,
University of Rochester

"Kohn, arguing that . . . [rewards] kill people's desire to do their best, . . . is able to back up his criticism of our motivational practices with solid, exhaustive evidence."

— *Los Angeles Times*

"Wonderfully clear, provocative, and satisfying. Alfie Kohn's groundbreaking exploration of the harmful effects of rewards should be mandatory reading for every parent and teacher."

— Adele Faber, coauthor, *How to Talk So Kids
Will Listen and Listen So Kids Will Talk*

To Alisa

CONTENTS

PREFACE

I came very close to failing Introduction to Psychology. This was at a school, you should understand, where the word *psychology* meant "the experimental study of animal physiology and behavior," and the only thing we students were required to do, apart from sitting through lectures, was to train caged rats to press a little bar. We reinforced them with Rice Krispies for doing this, and since they had been starved to 80 percent of normal body weight, they would have done almost anything for a little cereal.

I was successful, then, in carrying out the assignment, but less successful in figuring out the reason I was doing it. In a rather sophomoric act of rebellion (which was only appropriate given that I was in my second year of college at the time), I turned in a lab report written from the rat's point of view. The report described how, merely by pressing a bar, it had trained a college student to engage in breakfast-feeding behavior.* The instructor was not amused, and as I say, I barely passed the course. But that didn't stop me from immediately writing a parody of a psychology journal article for the school paper. I had the article's author claiming a 100 percent success rate in conditioning his rats to avoid pressing Lever B (which caused a three-hundred-pound anvil to drop suddenly from the top of the cage), proudly noting that not a single rat had touched that lever more than once.

In retrospect, I think it can fairly be said that I did not take well to behaviorism when first introduced to it. Nor did it grow on me as the years went by. By the time I had moved to Cambridge, home of B. F. Skinner, I decided it was time to ask him some of the questions that I had furiously scrawled in my copies of his books. I invited him

---

*Only much later did I learn that essentially the same joke had appeared decades earlier in the form of a cartoon (much beloved by behaviorists with a sense of humor) in the Columbia University newspaper.

to come speak to a class I was teaching and, to my surprise, he agreed and even gamely smiled for the Instamatics held by awed students.

A few months later I hit on the idea of writing a profile of Professor Skinner for a magazine, which gave me the opportunity to interview him twice more. In these sessions he patiently answered all my questions. I found myself admiring the fact that while his age had dulled his eyesight and hearing, it had not muted his evangelical fervor for behaviorism. (Excerpts from those interviews are reprinted in Appendix A of this book.)

Eventually I recovered from my preoccupation with Skinner's ideas, but then only to become increasingly concerned about the popular version of behaviorism, whereby we try to solve problems by offering people a goody if they do what we want. When, for example, I began to discover in my researches an extensive collection of evidence demonstrating that competition holds us back from doing our best work, it soon became clear that one of the reasons for its surprising failure is its status as an extrinsic motivator — a Rice Krispie, if you will. Later, investigating the question of altruism, I found studies showing that rewarding children for their generosity is a spectacularly unsuccessful way of promoting that quality.

Gradually it began to dawn on me that our society is caught in a whopping paradox. We complain loudly about such things as the sagging productivity of our workplaces, the crisis of our schools, and the warped values of our children. But the very strategy we use to solve those problems — dangling rewards like incentive plans and grades and candy bars in front of people — is partly responsible for the fix we're in. We are a society of loyal Skinnerians, unable to think our way out of the box we have reinforced ourselves into.

I headed back to the libraries and found scores of studies documenting the failure of pop behaviorism, studies whose existence remains unknown to all but a few social psychologists. No wonder there had never been a book written for a general audience that showed how rewards undermine our efforts to teach students or manage workers or raise children — much less a broader critique that looked at all three arenas. This is what I set out to write, well aware that such a challenge to conventional thinking would be even more unsettling than a lab report written from the rat's perspective.

Of this book's twelve chapters, the first six lay out the central argument. Chapter 1 briefly reviews the behaviorist tradition, the prevalence of pop behaviorism in our society, and some reasons for its widespread acceptance. Chapter 2 weighs arguments about the intrinsic desirability of rewarding people, first challenging the claim that doing so is morally or logically required, and then proposing that there is actually something objectionable about the practice.

Chapter 3 moves from philosophical arguments to practical consequences, summarizing the research evidence showing that rewards simply do not work to promote lasting behavior change or to enhance performance; in fact, they often make things worse. Then, in chapters 4 and 5, I explain why this is true, offering five key reasons for the failure of rewards, all of which amount to serious criticisms of the practice apart from their effects on performance. Chapter 6 examines one particular reward that few of us would ever think to criticize: praise.

The second half of the book examines the effect of rewards, and alternatives to them, with respect to the three issues I've mentioned: employees' performance, students' learning, and children's behavior. This part of the book is arranged so that readers primarily interested in only one of these topics won't have to wade through discussions of the other two. Workplace issues are discussed in chapters 7 and 10, educational issues in chapters 8 and 11, and the question of children's behavior and values (which is relevant to teachers as well as parents) in chapters 9 and 12. Serious readers will find that the endnotes provide not only citations for the studies and quotations but additional thoughts, qualifications, and discussion of the issues raised in the text.

Because this project is both ambitious and controversial, the only sensible thing to do at this point is try to place some of the blame for my conclusions on the people who helped me. I was first introduced to research on the detrimental effects of rewards (particularly with respect to creativity) by Teresa Amabile. My views on raising and teaching children have been mightily influenced by the wisdom of Eric Schaps and Marilyn Watson. I continue to take advantage of every chance I get to exchange ideas with these three people, all of whom I consider friends.

I have also spent hours badgering a number of other writers and researchers, picking their brains, challenging their ideas and inviting them to reciprocate. For some reason they agreed to this, even though most of them didn't know me. I'm very grateful to Rich Ryan, Barry Schwartz, John Nicholls, Ed Deci, Mark Lepper, Carole Ames, and the late B. F. Skinner (who, of course, would have been appalled by the result). Friends who have pressed me to think harder about these issues over the years include Lisa Lahey, Fred Hapgood, Sarah Wernick, and Alisa Harrigan.

An entirely different commitment of time and energy was involved in reading and criticizing drafts of my chapters. Here profuse thanks are due to Eric Schaps, Teresa Amabile, Alisa Harrigan, Phil Korman, John Nicholls, Carole Ames, Ed Deci, and most of all, to three people who took the time to read virtually the entire manuscript, offering one incisive comment after another: Barry Schwartz, Rich Ryan, and Bill Greene. Bill, who has done this for me four times now, has long since gone beyond the call of duty or friendship. Actually, *you* ought to be thanking him since he has spared you from having to read my first drafts.

Finally, let me acknowledge the assistance and support provided by Ruth Hapgood and Betsy Lerner, my editors, and John Ware, my agent, as well as all the people who, having heard me speak about rewards, asked hard questions that forced me to rethink my critique, refine my presentation, and reconsider the evidence. They've done me a great service by challenging some of my assumptions. I hope I can return the favor.

· *Part One* ·

THE CASE
AGAINST REWARDS

~ 1 ~

SKINNER-BOXED:
The Legacy of Behaviorism

For the anthropomorphic view of the rat, American psychology substituted a rattomorphic view of man.
— Arthur Koestler, *The Act of Creation*

THERE IS A TIME to admire the grace and persuasive power of an influential idea, and there is a time to fear its hold over us. The time to worry is when the idea is so widely shared that we no longer even notice it, when it is so deeply rooted that it feels to us like plain common sense. At the point when objections are not answered anymore because they are no longer even raised, we are not in control: we do not have the idea; it has us.

This book is about an idea that has attained just such a status in our society. The idea is that the best way to get something done is to provide a reward to people when they act the way we want them to. Scholars have debated the meaning and traced the development of the intellectual tradition known as behaviorism. What interests me, though, is the popular (or pop) incarnation of this doctrine, the version that lives in our collective consciousness and affects what we do every day.

The core of pop behaviorism is "Do this and you'll get that." The wisdom of this technique is very rarely held up for inspection; all that is open to question is what exactly people will receive and under what circumstances it will be promised and delivered. We take for granted that this is the logical way to raise children, teach students, and manage employees. We promise bubble gum to a five-year-old if he keeps quiet in the supermarket. We dangle an A before a teenager to get her to study harder. We hold out the possibility of a Hawaiian vacation for a salesman who sells enough of the company's product.

It will not take more than a few paragraphs to make the case that we are deeply committed to this way of thinking and behaving. But my aim is considerably more ambitious. I want to argue that there is something profoundly wrong-headed about this doctrine — that its assumptions are misleading and the practices it generates are both intrinsically objectionable and counterproductive. This last contention in particular, that from a purely pragmatic point of view pop behaviorism usually fails to produce the consequences we intended, takes up most of the pages that follow.

To offer such an indictment is not to suggest that there is something wrong with most of the things that are used as rewards. It is not bubble gum itself that is the problem, nor money, nor love and attention. The rewards themselves are in some cases innocuous and in other cases indispensable. What concerns me is the practice of using these things *as* rewards. To take what people want or need and offer it on a contingent basis in order to control how they act — this is where the trouble lies. Our attention is properly focused, in other words, not on "that" (the thing desired) but on the requirement that one must *do this in order to get* that.

My premise here is that rewarding people for their compliance is not "the way the world works," as many insist. It is not a fundamental law of human nature. It is but one way of thinking and speaking, of organizing our experience and dealing with others. It may seem natural to us, but it actually reflects a particular ideology that can be questioned. I believe that it is long past time for us to do so. The steep price we pay for our uncritical allegiance to the use of rewards is what makes this story not only intriguing but also deeply disconcerting.

Pigeons and Rodents and Dogs

Rewards were in use long before a theory was devised to explain and systematize their practice. John B. Watson suggested that behaviorism, of which he is known as the father, began with a series of lectures he gave at Columbia University in 1912. But a summary statement very similar to "Do this and you'll get that" — the so-called Law of Effect, which states that behavior leading to a positive consequence will be repeated — was set out by psychologist Edward Thorndike back in 1898.[1] What's more,

• One year before Watson's lectures, Frederick W. Taylor published his famous book, *The Principles of Scientific Management,* which described how tasks at a factory should be broken into parts, each assigned to a worker according to a precise plan, with financial rewards meted out to encourage maximum efficiency in production.[2]

• A full century earlier, a system developed in England for managing the behavior of schoolchildren assigned some students to monitor others and distributed tickets (redeemable for toys) to those who did what they were supposed to do.*

• For as long as animals have been domesticated, people have been using rudimentary incentive plans to train their pets.

In short, pop behaviorism might be said to predate and underlie behaviorism proper, rather than the other way around. But a few words about the more academic version, and the remarkable beliefs of its founders, will help us understand just what is involved when rewards are offered in everyday life.

Survivors of introductory psychology courses will recall that there are two major varieties of learning theory: classical conditioning (identified with Pavlov's dogs) and operant, or instrumental, conditioning (identified with Skinner's rats). Classical conditioning begins with the observation that some things produce natural responses: Rover salivates when he smells meat. By pairing an artificial stimulus with the natural one — say, ringing a bell when the steak appears — Rover comes to associate the two. Voilà — a response has been conditioned: the bell alone is now sufficient to elicit dog drool.†

Operant conditioning, by contrast, is concerned with how an action may be controlled by a stimulus that comes after it rather than before it. When a reward — Skinner preferred the term "reinforcement"[4] — follows a behavior, that behavior is likely to be repeated. A good deal of research has refined and embellished this straightforward principle, focusing on such issues as how to time these rewards for best effect. But Skinnerian theory basically codifies and bestows solemn scientific names on something familiar to all of us: "Do this and you'll get that" will lead an organism to do "this" again.

Virtually everyone who has thought about the matter agrees that both of these principles are useful for describing how some learning takes place. There is no shortage of familiar examples to flesh out the concepts. Anyone who has ever heard a toilet flush while taking a shower and immediately jumped backward provides a living illustra-

---

*This plan, similar to what would later be called a "token economy" program of behavior modification, was adopted by the first public school in New York City in the early years of the nineteenth century. It was eventually abandoned because, in the view of the school's trustees, the use of rewards "fostered a mercenary spirit" and "engendered strifes and jealousies."[3]

†Actually, Pavlov did not set out to investigate laws of behavior. He was studying the physiology of digestion when he noticed, at first to his annoyance, that the dog in his laboratory was drooling before being able to smell any meat.

tion of how one stimulus (a flushing sound) can come to be associated with another (scalding water). Anyone who has ever watched a child settle down in a hurry when promised a treat for doing so knows that rewards can affect behavior.

This book is more concerned with the second sort of learning, operant conditioning. To begin with, though, it focuses on a set of beliefs about this phenomenon and, by implication, about human beings. Skinnerians are not only interested in figuring out how rewards work; they are apt to argue that virtually everything we do — indeed, who we are — can be explained in terms of the principle of reinforcement. This is the essence of behaviorism, and it is the point of departure for our investigation.

B. F. Skinner could be described as a man who conducted most of his experiments on rodents and pigeons and wrote most of his books about people. This fact did not give him pause, because people to him were different from other species only in the degree of their sophistication. As a behaviorist sees it, you are more complex than a pigeon (in large part because you have vocal cords), but the theory of learning that explains how a bird trapped in a laboratory apparatus called a Skinner box comes to peck repeatedly at a disk also suffices to explain how you and I come to understand symbolism. "Man is an animal different from other animals only in the types of behavior he displays," Watson announced on the very first page of *Behaviorism*,[5] the book that convinced Skinner to become a psychologist. Thus it is that behaviorists speak sweepingly of how "organisms" learn.

For most of us, the existence of uniquely human capacities would raise serious questions about this theory. But Burrhus Frederic Skinner, who died in 1990 at the age of eighty-six, was not most people. One of the first things you realize when reading his books is that it is hard to offer an unfair caricature of the man's views. It is also difficult to use the technique of reductio ad absurdum in challenging them. Critics have exclaimed, "But if that's true, then here's the [obviously ludicrous] conclusion that follows." And instead of backpedaling and becoming flustered, Skinner would nod and cheerfully say, "Right you are." For example, he insisted that organisms (including us, remember) are nothing more than "repertoires of behaviors," and these behaviors can be fully explained by outside forces he called "environmental contingencies." "A person is not an originating agent; he is a locus, a point at which many genetic and environmental conditions come together in a joint effect."[6] But this would seem to imply that there is no "self" as we usually use the term, would it not? Yes indeed, replied Skinner.

But surely Fred Skinner the man — not the scientist, but the fellow who ate his breakfast and told a good joke and became lonely sometimes — surely *he* was a self. Amazingly, poignantly, he said no. In the epilogue to Skinner's memoirs we read:

> I am sometimes asked, "Do you think of yourself as you think of the organisms you study?" The answer is yes. So far as I know, my behavior at any given moment has been nothing more than the product of my genetic endowment, my personal history, and the current setting. . . . If I am right about human behavior, I have written the autobiography of a nonperson.[7]

Sure enough, over the course of four hundred pages, the book gives the impression that someone else is telling the story — someone who doesn't care much about him, in fact. (His mother's death is related without feeling, and the process of raising his two daughters is described as if it were one of Frederick Taylor's efficiency studies.) This uncanny detachment permeated his life. "When I finished *Beyond Freedom and Dignity*," Skinner once said, "I had a very strange feeling that I hadn't even written the book. . . . [It] just naturally came out of my behavior and not because of anything called a 'me' or an 'I' inside."*

Once the self has been dispatched, it requires only a minor mopping-up operation to finish off the features of being human that we treasure, such as creativity, love, morality, and freedom. Talking, after all, is only "verbal behavior," and thinking is only silent talking.[8] So it is not much of a reach to reduce creativity to a series of novel behaviors selected by the environment. "Beethoven," Skinner said (or verbally behaved),

> was someone who, when he was very young, acquired all the available music at the time, and then, because of things that happened to him personally as accidents and variations, he introduced new things which paid off beautifully. So he went on doing them, and he wrote because he was highly reinforced for writing. . . .

---

*This comment and other unattributed quotations that follow are taken from a series of interviews I conducted with Skinner in 1983 and 1984. Excerpts from those interviews are contained in Appendix A.

And love? Brace yourself. When two people meet,

> one of them is nice to the other and that predisposes the other to be nice to him, and that makes him even more likely to be nice. It goes back and forth, and it may reach the point at which they are very highly disposed to do nice things to the other and not to hurt. And I suppose that is what would be called "being in love."[9]

Morality, for Skinner and other behaviorists, has been reduced to the question of whether society deems an action appropriate or inappropriate, adaptive or maladaptive; it is never inherently right or wrong.

> To make a value judgment by calling something good or bad is to classify it in terms of its reinforcing effects. . . . The only good things are positive reinforcers, and the only bad things are negative reinforcers. . . . "You should (you ought to) tell the truth" . . . we might translate . . . as follows: "If you are reinforced by the approval of your fellow men, you will be reinforced when you tell the truth."[10]

Philosophers distinguish between this nonmoral use of the word *good* (as in "It's good to take out the trash before the bag gets too full") and a moral use ("It's good to tell the truth"). Skinner eliminated the latter altogether, collapsing it into the former.

His view of freedom, meanwhile, is better known since this is one of the two concepts behaviorism helps us to move beyond, according to the title of his best-selling book published in 1971. Some years ago, Skinner accepted my invitation to give a guest lecture at a class I taught. At the conclusion of his remarks, I couldn't resist a bit of flippant humor. "We certainly want to thank the environmental contingencies responsible for your being here this afternoon," I said. He didn't laugh. Smiling courteously, he replied, "I'm very glad they occurred."

Skinner believed that he had "chosen" to visit my class — and that all of us "choose" our actions — about as much as a rock in an avalanche chooses where to land. But then, the notion that a self freely decides is not likely to make much sense to a man who has repudiated the very idea of a self in the first place. If the rest of us presumptuously persist in talking about "intending" to do something, it is either because we derive comfort from thinking of ourselves as being in control or because we are ignorant, individually and collectively, of the forces that actually determine our behavior. Freedom's just another word for something left to learn: it is the way we refer to the ever-diminishing set of phenomena for which science has yet to specify the causes.[11]

And now we have the key to understanding the essence of behaviorism: it proceeds from a boundless faith in science — and specifically, a narrowly defined version of science that never caught up with modern physics — to tell us everything we need to know. This is described by some philosophers as "scientism," by which is meant the assumption that all true knowledge is scientific knowledge. Human beings are to be analyzed in precisely the same way as we would analyze "a chemical compound or the way a plant grows," said Watson. If there are parts of our humanity beyond the grasp of science, so much the worse for those parts. Anything that is not observable, testable, and quantifiable either is not worth our time or does not really exist. Psychologists who talk about consciousness put Watson in mind of "the ancient days of superstition and magic."[12] If anything, Skinner was even more emphatic in articulating these ideas.

The consequence of patterning psychology after the natural sciences is predictable: psychology's subject matter (us) is reduced to the status of the subject matter of physics and chemistry (things). When we try to explain *things*, we appeal to causes. When most of us try to account for human behavior, though, we talk about reasons; a conscious decision, rather than an automatic response to some outside force, usually plays a role. But for Skinner, our actions, too, can be completely described in terms of causes. Freedom is just an illusion. Remember, there is no "self" to *be* free: what we are is nothing other than what we do. This is the belief that gives behaviorism its name.

It is not only academic behaviorists who believe that only measurable behavior is real. A few years ago, a group of businessmen accepted a researcher's offer of a free meal in exchange for their comments on her new psychological questionnaire. One of the men, on his third cigarette before dinner, was scornful of a question that referred to a "feeling of trust" in the workplace. He said he didn't understand what the word *trust* meant, apart from its most literal denotation: "I 'trust' that you are writing down what I'm saying right now." Later he spoke up to object to another item, this one asking whether "failure is acceptable if a good effort has been made." This, he declared, was a contradiction in terms; all that matters is measurable outcome, and if that is judged a failure, the effort by definition was not good enough. In fact, if it can't be quantified, it's not real.[13]

This view reflects a thoroughly American sensibility. It is no accident that behaviorism is this country's major contribution to the field of psychology, or that the only philosophical movement native to the United States is pragmatism. We are a nation that prefers acting to thinking, and practice to theory; we are suspicious of intellectuals, worshipful of technology, and fixated on the bottom line. We define ourselves by numbers — take-home pay and cholesterol counts, percentiles (how much does your baby weigh?) and standardized test scores (how much does your child know?). By contrast, we are uneasy with intangibles and unscientific abstractions such as a sense of well-being or an intrinsic motivation to learn.

A thorough criticism of scientism would take us too far afield. But it is important to understand that practice does rest on theory, whether or not that theory has been explicitly identified. The overwhelming majority of teachers, according to one survey, are unable to name or describe a theory of learning that underlies what they do in the classroom,[14] but what they do — what any of us does — is no less informed by theoretical assumptions just because these assumptions are invisible. Behind the practice of presenting a colorful dinosaur sticker to a first grader who stays silent on command is a theory that embodies distinct assumptions about the nature of knowledge, the possibility of choice, and what it means to be a human being. If the premises of behaviorism trouble us once they have been laid bare, perhaps that is an invitation to question the specific practices that rest on those premises.

Is it unfair to indict all of behaviorism on the basis of what Watson and Skinner had to say? Yes and no. It is true that they were more extreme than subsequent researchers and therapists on certain issues, such as the status of an inner life. Feelings, attitudes, and intentions were suspect to them — useless for explaining anything people do, completely determined by external factors, largely irrelevant to their version of psychology. In many intellectual movements, the pioneers are unreconstructed and immoderate; it is left to the next generation to temper and qualify and blend in what is useful from other theories. To some extent, behaviorism did move on while Skinner stood still. Long before his death, he was spinning in his house from what was being offered under the name of behavior therapy. (In his last paper, completed the night before he died, Skinner reiterated that "there is no place in a scientific analysis of behavior for a mind or self.")[15]

But if more restrained and less quotable behaviorists have trimmed off the rough edges of Skinnerian psychology, they are carrying on a tradition that is fundamentally consistent with what I have been describing, at least with respect to the issues that matter most. They may have fastened on the finding that we also learn from watching other people receive rewards, or that attitudes as well as behaviors can be reinforced, but these are not decisive departures from Skinner with regard to what concerns us here.

More important, *we* can depart from Skinner at this point and begin to address ourselves to contemporary pay-for-performance plans in the workplace or the technique of pasting a gold star on a chart each time a child complies with her parents' demands. To repeat, this book is intended as a critique of these sorts of practices, of pop behaviorism rather than of Skinner, so whether the vision of a seamlessly controlled utopia like Walden Two chills you is beside the point. There is reason enough to be concerned once we reflect seriously on the implications of "Do this and you'll get that."

Bring In the Reinforcements

Some social critics have a habit of overstating the popularity of whatever belief or practice they are keen to criticize, perhaps for dramatic effect. There is little danger of doing that here because it is hard to imagine how one could exaggerate the extent of our saturation in pop behaviorism. Regardless of political persuasion or social class, whether a Fortune 500 CEO or a preschool teacher, we are immersed in this doctrine; it is as American as rewarding someone with apple pie.

To induce students to learn, we present stickers, stars, certificates, awards, trophies, membership in elite societies, and above all, grades. If the grades are good enough, some parents then hand out bicycles or cars or cash, thereby offering what are, in effect, rewards for rewards. Educators are remarkably imaginative in inventing new, improved versions of the same basic idea. At one high school in Georgia, for example, students were given gold ID cards if they had an A average, silver cards for a B average, and plain white cards if they didn't measure up — until objections were raised to what was widely viewed as a caste system.[16] This objection has not deterred a number of schools across the country from using a program that not only issues color-coded ID cards but also gets local merchants to offer discounts to students on the basis of their grade point average.[17]

A few years ago, some executive at the Pizza Hut restaurant chain decided — let us assume for entirely altruistic reasons — that the company should sponsor a program to encourage children to read more. The strategy for reaching this goal: bribery. For every so many books that a child reads in the "Book It!" program, the teacher presents a certificate redeemable for free pizza. This program and others like it are still in operation all over the country.

But why stop with edible rewards? Representative Newt Gingrich congratulated West Georgia College for paying third graders two dollars for each book they read. "Adults are motivated by money — why not kids?" he remarked, apparently managing to overcome the purported conservative aversion to throwing money at problems.[18] Nor is the use of rewards confined to a particular ideology. Proposals to rescue American education, offered by public officials and corporate chieftains (the latter having been permitted a uniquely privileged role in this discussion), are uniformly behavioristic, regardless of whether they come from liberal Democrats or conservative Republicans. Politicians may quibble over how much money to spend, or whether to allow public funds to follow students to private schools, but virtually no one challenges the fundamental carrot-and-stick approach to motivation: promise educators pay raises for success or threaten their job security for failure — typically on the basis of their students' standardized test scores — and it is assumed that educational excellence will follow.

To induce children to "behave" (that is, do what we want), we rely on precisely the same theory of motivation — the only one we know — by hauling out another bag of goodies. At home, we offer extra time in front of the television or a special dessert or money when children comply with our requests. At school, teachers promise extra recess or special parties for obedient classes. In an Indiana elementary school, children demonstrating exemplary docility in the cafeteria are rewarded with a fancy dress-up meal.[19] In a Texas junior high school, "excellent behavior" (defined as "any . . . act that the teacher deems appropriate") earns a "Good as Gold" card that entitles the holder to movie passes, T-shirts, or other prizes.[20]

These examples can be multiplied by the thousands, and they are not restricted to children. Any time we wish to encourage or discourage certain behaviors — getting people to lose weight or quit smoking, for instance — the method of choice is behavioral manipulation. Thus, when several Planned Parenthood chapters wanted to get serious about teenage pregnancy, they naturally reached for the reinforcements, in this case by paying young mothers a dollar for every day they avoided getting pregnant again. "The Federal Government pays farmers not to plant crops," reasoned the psychologist who came up with the idea. "Why shouldn't we pay teenagers not to have babies?"[21]

American workplaces, meanwhile, are enormous Skinner boxes with parking lots. From the factory worker laboring for piecework pay to top executives prodded by promises of stock options, from special privileges accorded to Employees of the Month to salespeople working on commission, the recipe always calls for behaviorism in full-strength concentrate. Depending on the size and type of the organizations surveyed and the way the question is framed, recent estimates of the number of U.S. companies using some form of incentive or merit-pay plan range from 75 to 94 percent, and many of these programs apparently have just been adopted during the last few years.[22] The livelihood of a veritable herd of consultants is based on devising fresh formulas for computing bonuses or dreaming up new money substitutes to dangle in front of employees: vacations, banquets, special parking spaces, cute plaques — the list of variations on a single, simple model of motivation is limitless. To page through business books today is to encounter repeated assertions such as this one: "What gets measured, gets produced. What gets rewarded, gets produced again."[23] Magazines and journals offer more of the same. One article, entitled "If Employees Perform, Then Reward 'Em," declares flatly, "The more money you offer someone, the harder he or she will work."[24]

No survey of the pervasiveness of pop behaviorism would be complete without mention of the one practice that is common to all arenas (school, work, and home) and used for all conceivable objectives (enhancing learning, improving productivity, and changing people's attitudes or behavior). I am speaking of praise, which Skinner called "the greatest tool in behavior modification." Books and seminars on parenting and classroom management urge adults to catch children doing something right and praise them for it — one article reminded mothers that "no matter how much [praise] you give, you can always give more"[25] — and corporate managers are offered similar advice. Even people who have concerns about piling on tangible rewards show no hesitation about the indiscriminate use of verbal rewards, which are, of course, another manifestation of the same principle. Approval or pleasure is often not merely expressed but doled out deliberately, conditionally, as part of a calculated strategy to shape others' behavior. (I will have more to say about the distinction between useful positive feedback and praise as an instrument of manipulation in chapter 6.)

Behind the Appeal of Behaviorism

Like most things that we and the people around us do constantly, the use of rewards has come to seem so natural and inevitable that merely to pose the question, Why are we doing this? can strike us as perplexing — and also, perhaps, a little unsettling. On general principle, it is a good idea to challenge ourselves in this way about anything we have come to take for granted; the more habitual, the more valuable this line of inquiry.

It is not by accident that pop behaviorism has come to suffuse our lives. There are identifiable reasons to account for its popularity, beginning with the belief systems already in place which it complements. One of these I mentioned earlier: our pragmatism, and specifically our tendency to favor practical techniques for getting the job done as opposed to getting bogged down with theories and reasons. A nation of busy pioneers and entrepreneurs has no time for figuring out the source of a problem; much more compatible with the American spirit is a simple declaration that would seem to assure results: "Do this and you'll get that."

Promising goodies to people we want to change seems comfortably familiar to us because other traditions and beliefs are based on a similar way of thinking. It may seem a bit of a stretch to compare pay-for-performance plans to religious notions of redemption or enlightenment or karma, which are decidedly different from behaviorism, but the if-then contingency is just as salient in the latter set of ideas. We have been taught that ethical conduct will be rewarded and evil acts punished, even if it does not happen in this lifetime: "When thou makest a feast, call the poor, the maimed, the lame, the blind: And thou shalt be . . . recompensed at the resurrection of the just" (Luke 14:13–14). We have also been taught that good acts or hard work *should* be rewarded, and this position, as I will argue later, leads some people to incline toward pop behaviorism regardless of the results it produces.

Ironically, rewards and punishments not only lie at the core of faith but are central to our idea of rationality as well, particularly as it makes its presence felt in economic choices. Rational decision-makers, by definition, are said to seek what is pleasurable and to avoid what is aversive or costly. Rationality, in turn, is central to what it means to be human, at least to many Western thinkers. A number of writers have recently challenged both steps of this argument, but pop behaviorism makes intuitive sense to us as a result of the assumptions built into our economic system.

In fact, behavioral psychology and orthodox economic theory have established a sort of mutual admiration society that flatters both fields, but only by creating a truncated picture of the human being whose actions they seek to analyze. On the first pages of their text-books, economists often nod in the direction of behaviorism to justify their fundamental assumptions about what motivates consumers or workers. Psychologists in turn assume that the process of weighing costs and benefits that describes how we go about purchasing an appliance is also what we are doing when talking with a lover. Among the features common to both disciplines, moreover, is the assumption that the reward-seeking, punishment-avoiding impulse that drives all our behavior is necessarily and exclusively dictated by self-interest.[26]

What we believe in other contexts, then, from religion to economics, may pave the way for behaviorism by making us receptive to its premises. But what we see and do is also critical. What we see from our earliest days is the use of the carrot-and-stick model of motivation; most of us were raised this way, and it is easy to swallow such theories whole and pass along the practices to our own children. Many new parents are startled when they open their mouths and hear their own parents' expressions come out, right down to the inflection. But even those who want to know how their mothers managed to sneak into their larynxes may not recognize how they have also absorbed basic assumptions from which their approach to raising children derives.

Pop behaviorism is perpetuated through the example of other significant individuals in our lives, too, including teachers and powerful people in the workplace. Frederick Herzberg observed that managers who emphasize rewards and punishments "offer their own motivational characteristics as the pattern to be instilled in their subordinates. They become the template from which the new recruit to industry learns his motivational pattern."[27] More generally, if we constantly see people being manipulated with rewards, we may come not only to accept this as natural but also to assume the tactic can be generalized: if we pay adults for working, why not children for reading? And when we reward children, they may absorb the message that the way to get other people to do what they want is to bribe them.[28]

Of course, our own experience with the use of rewards also helps to explain why we continue to use them. In a very limited sense — and just how limited is the subject of much of the rest of this book — rewards and punishments do work. In the short term, we can get people to do any number of things by making it worth their while. If I offer you an inducement that you find sufficiently rewarding, you will act in ways you would not otherwise consider. (Children, in fact, love to entertain themselves by pondering just how much they would have to be paid to perform various unappetizing feats.) If I make the reward contingent on your not only doing what I want but doing it immediately or quickly or repeatedly, you may well comply. Rewards, like punishments, are very effective at producing compliance.

If you are a parent who has found that your children promptly make their beds when you promise them ice cream cones for doing so, you may conclude that rewards are effective. You may even decide that it is unrealistic to expect children to do such things if you don't use them. Research by Ann Boggiano and her colleagues has shown that American adults, including parents, are firm believers in rewards. Typically, it is assumed that rewards will increase children's interest in an academic assignment or their commitment to altruistic behavior. Even when presented with data indicating that the reverse is true, 125 college students in one experiment continued to insist that rewards are effective.[29] (As we shall see, some research psychologists who champion behaviorism are just as likely to wave away data that contradict what they are sure is true.)

Attend to your experience and you will notice not only that rewards work (in this very circumscribed sense), but also that they are marvelously easy to use. In the middle of a lecture on behaviorism a few years ago in Idaho, one teacher in the audience blurted out, "But stickers are so easy!" This is absolutely true. If she finds herself irritated that children in her class are talking, it takes courage and thought to consider whether it is really reasonable to expect them to sit quietly for so long — or to ask herself whether the problem might be her own discomfort with noise.[30] It takes effort and patience to explain respectfully to six-year-olds the reason for her request. It takes talent and time to help them develop the skill of self-control and the commitment to behave responsibly. But it takes no courage, no thought, no effort, no patience, no talent, and no time to announce, "Keep quiet and here's what you'll get. . . ."

Exactly the same is true in the office. Good management, like good teaching, is a matter of solving problems and helping people do their best. This too takes time and effort and thought and patience and talent. Dangling a bonus in front of employees does not. In many workplaces, incentive plans are used as a substitute for management: pay is made contingent on performance and everything else is left to take care of itself.[31]

Another way of framing this issue is to say that while authority figures can unilaterally dispense rewards, they must acknowledge their lack of absolute control with respect to things like motivation. "Management can provide or withhold salary increments authoritatively, while it can only create conditions (or fail to) for individuals to achieve satisfaction of their higher-level needs," as Douglas McGregor put it.[32] The same thing is true in the classroom or at home: there is comfort in sticking to what we have power over, and the use of punishments and rewards is nothing if not an exercise of power. All told, this may be the single most powerful reason to explain the popularity of pop behaviorism: it is seductively simple to apply.

But doesn't the widespread use of rewards suggest (contrary to what I have been promising to show in later chapters) that they work? Why would a failed strategy be preferred? The answer to this will become clearer, I think, when I explain exactly how and why they fail to work. For now, it will be enough to answer in temporal terms: the negative effects appear over a longer period of time, and by then their connection to the reward may not be at all obvious. The result is that rewards keep getting used.[33]

By the same token (so to speak), it rarely dawns on us that while people may seem to respond to the goodies we offer, the very need to keep offering these treats to elicit the same behavior may offer a clue about their long-term effects (or lack of them). Whacking my computer when I first turn it on may somehow help the operating system to engage, but if I have to do that every morning, I will eventually get the idea that I am not addressing the real problem. If I have to whack it harder and harder, I might even start to suspect that my quick fix is making the problem worse.

Rewards don't bring about the changes we are hoping for, but the point here is also that something else is going on: *the more rewards are used, the more they seem to be needed.* The more often I promise you a goody to do what I want, the more I cause you to respond to, and even to require, these goodies. As we shall see, the other, more substantive reasons for you to do your best tend to evaporate, leaving you with no reason to try except for obtaining a goody. Pretty soon, the provision of rewards becomes habitual because there seems to be no way to do without them. In short, the current use of rewards is due less to some fact about human nature than to the earlier use of rewards.[34] Whether or not we are conscious that this cycle exists, it may help to explain why we have spun ourselves ever deeper into the mire of behaviorism.

Here, then, we have a portrait of a culture thoroughly and unreflectively committed to the use of rewards. They offer a temptingly simple way to get people to do what we want. It is the approach we know best, in part because it likely governed how we ourselves were raised and managed. It fits neatly with other institutions and belief systems with which we are familiar. But aside from some troubling questions about the theory of behaviorism, what reason do we have for disavowing this strategy? That is the question to which we now turn.

2

IS IT RIGHT
TO REWARD?

The interest of the behaviorist in man's doings is more than the
interest of the spectator — he wants to control man's reactions as
physical scientists want to control and manipulate other natural
phenomena.
>   — John B. Watson,
>   *Behaviorism*

What a fascinating thing! Total control of a living organism!
>   — B. F. Skinner, 1983

WHEN TWO PEOPLE find themselves at odds over an issue like
capital punishment, the disagreement may concern the intrinsic right-
ness or wrongness of the policy as opposed to its empirical effects. An
opponent of the death penalty may argue, for example, that there is
something offensive about the idea of killing people in the name of
justice. Evidence regarding the effect of executions on the crime rate
probably would not be seen as relevant to this objection.

The same distinction can be made with respect to a discussion about
pop behaviorism. Separate from the question of whether rewards do
what we want them to do is the question of whether there is something
fitting or troubling about their use. Some believe it is inherently desirable to give rewards, that people *ought* to get something for what they
do quite apart from the consequences this may bring.* Others believe
there is something objectionable about the whole idea of giving rewards. Lest these opposing values get buried under a mound of studies
(and become confused with factual findings), this chapter will carefully examine each of them in turn.

---

*This position, I should note, was not taken by Skinner, nor is it offered as a rule by
other behaviorists.

Saving Room for Just Deserts

It is an integral part of the American myth that anyone who sets his mind to it can succeed, that diligence eventually pays off. It seems to follow, then, that people who do not succeed can be held responsible for their failure. Failure, after all, is prima facie evidence of not having tried hard enough. This doctrine has special appeal for those who are doing well, first because it allows them to think their blessings are deserved, and second because it spares them from having to feel too guilty about (or take any responsibility for) those who have much less.

The belief that rewards will be distributed fairly, even if it takes until the next lifetime to settle accounts, is one component of what is sometimes referred to as the "just world" view. Social psychologists have found that those who hold this position are indeed likely to assume that apparently innocent victims must have done something to deserve their fate; to face the fact that suffering is visited upon innocent people is, of course, to recognize that the world is not particularly just at all. It does not take much imagination to see where this sort of thinking can lead: one group of children, after watching a film about the Nazis, were reported to have said, "But the Jews must have been guilty or they wouldn't have been punished like that."[1]

The belief I have been describing can be summarized as follows: deserving people will be rewarded. Underpinning this idea is an even more basic and widely held premise: deserving people *should* be rewarded. In theory, these two views can be separated, but in practice the latter often drives the former. Many people assume, at least with respect to important issues, that things eventually work out the way they ought to. It is terribly unsettling, after all, to acknowledge that our society, much less life itself, is not especially fair. The sheer wish that it were can produce in some people a belief that things are, or in time will become, what they should be.

Let us look a little more closely at the idea that rewards should be bestowed on those who merit them. For many people, the moralistic corollary to this assumption is that bad things should be bestowed on, or good things withheld from, those who are undeserving. Many of us have watched people become uneasy, if not positively furious, when they believe some offense — including one committed by a child — has not been punished severely enough. Later in this book I will argue that a child's misbehavior is best construed as a "teachable moment," a problem to be solved together rather than an infraction that calls for a punitive response. I will try to show that this approach is not only more respectful and humane but also much more effective over the long haul at helping children develop a sense of responsibility. But I have seen people brush aside such arguments, sometimes becoming visibly disturbed at the prospect that a miscreant will not have to suffer any consequences for her action. *Consequences* may be a code word for punishment, and punishment may produce resentment rather than responsibility, but never mind. The important thing, on this view, is that Justice is served, and cosmic balance restored, by cracking down on a wrongdoer.*

The entirely reasonable ideal of personal responsibility has been transformed in our culture into a terror of permissiveness that extends beyond child-rearing to a general fear of social laxity.[2] We see it in outraged reactions to prisons that are judged too comfortable, or even to organizations that compensate employees on any basis other than achievement. When pay is not conditioned on performance we are sometimes said to be rewarding incompetence (or laziness) and giving some people a free lunch — a prospect that sends shudders through executive dining rooms.

When stripped of this harsh rigidity, of course, the basic idea that people should get what they deserve, which social scientists refer to as the equity principle, seems unremarkable and, indeed, so intuitively plausible as to serve for many people virtually as a definition of fairness. Rarely do we even think to question the idea that what you put in should determine what you take out.

But the value of the equity principle is not nearly as self-evident as it may seem. Once we stop to examine it, questions immediately arise as to what constitutes deservingness. Do we reward on the basis of how much effort is expended (work hard, get more goodies)? What if the result of hard work is failure? Does it make more sense, then, to reward on the basis of success (do well, get more goodies)? But "do well" by whose standards? And who is responsible for the success? Excellence is often the product of cooperation, and even individual achievement typically is built on the work of other people's earlier efforts. So who "deserves" the reward when lots of people had a hand in the performance?

---

*A popular way to express this position is to say that the offender must be made to "pay" for what he did — a locution suggesting that we often conceive of justice in economic terms.

These questions lead us gradually to the recognition that equity is only one of several ways to distribute resources. It is also possible for each person to receive an equal share of the goods — or for need to determine who gets what. Different circumstances seem to call for different criteria. Few school principals hand out more supplies to the teachers who stayed up longer the night before to finish a lesson plan; rather, they look at the size and requirements of each class. Few parents decide how much dinner to serve to each of their children on the basis of who did more for the household that day. Few policymakers and moral theorists, struggling with the knotty question of how to distribute scarce health care resources, automatically assume that the most productive contributors to society (whatever that means) should get the most care.

In short, the equity model, as social psychologist Melvin Lerner put it, "applies to only a limited range of the social encounters that are affected by the desire for justice."[3] Specifically, it is the favored mode of "impersonal, economic relations."[4] To assume that fairness always requires that people should get what they "earn" — that the law of the marketplace is the same thing as justice — is a very dubious proposition indeed. What's more, as Morton Deutsch warns, "the danger of conceiving of personal relations in terms appropriate to marketplace exchanges is that it hastens the depersonalization of personal relations by fostering the intrusion of economic values into such relations."[5]

Just as important as the realization that principles other than equity could legitimately be invoked in many situations is the fact that principles other than equity *are* invoked in many situations. If we want to predict how people will choose to distribute resources, the most important thing we need to know is what kind of relationship exists among those involved. The equity principle, not surprisingly, is more likely to be the first choice of strangers.[6] (This is why it is a little suspicious that assumptions about the universality of that principle are largely based on contrived experiments in which the subjects have never met each other before.)[7] Other factors also help to determine which principle is used. For example, cultural background matters: where people are accustomed to thinking in communal rather than individualistic terms, they are more likely to distribute rewards equally rather than on the basis of who performed better.[8] Women are more likely than men to share this preference for equality as the basis for distribution.[9] Finally, there are differences on the basis of individual personality.[10] It is interesting to reflect on what kind of person might be expected to insist that what someone gets must be based on what he produced.

Edward E. Sampson, a psychologist who frequently writes about American culture, observed that we have been led to "take equity as the natural state and deviations from it as unnatural." However, the assumption that people should be rewarded on the basis of what they have done is "not as much a psychological law about human nature as it is a psychological outcome of a culture's socialization practices."[11] This doesn't mean that it is impossible to defend the view that people who have done something should be rewarded; rather, it suggests that this view must be defended, as opposed to taken for granted as obviously true.

To this point, I have been referring to rewards as resources to be distributed, which may be an appropriate way to think about, say, what to do with a company's profit at the end of the year. But this does not accurately describe many other kinds of rewards, such as grades or gold stars or praise. Many goodies have been invented for the express purpose of rewarding certain kinds of behavior. If the equity model applies here, it cannot be assumed on the basis of rules for deciding how much to pay employees.

Not long ago, I heard a teacher in Missouri justify the practice of handing out stickers to her young students on the grounds that the children had "earned" them. This claim struck me as an attempt to deflect attention away from — perhaps to escape responsibility for — the decision she had made to frame learning as something one does in exchange for a prize rather than as something intrinsically valuable. How many stickers does a flawless spelling assignment merit? One? Ten? Why not a dollar? Or a hundred dollars? After the fact, one could claim that any reward was "earned" by the performance (or performer), but since these are not needed goods that must be handed out according to one principle or another, we must eventually recognize not only that the size of the reward is arbitrarily determined by the teacher but that the decision to give any reward reflects a theory of learning more than a theory of justice.

When such individuals are pressed on their insistence that it is simply right to reward people for what they do, it sometimes turns out that their real concern is with the results they fear would follow the abolition of rewards. One business consultant, for example, writes that he was horrified to learn about a company that allocated bonuses equally to all employees; "mediocrity would receive the same rewards as excellence," he exclaims. But as we read on, we find that what at first appears to reflect a moral stance (you should pay for what you get) is ultimately based on expectations about the consequences (you'll get what you pay for) — a very different sort of objection. His suspicion is that workers will come to ask, "Why work harder" if there is no tangible benefit to doing so?[12] This, of course, is a question that can be addressed by looking at evidence about what actually motivates people and what happens when rewards are (and are not) used.

Treating People Like Pets

As behaviorists cheerfully admit, theories about rewards and various practical programs of behavior modification are mostly based on work with rats and pigeons. The underlying assumption, according to one critic, seems to be that "the semistarved rat in the box, with virtually nothing to do but press on a lever for food, captures the essence of virtually all human behavior."[13]

But it is not only researchers who make this assumption. We join them in taking "one giant leap toward mankind"[14] when we import the principles and techniques used to train the family pet to the realm of raising children. The way we sometimes talk about (or to) our daughters and sons reflects a view of parent-child relationships quite congenial to a committed behaviorist. Discussions about how to "handle" our kids are a case in point; on reflection, this seems a rather peculiar verb to use in the context of a relationship with another human being.[15] Likewise, when we call out a hearty "Good girl!" in response to a child's performance, the most appropriate reply would seem to be *Woof!* With respect to the workplace or public policy, we talk casually about the use of "carrots and sticks," and there is food for thought here, too. Before these words came to be used as generic representations of bribes and threats, what actually stood between the carrot and the stick was, of course, a jackass.[16]

Presumably most of us do not intend to compare ourselves — or more precisely, the people to whom we are administering these inducements — to poodles or donkeys. Surely we know that human beings can reflect on rewards and develop complicated expectations and opinions about them (and about the activities for which they are being dispensed) in a way that animals cannot. Yet it is not an accident that the theory behind "Do this and you'll get that" derives from work with other species, or that behavior management is frequently described in words better suited to animals.

My claim is that pop behaviorism is by its very nature dehumanizing. But I do not mean by that word merely that we are treated or understood as being on a par with other species; this is just a symptom. In the case of Skinnerian theory, the human self has been yanked up by its roots and the person reduced to a repertoire of behaviors. It is hard to imagine what could be more dehumanizing than the removal of what defines us as human. In fact, even to suggest that we learn or work only in order to obtain rewards — an assumption held by behaviorists less extreme than Skinner — is not only inaccurate but demeaning as well.

Some observers think that to manipulate workers with incentives is to treat them like children.[17] In a way this is true, but there is something problematic about treating people of any age this way. For other critics, the more apt comparison is to how we train animals. But again, this characterization does not go far enough because the assumption that an organism's behavior is wholly dependent on, and controlled by, reinforcements has been shown to be inaccurate even for rodents. Perhaps, then, as sociologist William Foote Whyte proposed, what reward systems finally suggest is an implicit comparison to nonliving things:

> Management also seems to assume that machines and workers are alike in that they are both normally passive agents who must be stimulated by management in order to go into action. In the case of the machines, management turns on the electricity. In the case of workers, money takes the place of electricity.[18]

The behaviorist's conception of humans as passive beings whose behavior must be elicited by external motivation in the form of incentives[19] is, by any measure, outdated. Although the work done by some modern psychologists continues to rely implicitly on this assumption, more and more researchers have come to recognize that we are beings who possess natural curiosity about ourselves and our environment, who search for and overcome challenges, who try to master skills and attain competence, and who seek to reach new levels of complexity in what we learn and do. This is more true of some people than others, of course, and in the presence of a threatening or deadening environment, any of us may retreat to a strategy of damage control and minimal effort. But in general we act on the environment as much as we are acted on by it, and we do not do so simply in order to receive a reward.

Within the discipline of psychology, the passive-organism view has faded along with the influence of behavior theory itself. But in everyday life, in the workplace and the classroom and the home, this view continues to make its presence felt through the practices of pop behaviorism. To put this the other way around, our everyday practices rest on an implicit theory of human nature that fails to do us justice. When we repeatedly promise rewards to children for acting responsibly, or to students for making an effort to learn something new, or to employees for doing quality work, we are assuming that they could not or would not choose to act this way on their own. If the capacity for responsible action, the natural love of learning, and the desire to do good work are already part of who we are, then the tacit assumption to the contrary can fairly be described as dehumanizing.*

The underlying theory of human nature, however, is not the only reason that handing out rewards (or, for that matter, punishments) is dehumanizing. That description also seems to apply because the practice is, at its core, neither more nor less than a way of trying to control people. Now there are circumstances, especially where children are involved, in which it is difficult to imagine eliminating all vestiges of control. (I will say more about this later.) But anyone who is troubled by a model of human relationship founded principally on the idea of one person controlling another must ponder whether rewards are as innocuous as they are sometimes made out to be.

Clearly, punishments are harsher and more overt; there is no getting around the intent to control in "Do this or else here's what will happen to you." But rewards simply "control through seduction rather than force."[20] In the final analysis, they are not one bit less controlling since, like punishments, they are "typically used to induce or pressure people to do things they would not freely do"[21] — or rather, things that the controller believes they would not freely do. This is why one of the most important (and unsettling) things we can recognize is that the real choice for us is not between rewards and punishments but between either version of behavioral manipulation, on the one hand, and an approach that does not rely on control, on the other.[22]

In the workplace, there is no getting around the fact that "the basic purpose of merit pay is manipulative."[23] One observer more bluntly characterizes incentives as "demeaning" since the message they really convey is, "Please big daddy boss and you will receive the rewards that the boss deems appropriate."[24] The use of treats at home, mean-

---

*To the extent that we sometimes do seem to be driven by rewards, this may be attributed, at least in part, to the way pop behaviorism creates a dependence on itself (see page 17).

while, offers exactly the same message, except here "big daddy boss" may literally be Big Daddy.

Sometimes the controlling nature of rewards is too obvious to miss. Consider the so-called token economy, which is used primarily with captive, dependent populations such as patients in psychiatric hospitals or children in school. The idea — again, explicitly derived from work with laboratory animals[25] — is that when the people in charge notice the patients or children engaging in the "correct" sort of behaviors, chips or other markers are handed out that can be exchanged later for privileges or treats. Even at the height of their popularity,* these programs offended a number of people for a number of reasons.[27] But specific objections aside, it is difficult to imagine a more flagrant example of control than one person's giving another a token redeemable for candy or privileges to reward him for being "cooperative."

We don't need critics of this approach to teach us this, however; the reliance on crude control is a point made more convincingly (albeit unintentionally) by the vocal proponents of token economies. In an article for school psychologists, a pioneer of such plans writes that "children need to be reminded frequently that they are working for reinforcers" and that "a teacher must always keep in mind that the teacher is the manager of the classroom." If a child is sneaky enough to save up tokens rather than feeling driven to keep earning new ones, we are warned that "the child and not the teacher is in control" of her behavior (a prospect evidently regarded as appalling on its face). Any complaints from children who think the administration of the rewards is unfair "can be easily handled by ignoring or redirecting"; if such concerns are "simply not reinforce[d] . . . they will extinguish."[28]

Just as threats are simply a more blatant version of control than bribes are, so token economies merely exaggerate the manipulation that describes other, less systematic, applications of rewards. The point to be emphasized is that all rewards, by virtue of *being* rewards, are not attempts to influence or persuade or solve problems together, but simply to control. In fact, if a task is undertaken in response to the

---

*The first institutional token economies in the United States were developed in the 1960s; after being in vogue for perhaps a decade, their use declined to the point that few hospitals now have them in place.[26] How widely these programs are still used in schools is difficult to determine, but probably the single most popular program of classroom management (Assertive Discipline) is clearly a behavior modification plan even if it is not strictly a token economy.

contingency set up by the rewarder, "the person's initial *action* in choosing the task is constrained."[29]

This feature of rewards is much easier to understand when we are being controlled than when we are doing the controlling. This is why it is so important to imagine ourselves in the other position, to take the perspective of the person whose behavior we are manipulating. It is easy for a teacher to object to a program of merit pay — to see how patronizing it is to be bribed with extra money for doing what some administrator decides is a good job. It takes more effort for the teacher to see how the very same is true of grades or offers of extra recess when she becomes the controller. Exactly the same is true of the worker, chafing under the burden of a manipulative compensation plan, who comes home and manipulates his child with a Skinnerian system that differs only in the type of reward.

By definition, it would seem, if one person controls another, the two individuals have unequal status.[30] The use of rewards (or punishments) is facilitated by this lack of symmetry but also acts to perpetuate it. Naturally, the impact of this fact is different in the relationship between two adults than it is in that between an adult and a child, but the fact itself is worth pondering. If you doubt that rewarding someone emphasizes the rewarder's position of greater power, imagine that you have given your next-door neighbor a ride downtown, or some help moving a piece of furniture, and that he then offers you five dollars for your trouble. If you feel insulted by the gesture, consider why this should be, what the payment implies. Again, this feeling of resentment in response to the status differential between giver and receiver should be kept firmly in mind when the roles have been reversed and we are the ones doing the rewarding.*

If rewards not only reflect differences in power but also contribute to them, it should not be surprising that their use may benefit the more powerful party — that is, the rewarder. This point would seem almost too obvious to bother mentioning except for the fact that, in practice, rewards are typically justified as being in the interests of the individuals receiving them. We claim to reinforce people to teach them things that they need to be taught. But one writer, after ticking off the specific objectives of behavior modification programs, asks, "In whose inter-

---

*Another example was provided by accounts of a magazine editor who, after disagreements with others on the staff, was given to handing out bottles of wine or gift certificates. This, according to one former associate editor, "made us feel like a McDonald's Employee of the Month."[31] Perhaps we should ask why anyone, even an employee at McDonald's, should be made to feel that way.

ests is it for a prisoner, a student, or a patient to be less complaining, more attentive, submissive, and willing to work?"[32] Who really benefits when a child quiets down and sits still?

To be sure, some behavior managers — the parent who tries to reinforce a child's display of good values, or the teacher who attempts to interest students in doing research by offering extra credit for a report — may genuinely be concerned to improve the lives of those they reward. In such cases we can proceed directly to ask whether these rewards have the intended effects. But it is possible that others who use rewards or punishments are being less than honest with themselves when they insist they are only trying to help whomever they are controlling. It may be their own convenience (or continued capacity to control) that is really at stake.

Cui bono? — Who benefits? — is always a useful question to ask about a deeply entrenched and widely accepted practice. In this case, it is not merely the individual rewarder who comes out ahead; it is the institution, the social practice, the status quo that is preserved by the control of people's behavior. A pair of psychologists who reviewed token economies and similar plans in classroom settings observed that those peddling such systems "have used their procedures to serve the goals and values of the existing school system." More generally, these psychologists encourage us to ask, "To what extent is behavior modification . . . helping the existing institutional system achieve its present goals, e.g., goals of control for the sake of control, order and (misleading) tranquility, thus preventing rather than producing needed change?"[33]

But we do not have to rely on critics to make this point. The father of behaviorism, John Watson, made it himself, candidly acknowledging that he and his colleagues

> are constantly manipulating stimuli, dangling this, that and the other combination in front of the human being in order to determine the reactions they will bring forth — hoping that the reaction will be "in line with progress," "desirable," "good." (And society really means by "desirable," "good," "in line with progress," reactions that will not disturb its recognized and established traditional order of things.)[34]

If rewards bolster the traditional order of things, then the psychologist Mihaly Csikszentmihalyi is right to warn (or promise) that "to deemphasize conventional rewards threatens the existing power structure."[35] The thrust of a book like this one is rightly viewed as political insofar as it raises questions about systems that support the status

quo, but it is no more political than pop behaviorism, which turns out
to be a profoundly conservative doctrine posing as a value-free technique.

In one sense, this conclusion is paradoxical: most people who call
themselves conservative emphasize the agency and responsibility of
the individual, whereas Skinner spent his life denying the idea of
choice and urging us to control reinforcers in the environment since
they, in turn, control us.* Indeed, some social reformers have been
enamored of the behaviorist vision (derived by Watson from John
Locke) of human beings as blank slates that can be written on as one
pleases.[36]

Paradoxical or not, though, it is difficult to deny the conservatism
of behavior control. In a very practical sense, applied behaviorists are
anxious not to offend their clients, and they therefore offer a system
of control that helps sustain the institutions and programs that currently exist. But I am making a more fundamental point. While it may
seem that reward-and-punishment strategies are inherently neutral,
that any sort of behavior could, in principle, be encouraged or discouraged, this is not completely true. If it were, the fact that these
strategies are invariably used to promote order and obedience would
have to be explained as a remarkable coincidence.

More realistically, we must acknowledge that because pop behaviorism is fundamentally a means of controlling people, it is by its
nature inimical to democracy,[37] critical questioning, and the free exchange of ideas among equal participants. Rewarding people for making changes in the existing order (which might include the very order
that allows some individuals to be controllers and others controlled)
is not merely unlikely but a contradiction in terms. "The master's tools
will never dismantle the master's house," as one writer put it.[38] This
point may seem far removed from the act of promising a child a
weekend trip to the zoo if he gets to bed on time all week, but that is
all the more reason to think seriously about the connection, which is
to say, about the implications of any system of control.

Before concluding this discussion, I want to consider three objections
that might be offered to these remarks concerning control. The first

---

*According to Skinner, the reason we have no cause to fear abuse by behaviorists and
their surrogates — the reason Walden Two will not come to resemble the world of
Nineteen Eighty-four — is that the Chief Reinforcer "doesn't control others; he designs
a world that controls others." This line of reasoning has not reassured everyone.

is the relatively modest point that it may be misleading to speak of rewards as inherently controlling, since some rewards are more controlling than others. To some extent this is true. In fact, I would expand on this comment by proposing a rough guideline for determining degrees of control: we need to look at the intention of the rewarder, the perception of the rewardee, and various characteristics of the reward itself.

Suppose, therefore, that we wish to present someone with a reward but also to reduce the extent to which the transaction is controlling. The first step is to examine our own motivation: are we ultimately trying to teach a skill, promote a value, boost self-esteem, or are we mostly interested in making someone do what we want? Next, we might try to put ourselves in the reward recipient's shoes and imagine whether she might *feel* manipulated, irrespective of our intentions. (An expression of positive feedback might be construed as useful information by one person and as a clever attempt to control what she does tomorrow by another.) Finally, we ought to look at various objective features of the reward experience — how much emphasis the incentive has been given, how large or attractive it is, how closely it is tied to the quality of performance, and so on — with an eye to minimizing the extent to which the recipient will see the reward as driving his actions.

While I think it makes sense to attend to these features, we have to be careful about assuming that doing so can eliminate the problem entirely. Inflating the manipulative features of a reward may make a bad thing worse, but there is no getting around the fact that any time we say "Do this and you'll get that," we are attempting to control the behavior of the person we are addressing. Probably all a rewarder can do is minimize — or more disturbing, distract people from noticing — what is really going on.

This may suggest a second, more sweeping objection, one that has been made not only by Skinner and Skinnerians but also by social theorists with whom they have little in common: control is an unavoidable feature of human relationships; all that actually varies is the subtlety of the system of reinforcement. A brief smile and nod are just as controlling as a dollar bill — more so, perhaps, since social rewards may have a more enduring effect than tangible rewards. Just because we cannot readily identify the operative operant doesn't mean it isn't there.

The introduction to a book entitled *Man Controlled* pretty well captures this perspective. Those who raise concerns about what the title suggests, we are told, simply have a "fear of new knowledge" that has been cultivated by "alarmists." Realists recognize that "the technology of behavior control is not good or bad, but neutral" — therefore "not even an issue" — for the simple reason that there is no freedom (in fact, this word appears only within quotation marks) to be lost. Whether we like it or not, "all behavior is controlled. . . . The world is, in a sense, one large 'Skinner box.' "[39]

Here, I think, we have to be very careful to tease apart what are actually quite different claims. That subtler reinforcers too can be controlling is quite true; in fact, I argued earlier that rewards are just as controlling as punishments, and delicate rewards as controlling as heavy-handed ones. But to conclude from this that all human interaction is therefore best described as an exercise in control seems to me a grave mistake. People who believe this have done one of two things: either they have taken on faith that selfhood and choice are illusions and we do only what we have been reinforced for doing, or they have stretched the word *control* until it encompasses many other kinds of interaction, such as trying to convince someone of the value of one's point of view. At this point, the word has become so broad and imprecise as to be of little use. If I decide that whenever two people talk about something, each is really trying to control the other, then this is true only because of my rather contrived definition of *control,* which doesn't help us understand very much.

A far more defensible position, it seems to me, is that some forms of human interaction are controlling and some are not. The line might not be easy to draw in practice, but the distinction is still meaningful and important. Consider an analogy: the line between truth and falsehood isn't always easy to draw either (as in the case where a possibly relevant true statement is omitted). Likewise, lots of people tell small lies. But we are not entitled to conclude from this that all human communication is fraudulent and that it makes no sense to oppose categories of talk that are inherently misleading. My point, of course, is that we can say the same about control.

The last objection we might anticipate is that even if it is possible to avoid controlling other people, control is sometimes an appropriate, even desirable, mode of interaction, whether we use rewards or some other technique. It could even be argued that parents who fail to control their children are not living up to their responsibilities.

I will have a number of things to say on this subject in chapters 9 and 12, but a few words at this point may not be out of place. To begin with, when people talk about the need to control children, they very often mean that children cannot be left entirely to their own devices. It is hard to imagine how anyone could disagree with this. But to say that children need structure or guidance is very different from saying they have to be controlled. In everyday conversation, we tend to confuse these different kinds of interventions; once we clarify them, it is not clear that many situations actually call for measures that most of us would see as controlling or manipulative.

I think it is true that very young children may sometimes require controlling responses; the bottom line is that a three-year-old cannot be permitted to toddle out into the street at will. But before we resort to control, we should be absolutely certain that less intrusive, more respectful interventions cannot work. We should also think about how an act of control is exercised: Do we justify it with a reasonable explanation ("Cars come by here very fast sometimes and I love you so much that I have to make sure you don't get hurt")? Do we pause to ask whether what we are getting the child to do (or stop doing) is really necessary? Are we thinking about how best to help the child become a responsible person (as opposed to just how to get her to obey)?

Parents and teachers who defend the use of control without reservation do not, as a rule, pause to ask these sorts of questions. Often this is because they see the world in dichotomous terms: either you are controlling or you are permissive; either you crack down hard or you let kids get away with anything. To devise flexible and reasonable rules for children, preferably by working *with* them to solve problems rather than imposing these rules *on* them, is very different from control on the one hand and a laissez-faire approach on the other.

Some who support more coercive strategies assume that children will run wild if they are not controlled. However, the children for whom this is true typically turn out to be those accustomed to being controlled — those who are not trusted, given explanations, encouraged to think for themselves, helped to develop and internalize good values, and so on. Control breeds the need for more control, which then is used to justify the use of control.

The thoughtful pursuit of reasonable ends requires far less use of control for children, let alone adults, than many of us assume. If someone persists in controlling others, something else may be at work — a set of values and a view of relationship that no argument or evidence will suffice to challenge. In the end, we may just have to take our stand with one or another vision of human life. Hugh Lacey and Barry Schwartz put it well:

There has always been a moral impulse behind Skinner's driven and unrelenting commitment to behaviorism, a belief that the implementation of systematic behavioral controls will contribute quickly to solving the big social problems of the modern world. And much of his philosophical writing has been devoted to arguing that persons are the kind of beings defined by relations of control. We too have a moral motive. It is that relations of dialogue in all aspects of life are better for everyone than relations of control.[40]

The thrust of this chapter, then, has been that giving people rewards is not an obviously fair or appropriate practice across all situations; to the contrary, it is an inherently objectionable way of reaching our goals by virtue of its status as a means of controlling others. Some readers will respond to this by saying that regardless of whether rewards are good, bad, or neutral from a moral point of view, the most important reason we use them is that they work. Let us now see whether this is true.

3

IS IT EFFECTIVE
TO REWARD?

[Rewards] have effects that interfere with performance in ways
that we are only beginning to understand.
— Janet Spence, 1971

LEON IS ON HIS WAY out the door to take a walk when Pam calls
out to him. If you help me clean the kitchen this afternoon, she says,
I'll take you to your favorite restaurant tonight. Leon closes the door
and finds a sponge.

On Nora's list of favorite activities, working on math homework
ranks just below having a root canal. So Phil announces that if she
finishes the problem set on page 228 before eight o'clock, he will give
her five dollars. Nora pulls out her book.

What has happened here? Both Leon and Nora complied with
someone else's wishes, engaging in an activity they were otherwise not
planning to do (at least not at the moment) in order to obtain something they valued. In each case, one person used a reward to change
another's behavior. The plan worked, and that, most of us say, is all
we need to know.

But let's probe further. Rewards are often successful at increasing
the probability that we will do something. At the same time, though,
as I will try to show in this chapter and the two that follow, they also
change the *way* we do it. They offer one particular *reason* for doing
it, sometimes displacing other possible motivations. And they change
the *attitude* we take toward the activity. In each case, by any reasonable measure, the change is for the worse. Most behaviorists are not
fond of punishment; as one Skinnerian has written, the trouble "may
be not that it doesn't work but that it works only too well."[1] I think
exactly the same thing can be said of rewards: we pay a substantial
price for their success.

However, even that statement concedes too much because the success of rewards is, in truth, widely misunderstood and vastly overrated. Here is where we begin our investigation, then: with a close look at the belief that rewarding people produces changes in behavior, and (in the following section) at the belief that rewards improve performance on a variety of tasks.

Do Rewards Change Behavior?

To examine the claim that rewards are effective at altering behavior, we pose three questions: First, for whom are they effective? Second, for how long are they effective? And third, at what, exactly, are they effective? (I have already hinted at a fourth question — At what cost are they effective? — but this we will set aside for the time being.)

1. For whom are rewards effective? Perhaps we should instead ask, For what . . . ? given that their most impressive successes take place in animal laboratories. But when we look at the probability that rewards will change human behavior, a pattern begins to emerge, as two management specialists have noticed:

> Many of the early (and highly successful) applications of the principles of behavior modification have involved animals (such as pigeons), children, or institutionalized adults such as prisoners or mental patients. Individuals in each of these groups are *necessarily* dependent on powerful others for many of the things they most want and need, and their behavior usually can be shaped with relative ease.[2]

Notice that this is not a moral objection; it is a statement of fact about how behavior is easier to control when the organism you are controlling is already dependent on you. In part, this is true because a dependent organism can be kept in a state of need. Laboratory animals are typically underfed to ensure their responsiveness to the food used as a reinforcer. Likewise, "in order to make people behave in a particular way . . . they must be . . . needy enough so that rewards reinforce the desired behaviour."[3] People who have some degree of independence, such as Leon, will also respond to rewards on occasion, but it is more difficult to make this happen in a predictable, systematic way.

2. For how long are rewards effective? The short answer is that they work best in the short term. For behavior changes to last, it is usually necessary to keep the rewards coming. Assuming your child is reinforced by candy, you can induce him to clean up his room for as long as you keep providing sweets. In practice, however, this raises several problems. What if he becomes satiated with sugar so that the reward eventually stops being rewarding to him?* Alternatively, what if his demands to be paid off escalate (in frequency if not in quantity) beyond your desire or ability to meet them? Most important, do you really want him to help out around the house only as long as you have a supply of M&M's on hand?

In the real world, even if not in the laboratory, *rewards must be judged on whether they lead to lasting change — change that persists when there are no longer any goodies to be gained.* This is the key question to pose to a manager who claims that performance in her division jumped after an incentive plan was introduced, or to a teacher who brags that his students read more books when they are given treats for doing so. We want to know what happens to productivity, or to the desire to read, once the goodies have run out.

In theory it is possible to keep handing out reward pellets forever. In practice, though, this is usually impractical, if not impossible, to sustain. What's more, most people with an interest in seeing some behavior change would say it is intrinsically better to have that change take root so that rewards are no longer necessary to maintain it. Even behaviorists generally accept this criterion.[4] Virtually every behavior for which children are rewarded, from brushing their teeth to acting altruistically, is something we'd like them to keep doing when they are no longer rewarded. At work, people usually continue to get paid for what they do, but if the goal is to help people change their behavior — for example, by improving the quality of their work — a continued dependence on rewards can create a range of practical problems, including an increase in demands (for money rather than M&M's), as managers trying to implement incentive programs on a permanent basis have discovered.

If it does make sense to measure the effectiveness of rewards on the basis of whether they produce lasting change, the research suggests that they fail miserably. This news should not be shocking; most of us, after reflecting carefully, will concede that our own experience bears this out. However, what is not always recognized is, first, just how utterly unsuccessful rewards really are across various situations, and second, just how devastating an indictment is contained in this fact.

---

*The same point applies, of course, to other rewards, such as grades.

Token economy programs To start with, let us consider elaborate behavior modification plans such as token economies (where markers that can be redeemed for privileges or treats are dispensed when people act "appropriately"). Theoretically, these programs should have unusually high prospects for success since they are typically implemented in laboratory-like settings — closed environments with dependent subjects.* In the first systematic review of the research on token economies, conducted in 1972, two avid proponents of the idea stated that

> the generalization of treatment effects to stimulus conditions in which token reinforcement is not given might be expected to be the *raison d'être* of token economies. An examination of the literature leads to a different conclusion. There are numerous reports of token programs showing behavior change only while contingent token reinforcement is being delivered. Generally, removal of token reinforcement results in decrements in desirable responses and a return to baseline or near-baseline levels of performance.

Translation: when the goodies stop, people go right back to acting the way they did before the program began. In fact, not only does the behavior fail "to generalize to conditions in which [reinforcements] are not in effect" — such as the world outside the hospital — but reinforcement programs used each morning generally don't even have much effect on patients' behavior during the afternoon![5]

Ten years later, one of these authors, Alan Kazdin, checked back to see if anything had changed. Was the initial failure due only to inadequate implementation of a basically sound idea? After reviewing another decade's worth of research, the best he could offer was the rather tepid statement that the gains produced by token economies "are not inevitably lost." In some programs, "intervention effects are at least partially maintained"; in others, they are not. On closer inspection, though, even this modest claim couldn't be defended. It turned out that the programs that seemed most successful often had been combined with other, more substantive reforms (including, in the case of schools, reducing the size of classes, getting parents more involved, and so forth). These other changes, of course, might well have been responsible for any beneficial effects. "As a general rule," Kazdin wrote, with an almost audible sigh, "it is still prudent to assume that

---

*Of course, it could be argued that the very dissimilarity between such artificial milieus and the rest of life makes it even more difficult to create lasting change.

behavioral gains are likely to be lost in varying degrees once the client leaves the program."[6]

One study conducted in a classroom should convey a feel for the kind of research he reviewed. Over the course of twelve days, fourth and fifth graders were rewarded for playing with certain math-related games and were not rewarded for playing with others. (None of these activities was inherently more interesting than any other.) When the rewards started, the kids promptly gravitated to the games that led to a payoff. When the rewards disappeared, their interest in those games dropped significantly, to the point that many were now less interested in them than were children who had never been rewarded in the first place. The researchers concluded that

> the use of powerful systematic reward procedures to promote increased engagement in target activities may also produce concomitant decreases in task engagement, in situations where neither tangible nor social extrinsic rewards are perceived to be available.[7]

Other reviewers surveying the landscape, including committed behaviorists, have reached a conclusion similar to Kazdin's, finding plenty of reason to doubt the long-term effectiveness of token economy programs or, at best, claiming that there still isn't enough research to know for sure that they work.[8] Perhaps most telling is the finding that in those cases where behavior change did continue after the initial rewards were withdrawn, it was only because new rewards were substituted for the original ones.[9]

Is this failure to promote enduring change restricted to token economies? These programs are rarely used today, but behaviorists are still called in to help people develop good habits or break bad habits. Three areas where there is enough evidence to permit at least provisional judgments about their success are losing weight, quitting smoking, and using seatbelts.[10] Here's what the data show:

Losing weight   In one dieting study, some subjects were promised a twice-a-week reward of five dollars each time the scale showed good news, while others got nothing. Those who were paid did make more progress at the beginning, but then gained back the weight — and then some — over the next five months. By contrast, those who had not been rewarded kept getting slimmer.[11] This study was quite small, and a lot of the subjects were unavailable for measurement at the end, so we probably shouldn't give it too much weight. But a similar study published ten years later offered little solace for behaviorists: after a year, no difference was found between the payment and nonpayment groups. (Actually, there was one difference: many of those who had been promised money for shedding pounds failed to show up for the final weigh-in.)[12]

Quitting smoking   Losing weight and keeping it off are inordinately difficult, so it may be unfair to reject pop behaviorism just because it hasn't worked miracles here. The trouble is that it hasn't done much better elsewhere, assuming we are looking for long-term gains. Take smoking cessation. A very large study, published in 1991, recruited subjects for a self-help program designed to help people kick the habit. Some were offered a prize for turning in weekly progress reports; some got feedback designed to enhance their motivation to quit; everybody else (the control group) got nothing. What happened? Prize recipients were twice as likely as the others to return the first week's report. But three months later, they were lighting up again more often than those who received the other treatment — and even more than those in the control group! Saliva samples revealed that subjects who had been promised prizes were twice as likely to lie about having quit. In fact, for those who received both treatments, "the financial incentive somehow diminished the positive impact of the personalized feedback." Not only were rewards unhelpful; they actually did harm.[13]*

Using seat belts   Even more research has been done on applying behaviorism to the promotion of seat belt use. In fact, an enthusiastic partisan of behaviorism and his colleagues reviewed the effects of twenty-eight programs used by nine different companies to get their employees to buckle up; nearly half a million vehicle observations were made over six years in this research. The result: programs that rewarded people for wearing seat belts were the *least* effective over the long haul. In follow-up measures ranging from a month to more than a year later, programs that offered prizes or cash for buckling up found changes in seat belt use ranging from a 62 percent increase to a 4 percent decrease. Programs without rewards averaged a 152 percent increase. The authors, who clearly did not expect this result, had to confess that "the greater impact of the no-reward strategies from both

---

*Recall that rewards were also positively harmful in the program that promised goodies to children for playing with certain math games. There, interest in the games dropped below what was found at the beginning; here, getting a prize for quitting smoking was worse than getting nothing at all. This sort of thing happens often enough that behaviorists have had to invent a neutral-sounding name for it: it is technically known as the "contrast effect."

an immediate and long-term perspective . . . [was] not predicted and [is] inconsistent with basic reinforcement theory."[14]

Other uses Some psychotherapists and couples counselors also use rewards to change behavior. One behaviorist, for example, actually suggests that spouses "use tokens with each other to encourage conversation [or] to control excessive talk."[15] An attempt to assess the effectiveness of rewards here would pull us into a long and complicated discussion about how therapy works and how its success can be measured. What stands out, though, in any evaluation of the topic is that plans to solve problems by rewarding certain behaviors can only be expected to work for as long as these rewards are still in effect. Moreover, "eliciting desired behaviors is not the only, indeed, not even necessarily the most important outcome of psychotherapy"; what matters more are "the underlying psychological processes," which behavioral approaches refrain from addressing.[16]

In chapter 9 I will argue that precisely the same is true with respect to our efforts to help children become responsible and caring: there is no reason to expect rewards (or punishments) to contribute anything to these goals, because a child promised a treat for acting responsibly has been given no reason to keep behaving that way when there is no longer a reward to be gained from doing so.

3. **At what, exactly, are rewards effective?** To ask how long rewards last, and to learn that they rarely produce effects that survive the rewards themselves, is to invite curiosity about just what it is that rewards are doing. Why don't people keep acting the way they were initially reinforced for acting? The answer is that reinforcements do not generally alter the attitudes and emotional commitments that underlie our behaviors. They do not make deep, lasting changes because they are aimed at affecting only what we *do*. If, like Skinner, you think there is nothing to human beings other than what we do — that we are only repertoires of behavior — then this criticism will not trouble you; it may even seem meaningless. If, on the other hand, you think that actions reflect and emerge from who a person is (what she thinks and feels, expects and wills), then interventions that just control actions wouldn't be expected to help a child grow into a generous person or even help an adult decide to lose weight.

What rewards and punishments do is induce compliance, and this they do very well indeed. If your objective is to get people to obey an order, to show up on time and do what they're told, then bribing or threatening them may be sensible strategies. But if your objective is to get long-term quality in the workplace, to help students become careful thinkers and self-directed learners, or to support children in developing good values, then rewards, like punishments, are absolutely useless. In fact, as we are beginning to see, they are worse than useless — they are actually counterproductive.

Do Rewards Improve Performance?

In 1961, a graduate student at the University of Kentucky found something she didn't expect. For her dissertation, Louise Brightwell Miller arranged a series of simple drawings of faces so that pairs of nearly identical images would be flashed on a screen. Then she brought 72 nine-year-old boys into her laboratory one at a time and challenged them to tell the two faces apart. Some of the boys were paid when they succeeded; others were simply told each time whether or not they were correct.

Miller expected that the boys would do a better job when there was money at stake. Instead, she found that those who were trying to earn the reward made a lot more mistakes than those who weren't. It didn't matter how much they were paid (one cent or fifty cents) or whether they were highly motivated achievers (as measured by a personality test). The discovery left her scratching her head: "The clear inferiority of the reward groups was an unexpected result, unaccountable for by theory or previous empirical evidence," she and her adviser confessed.[17]

The following year, another graduate student, Sam Glucksberg, published the results of his own dissertation research at New York University in the same journal. This time it was undergraduates, 128 of them in all, who were brought into a lab individually. Each was given matches, thumbtacks, and the boxes they came in and told to mount a candle on a wall using only these materials. (They were supposed to figure out that an empty box could be tacked to the wall and the candle placed on top of it.) Some of the students were given empty boxes, with matches and tacks on the side; others got full boxes, which made the solution much less obvious.

As with Miller's experiment, some of the students were informed that they could earn anywhere from $5 to $20 — quite a lot of money in 1962 — if they succeeded; others weren't promised anything. Even though the subjects were older and the assignment quite different, Glucksberg's results echoed Miller's: when the task was more challenging, those who were working for the financial incentive took nearly 50 percent longer to solve the problem.[18]

Nobody paid much attention to these studies at the time — or since, for that matter. But because most of us assume that better work is done by people who know they are going to be rewarded for doing it, this early research takes on a certain retrospective significance. Those graduate students may not have realized it, but they had stumbled onto something enormously important.

In the early 1970s, a batch of new reports came out that showed the early results were no flukes. Janet Spence, a psychologist at the University of Texas who later became the president of the American Psychological Association, published two studies in which children were asked to remember which of two words was "right" (as arbitrarily determined by the experimenter) and then choose that one over others when it came up again later. Some of the children simply saw a light come on (or a bean drop down a chute) when they chose correctly; others got either an M&M or a token that could be exchanged for an M&M when they were finished. It turned out that the children who received candy or the promise of candy got fewer right than those who received nothing more than information about how well they were doing — a result that led her to make the comment that appears at the beginning of this chapter.[19]

Four other studies, each conducted by a different experimenter and published in a different journal, were reported that same year:

• One researcher asked undergraduates to "select the pattern on each page that was least like the other two patterns on that page." To his surprise, he found that students "who were not offered money performed significantly better than those who were paid." So he doubled the amount of the reward — and got exactly the same result.[20]

• In an experiment that ventured outside the psychology laboratory, college students who worked on the school newspaper were observed as they learned to "writ[e] headlines according to prescribed rules." As they got better over time, they were able to work more quickly. For a while some students were paid for each headline they turned out — with the result that their performance stopped improving. Those who received no money kept getting better.[21]

• Fourth graders performed more poorly on a task when they were offered the very reward (some sort of toy or candy) that they had earlier indicated they especially liked. The experimenter pronounced the results "puzzling."[22]

• High school students were given five different tasks, some testing their memory and some requiring true creativity. Once again, some were promised a reward while others were not. And once again, regardless of the task, the rewarded subjects didn't do nearly as well.[23]

As the 1970s wore on, still more evidence accumulated. Preschoolers who expected an award for drawing with felt-tip pens drew at least as many pictures as those who didn't expect an award, but the quality of their drawings was judged to be appreciably lower.[24] (That rewards can have one effect on quantity and another on quality has been noticed by other researchers, too.)[25]

Another group of college students took longer to solve a problem requiring creativity when they were rewarded for doing so.[26] And in a particularly intriguing experiment, sixth-grade girls who were promised free movie tickets for successfully teaching younger girls to play a new game wound up doing a lousy job as tutors: they got frustrated more easily, took longer to communicate ideas, and ended up with pupils who didn't understand the game as well as those who learned from tutors who weren't promised anything.[27]

By the 1980s, anyone who kept up with this sort of research would have found it impossible to claim that the best way to get people to perform well is to dangle a reward in front of them. As the studies became more sophisticated, the same basic conclusion was repeatedly confirmed. College students exhibited "a lower level of intellectual functioning" when they were rewarded for their scores on the more creative portions of an intelligence test. (Their scores on the portions of the test requiring less insight and discovery were neither hindered nor helped by rewards.)[28] In a separate study, third graders who were told they would get a toy for working on some "games" (which, in reality, were also IQ tests) didn't do as well as those who expected nothing.[29] In research by Barry Schwartz, adults who had to figure out the rules to another sort of game, in effect trying to think like scientists, were less successful if they had been trained at the task earlier and promised a monetary reward for doing well. (They had trouble breaking out of the fixed pattern of behavior that had succeeded in producing rewards for them before.)[30]

A few years later, Teresa Amabile, a leading student of creativity, published two reports that clinched the case against the use of rewards. In the first, young creative writers who merely spent five minutes *thinking* about the rewards their work could bring (such as money and public recognition) wrote less creative poetry than others who hadn't been reflecting on these reasons for pursuing their craft.

The quality of their writing was also lower than the work that they themselves had done a little while earlier.[31] Then Amabile conducted a series of studies with children and adults that involved such tasks as making collages and inventing stories. Some subjects were promised rewards — real ones this time — and others weren't. Again, rewards killed creativity, and this was true regardless of the type of task, the type of reward, the timing of the reward, or the age of the people involved.[32]

As recently as 1992, researchers were still finding that rewards undermine different kinds of performance. Amabile and her associates discovered that professional artists do less creative work when that work is commissioned — that is, when they have contracted in advance for a reward.[33] And Mark Lepper, who was once Amabile's adviser, conducted a study with a graduate student in which fourth and fifth graders were given a problem-solving task similar to the board game Clue. Those who were promised a toy for doing well "formulated hypotheses in a much less systematic fashion" and took longer to get the solution than those who weren't promised anything. Even more disturbing, those anticipating a reward also did a poorer job on an entirely different task a week later.[34]

Still other researchers, approaching the topic from different angles, have found additional reasons to question the wisdom of pop behaviorism. One series of investigations considered the basis on which people are rewarded. After conducting six separate studies, Morton Deutsch concluded that "there is no evidence to indicate that people work more productively when they are expecting to be rewarded in proportion to their performance than when they are expecting to be rewarded equally or on the basis of need."[35] (In later chapters I will cite other evidence suggesting that pay-for-performance in the workplace and an emphasis on grades in the classroom are both counterproductive, exactly as Deutsch's data would lead us to predict.)

Other investigators, meanwhile, have been looking at people's attitudes toward rewards. Ann Boggiano and Marty Barrett found that children who are extrinsically motivated — that is, concerned about things like the rewards and approval they can get as a result of what they do in school — use less sophisticated learning strategies and score lower on standardized achievement tests than children who are interested in learning for its own sake. The reward-driven children do more poorly even when they are compared with children whose scores the previous year were identical to their own.[36]

·   ·   ·

I have described these studies individually rather than just summarizing the basic finding because without the supporting details of the research the conclusion might be hard to accept. After all, it was hard for the researchers themselves to accept — at least, until the results appeared so consistently that they had no choice. But before going on to examine the reasons for these results, let us take a moment to sort them out and think about what they imply and why they seem so startling.

Recall the three questions posed at the beginning of this chapter: For whom are rewards effective, for how long, and at what? We know that some people will do a better job at some things when there's a goody at stake, but few of us have stopped to consider just how limited the circumstances are in which this is true. For whom do rewards work best? For those who are "alienated from their work," according to Deutsch.[37] If what you've been asked to do seems silly or simple, you might decide to make a real effort only when there is something else, something outside the task itself, to be gained. (It shouldn't be surprising, then, that researchers find rewards are least effective — in fact, positively counterproductive — when people get these rewards for doing things that are optimally challenging for them, neither too hard nor too easy.)[38] This, of course, says something about the task as much as about the individuals involved; more accurately, it speaks to the relation between the two.

For how long do rewards work? Most of the research on this question concerns behavior change, the sort of effects discussed in the preceding section. Virtually all of the studies concerned with performance look at how well people do at a task immediately after getting, or being promised, a reward. In order for rewards to have any hope of boosting performance over a long period of time, we typically have to continue giving them out, or at least holding out the possibility that more will follow.

We come, finally, to the key questions: At what sort of tasks do people do a better job when they are rewarded? And "better" in what sense? By now we have already seen enough evidence to guess the answers. *Rewards usually improve performance only at extremely simple — indeed, mindless — tasks, and even then they improve only quantitative performance.* The unexpected results from those first dissertation studies by Miller and Glucksman appeared against a backdrop of research by behaviorists that counted things like an increase in the number of times an organism pressed a lever as proof that reinforcement improves performance. If you were given an enormous pile of envelopes to seal, you would probably lick them a lot faster if you were paid to do so. The trouble is that we have incorrectly inferred from this fact a general law of human nature — Reward people and they'll do a better job — and applied it in our workplaces and schools. This faulty application (which a behaviorist might refer to as "response overgeneralization") goes a long way toward explaining why so many of our workplaces and schools are now in trouble.

One of the most influential papers on the topic of rewards (influential, that is, for the very few social psychologists who are specialists in the field) reached the following conclusion based on research conducted up until the mid-1970s:

> Incentives will have a detrimental effect on performance when two conditions are met: first, when the task is interesting enough for subjects that the offer of incentives is a superfluous source of motivation; second, when the solution to the task is open-ended enough that the steps leading to a solution are not immediately obvious.[39]

This analysis by Kenneth McGraw provides us with a good point of departure from which to figure out when rewards are likely to fail. Subsequent investigations, for example, have confirmed that a Skinnerian approach is particularly unlikely to prove useful when it is creativity that we are trying to promote.[40]

But McGraw's rule may understate the failure of rewards by suggesting that they will miscarry only when used with interesting and creative tasks. I think it is more accurate to say that they are *most likely* to have a detrimental effect, or to have the *most pronounced* detrimental effect, with these tasks. It is true that some studies have found that people's performance at very basic things, such as multiplication, may improve when they are expecting to receive a reward. But the research I have described in this section includes enough examples of impaired performance at rather straightforward tasks — or at least a failure to enhance performance at these tasks — that we cannot casually assume it makes sense to reach for the reinforcements for everything that doesn't demand creativity.

"Do this and you'll get that" turns out to be bad news whether our goal is to change behavior or to improve performance, whether we are dealing with children or adults, and regardless of whether the reward is a grade, a dollar, a gold star, a candy bar, or any of the other bribes on which we routinely rely. Even assuming we have no ethical reservations about manipulating other people's behavior to get them to do what we want, the plain truth is that this strategy is likely to backfire.

As one psychologist read the available research, people who are offered rewards tend to

> choose easier tasks, are less efficient in using the information available to solve novel problems, and tend to be answer oriented and more illogical in their problem-solving strategies. They seem to work harder and produce more activity, but the activity is of a lower quality, contains more errors, and is more stereotyped and less creative than the work of comparable nonrewarded subjects working on the same problems.[41]

In the next two chapters we examine why all this is true.

4

THE TROUBLE WITH CARROTS:
Four Reasons Rewards Fail

It is better not to make merit a matter of reward
Lest people conspire and contend.

— Lao-tzu

CONFRONTED WITH IRREFUTABLE EVIDENCE that people who are trying to earn a reward end up doing a poorer job on many tasks than people who are not, researchers at first could only scratch their heads in puzzlement. A few tentatively suggested — or in one case, tried to prove — that the paradoxical effect of rewards must be due to the fact that they distract people from the task at hand.[1]

Indeed, it makes sense that the tantalizing prospect of receiving something we like might prevent us from focusing on what we are doing and thereby prevent us from doing it well. But subsequent research has shown that a lot more is involved than simple distraction. Thinking about a reward, as it turns out, is worse than thinking about something else equally irrelevant to the task.[2] Evidently rewards have a peculiarly detrimental effect on the quality of our performance.

There are, I believe, five core reasons for this failure, four of which are described in the sections that follow, with the fifth occupying the whole of the next chapter. (The second half of the book will play out the implications of these five points in the workplace, the classroom, and the family, and then discuss alternatives to the use of rewards.) Not all of these reasons pertain to the results of the laboratory studies described earlier; some account for the detrimental effects on achievement found in the real world. In any case, the problems I describe are more than explanations for why people don't perform as well when they expect to be rewarded. They are also serious indictments in their own right, raising concerns about the use of rewards beyond what they do to productivity. Collectively they constitute the central case against pop behaviorism.

I. Rewards Punish

A growing number of parents, teachers, and managers have come to believe that punishment, defined as any attempt to change someone's behavior by forcing him or her to undergo something unpleasant, is bad news. Later in this book, I will defend the position that punishing people should indeed be avoided whenever possible, both for practical and moral reasons. For now, I want to address readers who already share this view, and who therefore try to use rewards instead.

In certain circles, it has come to be taken as revealed truth that we are supposed to stop punishing and criticizing and instead attempt to "catch people doing something right" and reward them with privileges or praise. It is nearly impossible to open up a book on management, or scan an article on raising children, or attend a seminar on teaching without coming across this counsel. The underlying assumption is that there are exactly two alteratives: punitive responses or positive reinforcement, sticks or carrots, "slaps or sugar plums."[3]

When the choice is framed this way, of course, only a sadist or a simpleton would fail to pick the latter in each pair. Rewards are less destructive than punishments, and the difference between the two becomes more important as the punishment in question becomes more harsh. But the dichotomy is a false one: our practical choices are not limited to two versions of behavior control. And that is very good news indeed because despite the relative superiority of rewards, the differences between the two strategies are overshadowed by what they share. The troubling truth is that *rewards and punishments are not opposites at all; they are two sides of the same coin.* And it is a coin that does not buy very much.

In respects major and minor, rewards and punishments are fundamentally similar. As Kurt Lewin, the founder of modern social psychology, recognized, both are used when we want to elicit "a type of behavior which the natural field forces of the moment will not produce."[4] Moreover, the long-term use of either tactic describes the very same pattern; eventually we will need to raise the stakes and offer more and more treats or threaten more and more sanctions to get people to continue acting the way we want.

Underlying these two features is an even more critical fact: punishment and reward proceed from basically the same psychological model, one that conceives of motivation as nothing more than the manipulation of behavior. This is not to say that behaviorists fail to distinguish between the two; in fact, Skinner argued fervently against the use of punishment in most circumstances. But the theory of learning and, ultimately, the view of what it is to be a human being are not significantly different for someone who says "Do this and you'll get that" and someone who says "Do this or here's what will happen to you."

The correspondence is no less striking when we turn from theory to practice. Although many people counterpose rewards to punishments, it is interesting to observe that the two strategies often go hand in hand in the real world. In a study reported in 1991, elementary school teachers from thirteen schools were observed carefully over a period of four months. It turned out that the use of rewards and punishments in the classroom were very highly correlated; the teachers who used one were more, not less, likely to use the other.[5] A survey of several hundred mothers of kindergarten-age children revealed a significant positive relationship between the frequent use of rewards and the frequent use of physical punishment.[6] Other studies have found that even praise, the form of reward usually viewed as the least objectionable, is often favored by people whose style of dealing with children is conspicuously controlling or autocratic.[7] These findings don't prove anything about the inherent nature of rewards, but they do offer one kind of answer to the question of how rewards and punishments are related.

The most compelling aspect of that relationship, though, can be succinctly described in two words: rewards punish. Those who dispense rewards in order to avoid punishing people may not have thought about the punitive features that are built into the process of rewarding. Two such features come to mind. The first derives from the fact that rewards are every bit as controlling as punishments, even if they control by seduction. I made this argument at some length in chapter 2 in the course of identifying what might be seen as an intrinsically offensive aspect of rewards. Philosophical objections aside, though, if reward recipients feel controlled, it is likely that the experience will assume a punitive quality over the long run, even though obtaining the reward itself is usually pleasurable.[8]

One education writer compares the tendency of teachers to "blithely administer . . . knee-jerk jolts of positive reinforcement" to the use of electric cattle prods,[9] a comparison that may seem far-fetched until we pause to consider the ultimate purpose of rewards and how manipulation is experienced by those on the receiving end. Or try a different analogy: the question is not whether more flies can be caught with honey than with vinegar, but *why* the flies are being caught in either case — and how this feels to the fly.

That rewards punish is not due only to the fact that they are controlling. They also have that effect for a second, even more straightforward, reason: some people do not get the rewards they were hoping to get, and the effect of this is, in practice, indistinguishable from punishment. Many managers and teachers make a point of withholding or withdrawing a reward if their charges do not perform as instructed. The goody is dangled and then snatched away. In fact, this is precisely what many behaviorists recommend doing. While taking care to urge that children not be punished (by which is meant making something bad happen to them), they freely prescribe the use of "response costs" (by which is meant making something good *not* happen to them).* Unfortunately, those who haven't been trained to make such distinctions might fail to understand that when something desirable has been taken away they are not supposed to feel punished.

A parent tells a child that continued good behavior will be rewarded with a visit to the circus on Sunday. On Saturday, the child does something that annoys the parent, which prompts a familiar warning: "Keep this up and you can forget the circus tomorrow." Can there be any doubt that this threat to remove a reward is functionally identical to a threat to employ a punishment?

But even when the person with the power does not deliberately withdraw the reward — when meeting a clear set of criteria does result in the payoff — it often happens that some people won't meet these criteria and therefore will not get the reward. The more desirable the reward, and the more possible it once seemed to attain, the more demoralizing it will be to miss out. Given that there are disadvantages to the use of rewards even when people do manage to get them, and to the use of contests even for the winners, "imagine the effects of working for a reward and not getting it or of competing and losing!"[10]

There are, it would seem, only two ways around this problem. The first is to give a reward to people regardless of whether they fulfilled

---

*"Negative reinforcement" is different from either of these. It means making a bad thing not happen to someone — that is, removing something unpleasant. Contrary to common usage, it is thus closer to positive reinforcement (making a good thing happen to someone) than it is to punishment.

the stated requirements. Champions of equity theory, whose war cry is "Everything must be earned! No free lunches!" find this horrifying. (In fact, a number of criticisms of rewarding children that have appeared in the popular press over the last few years turn out to be criticisms only of giving rewards too frequently or too easily.) I have a different sort of objection: a goody given unconditionally is not really a reward at all. A reward, by definition, is a desired object or event made conditional on having fulfilled some criterion: only if you do this will you get that. If I promise to give you a banana tomorrow, that is not a reward. If I promise to give you a banana tomorrow for helping me out today, that is a reward — and if I don't give it to you, you will probably feel as if you are being punished. To avoid having this happen, I must avoid giving you things on a contingent basis.

The only other alternative is not to set out any criteria or promise any rewards in advance. Instead, the person in charge could present something after the fact: "For having helped me out yesterday, here's a banana." As it happens, most studies have found that unexpected rewards are much less destructive than the rewards people are told about beforehand and are deliberately trying to obtain. But apart from the practical problems of trying to keep people from expecting another reward tomorrow, it is no coincidence that the great majority of rewards *are* promised in advance. The whole point is to control people's behavior, and the most effective way to do this is to describe what will be given to them if they comply — or done to them if they don't comply. For this very reason, the possibility of ending up without the reward, which makes the process essentially punitive, is always present. The stick is contained in the carrot.

The objection here is anything but academic. Most businesspeople can remember an instance when they, or their colleagues, were expecting a bonus, only to become demoralized when they ended up, for whatever reason, not getting it. Parents readily tell stories of exactly the same thing happening when their children failed to get some reward at school that they were counting on. Most of us are familiar with this phenomenon, but few of us have considered that it is not merely widespread but endemic to the use of rewards.

The new school, which exhorts us to catch people doing something right and reward them for it, is therefore not all that much of an improvement over the old school, which had us catching people doing something wrong and threatening to punish them if they ever did it again. What is mostly taking place in both approaches is that a lot of people are being caught. This is more than a play on words. What we are talking about is the experience of being controlled and feeling punished. These are problematic realities in their own right, and they also happen to be impediments to working or learning effectively.

II. Rewards Rupture Relationships

Earlier I suggested that rewards and punishments flourish in asymmetrical relationships, where one person has most of the power. Even more troubling, rewards and punishments create, or at least exacerbate, that imbalance. If, as a matter of principle, we would like to see disparities in power among people minimized whenever possible, we already have reason to turn away from applied behaviorism.

But this general principle is only the beginning of the story. Rewards also disrupt relationships in very particular ways that are demonstrably linked to learning, productivity, and the development of responsibility. They have these effects both with respect to horizontal relationships (those among peers) and vertical relationships (those among people whose status is different, such as teacher and student, parent and child, supervisor and employee).

In considering the question of relationships among workers or students, we need to begin by recognizing that cooperation does not just make tasks more pleasant; in many cases, it is virtually a prerequisite for quality. More and more teachers and managers are coming to recognize that excellence is most likely to result from well-functioning teams in which resources are shared, skills and knowledge are exchanged, and each participant is encouraged and helped to do his or her best.

Rewards, by contrast, are typically based on the faulty assumption "that the organization's effectiveness is the simple additive combination of individuals' separate performances," in the words of organizational psychologist Jone L. Pearce[11] — a reductive view that overlooks the nature and value of group interaction. In the classroom, one of the central messages communicated by teachers, especially those enamored of rewards and punishments, is that tired old slogan "I want to see what you can do, not what your neighbor can do." This training in individualism persists despite considerable evidence that when students learn together in carefully structured groups, the quality of their learning is typically much higher than what even the sharpest of them could manage in solitude. As one pair of educational psychologists likes to say, "All of us are smarter than any of us."[12]

At best, rewards do nothing to promote this collaboration or a sense of community. More often, they actually interfere with these goals: an undercurrent of "strifes and jealousies" is created whenever people scramble for goodies, as educators in New York City found nearly two centuries ago after watching a behavior modification program in action (see footnote at page 5). "Complaints of unequal treatment" and "playing favorites" are common.[13]

As a rule, rewards are not conducive to developing and maintaining the positive relationships that promote optimal learning or performance. But two common arrangements for rewarding people take a bad thing and make it much worse by explicitly setting people against each other. The first of these is a condition of artificial scarcity. Imagine that you are one of twenty or thirty students in a classroom. The teacher announces at the beginning of the year that whoever makes the highest score on each Friday's quiz will be eligible to wear a GENIUS OF THE WEEK badge and enjoy a set of privileges that go with it. How is this likely to affect the way you view your fellow students? How inclined will you be to help someone else with an assignment? How easy will it be for a sense of community to take root in that room?

In this scenario, no matter how well everyone in the class does on each test, only one student is permitted to get the prize. The central message that is taught here — the central message of all competition, in fact — is that everyone else is a potential obstacle to one's own success. If the reward system sets people up as one another's rivals, the predictable result is that each will view the others with suspicion and hostility and, depending on their relative status, perhaps with contempt or envy as well.[14]

Of all the ways by which people are led to seek rewards, I believe the most destructive possible arrangement is to limit the number that are available. To do so is to replace the possibility that people will try to assist each other with the near certainty that they will try to defeat each other. But whether it is simply permitted by a standard individual incentive system* or actually required by a race for awards, contests are destructive for several reasons beyond the fact that they preclude the sort of teamwork that leads to success.

---

*Some writers have acknowledged many of these problems and suggested that the solution is to stop rewarding individuals and use small group incentives instead, either in the workplace or the classroom. Unfortunately, offering goodies to teams simply shifts the rivalry to another level, maximizing the competition and thereby minimizing the coordination among groups. Moreover, the four other major problems discussed in this chapter and the next are not alleviated by changing how many people receive a reward. There is research to show that "shared incentives do not ameliorate the negative effects of performance-contingent rewards."[15]

First, most competition creates anxiety of a type and level that typically interferes with performance.[16] Second, those who believe they don't have a chance of winning are discouraged from making an effort; having been given no reason to apply themselves except to defeat their peers, and convinced that they cannot do so, these people are almost by definition demotivated.[17] Third, according to a series of studies by psychologist Carole Ames, people tend to attribute the results of a contest, as contrasted with the results of noncompetitive striving, to factors beyond their control, such as innate ability or luck. The result is a diminished sense of empowerment and less responsibility for their future performance.[18]

But competition is only one variation on the behaviorist theme that practically guarantees enmity. The other is the deployment of a collective reward. "If all of us stay on our very best behavior," intones the teacher (speaking here in the first person even though the teacher's own behavior is never at issue), "we will have an ice cream party at the end of the day!" An excited murmur in the room soon fades with the realization that any troublemaker could spoil it for everyone else. This gambit is one of the most transparently manipulative strategies used by people in power. It calls forth a particularly noxious sort of peer pressure rather than encouraging genuine concern about the well-being of others.[19] And pity the poor child whose behavior is cited that afternoon as the reason that "the party has been, I'm sorry to say, boys and girls, canceled." Will the others resent the teacher for tempting and then disappointing them, or for setting them against one another? Of course not. They will turn furiously on the designated demon. That, of course, is the whole idea: divide and conquer.

Collective punishment is widely seen as unfair, but collective reward is not much better. What's more, neither collective nor artificially scarce rewards are confined to elementary school. Many corporations explicitly rank employees against each other or hold out the possibility of an incentive based on an entire department's performance. In this setting there is no need to announce who was responsible for the disappointing results last quarter. Someone will be found to take the blame, irrespective of whether it is deserved. Furthermore, general distrust and stress flourish in just such a system. At one company where "the pay of all depends on everyone's efforts . . . peer pressure can be so high that the first two years of employment are called purgatory."[20]

Several studies have examined the way we come to regard others when their actions determine whether we get a reward. When older girls were promised a reward for tutoring younger girls (see page **44**), they not only became less effective teachers but also "valued the younger child as a function of her utility in obtaining the desired goal": if she wasn't learning fast enough, she came to be viewed negatively.[21] In a very different kind of experiment, merely calling the attention of young adults to the possible rewards of being involved in a romantic relationship (for example, impressing one's friends) led them to report less love for their partners than was expressed by people who hadn't focused on those factors.[22]

The major point here is that whether or not people are offered a direct incentive to wish each other ill, the very fact that they have been led to see themselves as working or learning in order to get something means that they are not very likely to feel well disposed toward others and to put their heads together.[23] Some reward programs promote competition and inhibit cooperation more than others do. But to whatever extent they have this effect, the result is ultimately likely to be to the detriment of quality.

So far I have been talking about the effects of rewards on relationships among people of comparable status. The other sort of relationship affected by a reward is that between the person who gives it and the one who gets it. Even in situations in which we have no objection to the fact of this unequal status, we need to understand what the process of rewarding does to the interaction between giver and receiver. Someone who is raising or teaching children, for example, probably wants to create a caring alliance with each child, to help him or her feel safe enough to ask for help when problems develop. This is very possibly the single most fundamental requirement for helping a child to grow up healthy and develop a set of good values. For academic reasons, too, an adult must nurture just such a relationship with a student if there is to be any hope of the student's admitting mistakes freely and accepting guidance. The same goal applies to the workplace, where it is critical to establish a good working relationship characterized by trust, open communication, and the willingness to ask for assistance.

This is precisely what rewards and punishments kill. If your parent or teacher or manager is sitting in judgment of what you do, and if that judgment will determine whether good things or bad things happen to you, this cannot help but warp your relationship with that person. You will not be working collaboratively in order to learn or grow; you will be trying to get him or her to approve of what you are doing so you can get the goodies. If, for example, "the principal basis for compensation is the boss' whim, the only real incentive is to stay on his good side."[24] A powerful inducement has been created to conceal problems, to present yourself as infinitely competent, and to spend your energies trying to impress (or flatter) the person with power. At least one study has confirmed that people are less likely to ask for help when the person to whom they would normally turn wields the carrots and sticks.[25] Needless to say, if people do not ask for help when they need it, performance suffers on virtually any kind of task.

This result is somewhat easier to see when the individual in charge is perceived as a punisher: the parent who might send the child to her room, the teacher who might write a zero in his book, the supervisor who might turn in a negative performance appraisal. If you are the person who might be punished, you are approximately as glad to see that person coming as you are to see a police car in your rearview mirror. (This is one price that parents pay for presenting themselves as enforcers of "consequences" for misbehavior.)

What some observers have missed is that relationships are ruptured just as surely when we see the powerful person as someone to be pleased as when we see him or her as someone to be feared. William Glasser has labored for a quarter of a century to transform schools into places where students are not perpetually punished and made to feel like failures. But he errs in suggesting that teachers can "reduce the adversarial atmosphere" if they use "rewards instead of punishment."[26] Such a shift will not produce a different atmosphere; at least, it will not be different in the ways that matter. Both rewards and punishments induce a behavior pattern whereby we try to impress and curry favor with the person who hands them out. Whether we are looking to secure a reward or avoid a punishment is almost beside the point. Either way, what we *don't* have is the sort of relationship that is defined by genuine concern and that invites us to take the risk of being open and vulnerable — the sort of relationship that inspires people to do their best and can truly make a difference in their lives.

Just as the essentially controlling nature of rewards is most easily noticed by those who are being controlled, so the effects of rewards on relationships are most readily seen by those who must depend on others to get what they want. This is why it is important once again for someone who dispenses rewards to imaginatively put herself in the position of whoever is dependent on her, and to reflect on the kind of relationship that now exists between the two of them (and the consequences to the other person of not having a different kind of relationship). This act of perspective taking is easier for someone who plays both roles at once, someone who is responsible for deciding what happens to his subordinates while simultaneously remaining at the mercy of a superior for his own rewards.

The presence or absence of rewards is, of course, only one factor among many that affect the quality of our relationships. But it is a factor too often overlooked in its tendency to cause flattery to be emphasized in place of trust and to create a feeling of being evaluated rather than supported. This, combined with its impact on the relationships among those seeking the goodies, goes a long way toward explaining how rewards often reduce achievement.

III. Rewards Ignore Reasons

Except for the places where their use has become habitual, punishments and rewards are typically dragged out when somebody thinks something is going wrong. A child is not behaving the way we want; a student is not motivated to learn; workers aren't doing good work — this is when we bring in the reinforcements.

What makes behavioral interventions so terribly appealing is how little they demand of the intervener. They can be applied more or less skillfully, of course, but even the most meticulous behavior modifier gets off pretty easy for one simple reason: *rewards do not require any attention to the reasons that the trouble developed in the first place.* You don't have to ask why the child is screaming, why the student is ignoring his homework, why the employee is doing an indifferent job. All you have to do is bribe or threaten that person into shaping up. (Notice that this too describes a fundamental similarity between punishments and rewards.)

A mother in Virginia wrote to me not long ago to challenge my criticism of behavioral manipulation. "If I cannot either punish (or allow consequences) or reward (bribe) my children . . . what do I do when my almost three year old . . . wanders out of her room again and again at bedtime?" she asked. Fair enough: let us consider three possible ways of dealing with a child who will not stay in bed. Behaviorist A favors "consequences": "If you're not back in that bed by the time I count to three, young lady, you won't be watching television for a week!" Behaviorist B favors rewards: "If you stay in bed until morning for the next three nights, honey, I'll buy you that teddy bear you wanted."

But the nonbehaviorist wonders how anyone could presume to propose a solution without knowing *why* the child keeps popping out of bed. With very little effort we can imagine several possible reasons for this behavior. Maybe she's being put to bed too early and simply isn't sleepy yet. Maybe she feels deprived of quiet time with her parents, and the evening offers the best opportunity for her to cuddle or talk with them. Maybe she's still wound up from what happened a few hours earlier and needs to rehearse and clarify the day's events to try to make sense of what happened. Maybe there are monsters under her bed. Or maybe she can just hear people talking in the living room. (Is there anyone too old to remember how all the excitement seemed to start after we were put to bed?)

The point is we don't yet know what's really going on. But the behaviorists' solutions don't *require* us to know. Echoing a beer commercial of the late 1980s, their credo seems to be "Why ask why?" That posture helps to explain the popularity of the reward-and-punishment model — and also its ineffectiveness over the long run. Each of the possible explanations for why this girl doesn't stay in bed at night would seem to call for a different solution. (This is one reason it is difficult to give a simple reply to people who demand to know what "the alternative" is to using rewards.) Rewards are not actually solutions at all; they are gimmicks, shortcuts, quick fixes that mask problems and ignore reasons. They never look below the surface.*

From one perspective, this sort of criticism is not new. It was offered decades ago by Freudians, who argued that behavioral therapy in effect addressed only the symptoms of deeper problems. It was said that the underlying emotional issues would force their way up again in the form of a new symptom. But one doesn't have to be a psychoanalyst to see what is deficient about the behavioral approach. It is not necessary to attribute our actions to unconscious wishes and fears or repressed childhood events to recognize that merely controlling an individual's behavior with bribes or threats misses most of what is going on.

---

*Things are happening beneath the surface even when we think the reason for a behavior is straightforward. A child eats candy after being told not to do so, and we assume the motive is obvious: candy tastes good. But perhaps there is more than meets the eye here. Did lunch at school not fill him up? Is his blood sugar low? Are other, healthier snacks unavailable? Is he reaching for something forbidden as a way of expressing anger about something else? Even when we are sure that nothing complicated is going on and the cause of the objectionable behavior is really as obvious as it seems, we nevertheless need to address that cause somehow rather than just trying to change the behavior.

Let's say that a student repeatedly comes to class late or daydreams while the teacher is talking. Such behavior might signal that the student has given up on the subject matter after having struggled unsuccessfully to understand the assignments — perhaps for lack of adequate study skills, perhaps because of how the teacher presents the material, perhaps for some other reason. Whatever the real problem is, it remains unsolved if our intervention consists of promising a reward for an improvement in punctuality and attentiveness (or threatening a punishment if there is no improvement). Moreover, this reward will not be delivered if the student doesn't show sufficient progress, in which case the entire exercise is likely to lead to further alienation, an even more negative self-image, and a spiral of defeat.

The same goes for adults at work, regardless of the kind of work they do. A sudden deterioration in performance frequently turns out to be due to problems at home. A chronic record of mediocre performance, meanwhile, may indicate, among many other possibilities, that there is something wrong with the job itself or with an organizational structure that holds employees responsible for things that they are powerless to control. Turning the workplace into a game show ("Tell our employees about the fabulous prizes we have for them if their productivity improves . . .") does exactly nothing to solve these underlying problems and bring about meaningful change. Often it takes no great psychological sophistication to identify what is going on — only a willingness to do something other than dangle a goody in front of people.

Take another example, this one from the pages of public policy. Some politicians, noting that poor teenagers often give up on high school, have resorted to rewarding them with additional public assistance payments if they attend classes regularly, punishing them by cutting their benefits if they drop out, and sometimes even threatening to stop the checks to their parents in order to generate sufficient family pressure to get the teenagers back in school. Apart from concerns about the fairness of these tactics,[27] what interests me is the failure to consider the underlying reasons that someone, particularly in the inner city, might decide not to continue attending school. Rather than addressing the structural causes of poverty or the lack of perceived relevance of what the curriculum has to offer, the inclination is simply to manipulate people's behavior with a carrot or stick. If the money is needed desperately enough, the manipulation may succeed in increasing school attendance for a while. It will, of course, do nothing about the deeper issues.

Some people use rewards because they are impatient for results, however fleeting or superficial: their attention is focused on the bottom line and they don't particularly care about "deeper issues." But others are guided by the view that these issues actually make no difference. The core of behaviorism, on which some decisions to use behavioral strategies are based, is that human beings are no more than what they do. Change what they do and you have dealt with the problem. One writer concisely describes behaviorism as the "confusion of inner motives with their outward expression."[28] But my point is not just that the psychological theory is inadequate; it is that the practice is unproductive. If we do not address the ultimate cause of a problem, the problem will not get solved.

This is not to say that people who resort to incentives are necessarily so dull or insensitive that they will fail to see or care about other factors. A teacher who brandishes a grade book (on the theory that an appetite for A's or a fear of F's is "motivating") may nevertheless realize that a student is failing because of an abusive home environment, and may even endeavor to do something about this. My purpose, therefore, is not to generalize about the kind of people who use rewards but to examine the implications of the strategy itself. In principle, behavioral interventions *exclude* from consideration the factors that may matter most. In practice, behavioral interventions *distract* those who use them from attending to such factors. This gives us one more explanation for why trying to motivate people by rewarding them is not a very useful strategy.

IV. Rewards Discourage Risk-taking

Rewards can sometimes increase the probability that we will act the way someone wants us to act. But they do something else at the same time that many of us fail to recognize: they change the way we engage in a given behavior.[29] To start with, when we are driven by rewards, our focus is typically more narrow than when no rewards are involved; we are less likely to notice or remember things that aren't immediately relevant to what we are doing.

Say you are handed a pile of index cards, each of which has a different word printed on it. Each card also happens to be a different color. You are told that you will win a prize for successfully memorizing all of the words, and you set to work learning them. Later, after reciting as many as you can remember, you are unexpectedly asked to try to recall the color of the card that corresponds to each word. Chances are you will not do nearly as well on this task as someone who was given the identical instructions but wasn't promised a prize.[30]

This is an example of what researchers call "incidental learning," a type of performance that rewards invariably undermine. But the reason this happens is even more important than the effect itself. The underlying principle can be summarized this way: *when we are working for a reward, we do exactly what is necessary to get it and no more.* Not only are we less apt to notice peripheral features of the task, but in performing it we are also less likely to take chances, play with possibilities, follow hunches that might not pay off. Risks are to be avoided whenever possible because the objective is not to engage in an open-ended encounter with ideas; it is simply to get the goody. One group of researchers explained that when we are motivated by rewards, "features such as predictability and simplicity are desirable, since the primary focus associated with this orientation is to get through the task expediently in order to reach the desired goal."[31] Another psychologist was more succinct: rewards, he said, are the "enemies of exploration."[32]

This doesn't mean that we can't get people to take some kinds of risks by holding out the possibility of a reward if they are successful. The sports section and the business section of the newspaper are full of activities on which people gamble money in the hopes of making more. But notice how narrow this sort of risk-taking is. First, gamblers try to maximize their winnings by minimizing the risks: this is why they study horses or stocks carefully before betting on them. The more they are concerned about the payback, the more certainty they seek — even within an activity that, by definition, cannot provide absolute certainty. Second, gamblers are engaged in doing something where the nature (and sometimes even the precise extent) of the risks has been clearly laid out. They are not involved in challenging the bounds of an activity by approaching it from a new direction. By playing the odds, they are, paradoxically, doing something quite straightforward.

By contrast, the far more meaningful kind of risk-taking entailed by exploring new possibilities is precisely what people are unlikely to do when they are trying to obtain a reward. Far more common in most activities is an orientation of unreflective expedience — the very opposite of what creativity requires.

Teresa Amabile, who specializes in this topic, asks us to picture a rat in the behaviorist's maze trying to find its way to the cheese. The rat does not stop to weigh the advantages of trying another route, starting off on a path where the cheddar smell is less pronounced in the hope of finding a clever shortcut. No, it just runs toward where it thinks its breakfast waits, as fast as its tiny legs can take it. "The safest, surest, and fastest way out of the maze [is] the well-worn pathway, the uncreative route," says Amabile. "The more single-mindedly an external goal is pursued, the less likely ... that creative possibilities will be explored." The narrow focus induced by rewards is similarly worrisome, she adds, since being open to "the seemingly irrelevant aspects [of a task] might be precisely what is required for creativity."[33] Incidental learning may turn out to be integral.

But what if creativity is built into the process? If people will do whatever is required to obtain a reward, won't they think creatively if that's what it takes to get it? Alas, it's not that easy, as Barry Schwartz discovered. Using reinforcements, he tried unsuccessfully to get pigeons to peck in a sequence that was different from their pecking pattern in the preceding session. Eventually, he concluded that it was possible to produce variation, but only in the form of random responses. The difficulty of trying to operantly condition genuinely novel behavior, he argued, is not due to the fact that pigeons aren't very smart. It is inherent in the nature of reinforcement. We have to be able to specify a set of characteristics shared by certain behaviors so that we can offer a reward when they (and only they) appear. But this is impossible to do when what we are looking for is something new.[34]

Schwartz then switched to human subjects and more complicated tasks (see page 44). He found that rewards sometimes seemed to elicit a "stereotypic" or repetitive approach to doing things. After all, "once one finds some response pattern that works reliably [to secure a reward], it is pointless, even foolish, to deviate from it."[35] Unfortunately, Schwartz found, when we are rewarded for what we are doing, we are less likely to be flexible and innovative in the way we solve problems — even very different problems — that come along later. Why? "Reinforcement encourages the repetition of what has worked in the past, in part because the aim of the activity is not to produce something like a general principle or a rule, but to produce another reinforcer."[36]

To be a good scientist, behavioral or otherwise, one has to expect and even welcome some negative results. It is only by comparing events that lead to a certain outcome with those that don't lead to it that we can figure out what is going on and why. But, as Schwartz observes, people working for rewards don't want to risk negative results; they want to succeed as often and as quickly as possible. This, of course, has important implications not only for how we train physicists but also how we set up organizations and classrooms in which we want to encourage people to think systematically about anything.

It is not entirely accurate, though, to say that when we are working for rewards we just want fast and frequent success. The truth is even worse than that. Our objective is not really to succeed at the task at all (in the sense of doing it well); it is to succeed at obtaining the reward. If it were somehow possible to obtain it without finishing the assignment, we would abandon the task in a minute. Kurt Lewin said as much in the 1930s; two researchers confirmed this effect empirically in the 1980s.[37]*

If we do usually complete the task, it is only because doing so is a prerequisite for getting the goody. But even when this is true, we will, given a choice, select the easiest possible task. At least ten studies have found just that, with preschoolers working for toys, older children working for grades, and adults working for money all trying to avoid anything challenging.[39] Furthermore, research indicates that (1) the bigger the reward, the easier the task that people choose;[40] (2) when the rewards stop, those who received them earlier continue to prefer to do as little as possible;[41] and (3) easier tasks are selected not only in situations where rewards are offered but by people who are, as a general rule, more reward oriented.[42]

The basic proposition here makes logical sense. If you have been promised a reward, you come to see the task as something that stands between you and it. The easier that job is, the faster you can be done with it and pick up your prize.[43] It's logical, all right, but the practical implications are staggering. Our workplaces and classrooms, saturated in pop behaviorism as they are, have the effect of discouraging people from taking risks, thinking creatively, and challenging themselves.

Consider the popular program that offers free pizza to children for reading a certain number of books. If you were a participant in this program, what sort of books would you be likely to select? Probably short, simple ones. And what would be the likely effect of this prefer-

---

*By contrast, from the perspective of the individual doling out the rewards, "the ultimate goal of behavior modification should always be to get the maximum behavior for the minimum reinforcement," as two advocates of token economies put it.[38] The very essence of rewarding people, then, sets the reward giver and recipient to working at cross-purposes — another way to think about its effects on relationships.

ence on your reading skills and your attitude toward books? The answer is distressingly obvious. If we want children to read more, to read carefully, and to care about reading, then offering them bribes — edible or otherwise — is exactly the wrong way to go about it.

Likewise, in getting students to concentrate on the grades they will receive for successfully completing an assignment, we may manage to get them to do it. But what sort of tasks will they come to prefer as a result? Every time a teacher reminds the class what an assignment is "worth" (not in terms of its meaning, of course, but in terms of how many points toward a grade it represents), every time a parent asks a child what he "got" on a paper (rather than what he got from the act of writing it), an important lesson is being taught. The lesson is that school is not about playing with ideas or taking intellectual risks; it is about doing what is necessary, and only what is necessary, to snag a better letter or number. Most students will quickly accommodate us, choosing "to do that which will maximize the grade and not attempt[ing] tasks in which they might fail, even though they would choose to challenge themselves to a greater degree under other circumstances."[44]

The last part of that quotation is critical. If it has escaped our notice up until now that rewards — grades, of course, being only one example — have these unhappy effects, this may be because we assume that people naturally avoid challenging themselves, that it is "human nature" to be lazy. The evidence shows that if anything deserves to be called natural, it is the tendency to seek optimal challenge, to struggle to make sense of the world, to fool around with unfamiliar ideas. Human beings are inclined to push themselves to succeed at something (moderately) difficult.[45] As a rule, we retreat from doing so and take the easy way out only when something else intervenes — something like rewards. If people all around us generally pick the easy task, it may be because rewards are all around us too.

Just as it is possible for a behaviorally oriented teacher to think about the deeper reasons for a student's actions, so it is conceivable that someone promised a reward could choose to take risks and work on challenging tasks. Theoretically, for that matter, almost any psychological effect can be overcome by someone who is sufficiently determined. But for this to happen, one must swim upstream, attempting to transcend the mindset that rewards, by their very nature, tend to induce. Most people prodded by the promise of a reward will approach tasks in the manner described here. If that orientation disturbs us, then urging people to "be creative" or "go the extra mile" is apt to be far less effective than taking a hard look at our use of rewards to get people to perform.

"Do this and you'll get that" makes people focus on the "that," not the "this."[46] Prompting employees to think about how much will be in their pay envelopes, or students to worry about what will be on their report cards, is about the last strategy we ought to use if we care about creativity. We can summarize this discussion as follows: *Do rewards motivate people? Absolutely. They motivate people to get rewards.*

~ 5 ~

CUTTING THE
INTEREST RATE:
The Fifth Reason Rewards Fail

*Who would have thought that play could be turned into work by
rewarding people for doing what they like to do?*
— Rosemarie Anderson et al., 1976

W E C O M E N O W to what is probably the most tragic single consequence of applied behaviorism and, at the same time, the most important reason for its failure: how rewards change the way people feel
about what they do.

Psychologists sometimes refer to rewards and punishments as "extrinsic" motivators, because they are inducements outside of the task
itself. People who have been led to think in terms of what they will get
for doing something can be described as extrinsically motivated. The
opposite of this is *intrinsic* motivation, which basically means enjoying what one does for its own sake.*

If our goal is quality, or a lasting commitment to a value or behav-
ior, no artificial incentive can match the power of intrinsic motivation.
Think about someone you know who is truly superlative at his job.
Now ask yourself whether he has a bumper sticker on his car that says
I OWE, I OWE . . . IT'S OFF TO WORK I GO or THANK GOD
IT'S FRIDAY or WORK SUCKS, BUT I NEED THE BUCKS.
(One could scarcely imagine more vivid signs of an economic system
in crisis.) Clearly, this is not the sort of sentiment we associate with
people who do excellent work. Such people may be glad to be paid,
and even more glad to be well paid, but they do not see themselves as

---

*For a fuller discussion of the concept of intrinsic motivation, see Appendix B.

· 68 ·

working primarily in order to collect a paycheck. They love what they do. Sometimes they even keep doing it on their own time.

This doesn't mean that our interest in a task fully accounts for how well we do it[1] — or even completely explains why performance drops in the presence of rewards.[2] But intrinsic motivation remains a powerful predictor of how good a job someone will do in the workplace or how successfully he or she will learn in school. As one group of researchers summed up the available evidence, "Intrinsically motivated people function in performance settings in much the same way as those high in achievement motivation do: They pursue optimal challenges, display greater innovativeness, and tend to perform better under challenging conditions."[3]

Few readers will be shocked by the news that extrinsic motivators are a poor substitute for genuine interest in what one is doing. What is likely to be far more surprising and disturbing is the further point that rewards, like punishments, actually undermine the intrinsic motivation that promotes optimal performance. I have already offered hints about this phenomenon in describing how coming to see ourselves as engaging in a task to get a reward typically alters the way we view that task. We will now explore this effect more carefully.

The Old Man's Plan

Psychology, and social psychology in particular, is often accused of doing little more than ratifying common sense and describing what we already knew to be true in more impressive-sounding language. When researchers find something that upsets the conventional wisdom, it is therefore worth paying attention. The discovery of how rewards affect achievement offers a textbook example of such a counterintuitive finding (even if it is still ignored by many psychology textbooks). And if we peel back the effect on achievement, we find ourselves looking at something no less fundamental and significant: the effect of rewards on interest.

This research first appeared in the early 1970s, with two investigators stumbling onto the same finding independently, as often happens in science. In this case, the two were psychologists in their late twenties who lived across the country from each other and favored different experimental approaches. Edward Deci, at the University of Rochester, performed the first of what turned out to be a series of experiments with college students. The basic design was ingeniously simple and, as tends to be the case in social psychology, a little deceptive. Each subject was asked to work on an interesting spatial-relations puzzle. Half were promised money; the other half weren't. Then the experimenter announced that it would be a few minutes before the next phase of the study got started. The subject was left alone in a room to wait, where he or she could continue playing with the puzzle, read a magazine, or daydream.

Actually, this *was* the next phase of the study; the subjects were secretly watched to see how long they worked on the puzzle when they had a choice. Those who had been paid, it turned out, now spent less time on it than those who hadn't been paid. It appeared that working for a reward made people less interested in the task. Or, as Deci put it, "money may work to 'buy off' one's intrinsic motivation for an activity."[4]

When the published report of this experiment arrived with his mail, Mark Lepper of Stanford University was already busy writing up the results of his own study. Lepper's interest in the subject had been kindled in the late 1960s, when he observed young children in Head Start classrooms. Many teachers there used rewards to induce children to play with learning games, which they dutifully did. But when the rewards were no longer available, Lepper noticed that the kids wanted nothing to do with these activities anymore — whereas in classrooms that left it up to the children to decide what to play with, lots of them eagerly played with the very same games.

"You didn't have to be a psychologist to see that the rewards worked — they really controlled kids' behavior," Lepper remarked many years later. "But the negative effects were harder to see. I'm not sure I would have noticed them myself if I hadn't gone to these other schools [that didn't use rewards] where kids were loving the activities."[5]

Lepper and his colleagues set about conducting an experiment to figure out what had been going on in those Head Start classrooms. They gave fifty-one preschoolers a chance to draw with Magic Markers — something that most children of that age find very appealing. Some of them, however, were told that if they drew pictures they would each receive a special, personalized certificate, decorated with a red ribbon and a gold star. Between a week and two weeks later, the children were observed in their classrooms. Those who had been told in advance of the certificate they would receive, Lepper discovered, now seemed to be less interested in drawing with Magic Markers than the other children were — and less interested than they themselves had been before the reward was offered.[6]

Deci's study looked at the immediate effects that a financial reward had on adults' interest in a puzzle. Lepper's study looked at the delayed effects that a symbolic reward had on children's interest in drawing. Despite the differences in design, the two experiments converged on a single conclusion: *extrinsic rewards reduce intrinsic motivation*. People's interest in what they are doing typically declines when they are rewarded for doing it. Over the next two decades, scores of other studies confirmed this conclusion.[7] Although various factors, which I will talk about later, do have an impact on the strength of this effect, and while criticisms of varying degrees of persuasiveness have been leveled against this body of research (see Appendix C), the central finding has been documented beyond any reasonable doubt. Remarkably, however, it is not widely known even in the neighboring fields of educational and organizational psychology, much less in the culture at large.

On the one hand, most people are surprised to learn that rewards kill interest. It is widely and erroneously assumed that if you add an inducement (such as money or grades) to do something, an individual's motivation to do it will automatically increase. On the other hand, once the finding is described and explained, many people immediately recognize its plausibility.[8] Most of us, after all, can think of something we used to do just because we found it enjoyable — until we started getting paid for engaging in the activity, after which there was no way we would consider doing it for free. Somehow our intrinsic interest evaporated after rewards were introduced.

An old joke captures this phenomenon as well as any study could. It is the story of an elderly man who endured the insults of a crowd of ten-year-olds each day as they passed his house on their way home from school. One afternoon, after listening to another round of jeers about how stupid and ugly and bald he was, the man came up with a plan. He met the children on his lawn the following Monday and announced that anyone who came back the next day and yelled rude comments about him would receive a dollar. Amazed and excited, they showed up even earlier on Tuesday, hollering epithets for all they were worth. True to his word, the old man ambled out and paid everyone. "Do the same tomorrow," he told them, "and you'll get twenty-five cents for your trouble." The kids thought that was still pretty good and turned out again on Wednesday to taunt him. At the first catcall, he walked over with a roll of quarters and again paid off his hecklers. "From now on," he announced, "I can give you only a penny for doing this." The kids looked at each other in disbelief. "A penny?" they repeated scornfully. "Forget it!" And they never came back again.

The old man's plan was sly but also elegantly simple. He rewarded the children for something they had been doing voluntarily, something they thought was fun, and right away they came to see themselves as harassing him in order to get paid. As soon as the reward was no longer there, neither were they. This, of course, was the whole idea: to sap their intrinsic motivation. But that is also what millions of us — well-meaning parents, teachers, and managers — are doing to the people *we* reward, whether we realize it or not: killing off their interest in the very things we are bribing them to do.

One of the most memorable studies to confirm this effect was conducted by a researcher whose specialty is the investigation not of rewards but of food preferences. Leann Lipps Birch and her colleagues at the University of Illinois took a group of children and got them to drink kefir, a fruit-flavored yogurt beverage they had never tasted before. The children were divided into three groups: some were just handed a full glass, some were praised ("That's very good, you drank it all the way down"), and some were given a free movie ticket for drinking it.

Who drank more? Skinner, of course, would predict higher levels of consumption by those who received either verbal or tangible rein-forcement. Was he right? Whenever I put this question to a group of people who have just listened to an account of how rewards are bad news, most of them now assume that everything Skinner says must be wrong — or at least that I wouldn't bring up the study unless it refuted his prediction. In fact, though, his prediction is absolutely correct. If a reward is attractive enough, people will do almost anything to get it. A few extra gulps of liquid yogurt are surely worth a movie ticket.

But Birch was not interested in who would drink more kefir at the time the rewards were offered. What she wanted to know was how the incentives would affect the children's long-term preferences. What she found was that those who got nothing for drinking it liked the beverage just as much, if not more, a week later. But those who had received tickets — or, to her surprise, praise — now found the stuff much less appealing.[9]

With the possible exception of dairy farmers, no one particularly cares what children think about kefir. The point, of course, is that reinforcement can also kill a taste for creative writing or financial analysis or generous behavior or anything else we value. In fact, this effect is so predictable that rewarding people might even be regarded as a clever strategy for deliberately undermining interest in something. Recently I was told about a Sunday school teacher who handed out candy bars when her students correctly recited Bible verses. It occurred to me that this, given the probable long-term effects, would be a shrewd tactic for an ardent opponent of religion to use.

All those reading incentive campaigns inflicted on elementary school children across the country provide sobering evidence of just how many parents and educators are trapped by Skinnerian thinking. They also illustrate the consequences of extrinsic motivators more generally. Asked about the likely results of Pizza Hut's popular food-for-reading program, educational psychologist John Nicholls replied, only half in jest, that it would probably produce "a lot of fat kids who don't like to read."[10]

Consider the following excerpt from a recent article in *USA Today*:

> When school let out for the summer, a Philadelphia mother was concerned her 9-year-old son would take a three-month vacation from reading.
>
> "He has not learned to love books," Christina Long said then. "He only reads what's required of him."
>
> That was before Greg Prestegord learned he could earn packs of baseball cards and other prizes by reading books through his library's summer reading program.
>
> Two days later the avid baseball fan checked out six books.
>
> "That's why I'm doing it," Greg says. "I must have a million baseball cards."[11]

The article goes on to note that this summer program is similar to others around the country that offer movie parties, zoo passes, and other prizes to children who pick up enough books. Presumably the librarians who administer them and the parents who support them have the very best of intentions. But if Ms. Long is typical, they are not listening to what their children are telling them. Greg is both candid and unequivocal: the baseball cards are "why I'm doing it," he says. Thus, he is still reading (as his mother puts it) "only . . . what's required of him"; all that has changed is that reading is now required to get a card instead of a grade. A program that turns vacation reading into something one has to do to obtain a reward is hardly likely to produce children who have "learned to love books." Quite the contrary.

"But at least he's reading now," Ms. Long might protest. "At least he's being introduced to new books!" And this is true. The reward buys us a behavior — in this case, the act of checking out a book and reading it. But at what price? The quality of performance in general (as we saw in chapter 3) and of learning in particular (as we'll see in chapter 8) tend to decline significantly when people are extrinsically motivated. Once the library runs out of baseball cards, children are not only unlikely to continue reading; they are less likely to read than they were before the program began. Think about it: reading has been presented not as a pleasurable experience but as a means for obtaining a goody. The experience of children in an elementary school class whose teacher introduced an in-class reading-for-reward program can be multiplied hundreds of thousands of times:

> The rate of book reading increased astronomically . . . [but the use of rewards also] changed the pattern of book selection (short books with large print became ideal). It also seemed to change the way children read. They were often unable to answer straightforward questions about a book, even one they had just finished reading. Finally, it decreased the amount of reading children did outside of school.[12]

Notice what is going on here. The problem is not just that the effects of rewards don't last — although, as we saw in chapter 3, that is true in one sense: long-term change of the kind we want is not effected by manipulating people's behavior with incentives. The more significant problem is precisely that the effects of rewards do last, but these effects are the opposite of what we were hoping to produce. What rewards do, and what they do with devastating effectiveness, is smother people's enthusiasm for activities they might otherwise enjoy.

The Scope of the Effect

Further scientific examinations of how rewards affect intrinsic motivation have turned up additional evidence of the extent of their destructive power. A single, one-time reward for doing something you used to enjoy can kill your interest in it for weeks.[13] It can have that effect on a long-term basis, in fact, even if it didn't seem to be controlling your behavior at the time you received it.[14] The reward may also spill over to spoil your attitude about brand-new activities,[15] in effect making you more dependent on extrinsic incentives generally. And just as you don't have to be the one smoking a cigarette in order to be harmed by it, merely watching someone else get a reward for engaging in some activity can have at least a temporary motivation-killing effect.[16]

The scores of studies that have documented the harms of rewards have used many different types of incentives without any apparent difference in result. Candy can spoil one's appetite for the activity in question, but so too can money, a chance to play with a toy (for young children) or a camera (for older children), a certificate or award, a tour of a college psychology department (for high school students), movie tickets, and many other extrinsic incentives.

That doesn't mean that all rewards should be treated as if they were equal. There may be other reasons for objecting more strenuously to the use of certain goodies. For example, we should be especially concerned about presenting food as a prize on a regular basis if there is any chance that doing so could contribute to eating disorders. More important, some things ought to be made available unconditionally, such as love and affection for children or certain basic rights for people in institutions, and therefore should not be presented as rewards for acting in certain ways.

These specific concerns aside, though, any reward has the power to make a task seem less interesting. The basic demotivating effect, moreover, occurs with all kinds of people.

Age. Clearly, as we have seen, "the effects of rewards on intrinsic motivation have been found to be similar across the ages," from very young children to adults.[17] One is never too young or too old to have one's interest in a task reduced when that task is presented as a way of getting a reward.

Sex. Men and women, boys and girls, respond to rewards in pretty much the same way; most researchers have had no reason to expect different results on the basis of gender and have found none.[18] (The one exception to this trend concerns responses to praise, which tends to affect females more negatively than males, for reasons to be discussed in chapter 6.) There hasn't been much research on gender differences in overall extrinsic or intrinsic orientation, and that which has been published doesn't point to a clear conclusion.[19] Of course, males and females may respond differently to a particular reward (such as grades or money) depending on what they have been raised to value. But given rewards that are equivalently desirable, the tasks for which they are given will themselves be valued less by people of either gender.

Race and social class. As far as I can determine, no researcher has ever set out to investigate whether rewards affect one's interest in a task differently depending on race or social status. There are some data, however, on how rewards affect task performance. Studies in the 1950s and 1960s found that "lower-class" children, unlike their middle-class counterparts, tended to perform better on certain iso-lated tasks when given tangible incentives such as candy.[20] The reason, some theorists proposed, is that "the 'extrinsic context' is more com-mon in lower-income homes."[21] Since rewards can, in effect, displace an intrinsic orientation, it is conceivable that a steady diet of them (with or without punishments) could make someone more dependent on extrinsic motivators. But as of the 1970s, most researchers stopped finding these class differences: tangible rewards either didn't improve or actually impeded the quality of performance by black children of low socioeconomic status, just as they did with middle-class whites.[22] Moreover, surveys designed to measure the intrinsic motivation of students have found no differences by race or social class.[23] (Not surprisingly, though, adults in the workplace do tend to be a lot more concerned about money if they aren't making much of it and have very little say over what they do all day: "Man tends to live for bread alone when there is little bread," as Douglas McGregor once put it.)[24]

The Reason for the Effect

I have offered five separate reasons to account for the decline in performance associated with rewards, one of them being the decline in interest in the task. But how do we account, in turn, for *that* effect — for what rewards do to interest? Various explanations have been proposed over the years,[25] and it is probably impossible to prove once and for all that any one of them is correct. Two seem to stand out, though, as especially plausible and straightforward.

The first explanation has an appealing simplicity to it and seems to make sense on the basis of our real-life experience: *anything presented as a prerequisite for something else — that is, as a means toward some other end — comes to be seen as less desirable.* "Do this and you'll get that" automatically devalues the "this." The recipient of the reward figures, "If they have to bribe me to do this, it must be something I wouldn't want to do." Or as the educator A. S. Neill put it, promising a reward for an activity is "tantamount to declaring that the activity is not worth doing for its own sake."[26] Thus, a parent who says to a child, "If you finish your math homework, you may watch an hour of TV" is teaching the child to think of math as something that isn't much fun.

Nearly a decade after Mark Lepper killed preschoolers' interest in drawing with Magic Markers by giving them an award, he went back to the same school with a new plan. He noticed that children ordinarily love to draw not only with felt-tip pens but also with pastel crayons. So he told half of them that in order to be able to draw with the pens they would first have to spend some time drawing with the crayons; the other half were told the reverse. When he returned two to three weeks later, he found, sure enough, that whichever activity had been the prerequisite for the other was now something the children were less interested in doing.[27] Other researchers, meanwhile, have found that the greater the incentive we are offered, the more negatively we will tend to view the activity for which we received it.[28]

Even people can be devalued (as Kant realized) if human interaction is seen as a means to some other end. When children were invited to play with someone else in order that they might have access to one of that child's toys — or, in another study, when they were offered cookies for playing with a partner — they were less interested in future interactions with the other child. Similarly, college students, except those who were very shy, turned out to be less likely to continue talking with a stranger if they had been paid earlier for doing so.[29]

The same means-ends explanation probably accounts for the results of the kefir experiment: the beverage was instantly devalued by being presented, in effect, as something you got rewarded for drinking. Another pair of researchers subsequently confirmed that children were less likely to choose a snack food that had earlier been presented as something they had to finish in order to eat something else — even though the two foods were viewed as equally appealing before the experiment. (Just giving the children one snack before the other didn't have this effect.)[30] In fact, a mischievous researcher might be tempted to test the limits of this mechanism by telling a toddler, "No Brussels sprouts for you, young man, until I see every bit of ice cream gone from that dish."*

Even if prerequisites do come to seem less attractive, does that mean that ends become more attractive? Behaviorists observe that any activity we particularly enjoy can be used as a reinforcer (to get us to do something else); is it also true that anything used as a reinforcer will

---

*Actually, one graduate student has conducted such a study, and the major result was amused disbelief from her subjects. Presumably these children, three to four years old, had already been introduced to the same foods under the usual contingency pattern — vegetables as prerequisite, dessert as reward — so they just giggled at the reversal.[31] Ideally, the experiment would have to be conducted when these foods were first offered to them, assuming parents could bring it off with a straight face. Even then, it is likely that the inherent appeal of a sweet, fatty food like ice cream might override its status as a means to another end. (Likewise, nothing short of a miracle could make most people look forward to biting down on a Brussels sprout.)

become something we enjoy? When we hear "Do this and you'll get that," in other words, do we come to like the "that" more than we did before? This possibility, dubbed the "bonus effect," has received only limited support. One team of researchers did find that an activity looked better to children who were allowed to engage in it as a reward than it did to their peers.[32] When Lepper told children they had to draw with pens before they could draw with the crayons, however, interest in the pens went down but interest in the crayons didn't go up. Likewise, the two-snack study didn't find enhanced appeal for the reward snack — only diminished appeal for the prerequisite snack.

John Nicholls, who suggested that pizza-for-reading programs are likely to produce fat kids who don't like to read, later joked that we might be more successful at getting children hooked on reading if we offered "a free book for every pizza they eat." It's a clever line, but is it a promising strategy? Can we turn the destructive effects of rewards to our advantage simply by turning the behavior or object we want to promote into the goody to be gained? Probably not. The reason is that there is a second explanation for the loss of interest: *rewards are usually experienced as controlling, and we tend to recoil from situations where our autonomy has been diminished.* Simply exchanging the means and ends doesn't change this crucial feature of applied behaviorism and therefore will not mitigate its negative effect on intrinsic motivation.

For years Edward Deci, Richard Ryan, and others who have passed through the psychology department at the University of Rochester have been propounding and refining this explanation.[33] Its premise is that all of us have a basic desire to feel self-determining or, as Richard deCharms would have it, like an "origin" instead of a "pawn." We need to maintain a measure of control over our own destiny, to have some choice about what happens to us.[34] When something interferes with this sense of self-determination — when, for example, we are simply told what we have to do (and how and when to do it), various undesirable consequences follow. Later I will describe how controlling environments affect children's learning and behavior. For now, the point to be emphasized is that, all things being equal, we are less interested in doing things when we are made to feel like pawns. If we have very little discretion about what we do all day at work or school, there is a good chance we will spend the time wishing the weekend would arrive.

Deci, Ryan, and their colleagues argue that a reward for acting in a particular way does two things: it gives us information about what we have done, and it controls (or attempts to control) our future behavior. The more vividly we experience the latter, the more likely that we will lose interest in whatever we are doing. If we are drawing a picture in the hope of getting a prize, or writing a report in order to receive a favorable recommendation, we come to feel that our work is not freely chosen and directed by us; rather, the reward is "pulling" our behavior from the outside. "Intrinsic motivation is the prototypical form of self-determination,"[35] while "rewards in general appear to have a controlling significance to some extent and thus in general run the risk of undermining intrinsic motivation."[36]

If the problem with rewards is due to the fact that they are controlling, then other things that limit our ability to be self-determining should have exactly the same effect on how we feel about a task.[37] Some evidence even suggests that the extent to which we experience an environment as controlling is a better predictor of reduced interest than whether we have been offered a reward.[38] In any case, there is no question that intrinsic motivation is often corroded by circumstances other than receiving rewards, such as when we are

• **Threatened.** Warnings about what will happen if we don't do something well enough will make that activity a lot less appealing to us.[39] If there hasn't been much research on this point, it is probably because hardly anyone doubts that it is true. (The surprising discovery, after all, is that carrots aren't much better than sticks.)

• **Watched.** Studies with children as well as adults suggest that when we are carefully monitored as we work on a task, we tend to lose interest in it.[40] Later research indicates that this effect seems to occur only when the surveillance is perceived as controlling — for example, when we have reason to think that the observation is being conducted to check our performance or compliance with instructions (rather than, say, just out of curiosity).[41] The implications are disturbing, given the increased use of surveillance, now aided by computers, in the modern workplace.*

• **Expecting to be evaluated.** Closely connected to surveillance is evaluation; the purpose of watching, after all, is usually to see how

---

*In fact, the disadvantages of this practice extend beyond its effects on motivation. Back in the 1950s, an experiment found that merely instructing subjects to keep a close watch over their "subordinates" led them to assume (without any evidence) that those whose performance they were monitoring did their jobs only because they were under surveillance — in other words, that they were not to be trusted and therefore needed to be closely watched. Like rewards, this way of controlling people tends to feed on itself and create its own demand.[42]

good a job someone is doing. Letting people know their performance is going to be evaluated is sometimes said to provide "accountability" — a buzzword in both the public and private sectors — and to push people to do their best. (The strategy is particularly popular with those who assume motivation must come from outside the individual and that people always try to get away with doing as little as possible.) Once again, however, control backfires. When people think they will be evaluated, their intrinsic motivation suffers — even if no reward is offered for doing well, and even if the evaluation turns out to be positive.[43] Performance too declines, especially on tasks demanding creativity.[44] In fact, anytime we are encouraged to focus on how well we are doing at something (as opposed to concentrating on the process of actually doing it), it is less likely that we will like the activity and keep doing it when given a choice.[45] This simple, much-replicated finding has very significant implications for education, and I will return to it in chapter 8.

• **Forced to work under deadline.** Just as the performance of certain tasks can be artificially boosted (in the short run) by offering a reward, so the imposition of a deadline can sometimes light a fire under us, making it more likely that we will finish a job. Some people, for a variety of reasons, grow to depend on an externally imposed structure to the point that they wait until the last possible minute before starting a task. But how do deadlines affect long-term interest in — and, by extension, performance of — the task? I know of only two studies on this subject — both, by coincidence, conducted with male undergraduates; both found a reduction of interest as a result of imposed time pressures.[46]

• **Ordered around.** When parents talk to their children in ways that seem controlling, or intended to pressure them to do specific things, the activities in which they are engaged come to seem less appealing to these children as a result.[47] When adults are assigned performance goals with respect to a reasonably interesting task, they are apt to become less interested in that task than those allowed to work at their own pace.[48]

• **Competing against other people.** If we are concerned about intrinsic motivation, the only thing worse than scrutinizing people's performance, evaluating it, and making them worry about deadlines is to cause a reward or punishment to hinge on the outcome. And the only thing worse than that is to set up the activity so that one person can be successful only when someone else is not. When rewards are made scarce artificially — when success is turned into winning, an outcome available to only one person or team, by definition — the consequences include a drastic reduction in interest. That doesn't mean we necessarily stop engaging in the activity. We may continue because we know of no form of recreation except the kind that involves trying to defeat other people, because we are powerless to change the rules of the workplace or classroom, and so on. But typically we do so with less interest in the task itself. The dominant motivator is now the possibility of victory, or some other extrinsic factor: "one needs the reward of winning in order to persist." No wonder the data show "competitively contingent rewards . . . to be [the kind that is] most controlling (and thus most undermining of intrinsic motivation)," according to Deci and Ryan.[49]

Each of these various forms of control is bad enough on its own; putting them together just accelerates the loss of self-determination. The use of surveillance *and* rewards (either a tangible incentive or praise that is presented in a controlling manner) is worse than either by itself.[50] Rewarding children for playing a game makes them less interested in it; telling them which game they must play reduces its appeal further.[51] But rewards alone do plenty of damage, and they do it, in part, because of our reduced sense of autonomy.

"But If We Just . . ."

In some situations, we may be inclined to explain the consequences of using rewards by noting that whatever has to be done to get them is seen as just a prerequisite; in other situations, we may notice that people lose interest by virtue of feeling controlled. In either case, the reduction in intrinsic motivation is the same, and this fact makes it difficult to rescue pop behaviorism. I want now to consider a variety of claims that are frequently offered in defense of the use of rewards — or proposed modifications of their use — and why they fail to get at the crux of the problem. (In Appendix C, I deal with other responses, made mostly by researchers sympathetic to behaviorism, to the arguments and evidence presented here.)

"Two kinds of motivation are better than one." Outside of psychology departments, very few people explicitly distinguish between intrinsic and extrinsic motivation. But some who do make use of these concepts apparently assume the two can simply be added together for best effect.[52] Motivation comes in two flavors, these people seem to be saying, and both together must be better than either one by itself. What research (and, if we are attentive to long-term consequences, experience) makes quite clear is that things don't always work this way in the real world. You can combine different forms of control to make people less motivated, but it's not so easy to combine intrinsic and extrinsic motivation to make them more motivated. Finding a task interesting, which is both critical to excellence and highly desirable in itself, is usually eroded by the addition of a reward.

"As long as you don't use rewards permanently, there's no problem." The idea that extrinsic motivators are harmless if used only temporarily is favored by some teachers: give a child a chocolate bar for mastering writing skills and then, once the inherent appeal of using the language has taken hold, gradually reduce the frequency or size of the bribe. This technique, a variant of the old "bait and switch" gambit used by salespeople, is enormously appealing because it seems to offer someone who is skeptical about extrinsics a way of using them with impunity. Unfortunately, the evidence on how interest is undermined raises serious doubts about the idea that we can, so to speak, have our candy and eat it, too.

What are the underlying premises of this strategy? First, it assumes that a little bit of something cannot possibly do any real damage. (In reality, just because this is true of *eating* candy doesn't mean it's true of using candy as a reward.) Second, the practice proceeds from a model of human behavior that assumes we can do something to an individual and then, once we have stopped doing it, be assured that there is no lasting effect — rather like moving a piece of furniture into someone's living room and then moving it out again without having changed the room itself. Richard deCharms realized that the truth is quite different: giving someone an extrinsic reason for behaving in a certain way "changes the whole event; it does not just add a reward."[53] The Gestalt has been shifted; the perception of the task and of one's motives may no longer be what they were.

More specifically, the belief that we can offer rewards to jump-start a behavior and then simply fade them out presumes, according to Barry Schwartz, that "the effects of rewards do not carry over beyond acquisition into later occurrences of the activity in question and do not transfer to related, but different activities." And, he continues (consistent with the evidence already reviewed here), "there is no reason to believe that there is anything self-contained about the effects of a reinforcement regimen."[54] This doesn't mean that once we have rewarded people we have no choice but to keep doing so until they die. But we cannot simply provide rewards and expect to be able to withdraw them later without any complications.

"Rewarding people is not only inevitable but apparently desirable since people *want* the goodies we give them."   The trouble with this claim is that it confuses *what* we are offering people with *how* it is being offered. There is nothing objectionable about a teacher's throwing a popcorn party for her class; the problem is making the party contingent on students' behavior ("Do what I tell you and then you will get a treat"). To be sure, there is nothing wrong with offering a child acceptance and reassurance, but there is something very wrong with turning these into rewards that are provided only when the child acts in a certain way. There is no question that people want and need to be paid for the work they do; the danger comes from pushing money into people's faces by promising more of it for better performance. In short, just because we are interested in an object that is being used as a reward doesn't mean that the practice of using it as a reward is itself innocuous. In fact, *the more you want what has been dangled in front of you, the more you may come to dislike whatever you have to do to get it.*

In an earlier chapter I observed that the more we are rewarded, the more we may come to depend on rewards. Now, with the research of Deci and Lepper, with the kefir study and the logic of the old man's plan, it becomes clearer how this vicious circle works. When we are repeatedly offered extrinsic motivators, we come to find the task or behavior for which we are rewarded less appealing in itself than we did before (or than other people do). Thereafter, our intrinsic motivation having shrunk, we are less likely to engage in the activity unless offered an inducement for doing so. After a while, we appear to be responsive to — indeed, to require — rewards. But it is the prior use of rewards that made us that way!

> As rewards continue to co-opt intrinsic motivation and preclude intrinsic satisfaction, the extrinsic needs . . . become stronger in themselves. Thus, people develop stronger extrinsic needs as substitutes for more basic, unsatisfied needs. . . . They end up behaving as if they were addicted to extrinsic rewards.[55]

The teacher shrugs and says, "Hey, if I don't tell them this material will be on the test, they won't bother to learn it." The manager insists the job won't be done right unless she offers a bonus. The parent is convinced it's unrealistic to expect children to do what they're "supposed to" in the absence of an incentive. But look again: these are not arguments for pop behaviorism. They are signs that something is terribly wrong with how the classroom or workplace is arranged (or with what people are being asked to do). Given that rewards can undermine interest, the last thing we ought to be providing is more of the same. Promising a reward to someone who appears unmotivated — or demotivated — is like offering salt water to someone who is thirsty: it's not the solution; it's the problem.[56]

"Let people reward themselves." Giving children a book for each pizza they eat prevents reading from being seen as just a means to an end; in fact the book becomes the end. But this strategy doesn't solve the other problem with rewards, because the children are still deprived of self-control. Exactly the reverse is true of another, more commonly suggested idea: telling someone to administer his own rewards. This may solve the second problem (by letting him make decisions that would normally be made by someone else) but not the first (because the desired behavior is still framed as a prerequisite for — an obstacle to — getting the goody).

For many behaviorists, of course, there is no question of restoring self-control because there is no such thing as self-control;[57] there is only self-administration of reinforcements. In practice, many behaviorists have tried to devise a way by which people can be made to do what the controller wants while letting them pop M&M's into their own mouths — that is, allowing them to choose how or when to reward themselves.[58] Notice, though, that the ultimate goal is still compliance, and the process is therefore no less likely to be experienced as controlling. The result: once again, less intrinsic motivation.

Maybe this is why one behaviorist's review of research on "self-administered contingencies" found only a "weak" improvement with respect to how long such behaviors lasted compared to rewards administered by someone else.[59] Even when the objective isn't necessarily to conform to another person's demands, "people can — and presumably do — pressure themselves in much the same way that they can be pressured by external events, and the results of controlling themselves in these ways are similar to the results of being externally controlled," as Deci and Ryan have observed.[60]

Whatever the explanation, though — failing to change the means-end contingency, failing to change the goal of compliance, or failing to remove the unpleasant experience of pressure — two studies have found that just because we reward ourselves doesn't mean that our interest in the task stays high. Young children who were allowed to give themselves gold stars when they thought they had done a good job solving a maze lost interest in the activity, exactly as those receiving rewards from an adult did.[61] And college students who worked on a puzzle and then selected and read to themselves a statement reflecting the quality of their performance — a statement couched in controlling language (for example, "Good. I'm doing just as I should") — lost interest in the task to the same extent as students who heard a similar evaluation from the experimenter.[62]

If we are determined to use rewards, it does seem to make sense to let people have as much control as possible over what they will get and what they will have to do to get it. All things being equal, the more people retain a sense of autonomy, and the more they perceive the whole arrangement as fair, the less damage will be done. But behaviorism with a friendly face is still behaviorism, and many of its effects will be the same.

"The only problem is that we are offering incentives for the wrong behaviors. If we made rewards contingent on people's doing exactly what needs to be done, the problem would disappear." Two education researchers have stated (without any supporting data) that the "undesirable effects of rewards can be minimized by tying reward delivery to quality rather than mere quantity of performance."[63] Any number of management consultants have made the same assertion,[64] as have behaviorists eager to defend Skinnerian practices from the charge that they undermine motivation.[65] It is true, of course, that if I promised you a reward for every picture you drew, you would very likely dash off an impressive number of poorly drawn sketches. But can I turn things around just by making the reward dependent on *good* work? True, your art might be better than it was when you were paid for sheer quantity. But will it improve compared to a situation without any extrinsic motivator at all?

Of the five reasons that account for how incentives impede performance — their hidden punitive side, their effect on relationships, their failure to uncover and deal with the source of the problem, their tendency to discourage risk-taking, and their long-term negative effect on intrinsic motivation — not one will disappear just because we change the criteria for getting the reward. The problem does not result from the *application* of reinforcements; it resides at the very core of extrinsic motivation.

There has been a debate among researchers for some years about the relative effects of making rewards contingent on performance rather than on simply doing the task — a dollar for every puzzle a subject solves correctly versus a fixed payment for taking part in the study, for example. Some have argued that performance-contingent rewards (PCRs) ought to boost interest in a task since they offer evidence that a job has been done well, which makes the recipient feel competent, which is in turn highly motivating.[66]

The best that proponents of this view can do, however, is to cite evidence with major qualifications attached. In some research, interest wasn't undermined by PCRs, but neither was it enhanced.[67] In two studies, the effect on interest was positive, but only for boys (in one case)[68] and only for low-achieving students (in the other).[69] Generally, for PCRs to have even a neutral effect it is necessary that people be led to believe they are successful so they feel competent.[70] But if competence is a key to intrinsic motivation, what happens to the motivation of all those who are working for a PCR and don't get it? Moreover, if informational feedback is desirable, it's easy to tell people how well they've done without turning this into an exercise in Skinnerian manipulation. (One study found that people who got PCRs became less interested in the task than those who just received feedback about their performance.)[71]

Even with these qualifications, the studies showing *any* advantage to basing a reward on the quality of performance are in the minority. From Deci's first experiment in 1971 to an experiment that a student of Lepper's conducted in 1992, the research literature indicates that this technique usually undermines intrinsic motivation.[72] A study that is billed as the first to explicitly compare the effects of paying subjects just for taking part in an experiment with paying them on the basis of how good a job they did at a task found that their interest was significantly lower in the performance-contingent situation.[73] In short, PCRs are more destructive — or at best, no less destructive — than other rewards.

These results make perfect sense since, as Richard Ryan puts it, by making a goody contingent on performance, "not only do you control what I do but you control how well I have to do it before you reward me"[74] — a situation more destructive of autonomy (and therefore of motivation) than one where the reward is provided without reference to the quality of performance.* It also sets up a situation that virtually demands the use of other controlling strategies, such as surveillance and evaluation. In later chapters I will discuss the implications of this

---

*This helps to explain the destructive effects of competition, which is, of course, performance-contingent by definition.

research for the use of salary versus commissions, and for how we grade students.

"If we're worried about reducing intrinsic motivation, then what's the problem with giving people rewards for doing things they don't find interesting?" It is true that rewards are most likely to kill interest where there is the most interest to *be* killed; if intrinsic motivation is already at rock bottom, it's hard to lower it any further. It is also true that short-term interest in tedious (and extremely simple) tasks can sometimes be enhanced by offering a reward for working on them.[75] Finally, it is true that the most destructive way to use extrinsic motivators is to offer them for doing something that is potentially interesting in its own right.

(Perhaps a better way to put this last point is to say that it is most important to avoid rewarding people for engaging in an activity or behavior that we would *like* them to find intrinsically motivating. Thus, a regimen of positive reinforcement for potty-training a toddler is not likely to do lasting harm — putting aside for a moment the question of its manipulativeness and the issue of whether children should be induced to use the toilet before they are ready. Why? Because we are not terribly concerned to instill a lifelong love of defecation. But the use of rewards for reading, writing, drawing, acting responsibly and generously, and so on *is* cause for concern, not only because these things could be intrinsically motivating but because we want to encourage rather than extinguish that motivation. *Extrinsic motivators are most dangerous when offered for something we want children to want to do.*)

All of this is true. But does it amount to an invitation to reward people for doing things that are not very interesting? No. Here's why:

1. If we are concerned about performance as well as interest, remember that a number of studies have shown that while extrinsic motivators nearly always reduce creativity, they sometimes cause people to do a poorer job at fairly routine (and presumably uninteresting) tasks, too, such as memorizing, distinguishing between similar drawings and patterns, and so on. Recall also that rewards are generally ineffective at leading to the long-term adoption of uninteresting behaviors, such as using seat belts. Even when our sole concern is getting people interested in a boring task, rewards cannot always be counted on to help. In one study, for example, "extrinsic rewards were no more effective in increasing the motivation of children whose initial level of interest was low than were simple requests to work on the tasks."[76]

But let's take the point one step further. It is often possible to devise creative, interesting ways of doing things that are of themselves quite dull. A friend of mine managed the mind-numbing memorization of anatomy required in medical school by inventing elaborate fables in which different parts and systems of the body played starring roles.[77] One psychologist has described creative ways to make mowing the lawn less boring.[78] Clerical tasks can seem less tedious if they are turned into a game — devising more efficient techniques, coming up with inventive ways of keeping track of what is still to be done, and so forth.

I do not mean to imply that everything we have to do can be made enthralling, or that people who work at menial jobs have only themselves to blame when they become bored. Some tasks *are* less interesting than others. Rather, the point is that whatever opportunities do exist for reconfiguring a dull task are put at risk when rewards are used. Extrinsic motivators have the capacity to reduce interest not only in the task itself but in the strategies we might use to brighten the task.

Incidentally, it is important to distinguish between tasks that are inherently uninteresting from those that certain individuals happen not to be interested in. Even if people who are bored by a task seem to respond to a reward,[79] it seems unwise to use artificial inducements to try to interest someone in an activity that other people already enjoy on its merits.* It would be far more productive to ask why he or she is bored. (Perhaps the task is simply too easy or too hard for her, in which case adjusting the level of challenge would seem to make more sense than offering a bribe.) It also undermines the possibility that she will find herself intrinsically motivated at some later point.

> The suggestion has been [made] that extrinsic rewards may enhance the interest and thus the learning of a person with low initial interest in the problem or task at hand, even though their use with highly motivated individuals is unwarranted. This may be so; but if, as we suspect, these rewards create a context that elicits a different pattern of interaction with the task, they may be a poor way to "motivate" even uninterested children. If the offer of rewards produces . . . a more superficial interac-

---

*Ironically, some researchers have offered the opposite argument, attempting to justify the use of extrinsic motivators for tasks that people find highly motivating, or for people who are in general highly motivated. The argument is not that they are necessary in such cases but that interest levels may at some point be resistant to the effects of rewards.[80]

tion of subject with task — then we may be loath to use them even to encourage uninterested children to "learn."[81]

Look at it another way: someone who is obliged to work on something uninteresting may, in fact, experience precious little sense of self-determination.[82] The last thing this person needs is to be controlled further, which is what rewards do.

2. In practice, the idea that we can surgically carve out what is boring in life and use extrinsic motivators here (and only here) is naive. First, when teaching or managing a group of people, it is no easy matter to individualize the use of rewards so that they are offered only to those who are yawning. ("Bill gets a bonus for finishing his report because his intrinsic motivation is low. You're already interested in it, Hillary, so you get nothing.")[83]

Second, even if every individual had similar interests, a given topic will usually contain some elements that are much more interesting than others. Consider elementary school math. Memorizing the multiplication table is not a lot of fun, but exploring mathematical concepts is highly stimulating and very much like a game when presented by a talented teacher. How do we dangle A's in front of children to learn the former and abruptly cease giving grades so as not to kill intrinsic motivation in the latter? The practical problem is compounded when enjoyable and monotonous components are contained within a single task, such as writing a report.

If, therefore, we assume it is acceptable to offer rewards when intrinsic motivation is low, we will end up giving them to some people who are already motivated, or for some activities that are already motivating. Decreased interest is the likely result. Getting people to finish boring tasks more quickly (by promising a reward) is simply not worth it if in the process we turn potentially interesting tasks into boring ones.

3. The practice of rewarding people conveniently spares us from asking hard questions about why we are asking people to do things that are devoid of interest in the first place. Let me immediately concede that there may be tedious jobs that must be done in order for a society, or even a household, to function. Likewise, there may be things we decide children ought to learn that hold little appeal for them at the time. But to acknowledge such necessity in the abstract is very different from assuming that *every* deadening job to which people are consigned every working day of their lives has to be done (or has to be organized as it is at present), or that *every* fill-in-the-blank or

learn-by-heart assignment must be given to students just because that was what we had to do when we were in school.

We need to ask, Which boring tasks really are indispensable? And why? Instead, we take on faith that some people will have to chop up an endless conveyor belt of chicken carcasses regardless of what it does to their health and sanity. We accept without question that children have to memorize the state capitals even though they could look up that information whenever they need it. Like any other tool for facilitating the completion of a questionable task, rewards offer a "how" answer to what is really a "why" question. "Reach for the reinforcements if people find a task uninteresting" is a slogan that perpetuates the status quo and allows us, as teachers and managers and citizens in a democracy, to continue taking certain things for granted.

4. Even when we have decided that a particular uninteresting task simply must be completed, artificial inducements are not our only option. There are other ways, less manipulative and more respectful, to encourage people to do things that they are unlikely to find intrinsically motivating. The rule of thumb for getting people to internalize a commitment to working at such tasks is to minimize the use of controlling strategies. Deci and his colleagues have proposed a three-pronged approach: First, imagine the way things look to the person doing the work and acknowledge candidly that it may not seem especially interesting. Second, offer a meaningful rationale for doing it anyway, pointing, perhaps, to the long-term benefits it offers or the way it contributes to some larger goal. Third, give the individual as much control as possible over how the work gets done.[84]

The last of these suggestions brings us back full circle, since the deprivation of self-determination helps explain the damage that extrinsic motivators do. An affirmative emphasis on giving people choice will play a central role in the last three chapters of this book, which are concerned with laying out practical ways to achieve the advantages that cannot be realized through the use of behaviorist tactics.

"Some people are more extrinsically oriented than others. Why not give rewards to those who seem to want or need them?" At first glance, nothing could be more logical than matching a treatment to the personal predilection of the individual. This idea is particularly appealing to educators who support the recent emphasis on "learning styles," which recognizes that students have distinctly different skills and ways of knowing. The premise is difficult to dispute but not always appreciated: where teaching is concerned, one size just does not fit all.

There is something fundamentally troubling, however, about stretching this approach until it includes the provision of extrinsic motivators. I'm not referring here to the practical problems of trying to individualize rewards in a work or school setting; let us set those aside for the sake of the argument. Two questions that are even more important need to be asked in weighing whether to reward people just because they seem predisposed to respond to rewards: Where did this disposition come from? And what are our long-term goals for people — particularly children — with respect to motivation?

All of us start out in life intensely fascinated by the world around us and inclined to explore it without any extrinsic inducement. It is not part of the human condition to be dependent on rewards; in fact, there is no reason to think that *anyone* is born with an extrinsic orientation. If such a "trait" exists, it is only in the weakest sense of this word. We are not talking about an innate characteristic, or even necessarily an enduring one,[85] but something that is learned and, presumably, can be unlearned. It is a function of the way we have been treated, the extent to which we have been trained to think that the reason to learn or work or live according to certain values is to get a reward or avoid a punishment.

Ryan and his colleagues put it this way: "Given particular outer conditions and approaches to education, an inner world will eventually emerge which conforms to and matches it."[86] If people's "extrinsic-ness" is really a result of internalizing the orientation of their environments, then it should vary depending on one's experience. This is exactly what we find: teachers who use controlling techniques such as extrinsic motivators tend to produce students who are more extrinsic, while those who emphasize students' autonomy produce students who are more intrinsic.[87]

Most American schools marinate students in behaviorism, so the result, unsurprisingly, is that children's intrinsic motivation drains away. They typically become more and more extrinsically oriented as they get older and progress through elementary school.[88] For us to turn around and say of those students who are particularly dependent on extrinsic motivators that this is just their motivational orientation or "learning style" — something to which we must reconcile ourselves and to which we have to respond by providing more rewards — seems unsatisfying, to say the least.*

---

*The same is true regarding adult workers with an extrinsic orientation: there is evidence to suggest that this is simply a response to the deprivation of intrinsic satisfactions (see page 131).

The second question we should ask before dishing out more rewards for those who are lacking in intrinsic motivation concerns what we are hoping to achieve. Is our ultimate goal simply to effect a pleasing correspondence between the individual and the intervention? The result will be to ensure a continued lack of genuine interest in learning or acting responsibly, thus requiring an endless supply of extrinsic motivators. Two researchers have questioned the long-term benefits of relying on "educational practices matched to the particular motivational orientation of each student" since to do so

> further reinforces and maintains this extrinsic orientation. . . . [If] external teacher control of the classroom is not the ultimate long range objective . . . the teacher must . . . move beyond relying on punishment and reward . . . to more autonomous classroom environments . . . [in order] to encourage development of an [intrinsic motivation] orientation in [extrinsically motivated] students.[89]

If we see intrinsic motivation (and self-directed learning) as something worth promoting, then it will not do to say we should give rewards to those who seem to need them and leave it at that.

Minimizing the Damage

The point of the preceding section was that the detrimental effects of applied behaviorism, especially with respect to subsequent interest in the task for which people have been rewarded, are inherent in the very idea of "Do this and you'll get that." In Part Three I will talk about alternatives to extrinsic motivators in the context of the workplace, the classroom, and the family. But for people who must, or feel they must, continue to hand out rewards, it is possible to reduce the extent of the harm they do. Here are half a dozen practical suggestions for limiting the damage over the long haul:

• **Get rewards out of people's faces.**   If they must be given, at least reduce the salience of the rewards — that is, how conspicuous and relevant they are. Research suggests that the more prominent an extrinsic motivator is, the more intrinsic motivation is undermined.[90] Our challenge is to offer fewer of them, make each one smaller, give them out privately, and avoid making a big fuss over the whole process.

• **Offer rewards after the fact, as a surprise.**   People who protest that their intent is not to control people but only to "recognize excellence" (an idea taken up in the next chapter) or to show appreciation can demonstrate they mean what they say by taking care not to tell people in advance what they will get for doing something. Lepper and a colleague argue that the receipt of an unexpected reward "should not typically lead subjects to see their previous behavior as having been directed toward attainment of the reward," which means that intrinsic motivation is less likely to decline.[91] Indeed, most studies have found that being presented with an unexpected goody neither helped nor hurt.[92] The problem, of course, is that if people receive a surprise reward this time, they may come to expect another one next time; then, whether they get one or not, their interest in the task may drop.

• **Never turn the quest for rewards into a contest.** Extrinsic motivators, as I have noted, become more destructive when the number of them is artificially limited — that is, when performance is measured in relative rather than absolute terms.[93] If bonuses are to be handed out at work, they should be available to anyone who meets a given standard instead of making each person an obstacle to the others' success. Likewise, the tendency of some classroom teachers to grade on a curve is nothing short of immoral: it gratuitously limits the number of good grades just so the result will conform to an arbitrary, fixed distribution (few grades that are very bad, an equally small number that are very good, and a lot that are mediocre). This requires making meaningless distinctions between essentially comparable performances so that only a few students will receive a top mark. More important, it turns students into rivals, creating an atmosphere of hostility and sabotaging the possibility of cooperation that leads to higher-quality learning. Finally, in an organization or school that cares about excellence there is no place for awards assemblies or banquets. (These might be defined as public events that instantly transform most of the people present into losers.) Either people do not take them seriously, in which case there is no reason for them to exist, or people *do* take them seriously, meaning that watching someone else get an award is a powerful demotivator — in which case, again, there is no reason for them to exist.[94]

• **Make rewards as similar as possible to the task.** So-called endogenous rewards reduce the gap between what people are doing and what they are getting for it.[95] If you feel compelled to give a child something for having read a book, give her another book.

• **Give people as much choice as possible about how rewards are used.** Although rewards are basically mechanisms for controlling people, you can minimize the destructive consequences by including the potential recipients in the process of deciding what will be given out and how and to whom.[96] At the very least, they should play a major role in evaluating the quality of what they have done. Take care, though, that this process does not turn into such a major production that the rewards become more salient than they would otherwise be.

 • **Try to immunize individuals against the motivation-killing effects of rewards.** It is possible that in some circumstances people's intrinsic motivation can be shored up so that they are more resistant to the harmful effects of rewards. Some laboratory experiments have countered these effects by convincing people that they find the task interesting,[97] reminding them that they used to be interested in it,[98] or training them to focus on what is intrinsically motivating about it.[99] The implication is that in certain cases the act of offering an extrinsic motivator will not lower an individual's intrinsic motivation. However, the risks involved are too great, the legacy of rewards too ominous, and the findings of this research too tentative (and laboratory-bound) to choose such a strategy over simply minimizing rewards when the latter is an option. When it is not, we might as well do what we can to help people shrug off the implicit message offered by extrinsic motivators.

All of the reasons that rewards fail to improve the quality of performance are also more than that: they are arguments against pop behaviorism in their own right. This is most decisively true in the case of the explanation discussed in this chapter. Doing something in order to receive an extrinsic motivator makes us less interested in what we are doing.

The more tasks that are undermined in this way, the more tragic this phenomenon becomes. If it were only changing inner tubes that became boring to a bicycle repairman, if it were only history class that seemed to a teenager to last forever, that would be one thing. But financial incentives for the worker and an emphasis on making the honor roll for the student may turn the bulk of what they do from Monday through Friday into one long, dreary prerequisite. Granted that some kinds of work (and school curricula) are tedious in their own right; rewards are hardly the only reason that people lose, or never develop, interest in what they are doing. But add up the impact of what has been described in this chapter and you are looking at an enormous sacrifice for the dubious short-term gains offered by behaviorism. When "Do this and you'll get that" is the rule rather than the exception in our lives, we come to feel, in the words of one expert in motivation, "that psychic energy invested in new directions is wasted unless there is a good chance of reaping extrinsic rewards for it . . . [which means we] end up no longer enjoying life."[100]

And the psychological costs do not end there. Our sense of ourselves as basically competent and worthwhile, of being able to have an impact on the events that shape our lives — in short, our mental health — is in jeopardy when extrinsic motivation displaces intrinsic.[101] Recent research corroborates this by indicating that extrinsically oriented people, presumably as a result of having been subjected to extrinsic environments, tend to be more depressed and to feel more helpless than intrinsically oriented people; when things aren't going well, their reaction gets even worse. Helplessness is an understandable reaction, given that someone else is in a position to decide whether or not we get the reward for which we have been working.[102]

It is not a pretty picture, but it is one whose forms and shadings we know very well. What we don't always recognize is its connection to the Skinnerian landscape that surrounds us.

~ 6 ~

THE PRAISE PROBLEM

> Children have an intrinsic desire to learn. Praise and manipulation
> can only serve to stifle that natural motivation and replace it with
> blind conformity, a mechanical work style, or open defiance to-
> ward authority.
>
> — Randy Hitz and Amy Driscoll, 1988

IT IS ONE THING to consider abandoning the use of gold stars and
candy bars. But *praise?* All of us hunger for approval; many of us
wish we had gotten a lot more praise (and a lot less criticism) as
children. When the experts tell us to get in the habit of finding something about people's behavior that we can support with positive comments, this strikes us intuitively as sound advice. So what could
possibly be wrong with telling our children (or students or employees)
that they've done a good job?

In this chapter, building on what has gone before, I try to answer
that question, arguing that we need to look carefully at why we praise,
how we praise, and what effects praise has over time on those receiving it. I distinguish between various forms of positive feedback: on the
one hand, straightforward information about how well someone has
done at a task, or encouragement that leaves the recipient feeling a
sense of self-determination; on the other hand, verbal rewards that
feel controlling, make one dependent on someone else's approval, and
in general prove to be no less destructive than other extrinsic motivators.

If by the word *praise* we mean only the latter form of feedback,
then it would seem to follow that praising people is always problematic. If we prefer to define the word more broadly so that it takes in all
forms of positive feedback, then we can safely say that only some
versions of praise need to be avoided. Which definition we use doesn't
matter. The critical points are that some approving comments are not
only acceptable but positively desirable, and some are neither.

On its face, this thesis seems quite restrained — not to mention more moderate than what I have said about other sorts of rewards. But even such a qualified criticism may seem surprising in light of the widespread assumption that praise is always a good thing. Posters for one behavioristic classroom management system urge teachers to PRAISE EVERY CHILD EVERY DAY, and teachers are sometimes evaluated on the basis of how close they come to this standard. Most books on parenting offer no hint that positive comments could be anything but constructive.* Even some writers who warn about the overuse of tangible rewards imply that replacing them with praise will solve everything.

To try to make sense of the contrary claim that much praise, as distinct from welcome expressions of love and encouragement, is actually undesirable, we begin with a deceptively simple question: What is the purpose of praise? As with the use of rewards more generally, the real point often turns out to be a matter of benefiting the giver rather than the recipient. If we praise people, they are more likely to do what we want, which is not only advantageous to us in itself but also confers on us a sense of power. People whom we praise may come to like us better, too — another significant inducement. As one writer put it, "Often the change which praise asks one to make is not necessarily beneficial to the person being praised but will redound to the convenience, pleasure, or profit of the praiser."[1] Clearly, it is worth reconsidering the use of praise if it turns out to be something we need to say more than something they need to hear.

But let us assume that our primary motive truly is to help the person we are praising. What, specifically, are we trying to do? Three goals are mentioned most frequently: enhancing performance (learning, achievement, and so forth), promoting appropriate behavior or positive values, and helping the individual to feel good about himself or herself. Over the long haul, praise, at least in the form it usually takes, fails to achieve any of these objectives and may even prove counterproductive.

---

*Much of the relevant research, which challenges this unconditional endorsement and raises serious doubts about the way most of us actually praise people, has focused on the school setting. That work, however, is generally applicable to the way we treat children at home, too. In fact, although I will not use many such examples, most of the key points are also relevant to what we say to other adults.

"Good Work!" vs. *Good Work*

Studies on the relationship between praise and achievement are remarkably scarce. Apparently, blind faith in the Skinnerian model has convinced most people that telling someone what a good job she is doing will cause her to learn or perform more effectively in the future. For all the exhortations to praise one's employees that one finds in "how to manage" books, not a single study, to the best of my knowledge, has ever examined whether this practice really does improve performance on the job.

Two scholars, however, have reviewed the available research on classroom performance. One found that "praise does not correlate with student achievement gains,"[2] and the other concluded that "correlations between teachers' rates of praise and students' learning gains are not always positive, and even when correlations are positive, they are usually too low to be considered significant."[3]

Two recent experiments underscore the point. In one, fifth and sixth graders in Israel were asked to work on a task requiring creativity. Those who were praised for their performance went on to do lower-quality work on a similar task as compared to subjects who received more neutral comments. What's more, these children didn't do as good a job as they themselves had done before being praised.[4] In a series of studies with American college students, meanwhile, "praise consistently led to impairment in skilled performance. Indeed," the researchers conclude, "these results suggest that an effective way to disrupt skilled performance is to compliment the performer immediately beforehand."[5]

What's going on here? Why should praise not only fail to boost achievement but actually drag it down? In addition to the explanations suggested in chapter 4, four reasons come to mind. First, when someone is praised for succeeding at tasks that aren't terribly difficult, he may take this to mean he isn't very smart: that must be why someone has to praise him. This inference leads to "low expectations of success at difficult tasks, which may in turn result in decreased persistence and performance intensity at these tasks."[6]*

---

*Praising people's effort may signal that they have to try so hard because they aren't very good at what they are doing. For this reason, some researchers suggest praising ability instead, which is supposed to enhance one's feeling of competence. Unfortunately, encouraging people to attribute their success (or, by implication, their failure) to something that is outside their control, such as a fixed level of ability, may make matters

Second, telling someone how good she is can increase the pressure she feels to live up to the compliment. This pressure, in turn, can make her more self-conscious, a state that often interferes with performance. Sylvia Plath once commented that while she wanted her poetry to be accepted by others, the acceptance "ironically freezes me at my work."[8] The artist Andrew Wyeth observed that, on hearing expressions of approval for a painting in progress, "you become fearful you are going to lose it."[9] What is true for highly creative individuals surely applies to the rest of us. In fact, those of us without extraordinary talent may be even more susceptible to such praise-induced paralysis, particularly if the praise is explicitly tied to future performance — such comments as "Since you did so well on that, you should also be able to do well on this."[10]

Third, while Skinner declared that praise "encourages us to take the risks that expand our lives,"[11] there is reason to think that exactly the opposite often occurs. One classic classroom study, by Mary Budd Rowe, found that elementary school students whose teachers frequently used praise showed less task persistence than their peers.[12] Why? Perhaps because praise sets up unrealistic expectations of continued success, which leads people to avoid difficult tasks in order not to risk the possibility of failure. If we steer clear of situations in which we might fail, we eliminate any chance of being criticized by the very person who just praised us. Praise encourages some children to become dependent on the evaluations offered by their teachers — a point to which I will return shortly — and "those who are unable to meet their teachers' expectations . . . ultimately decide to give up trying."[13]

Finally, praise, like other rewards, often undermines the intrinsic motivation that leads people to do their best. I say "often" because the laboratory research is not entirely consistent on this point. One of the reasons for this inconsistency may be the fact that different researchers mean different things by "praise" (or "verbal reward," "social reward," or "positive feedback"). Sometimes the comment offered to subjects is nothing more than an exclamation ("Good work!"), and sometimes it includes specific information about how well they did on the task. It may involve a comparison to their earlier performance, or to the performance of others, or neither. The comment may focus on

---

worse by discouraging them from taking responsibility for working to improve their performance. It may be most sensible to avoid casting praise as a comment on either effort or ability.[7]

the person or only on the work itself. It may refer to ability ("You're very creative") or to effort ("I can see you're trying awfully hard"). These variations from one study to another could well be responsible for the different effects they have turned up.[14] In fact, even subtle differences in inflection can impart an entirely different flavor to a compliment: "That's very good" may be spoken with a pompous solemnity, with a note of surprise, accompanied by a slow, thoughtful nod, and so forth. Depending on the delivery, we might react with delight, indifference, or even irritation.

Whatever the reason, though, the research findings are not uniform. Before turning to the work that documents negative results, we should pause to consider the fact that a few studies have found that people seemed more interested in a task after being praised for what they were doing[15] and still others have found that praise neither helped nor hurt.[16]

Those impressed by this positive or neutral research have argued that praise isn't as bad as other extrinsic motivators for several reasons. First, it is less salient. Something you hear should have less of an impact than something physically handed to you, the latter serving as a lingering reminder that you got a goody for what you did and you may have done it for that very reason.[17] Second, praise is thought to be less controlling. You may not come away feeling that someone is trying to manipulate your behavior if that person gives you a compliment rather than money or M&M's.* Third, praise is less likely to be promised in advance. Rewards are most damaging when they are expected — that is, when "Do this and you'll get that" is heard before we do something — whereas praise generally comes as a surprise, after the fact.[18]

The case that praise is less harmful than other rewards rests mostly on these three claims. But what if any or all of these distinctive features don't apply? Surely praise can be plenty salient, making (and retaining) just as much of an impact as any tangible reward.[19] It can also be heard as an attempt to manipulate our behavior, not just as feedback on our performance. And it can be something we anticipate receiving, especially if it's been given to us in the past when we complied with someone's wishes. Whenever praise *is* salient, controlling, or expected,

---

*It is worth noting, incidentally, that subjects in laboratory studies are praised by people they don't know, which may not be experienced as controlling. This fact casts doubt on the assertion by some psychologists that praise is innocuous. In real life we may react quite differently to praise from our parents, teachers, and managers.

it should lower interest in what we are doing, just as other rewards do. We may persist with whatever we were working on in the hope of being complimented, but we would no longer be intrinsically motivated by the activity itself. (See Appendix B for more on this distinction.)

A good deal of research has found that intrinsic motivation does indeed decline as a result of praise. That's what happened in the Israeli study, which is probably why the children's creative performance declined as well. In the kefir experiment described in the previous chapter, children who were praised for drinking the beverage, like those who were rewarded with movie tickets, came to find it less appealing. Yet another study found that elementary school students who generally didn't see themselves as having much control over their own lives showed less interest in what they were doing after being told, "That's the best work you've done so far."[20]

When researchers deliberately erase the factors that are said to make praise harmless, the negative effects are particularly visible. If undergraduates are led to *expect* a "social reward," their interest in a task declines.[21] The same thing, according to three different studies, happens when children or adults are given positive feedback that sounds controlling (for example, "You're doing fine — as you should be doing").[22]

Here, then, we have four accounts of how praise may impede performance: it signals low ability, makes people feel pressured, invites a low-risk strategy to avoid failure, and reduces interest in the task itself. Regardless of which of these seems to be operating, the evidence suggests that praise "interacts with other variables in a manner analogous to tangible rewards."[23] That means it is a poor bet for enhancing the quality of what people do.

Hooked on Praise

We praise people, especially children, not only to get them to do good work but also to help them develop good values and healthy self-esteem. Here too, though, we must be careful. Parents must offer love and support as well as guidance and instruction, and in the following section I will elaborate on the ideas of informational feedback and encouragement, which contribute to these goals. But words of praise that take the form of verbal rewards generally do more harm than good, particularly when they are doled out as part of a deliberate strategy to reinforce certain ways of behaving.

"Giving praise for prosocial behavior" — that is, for caring, sharing, and helping — "is one of the most common ways parents try to encourage altruism in their children," psychologist Joan Grusec and a colleague observed recently.[24] Since the promotion of good values is the subject of chapters 9 and 12, I will confine myself here to pointing out that, for this purpose, praise again seems to be plagued by exactly the same problems we find with other rewards. Assuming that a child desires the parent's (or teacher's) approval, a supportive comment may alter behavior for a while. But it probably will not create a personal *commitment* to the value in question; in fact, it might actually reduce the likelihood that good behavior will continue when there is no longer anyone around to praise it. In a study of young children published in 1991, Grusec found that those who were frequently praised by their mothers for displays of generosity tended to be slightly *less* generous on an everyday basis than other children.[25]

Praise is no more effective at building a healthy self-concept. We do not become confident about our abilities (or convinced we are basically good people) just because someone else says nice things to us. One key question is whether the acknowledgment we receive helps us to feel as if we are responsible for — that is, the cause of — these admirable attributes. Rewards, including comments that sound like verbal rewards, lead us to feel just the opposite: our behavior seems to be a response to these controlling devices. Thus, the effect of praise may once again be counterproductive rather than merely ineffective.

Some people react quite negatively to positive reinforcement, either becoming openly defiant or withdrawing in a show of passive resistance. Are these acts of sheer perversity? Not at all. They are reactions to a very basic but rarely noticed fact: *the most notable aspect of a positive judgment is not that it is positive but that it is a judgment.* Older children and adults may hear praise as condescending, as a reminder of (or an attempt to bolster) the greater power of the person giving it. Suppose you are having a discussion about politics with some friends and one of them nods gravely after you say something and proclaims, "That is a very good point." Depending on a variety of factors, your reaction might well be intense annoyance rather than pleasure: "Who the hell is he to judge the value of my comment?"

"It is interesting to note here that when the work of a high-status person is praised by a low-status person, this is often seen as presumptuous or even insulting," one writer points out.[26] Precisely because praise usually implies a difference in position, it can produce resistance. Interestingly, some of the very people who recoil from the prospect of judging people or being judged — who speak the phrase "value judgment" as if it were an epithet — are enthusiastic proponents of praise. What they fail to see is that telling someone her work is good is every bit as much a value judgment as saying it is bad. Eventually the person being judged will catch on to what is happening.

Apart from the implied power imbalance, the recipients of praise may not be happy because they realize that the person offering a positive judgment could just as well be making a negative one: "Today she praises me, but will she start criticizing me tomorrow?"* Just as every carrot contains a stick, so every verbal reward contains within it the seed of a verbal punishment. The child may reason (even if not explicitly), "Better to repudiate the whole business so as to deprive her of the power to do me harm."[27]

Yet a third possibility is that praise may clash with what the recipient already thinks about himself.

> The person compares what he "knows" about his abilities and accomplishments with what he is being told about them. . . . In searching the evidence bearing on general praise, the person is more likely to encounter instances that are inconsistent with the evaluation contained in the praise. He must then either begin explaining such instances away or qualify the praise, perhaps rejecting it altogether . . . [perhaps inclining toward] active self-criticism or conscious attempts to sabotage performance.[28]

On the surface, a negative reaction to a positive comment seems bewildering. But this sort of sabotage makes perfect sense in light of the gap between what one is told and what one believes to be true. Another writer offers a concrete example:

> Suppose the teacher says, "What a good boy you are, Jack! You returned the book without my asking you." Does returning the book make Jack a good boy? Of course not! Jack knows this and may think the teacher is not too swift, and then try to show [her] that he can be a "bad" boy and still return books.[29]

As a general rule, we should expect more resistance when the praise is extravagant and very general ("What a good boy you are" rather than "That was nice how you shared your sandwich with Barbara") and

---

*That this is more than a reflection of suspiciousness or insecurity seems clear from the evidence that the same people who praise are indeed likely to criticize or act in a controlling manner (see page 51).

also when it clashes with the person's existing beliefs. The more self-doubt, the more difficult to reconcile the compliment with what one thinks about oneself.

Of course, only some children react to praise in this way. Others respond more cooperatively, more submissively, more "appropriately." We tell them how good they are and they light up, eager to please, and try to please us some more. These are the children we should really worry about.

The desire for approval is very nearly universal in young children. This fact is worth emphasizing in itself, especially by way of response to the assumption that reckless or inappropriate behavior must reflect malign motives. If we recognize that the simple absence of skills may explain what is going on — that children, so far from trying to make our lives miserable, basically yearn for our acceptance — we can avoid setting up the sort of self-fulfilling prophecy that comes from assuming they are up to no good. But at the same time this desire to please must be treated with caution. We have an enormous responsibility not to exploit it for our own ends.

Praise, at least as commonly practiced, is a way of using and perpetuating children's dependence on us. It gets them to conform to our wishes irrespective of what those wishes are. It sustains a dependence on *our* evaluations, *our* decisions about what is good and bad, rather than helping them begin to form their own judgments. It leads them to measure their worth in terms of what will lead us to smile and offer the positive words they crave. Rudolf Dreikurs saw this back in the 1950s: praise, he said, can "lead to a dependency on approval. Overdone, it promotes insecurity as the child becomes frightened at the prospect of not being able to live up to expectations."[30]

Not long ago, a teacher in Massachusetts listened to a critical presentation about praise and shook her head skeptically. Maybe some children can do without it, she said, but what about those whose self-esteem is in the basement? She went on to describe two students in her class who were continually insecure and seemed to need reassurance about everything. How could she be expected to withhold praise from them?

What had not occurred to this caring teacher was the possibility that her praise might be making these children *more* insecure. Every time she told them, "Good job! You really helped me out today!" the desire to please her grew. They were no closer to achieving the security that comes from confidence in their own decisions about how to act, or to developing a set of standards by which to judge their own behavior. Their eyes were on her and their mood soared or plummeted depending on whether she had reacted with sufficient enthusiasm to whatever they had done.

Mary Budd Rowe's study, the one that found less task persistence by children whose teachers praised them heavily, also discovered that these students seemed more tentative in their responses, more apt to answer in a questioning tone of voice. They were less likely to take the initiative to share their ideas with other students. And praise was one factor contributing to a tendency to back off from an idea they had proposed as soon as an adult disagreed with them.[31]

Praising children for the work they do may discourage self-directed learning, since it is our verbal rewards, and not love of what they are doing, that drive them. Praising children for the way they behave, meanwhile, gives them no reason to continue acting responsibly when no one is likely to say nice things to them after they do so, and it gives them neither the skills nor the inclination to make their own decisions about what constitutes responsible behavior.*

But let us return to the fact that not all children react the same way to praise. While utterances that are unmistakably manipulative lead predictably to certain reactions, positive feedback of a more ambiguous sort — the kind that could be perceived either as useful information about one's performance or as an attempt to control — will probably be interpreted differently depending on who hears it. At least two studies have found that "identical statements made by the same teacher under the same circumstances produce different results for different students."[32] This is an ideal illustration of the futility of searching for laws of learning or behavior that apply to all children (much less all organisms): people's various experiences and ways of making sense of the world transform the meaning and consequences of what they hear.

The likelihood that someone will respond positively to praise[33] — or for that matter, that he will be a frequent recipient of praise[34] — may vary according to a child's background and personality. The best single

---

*Some children will internalize that voice of adult approval so that it continues to govern their behavior when there is no authority figure in sight. This is sometimes regarded as evidence of successful socialization. But, as Deci, Ryan, and others have pointed out, some kinds of internal control raise troubling questions. If any internalization occurs as the result of controlling children's behavior with praise and other rewards, it is merely likely to replace an external sense of compulsion with an internal sense of compulsion. There is a world of difference between this and the experience of making one's own decisions and judgments. I will have more to say about this later.

predictor of response is gender: in general, praise is more likely to have undesirable consequences for females than for males. Two studies with college students found that women (but not men) who were praised for their work became less interested in it than those who weren't praised.[35] Deci speculated that this effect was due to the fact that women are more likely than men to view positive feedback as controlling, rather than just providing information about how they did. A later experiment with children supported this hypothesis,[36] while other research suggested that "girls were less able to attribute actions internally and perceive themselves as altruistic" precisely because adults are "more likely to praise girls for this type of behavior."[37]

Encouraging Words

In case any reader might be wondering whether these findings mean that we are supposed to scowl at kids all day, let me be very clear about what does and does not follow. My reading of the evidence is that it does not require us to stop smiling. It does not suggest that we ought to hold ourselves back from expressing enthusiasm about what other people have done. It does not imply that we should refrain from making positive comments. Apart from the fact that few of us are about to take such drastic steps regardless of what the data show, my point is that there is no reason we should.

On the other hand, I think we *are* obliged to think very carefully about the potential pitfalls of verbal rewards and how we can avoid them. This statement (and the arguments leading up to it) can be terrifically unsettling in itself. People sometimes react with nervous laughter, declaring, somewhat facetiously, that if they take all this seriously they will become paralyzed with fear: "What if I accidentally say the wrong thing and praise someone?" But it is important that this concern, which is a perfectly understandable reaction to being asked to question an automatic behavior, not be used as an excuse to continue doing something that doesn't make sense.

The problem with our praise is not, as some people seem to think, just that we overdo it. The problem is with the nature of the praise, with what we say and how. The solution I propose consists of keeping in mind two general principles that might be thought of as the standards against which all praise should be measured. The first principle is *self-determination*. With every comment we make — and specifically, every compliment we give — we need to ask whether we are helping that individual to feel a sense of control over his life. Are we encouraging him to make his own judgments about what constitutes a good performance (or a desirable action)? Are we contributing to, or at least preserving, his ability to choose what kind of person to be? Or are we attempting to manipulate his behavior by getting him to think about whether he has met our criteria? The other principle is *intrinsic motivation*. Are our comments creating the conditions for the person we are praising to become more deeply involved in what she is doing? Or are they turning the task into something she does to win our approval?

To determine the likely effect of praise with respect to these two guidelines, we need to examine, first, our own motives. Are we trying to control someone's behavior for our own convenience, or saying nice things just to have something to say, or hoping to get that person to like us more? Second, we need to think about how our comments sound to the individual who hears them. Our intent, for example, may be to offer useful feedback about the quality of someone's work, but he may interpret what we say as limiting his autonomy. (We can simply ask older children or adults how they perceive what we have said; people of any age can be observed for signs of resistance, dependency, or reduced interest.) Finally, we ought to attend to the objective characteristics of what we say and how we say it.

I want to offer some specific suggestions for how we might praise, but it's useful to remember first of all that giving feedback does not require us to offer praise at all. To put it another way, those of us who are disinclined to give verbal rewards are not obliged to stay silent. There is another alternative, at least in some circumstances, which is simply to provide information about how well someone has done. In the course of an intricate analysis of how teachers praise students, education researcher Jere Brophy says this:

> It is essential that students get feedback about their academic progress and classroom conduct, but this does not require the more intensive and evaluative reactions implied by "praise." Indeed, I see no strict *necessity* for any praise . . . at all. Students do not actually need praise in order to master the curriculum, to acquire acceptable student role behaviors, or even to develop healthy self-concepts.[38]

In fact, to the extent that praise *can* have a positive effect in the classroom or workplace, it may well be because of the information it provides (regarding one's success at performing the task) rather than the expression of approval. Some research on this question[39] — although not all of it[40] — has found that adults and children alike become more interested in what they are doing when they get straightforward feedback about how they are doing it.

Interpreting this finding, however, is somewhat complicated by the fact that the feedback offered by these researchers is almost always positive. If you perk up at the news that you've done well at something, it is probably due to the feeling of competence you derive from this information. In real life, of course, you often *don't* succeed, and there is reason to think that feedback about how you failed won't do much in itself to boost your intrinsic motivation.[41] The challenge for teachers and managers, in fact, is to avoid destroying people's motivation while letting them know they haven't done well — that is, to provide negative feedback in a way that doesn't kill interest. (One way to do this is to describe the failure "in terms of a problem to be solved" and to involve the person performing the task in figuring out ways to improve.)[42]

There's another problem with choosing to provide informational feedback rather than praise: the two can't always be separated. Even when we decide someone has done well and tell him so, it's not easy to strip that information of emotional weight: just as someone informed that he has done poorly may feel criticized, someone told he has done well may interpret this as a verbal reward, which is also undesirable. The trick is to help people regard feedback as information they can use. Someone who tends to be intrinsically motivated as a rule is more likely to see things that way.[43] Likewise, as I will argue later, we can help free students from the reward-and-punishment frame of reference by de-emphasizing the performance aspect of learning.

In all situations, though, I believe there are things we can do to blunt the damaging impact of praise. Here are four practical suggestions.

1. Don't praise people, only what people do. It's less likely that there will be a gap between what someone hears and what he thinks about himself if we don't make sweeping comments about what he is like as a person. "Too much global positive evaluation . . . trains children to think globally, to make their selves the issue in whatever they do, and thus to be prone to both grandiosity and self-contempt," as one child psychiatrist sees it.[44] Saying something about what the person has done (or is doing) makes more sense: "That's a really nice story" is better than "You're such a good writer."

2. Make praise as specific as possible. Not only should we focus on the act or product, but we should do so by calling attention to the specific aspects that strike us as especially innovative or otherwise worthy of notice. This "enables its recipient to judge for himself whether the evaluator's standards are appropriate,"[45] and it pulls him into the task itself rather than fixing his attention on the fact of our approval.[46] Even better than "That's a really nice story" is "That's neat at the end when you leave the main character a little confused about what happened to him."*

3. Avoid phony praise. A parent or teacher who is genuinely delighted by — or appreciative of — something a child has done should feel free to let that excitement show. Praise becomes objectionable when it is clearly not a spontaneous expression but a deliberate strategy, a gimmick that seems to have been picked up from a book or seminar. When we are instructed to "catch people doing something right" and praise them for it, or even to practice praising other people, we are being schooled in a technique. The result is unavoidably contrived.

One symptom of phony praise is a squeaky, saccharine voice that slides up and down the scale and bears little resemblance to the way we converse with our friends. Another is a pause before praising that suggests we have first decided to hand out a verbal reward and are now trying to find someone to whom it can be presented — or even worse, we are trying to control the behavior of a group of children by creating some suspense about who will be made the object of the praise. "I like the waaaaaaay [the syllable is drawn out while the teacher looks around the room and the children scramble to be the chosen one while she settles on the winner] . . . Stewart! is sitting so nice and quiet and ready to work."

A four-year-old can usually tell the difference between a genuine expression of pleasure and phony praise, between a sincere smile and one that is manufactured and timed for best effect. He is more likely to be warmed by the real thing — a fact that perplexes behaviorists since, in their parlance, it is precisely that which is not intended to reinforce that is most reinforcing. On the other hand, just because praise is genuine and spontaneous does not mean that it is guaranteed to be beneficial: the very fact that it means more to a child suggests

---

*Specificity is also useful for preserving interest (and self-respect) when giving criticism. Hearing about particular mistakes one has made is much less threatening than seeing an F, receiving a poor overall performance rating, or hearing a general dismissal of one's work. Feedback that pinpoints the source of the problem and offers suggestions for improvement is likely to minimize the dangers inherent in criticism. (Notice that pointing the way toward improvement is very different from future-oriented comments such as "You can do better," which are likely to be viewed as controlling and to create pressure.)

that it may be even more effective at creating a dependence on the praise giver. Fortunately, when our responses are genuine, the child will at least sense that our motive is not to control.

4. Avoid praise that sets up a competition. It is never a good idea to praise someone by comparing her to someone else. Phrases like "You're the best in the class" (or for adults, ". . . in this department") ought to be struck from our vocabulary. The research is quite clear that such comments undermine intrinsic motivation,[47] but their most pernicious effects are subtler: they encourage a view of others as rivals rather than as potential collaborators. What's more, they lead people to see their own worth in terms of whether they have beaten everyone else — a recipe for perpetual insecurity.[48]

Competition is also fostered by giving praise publicly. For example, the elementary school teacher who announces in front of the class "I like the way Stewart is sitting so nice and quiet and ready to work" has set up a contest for Nicest, Quietest Student, and everyone other than Stewart has just lost. This sort of praise is objectionable for three other reasons as well. First, it does Stewart no favors; his standing with his peers is unlikely to improve as a result of having been identified as Nicest and Quietest. Second, the most important word in that sentence is *I;* Stewart is not helped to reflect on the value of being nice or quiet but only to figure out how to please the teacher.[49] Last, the interaction is fundamentally fraudulent because the teacher, while pretending to address Stewart, is actually *using* Stewart to manipulate the behavior of others in the room. Making an example of someone is a troubling practice regardless of whether we do so with punishments or rewards, and public praise is really not much of an improvement over public criticism. This is why I join with a number of other educators in urging that positive comments be offered in private.[50]

I do so despite the fact that public praise, sometimes involving elaborate competitive ceremonies and awards, is often justified on the grounds that we are "recognizing excellence." Few of us stop to ask what that phrase really means and what our motives really are. *Why* is it important that excellence be recognized?

• If the idea is to let someone know that she has done good work (which presumes that she is unaware of this fact), such feedback can be offered without the trappings of behaviorism.

• If the idea is to convince the person being recognized to keep up the good work, we need to ask, first, whether this is really necessary (did he get this far out of a quest for recognition?), and second, whether offering a reward might actually undermine his motivation for all the reasons reviewed in previous chapters.

• If the idea is that other people will be motivated by watching one of their peers get rewarded, there is ample evidence that extrinsic motivators are more likely to demotivate and that losing in a competition (which is what selective "recognition" often feels like) is even worse.

• If the idea is to clarify and communicate to a wider audience what excellence consists of, this can be done without a lot of hoopla. Moreover, it ought to be done in a format that is more like a conversation than an announcement.

• If the idea is simply that it would be nice to show someone who did a good job that this has been noticed, there is no need to do so in a way that may stir up others' resentment and possibly even embarrass the person being publicly praised. Private comments, offered so as to promote self-determination and intrinsic motivation, are enough to let people know their work is appreciated. There is no reason to offer these comments from a stage or to weight them down with trophies or certificates.

Consider a situation where a large number of people attending a school, working in an organization, or participating in an event are grateful to someone who has worked hard for the benefit of everyone. If thanking that person in public does not seem particularly objectionable, this may be partly because the process of doing so is democratic. By contrast, in the typical ceremony for "recognizing excellence," the people in charge have unilaterally selected, at their own discretion and based on their own criteria, some people to recognize over, and in front of, others. It is their power to do so that is ultimately being recognized.

Rather than talking about how we can minimize the potential disadvantages of praise, Rudolf Dreikurs and his followers prefer to talk about responding to children in ways that "encourage" them.[51] Some of the suggestions for putting that approach into practice, as well as the reasons for doing so, overlap with what I have been talking about. Of course, whether we prefer to cast the issue as a contrast between bad praise and good praise or between praise and encouragement doesn't matter nearly as much as the substance of our responses.

What the Dreikursians contribute to this discussion is the critical point that *evaluative comments are often entirely unnecessary.** We

---

*In this connection, it is worth pointing out that praise appears to be entirely absent in some cultures — a fact that would seem to belie the assumption that the process of socialization requires that children receive selective verbal reinforcement.[52]

can be less judgmental and controlling — and in the long run, more effective at promoting self-determination and intrinsic motivation — by simply acknowledging what a child has done. Just pointing out an aspect of a child's essay or drawing that seems interesting (without saying that it's nice or that you liked it) will likely be sufficient to encourage her efforts.

I recently heard a third-grade student read an original story to her classmates. When she was finished, her teacher said, "You worked hard on that ending. You wrote that part three times." Presumably, the teacher had offered some feedback earlier on what worked and what did not work in the story in order to help the student improve (and encourage her to think critically about what constitutes improvement in story-writing). Now that she was done, it was sufficient to show that her efforts had been noticed and appreciated; the superlatives followed by exclamation points that we tend to lavish on children seemed to the teacher altogether unnecessary. (Notice, incidentally, that when the child turned in a paper that was unsatisfactory, she was given the opportunity to rewrite it rather than being penalized with a bad grade. The emphasis in this classroom was on improvement and learning rather than evaluation.)

Suppose that a young child finishes a drawing and shows it to you. I have said that it is better to focus on the art than on the artist, and better yet to be specific in our comments about the art. But whenever those comments amount to praise in the traditional sense, we run the risk of tilting a child toward the goal of eliciting our approval instead of his own, and making him more intent on the verbal reward than on the process of playing with color and design. These are risks we can minimize by offering observations and questions about what he has done ("Are these mountains over here near the water? Boy, this one is huge, isn't it? How come you decided to draw them in green? . . . What are you planning to draw next?")

Why do most of us respond instead with a barrage of compliments? First, because no thought is necessary to offer them; praise is cheap and easy. By contrast, it takes skill and care and attention to encourage people in such a way that they remain interested in what they are doing and don't feel controlled. (It is always easier to do things *to* people, or to take over and do things *for* them, than it is to work *with* them to help them make their own decisions.)

Second, it feels good to have someone, even someone very short, in the position of looking to us (figuratively and sometimes literally) for our approval. This motive does not play a part in everyone's praise, of course, but we might consider carefully whether it is just a coincidence that what we say has the effect of ensuring that others keep needing to hear what we think.

Third, many of us fear that there is something sterile and chilly about giving comments without compliments. It may feel at first as if we are withholding praise and therefore being stingy with our approval. What matters, though, is whether our responses are offered in such a way as to communicate warmth and concern. If so, children will be encouraged rather than frustrated by what we say. If not, then praise, too, no matter how lavish, is unlikely to be helpful.

These arguments often provoke resistance because they seem to challenge a widespread conviction that all children — indeed, all people — would be better off with more kind words. But when we contemplate the reality of emotionally impoverished families, or the effect of unrelenting criticism, let us keep in mind that the problem in such households is not too little praise. It is too little encouragement and support. To question the use of verbal rewards is not to favor verbal punishment or indifference. On the contrary, children ought to know they are so deeply cared about that their parents and teachers are willing to put their long-term interests ahead of the short-term compliance that extrinsic motivators can secure.

A teacher in Missouri wondered aloud not long ago how she could bring herself to stop praising her students since many of them came from desperate circumstances, from loveless, brutal homes. They *need* my support and approval, she exclaimed. And so they do. But they need it without strings attached; they require unconditional love. By contrast, praise, like all rewards, is conditional. (Only if you do this will you get that — "that" referring here to expressions of delight and support.) Moreover, children in distress need to feel not only loved but potent, capable of making choices and having some say about what happens to them. What they do not need is to be controlled, even by honeyed phrases.

Precisely because it is something that takes thought and effort, responding with encouragement rather than praise requires practice and cannot be taught in five easy lessons. We will need to make sure that this approach, like most suggestions for dealing with children, is not implemented mechanically, with the result that it comes to seem an affectation. We will need to keep in mind the age and capacities of the child to whom we are speaking. (With adults, even a response intended to encourage rather than judge may seem condescending.)

And we will need to be prepared for the fact that we may lapse back into praise sometimes; it is not an easy habit to break.

The Fear of Spoiling

I have not been reticent about criticizing rewards in general or praise in particular. But there is one complaint that I have not offered, and to avoid any misunderstanding, I want now to distance myself from it explicitly. This is the view that leads people to say we should stop rewarding children so often because we're spoiling them, and that kids today expect a goody, or at least a compliment, for everything they do.

The popularity of this criticism seems to have grown in recent years to the point that, while negative comments about rewards are not offered very frequently, the majority of those that are made tend to take this line. Thus, articles urge parents and teachers to "praise conservatively"[53] or "concentrate on giving truly deserved rewards"[54] or use "Tough Praise" predicated on "honest, diligent work," lest children be the recipients of "praise that comes too easily."[55] A cover story in *Newsweek* in early 1992 took aim at educational programs designed to enhance children's self-esteem, snickering at the use of gold stars and stickers and at adults who give "praise for walking across the room without falling over."[56]

Let us explore the sensibility reflected in this criticism. To begin with, it suggests that the problem with rewards is limited to how easily we give them; the title of a representative article written from this perspective complains that "Giveaways Have Gone Too Far!"[57] This seems to me a superficial analysis because it ignores what is at the heart of the trouble — the idea of extrinsic motivation.

More important, though, those who complain that we are spoiling children with rewards often betray a deeper reason for their discomfort: they seem to think that kids should just do what we want them to do because we tell them to do it. It would not surprise me to learn that many of these critics are equally unhappy with the idea that we ought to explain to children the reason for our requests. Anything other than automatic, unquestioning compliance is annoying to some people. There is no attention given to *what* we are asking children to do, whether the request is reasonable or the school assignment is worth doing. They should simply do what is expected of them without requiring encouragement or justification.

I object not only to this demand for obedience but also to the tendency to focus on how easy kids have it today. The real problem is not that children expect to be praised for everything they do; it is that adults are tempted to take shortcuts, to manipulate their behavior with the use of rewards instead of explaining, helping them to develop needed skills, fostering a commitment to good values, and bringing them in on the process of deciding how to learn and behave.

Traditionalists who ridicule attempts to boost self-esteem like to say that people feel good about themselves as a result of what they have achieved; they don't achieve because they feel good about themselves. There may well be some truth to this. At any rate, it is a hypothesis worth considering.* But lurking beneath the assault on such programs is a more visceral objection that might be identified as a fear that somebody is going to get a "psychological free lunch" and be pleased with himself without *earning* that right. (One imagines that last phrase being barked out while a fist is slammed on the table for emphasis.) If I am right about the ideology that is at work here, it is a difficult one to defend. Conservative economic principles are out of place when we are talking about what children need and deserve. What they need, as I have said, is unconditional approval and acceptance — the very opposite of verbal rewards, and especially of Tough Praise. What they deserve, I believe, is what they need.

Others couch the objection in more pragmatic terms. Children will become fat and lazy — they will stop doing schoolwork or acting responsibly — unless they have to jump through hoops to get adults' approval. This position is based on assumptions about learning and "human nature" that simply do not stand up under close scrutiny and which I have begun to address in talking about equity theory (chapter 2) and the futility of making rewards contingent on quality (chapter 5). Let me just say here that selective reinforcement and indiscriminate reinforcement are two versions of the same thing, two manifestations of the same theory of motivation. The trouble with rewards is not that

---

*Of course, both may be true: achievement fortifies self-esteem, and confidence in oneself also facilitates achievement. In any case, the fact that students need to achieve something of which they can be proud is not, as is often assumed, an invitation to go "back to basics" — that is, to a traditional curriculum emphasizing memorization and recitation. We ignore at our peril (and more important, our children's peril) the question of whether the material they are asked to learn is engaging and relevant to their life experience. What sort of achievement leads children to feel good about themselves is very much an open question.

we hand them out too easily; it is that they are controlling, ultimately ineffective, and likely to undermine intrinsic interest. That means they will be counterproductive even when — maybe especially when — they are most clearly contingent on what precedes them. Giving rewards less frequently or more stringently will not solve the underlying problem, because the problem is behaviorism itself.

· *Part Two* ·

REWARDS IN PRACTICE

7

PAY FOR PERFORMANCE:
Why Behaviorism Doesn't Work in the Workplace

[The fault does not lie] with the use of poor techniques in administering incentive systems. . . . [Rather,] there is something wrong with the theory of worker motivation upon which the policies and procedures are based.

— William Foote Whyte, 1955

EXECUTIVE SUMMARY

Not only are incentive systems and pay-for-performance plans pervasive in U.S. companies, but there exists a deep and rarely questioned commitment to the belief that offering people rewards will cause them to do a better job. The evidence, however, suggests that extrinsic motivators in the workplace are not only ineffective but often positively counterproductive. The most familiar reasons proposed to explain this failure deal with relatively minor issues that apply only to specific incentive programs. But several other reasons strike at the heart of the assumptions about motivation that underlie all such programs. The bottom line is that *any* approach that offers a reward for better performance is destined to be ineffective.

· 119 ·

Incentives Prevail

IF POP BEHAVIORISM were a religion, American managers would have to be described as fundamentalists. It is difficult to overstate the extent to which they, and the people who advise them, believe in the redemptive power of rewards. Certainly, the vast majority of corporations utilize some sort of program whose purpose is to motivate employees by tying pay (or other forms of compensation) to one or another index of performance.[1]

To get a better sense of the breadth and depth of this allegiance to the Skinnerian model, though, we might attend to what managers, as well as consultants and business school instructors, have to say on the matter. Tellingly, it does not occur to most of them even to question the value of extrinsic motivators. A typical handbook on compensation matter-of-factly states that to pay "correctly" is to pay "in relation to performance."[2] In business journals we regularly come across declarations like this one: "Organizations must give the greatest rewards to those who perform best. To do otherwise is inconsistent with concern for productivity."[3] And from an academic anthology on incentives: "The more closely pay is tied to performance the more powerful its motivational effect."[4] Such assertions have about them the flavor of obvious truths that need not be defended because no one doubts their veracity. They are talismans that the writer touches before moving on to deal with something controversial.[5]

Occasionally one comes across an article or book that attempts to bring some "psychological" perspective to bear on the field of management, drawing from humanistic or psychoanalytic theory, for example. Such works stand out in sharp relief against a background of thousands of other publications, but the truth is that all these other writings are also based on a psychological theory.[6] That theory happens to be behaviorism, which is so pervasive in the field that no one even regards it as a theory. Its precepts are axiomatic.*

This is not to say that no one criticizes incentive systems. Plenty of articles do just that, and they are often published under arresting titles: "Why Incentive Plans Fail," "How to Ruin Motivation with Pay," and so forth. But the problem with such plans, these authors

---

*Behaviorism, in turn, as I suggested in chapter 1, embodies certain assumptions about learning and human nature. Consider the recommendation by a group of consultants that employees be given "an incentive (an award) for learning. What is learned becomes worth knowing"[8] — the implication, of course, being that anything learned in the absence of an artificial inducement is not worth knowing.

eventually give us to understand, concerns nothing more than the details of their implementation.[9] Only fine-tune the calculations and delivery of the extrinsic incentive — or, perhaps, hire the author as a consultant — and all will once again be right with the world. Even researchers who have documented the utter failure of such programs rush to assure us that, of course, "merit pay is desirable in principle."[10] We just have to learn how to do it right.

> Anyone reading the literature on this subject published 20 years ago would find that the articles look almost identical to those published today. Most experts on the subject were then, and are still, decrying the fact that we are doing a poor job of administering merit pay plans. . . . [Despite the] new approaches . . . the results never seem to improve.[11]

That assessment, which could have been written this morning, was actually offered in 1975. Criticisms that dig deep enough to question our assumptions about what motivates people are published now and then, but mostly then. As a general rule, the more explicitly a business-related book or article challenges — or even identifies — the behaviorist underpinnings of incentive plans, the greater the probability that it was written more than twenty years ago. Notice the irony here: just as social psychologists were starting to recognize how counterproductive extrinsic motivators can be, this message was beginning to disappear from publications in the field of management.

The devotion to reward-and-punishment psychology is, if anything, even more apparent when we put down the journals of management and talk to managers themselves. Many denizens of the corporate world still seem to identify with the beliefs that Douglas McGregor referred to collectively as Theory X: people basically don't like to work and therefore need to be controlled and coerced — specifically, by having material rewards promised or withheld — if we expect them to get anything done.[12] This view is consistent with the behaviorist doctrine that motivation is a function of external reinforcements, on the one hand, and with the practice of paying for performance, on the other.

Thus, Tom Peters was quite correct when he summed up the current wisdom as follows: "Get the incentives right and productivity will follow. If we give people big, straightforward monetary incentives . . . the productivity problem will go away."[13] In point of fact, if we have seen anything "go away" as a consequence of relying on incentives, it has not been the productivity problem but productivity. Pop behaviorism, however, is not offered as a hypothesis to be tested. It more nearly resembles theological dogma, and it is connected to capitalism itself:

"The free enterprise system operates on the premise that rewards should depend on performance," as one consultant put it.[14] To this extent, criticism is viewed as an assault on fundamental values. After I offered a critique of incentive plans at a management conference not long ago, one businessman exclaimed, "Well, isn't that communism?"

I do not mean to imply that there has been no movement in the theory or practice of management over the last generation. A number of people have talked about, and in some cases even tried to implement, systems to promote teamwork, participative management, more thoughtful and responsive approaches to supervision, and an emphasis on continuous improvement. But it is precisely here, among the recommendations for change, that we can glimpse the hardiness of behaviorism: to institute and maintain these very reforms, it is often said, we must depend on rewards.

"If you want teamwork, you have got to recognize the team," says the influential management theorist Edward Lawler.[15] His main point is that we should shift rewards from individuals to groups, but the idea of moving beyond a reliance on rewards altogether — promoting cooperation without, in effect, bribing people to work together — is evidently unimaginable. Meanwhile, the use of competitive rewards for quality management, such as the Baldrige Award, "reinforces, one more time, extrinsic motivation rather than intrinsic," as one critic puts it.[16]

The same is true regarding the practice of rewarding employees when they acquire new skills or participate in programs to improve the organization. *What* we bribe people to do may have changed a bit; the reliance on bribes — on behaviorist doctrine — has not. Do we want "a continuous effort to improve"? Then people must "get paid more as they learn more," says one proponent of Total Quality Management.[17] Some consultants even argue that in order to get managers to use rewards with their employees, we must dangle rewards in front of the managers themselves.[18] This suggests a logo for the American workplace: a large dog holding out a biscuit to a smaller dog that holds one out to a still smaller dog, and so on until the dogs and biscuits vanish into insignificance.

Incentives Fail

Rewards in general do not enhance, and often impede, performance on many different kinds of tasks, especially those that require creativity. That was the clear consensus of the evidence reviewed in chapter 3. An incentive or merit pay plan, of course, depends on the use of rewards. Is there any reason to believe that such an application is somehow immune to the forces that cause other extrinsic motivators to fail?

No. Extrinsic motivation doesn't work in the workplace* any better than it works in any other context. Back in 1960, McGregor ticked off the consequences of incentive plans, noting that they may lead to

> deliberate restriction of output, hidden jigs and fixtures, hidden production, fudged records . . . antagonism toward those who administer the plan, cynicism with respect to management's integrity and fairness, indifference to the importance of collaboration with other parts of the organization (except for collusive efforts to *defeat* the incentive system).[19]

Some professionals who oversee these programs are able to see the consequences for themselves. At a conference presentation entitled "Human Resource Utilization" in which I participated, one of my copanelists, an executive at one of the big three auto companies, described the results of an informal survey she and her colleagues had conducted to see how people at various companies regarded their incentive programs. At best, she said, they reported that their programs didn't do *too* much damage.[20]

Consider the countries typically cited as competitors of the United States. Japan and Germany, to take two of the most successful, rarely use incentives or other behaviorist tactics to induce people to do a better job.[21] This fact not only debunks the idea that it is "human nature" to be motivated by extrinsic rewards, but also calls into question the usefulness of such rewards, given that these nations appear to be doing reasonably well. "If these successful countries do not need them, does America?" asks *The Economist.*[22]

But put aside the anecdotal evidence of failure and the experience of other countries. What does the research say? Apart from occasional surveys of how satisfied managers say they are with their incentive

---

*I am not concerned here with the sort of incentives that are offered to businesses as a matter of public policy, such as tax breaks that are awarded for controlling pollution or creating jobs. A corporate entity, for better or worse, is accountable only for the financial return it brings its investors and therefore is presumably responsive to financial incentives and penalties. The debate among economists typically counterposes this approach to direct regulation, which raises issues quite different from those addressed in this book. In fact, the use of financial incentives to manipulate a person's behavior may be objectionable and ultimately ineffective precisely because it reduces the psychology of human motivation to a branch of economics.

plans,[23] it is exceedingly difficult to find hard data on the question of whether these programs do any good. (The absence of empirical support, of course, prevents almost no one from adopting incentives — or even, in some cases, from claiming that such support does exist.)[24] According to researcher G. Douglas Jenkins, Jr., in fact, "the evidence that has been generated tends to focus on the effects of *variations* in incentive conditions, and not on whether performance-based pay per se raises performance levels."[25]

In a search for evidence on the effect of pay-for-performance programs, one may first stumble on a series of studies, beginning in the early 1960s, that have found a very weak or even negative relationship between pay and organizational performance, and especially between executive pay and corporate profitability measured over a period of time.[26] What is the significance of this finding? Typically, the absence of such a correlation is taken to mean that people are not really paid on the basis of how well they do their jobs. In other words, the compensation system has been poorly implemented.

But most of these data might just as well be used to support a different conclusion, one that reverses the causal arrow. Perhaps what they are telling us is that better performance does not *follow* from higher pay. In other words, the very idea of trying to reward quality may be a fool's errand. Two researchers explicitly tried to establish whether return to shareholders was any better for corporations that had incentive plans for top executives than it was for those without such plans. The researchers were unable to find any difference.[27]

Other studies too provide scant comfort for those who favor rewards in the workplace. In 1986, Jenkins tracked down twenty-eight previously published experiments that measured the impact of financial incentives, some in the laboratory and some in the field. Sixteen of them (57 percent) found a positive effect on performance. But this ratio overstates the benefit of incentives for several reasons. First, the improvement was judged on the basis of short-term measures, and there was no indication that it would have continued. Second, the tasks involved in the studies were mostly clerical or physical work, such as simple assembly jobs, tree planting, and card sorting. Third, and most telling, all of the performance measures were quantitative in nature: a good job consisted of producing more of something or doing it faster. Only five of the studies looked at the quality of performance. Of the five, how many showed a positive effect for incentives? None.[28]

One of the studies in that survey, conducted by Edwin A. Locke in the late 1960s, found that people who were paid on a piece-rate basis did not even turn out any more work than did those paid only for their participation.* (Locke also found that workers tended to choose easier tasks as the payment for success increased, a finding consistent with the argument that rewards discourage risk-taking [see pages 62–67].)[30]

The studies that Jenkins missed, or that appeared after his review was published, contain more bad news. One interesting bit of research took advantage of an unusual occurrence in a real workplace: the sudden elimination of an incentive system that had long been in effect for a group of welders. If a financial incentive supplies motivation, its absence should drive down production. And that is exactly what happened — at first. Fortunately, this researcher continued tracking production over a period of months, thus providing the sort of long-term data rarely collected in this field. In the absence of incentives, the welders' production quickly began to rise and eventually reached a level as high or higher than it had been before.[31]

One of the largest reviews of research looking at how various intervention programs affect worker productivity, a meta-analysis of some 330 comparisons from ninety-eight studies, was conducted in the mid-1980s by Richard A. Guzzo and his colleagues. The raw numbers seemed to suggest a positive relationship between financial incentives and productivity, but because of the huge variations from one study to another, statistical tests indicated that there was no significant effect overall. Financial incentives were also virtually unrelated to the number of workers who were absent or who quit over a period of time. By contrast, training and goal-setting programs had a far greater impact on productivity than did anything involving payment.[32]

Finally, consider the use of merit pay in the public sector. The most comprehensive attempt to implement such a program in the federal government, resulting from the Civil Service Reform Act of 1978, was judged a disaster even by the man who directed it.[33] In what was billed as the first direct test of the effects of performance-contingent pay for managers, a team of researchers at the University of California at Irvine looked at the performance of twenty offices of the Social Security Administration over more than four years. Using the very perfor-

---

*Whyte reported that piecework systems typically fail because workers "set a quota on what constitutes a fair day's work and refuse to go beyond this amount even when it is well within their ability to do so." This is not, he continued, a function of a poorly designed or administered incentive system but of the underlying theory of motivation.[29]

mance measures on which the managers' salary increases had been based, they found that "the implementation of merit pay had no significant effects on organizational performance."[34]

The same group of researchers surveyed managers at five diverse federal agencies, tapping their attitudes about merit pay at four different times and tracking the results of the program as it was implemented. Few of the managers said that financial incentives in general would make them work harder. Most thought it was difficult to document actual performance differences. And as this specific merit pay plan took effect, more and more of them concluded that it did not encourage them to do their jobs well.[35]

One other incentive system in the public sector has been investigated over the years: merit pay for teachers. Various objections to this idea have been offered, starting with the fact that it is fundamentally "manipulative and reflective of distrust."[36] But does it lead to better teaching? Disinterested researchers and even conservative policy analysts who are clearly attracted to the idea have found little or no evidence that it does. Neither objective measures nor the testimony of teachers or administrators offers any reason to think that the quality of instruction will improve as a result of merit pay — or even that a school district using such a program will be more likely to attract or retain good teachers.[37]

Why *Incentives Fail*

There are three possible ways to make sense of all this evidence that paying people for performance does not generally lead them to do a better job. The first is to assume that there must be other studies out there somewhere documenting positive results from such systems. I have spent a good deal of time looking for such findings without success, but I invite readers to search the literature and let me know if they discover any evidence that long-term improvements in the quality of work really do follow from the use of rewards. (Even more impressive — and improbable — would be data showing that rewards are more likely to produce such improvements than are substantive changes in the way workers are treated. One recent study appeared to show that an incentive plan that was provided to an entire organization rather than to individuals actually produced measurable benefits, but it turned out that the program also included increased employee involvement in decision making, a feature more likely than rewards to account for any positive effects.)[38]

The second possible reaction to these studies is to dismiss the consistent failure of incentives as reflecting nothing more than problems with these particular plans. "Someday we'll find a good one" is, of course, the dominant view in American business, and the consequence of holding it is twofold: an increasing use of pay-for-performance systems, and a continued inability to understand why they never seem to work.*

The third response is to conclude that what is wrong with incentive systems is not the way we are administering them but the fact that they *are* incentive systems. To try a different bonus plan, another reward, a new proposal from the same Skinnerian perspective, is about as sensible as treating cirrhosis of the liver by switching from vodka to gin. This section and the next two make the case that the source of the trouble is pop behaviorism itself. (Chapter 10 will propose suggestions for how we might think about motivation in a different way — and what practices follow from that alternative paradigm.)

Specifically, I want to offer fourteen reasons to account for the failure of incentive and merit pay plans, beginning with the easily repaired problems associated with particular programs and progressing to explanations that challenge the value of any such plan, regardless of how skillfully it is designed. The latter sort of analysis, especially when it involves a close look at the nature of human motivation, is far more disconcerting and subversive — and not coincidentally, appears far more rarely in the published literature. (Since I am concerned here only with reasons for the failure of incentive plans, I refrain from making moral objections to the way money is actually distributed when these plans are put into practice.)[40]

Let's start with a few relatively minor problems. Precisely because these have been described so often by others — and because they deal only with issues of implementation — we can list them quickly and move on:

1. Lack of necessity. Incentive programs, with all the attendant risks, are sometimes introduced unnecessarily — that is, when employees are already doing a fine job. Solution: leave well enough alone.

---

*We might ask, while we are at it, who has the greatest incentive to defend the idea of incentives. Who would naturally prefer to fiddle with the formulas used for compensation rather than question the very premise of paying for performance? Arguably, the answer is the thousands of consultants whose livelihoods would be jeopardized if that premise were challenged.[39]

2. Secrecy. When no one is supposed to know how much anyone else makes, people may overestimate what others actually earn or assume that inequities exist even when they don't. This lowers morale and throws the organization into turmoil.[41] Solution: stop keeping secrets.

3. Pay doesn't match performance. For a variety of organizational reasons, compensation often does not correspond to performance ratings even when there is high confidence in these ratings, and even when it has been decided that the two should be closely tied. Solution: do what you say you're going to do.

4. Expense. Some incentive plans are said to be too expensive. Solution: substitute noncash rewards.[42]

Other problems with incentives can be framed as dilemmas, such that either of two possible choices is undesirable.

5. Too big versus too small. If bonus payments are modest, they may not have much of an impact. If they are large enough to make an impact, fewer people will receive them.[43]

6. Short-term versus long-term. If an incentive is based on short-term performance, employees may make decisions counter to the long-term interests of the organization.[44]* If the incentive is based on performance over a longer period of time, the connection between behavior and reinforcement becomes fuzzy (a behaviorist's nightmare).

7. Objective versus subjective. If compensation is based on objective factors, the system may be rigid and unresponsive to those aspects of performance that defy reduction to a fixed protocol. If compensation is based on subjective factors, it becomes dependent on the whims and biases of the rater.[45]

The solution to these three dilemmas is far from obvious. But let us assume for the sake of the argument that we could steer a flawless course between each pair of traps that threaten to sink the system. Even so, we find ourselves facing a batch of even more serious problems with incentives.

8. "Performance evaluation is an exercise in futility."[46] A plan to pay on the basis of performance is only as good as the system for determining the quality of that performance. Unfortunately, such eval-

---

*For some years, critics have faulted top U.S. executives for concentrating on short-term profit and, as a result, running these organizations into the ground. Ironically, some of these same critics favor incentives of various kinds, even though rewards, by their very nature, are the ultimate short-term fix.

uations are typically far less accurate than we would like to believe. It is nearly impossible to quantify performance for many kinds of work, and in any case, most rating systems are accurate only at the extremes — that is, for identifying exceptionally good or bad performance.[47] That means gradations in compensation will be made that probably don't correspond to meaningful gradations in quality.

A performance rating may seem precise, but it actually masks many subtle distinctions in the way someone approaches his job; numbers simply cannot do justice to people's different styles and strengths.[48] Even when we try to allow for a more ambitious qualitative appraisal, that assessment will tell us as much about the appraiser as about the appraisee.[49] It tells us how harsh a critic she is, how good a job she expected the employee to do, how well the two of them get along, and sometimes, what basic values they share (or even whether their backgrounds are similar).[50]

Moreover, "any individual's performance is, to a considerable extent, a function of how he is managed," as McGregor put it, so the manager is in part evaluating herself without appearing to do so.[51] Assessments of individuals also overlook the extent to which any one person's performance grows out of an exchange of ideas and resources with colleagues and otherwise reflects the indirect contribution of the larger system.[52]

Finally, even if performance appraisals *were* adequate to gauge how well people are doing, their effects are usually so destructive that they shouldn't be used anyway. Not only is the fact of interdependence in the workplace ignored, but people are discouraged from cooperating in the future. ("Why help him when I'm being judged only on my own performance?") As McGregor pointed out, performance appraisals also elicit "rationalization, defensiveness, inability to understand, [and] reactions that the superior is being unfair or arbitrary" whenever people receive an evaluation that isn't as positive as what they think they deserve.[53]

The legendary statistical consultant W. Edwards Deming, with his characteristic gift for understatement, has called the system by which merit is appraised and rewarded "the most powerful inhibitor to quality and productivity in the Western world."[54] He adds that it "nourishes short-term performance, annihilates long-term planning, builds fear, demolishes teamwork, nourishes rivalry and . . . leaves people bitter."[55] To this we can add that it is simply unfair to the extent that employees are held responsible for what are, in reality, systemic factors that are beyond their control.

Money

9. "Pay is not a motivator."[56]   If an employee isn't especially interested in an in-kind incentive, this is not a serious problem; a stereo system can be substituted for a trip to Hawaii. But what if it turns out that the default reward, money, also lacks the motivational power most of us attribute to it?

That making money shouldn't be the driving force in our lives is a message that has echoed through all cultures and in all ages. That money isn't the driving force in our lives is another matter. Even when a man of Deming's stature makes the flat declaration that money isn't a motivator, we are skeptical — or at least puzzled.

Of course, all of us want to be paid. Money buys the things we need and the things we want. Moreover, the less someone is paid — or at least, the less control he has over his own work — the more concerned he is likely to be about financial matters.[57] In this respect, money is like sex, as James Baldwin remarked somewhere: we are preoccupied with it mostly when it is missing from our lives. It can be readily conceded, then, that everyone needs to earn a living, and that those who have trouble doing so are the most concerned about money.[58]

The problem is that from such facts questionable conclusions are drawn. For example, it doesn't follow that most of us think about our work chiefly in terms of the extrinsic rewards it brings. Several studies over the last few decades have found that when people are asked to guess what matters to their coworkers — or in the case of managers, to their subordinates — they assume money is at the top of the list. But put the question directly — "What do *you* care about?" — and the results look very different. To wit:

• When samples of industrial employees in 1946 and 1986 were asked what they looked for in a job, they ranked "good wages" fifth out of ten possible factors. In the more recent survey, "interesting work" was number one. Supervisors, however, assumed that workers cared most about money[59] — and presumably made managerial decisions on the basis of that erroneous belief.

• In a survey of more than fifty thousand utility company applicants over a period of thirty years, pay was ranked sixth out of ten job factors, well behind such considerations as "type of work." But when asked what they thought was important to others, most people picked pay.[60]

• Several large-scale national surveys have found that people who were unhappy with their jobs pointed to reasons like the lack of variety or challenge, conflicts with coworkers or the boss, and too much pressure. Salary simply was not a major issue.[61]

• Concern with intrinsic issues in the workplace, such as the chance to learn new skills, use one's talents fully, or make decisions, is not limited to only some kinds of people. Contrary to the view that an exclusive emphasis on extrinsic rewards is appropriate for certain categories of workers, research has shown that all people who work for a living, regardless of type of occupation or level of education, are "powerfully affected in their assessment of a job by the level of intrinsic rewards it offers. . . . Extrinsic rewards become an important determinant of overall job satisfaction only among workers for whom intrinsic rewards are relatively unavailable."[62]

• Even for salespeople, who are sometimes thought to be singularly money-driven, "increased compensation was the *least* commonly cited reason" for switching to another company, according to a poll conducted in 1991.[63]

The broader point here is that economists have it wrong if they think of work as a "disutility" — something unpleasant we must do in order to be able to buy what we need, merely a means to an end.[64] Work can be turned *into* something so wretched that we come to think of it that way, but this is an aberration.* Humans do not simply work to live but also live to work — to grow food, make things, solve problems. Even in a highly industrialized society where tasks have been split into fragments and our talents often lie fallow most of the day, most people say they are satisfied with their jobs.[66] What's more, most people continue to work even when suddenly freed of any financial need to do so.[67] Most surprising of all, perhaps, is the finding that the majority of the moments of pure, unselfconscious pleasure we experience take place at work.[68]

To this point, I have argued that money's role in the context of work is less prominent than we have assumed. When we widen our inquiry to look at the significance of money relative to life itself, the results are even more striking. As the sociologist Philip Slater once remarked, "The idea that everybody wants money is propaganda cir-

---

*Those who insist that we work only to make money not only confine their analysis to mind-numbing, dead-end jobs but also take as a given that these jobs must always remain so. People will always care about the money, these critics seem to be saying, so it is pointless to try to improve the quality of what they do all day. This, of course, is a self-serving as well as self-fulfilling prophecy. The belief that nothing can be done to make work more interesting leads to managerial action (or, more precisely, inaction) that *perpetuates* tedious jobs and a focus on money.[65]

culated by wealth addicts to make themselves feel better about their addiction."⁶⁹

Again, those who despair of being able to pay the bills often find their thoughts returning to financial matters. But notice how many people, regardless of how they feel about their jobs, or even how much they are paid, are apt to pour their souls into tasks that they pursue in their free time: making music, fixing cars, decorating rooms, puttering in a garden, and of course, tending to their children. This work is often hard and time-consuming, and it is done with no thought of remuneration. Overall, the point is that money isn't the point.⁷⁰

There are people, of course, who are relatively well off and yet whose lives seem to be geared principally to the accumulation of wealth. Understanding the nature and causes of this preoccupation properly requires a book in itself, but a few possible explanations might be reviewed here. People may express such sentiments by force of habit, or because they have been raised to think one's net worth is what matters in life, or in order to compensate for earlier days of deprivation. Others, recalling that old-time religion, may believe that wealth signifies divine election — a sign that one has "made it" in more ways than one. Money can also be pursued because it signifies power or status or provides a vague existential reassurance: I have, therefore I am. (This last interpretation comes to mind when one sees men compulsively jingling the change in their pockets.)

Frequently, though, the quest for ever-higher salaries can be interpreted as a symptom of a deeper longing. To listen to people who steer every conversation back to the subject of money, and who spend their lives grasping for more, is to speculate on what needs they are trying to fill with material satisfactions. There is a tendency to focus by default on the size of one's paycheck when work is bereft of more important features: deprive someone of a genuinely engaging and meaningful task, the capacity to exercise choice over what one does, social support, the chance to learn and to demonstrate one's competence, and that person will likely turn his attention to what he earns. (He may even dismiss as naive the suggestion that work could ever be about more than money.) The same is true, as a number of psychologists and social critics have argued, when a sense of meaning or deep connection to others is absent more generally from one's life: a plump bank account is made to substitute for authentic fulfillment.

That we are dealing with a substitute satisfaction here seems clear from the fact that no sum ever suffices: such people always "need" more than they are currently making — or buying. Add one more pair of shoes, a new electronic gizmo, or a higher salary with which to buy them, and it is still not enough. It is never enough.[71] Questioned about the choice to put money at the center of their lives, these individuals may respond defensively: "Hey, you've gotta eat." (True, but you don't have to go to France to do so. The question was why these wants have taken over one's life; the response attempts to justify them by repackaging them as needs.) It may not be surprising to learn that young adults for whom financial success is a central goal in life are likely to show evidence of "more depression and more anxiety" as well as "lower global [psychological] functioning, lower social productivity, and more behavior problems" than other people do.[72]

Money, then, is not as significant a factor in how we live, or even how we work, as is commonly believed. Even people who do seem to be obsessed with the subject — those who, like Oscar Wilde's cynic, know the price of everything and the value of nothing — may be confessing, in effect, their need for something more. But even if I am wrong about all this, even if people really are principally concerned with what they are being paid and money really is the focal point of our lives and our work, there is still no justification for believing that money is *motivating*. Specifically, we have no grounds for assuming that paying people more will lead them to do better-quality work — or even, over the long run, more work.

In part, this is true because individuals who are committed to excellence and likely to do the best work are particularly unlikely to respond to financial incentives. As one instructor at the Harvard Business School has pointed out, "the kind of people who make good leaders are not obsessed with money."[73] But there is an even more fundamental reason for the limited effect of financial incentives, an argument made some time ago by Frederick Herzberg. Herzberg had a great deal to say about work and motivation, and some of his claims have been criticized over the years. But one point was surely correct and vitally important: just because too little money can irritate and *demotivate* does not mean that more and more money will bring about more and more satisfaction, much less more motivation to do one's best.[74] If your take-home pay were cut in half, it is plausible to assume that the effect on your morale might be so devastating as to undermine your performance; you might even decide to quit.* But

---

*Even this seemingly obvious proposition is less cut-and-dried than it appears. Some evidence indicates that people are more concerned about whether they are being compensated fairly than about how much they are making in absolute terms.[75] Does the amount

this doesn't mean that if your pay were doubled you would do a better job than you do now.

Consider, by way of analogy, the claim that carrots are good for your eyes. This is true only in the very limited sense that they provide carotene, which your body turns into vitamin A; a complete deprivation of vitamin A would cause night blindness. But almost everyone has immense reserves of carotene stored in the liver, and eating more carrots, or otherwise ingesting vitamin A above the amount you need, doesn't improve your vision at all. So it is for a "carrot" like money: less of it may hurt, but that doesn't mean more of it will help.

None of this, I should emphasize, offers managers a justification for being stingy in paying their employees. Everyone wants to be compensated adequately and fairly; those who do the most monotonous or grueling work would seem, in fact, to have a particularly compelling claim to be paid well. But to assume that money is what drives people is to adopt an impoverished understanding of human motivation.[76] Since incentive plans are generally predicated on just such a model, it should not be surprising that they do not succeed. But "myths die hard. It is quite clear that money's reputation as the ultimate motivation is going to be a long time a-dying." So one writer put it — in 1963.[77]

The Five Problems with Rewards . . . at Work

Once more we play the game called "even if . . ." Assume that all nine of the reasons offered above to account for the inadequacy of incentive programs are correctable, based on faulty thinking, or supported by questionable evidence. Such programs, I believe, are nevertheless doomed because of the fundamental flaws of pop behaviorism itself. Trying to motivate people by extrinsic means is inherently a losing proposition, for the reasons discussed at length in chapters 4 and 5. I will take only a few pages to review these arguments and apply them

---

seem appropriate to the kind of work involved, the training and experience one brings to the job, what others doing similar work are making, and so forth? Even an appreciable loss of income will not necessarily reduce motivation. A number of factors come into play: Are you left with enough money to live? Was there a legitimate rationale for the reduction? Is everyone in the organization, including those at the top, sharing in the sacrifice? How much of a role did the individual play in making the decision to take a cut in pay? (Things that are done *to* us are always more demotivating than things we choose.)

to the workplace, but they stand as the most decisive explanations of the failure of programs that tie rewards to performance.

10. Rewards punish. In some circles, it is no longer necessary to make the case that punishment destroys motivation: this fact is already understood, and one can proceed directly to the seldom-noticed point that rewards have the same effect. But the people who run many large American corporations are still convinced that coercive and punitive tactics are useful. Sadly, a few words on this topic (before addressing the question of rewards) may not be superfluous.

Even today it is not very difficult to find business leaders who believe that fear motivates people to do good work. "I hope everybody here comes to work scared to death" about the fate of the company, said a top executive at AT&T.[78] "Making the bottom 10 percent uncomfortable is good business," declared a senior vice president of personnel at IBM, which recently adopted an evaluation system mandating that one of every ten employees must receive a poor rating every year and be given three months to improve or be fired.[79] Pay-for-performance systems, in order to "send the proper signals for good performance," must "withhold sufficient pay" when people's work is disappointing, according to a standard text on compensation.[80] Some behavioral psychologists defend the practice of punishing employees on the grounds that it helps to "clarify management's expectations of performance and promote goal setting."[81] (This is comparable to the claim that throwing employees out an office window helps to clarify what floor they work on.) One well-known business school professor and consultant on "organizational effectiveness" likes to conclude his lectures by quoting the bank robber John Dillinger: "You can get more cooperation with a smile and a gun than you can with just a smile."*

It is hard to imagine another philosophy of management so utterly at variance with everything research and experience teach us. I will reserve most of my comments about punishment for chapter 9, which deals with raising children. For now, let me point out what people on the receiving end of the stick surely know: punitive strategies, such as holding out the possibility of termination or demotion for inadequate performance, are counterproductive in the extreme — not to mention unpleasant, disrespectful, and in general, an intrinsically offensive way to deal with other human beings.

To begin with, punishment typically leads not to improvement but to defiance, defensiveness, and rage. Rather than relying on persua-

---

*By "cooperation," of course, he means obedience, not teamwork.

sion or problem-solving, the punisher engages in a naked exercise in power assertion. Given the chance, most people respond in kind rather than with a newfound determination to do a better job. At best, coercion elicits only resentful obedience, hardly a desirable state of mind over the long haul. An ironic motto posted in some offices and schools perfectly captures the illogic of this retrograde approach to management: THE BEATINGS WILL CONTINUE UNTIL MORALE IMPROVES.

The most charitable thing we can say about the use of punishment and fear is that it is psychologically naive. Threatening people can make them anxious about the consequences of doing poorly, but the fear of failure is completely different from the desire to succeed. The former distracts people from the task at hand; instead of reaching for excellence, they are more likely to play it safe and protect themselves. This, to put it mildly, is not where quality comes from. As Herzberg liked to say, a "KITA" — which, he coyly explained, stands for "kick in the pants" — may produce movement but never motivation.[82]

Even executives who know that punitive management is a contradiction in terms may fail to recognize just how similar rewards are to punishments, both in their underlying assumptions about motivation and in their practical consequences. "Why is it," Herzberg wondered, "that managerial audiences are quick to see that negative KITA is *not* motivation, while they are almost unanimous in their judgment that positive KITA *is* motivation?"[83]

As I have argued in previous chapters, both extrinsic tactics are controlling. Rewards feel punitive because they too amount to an effort to manipulate people's behavior. Moreover, employees may find a bonus or other incentive deliberately withheld or withdrawn from them (as urged by the compensation manual quoted above), or else they may simply fail to obtain it despite their best efforts. The effect is no less aversive than — and indeed, is effectively identical to — a punishment. Researchers have found exactly what one would expect in terms of motivational impact when people receive a performance evaluation poorer than they think appropriate.[84] Similarly, the failure to receive an anticipated bonus is bound to have an adverse effect on subsequent performance: "The achievers [who] were denied the merit award may react by producing at . . . even lower levels in the future."[85] In sum, reward systems fail because their overall effect is punitive.

11. Rewards rupture relationships. Horizontal relationships, such as those among employees of comparable status, are casualties of the scramble for rewards. As Deming and others have emphasized, incentive programs reduce the possibility that people will cooperate. And when cooperation is absent, so is quality. "We talk about teamwork at training sessions," one bank executive remarked, "and then we destroy it in the compensation system."[86]

The surest way to destroy teamwork, and therefore organizational excellence, is to make rewards scarce — that is, make people compete. Many companies continue to rank employees against each other;[87] the chairman of one of the largest corporations in the world, for example, continues to insist that this practice promotes "rigor,"* despite the widespread conviction on the part of the people who are ranked that such systems actually promote ruin.

Likewise, competitive recognition programs and other contests persist, despite evidence of the harm they do. For each person who wins, there are many others who carry with them the awareness of having lost, and who "come to feel that regardless of their efforts they will remain outside the winners' circle."[88] The more these awards are publicized, through the use of memos, newsletters, and award banquets, the more detrimental their impact. Furthermore, contests, rankings, and competition for a limited number of incentives cause each employee to see every colleague as an obstacle to her own success, which in turn discourages collaboration and erodes the social support and sense of belongingness that make for secure employees and an effective organization.[89] In fact, these results can attend any use of rewards; introducing competition into an incentive program just makes a bad thing worse.

Vertical relationships too, such as those between supervisors and subordinates, collapse under the weight of a reward structure. I have already made the point that when the person to whom you report decides how much money you will make (or what other goodies will

---

*In addition to the disadvantages it shares with other sorts of extrinsic motivators, ranking employees against each other is senseless for other reasons. It pretends to offer precision, even though the evaluations that determine each person's rank are inherently subjective — particularly when people who do very different sorts of jobs are measured on the same scale. (Do we seriously think that the performance of a typist, an accountant, and a chemist can all be judged on a single set of criteria so they can be ranked against each other?) But here is the decisive objection: *relative performance is ultimately irrelevant to any organizational concerns that count.* To be blunt about it, who cares if someone is in the top 10 percent of a company that is going down the toilet? Or for that matter, what difference does it make if someone is in the bottom tenth of a company where everyone is basically doing a good job? What matters are absolute, not relative, criteria. And if a forced-ranking system undermines teamwork, then it is not merely irrelevant to performance; according to the measures that matter, it makes things worse.

be awarded to you), you have a temptation to conceal any problems you might be having (see pages 57–58). Rather than asking for help, which is a prerequisite for optimal performance, you will be apt to spend your energies trying to flatter that person and convince him that you have everything under control.[90] Moreover, according to Dean Tjosvold, a professor of business administration, you will be less likely to challenge poor decisions and engage in the kind of conflict that is beneficial for the organization if you are concerned about losing out on a reward. Very few things are as dangerous as a bunch of incentive-driven individuals trying to play it safe.[91]

12. Rewards ignore reasons. The point here is remarkably simple: in order to solve problems in the workplace, we must know what caused them. Are employees inadequately prepared for the demands of their jobs? Is long-term growth being sacrificed to maximize short-term return? Are workers unable to collaborate effectively, with the result that one division is duplicating the work of another? Is the organization rigidly hierarchical so that the people who know what is needed are intimidated about making recommendations, and feel powerless and burned out as well? Each of these situations calls for a different response. But holding out a carrot — "Do better work and here's what you'll get" — is a pseudosolution; it fails to address the issues that are actually responsible for holding back the organization and the people who work there.[92]

More generally, incentive systems are frequently used as a substitute for giving workers what they need to do a good job. Treating workers well — which, as I will argue later, means providing useful feedback and meeting their needs for self-determination and social support — is the essence of good management. It establishes the conditions under which intrinsic interest in work can develop. But much less effort is required to dangle a bonus in front of employees and wait for the results to take care of themselves.

Indeed, there is evidence that pay-for-performance plans tend to displace careful management: where reward systems are employed, it is less likely that productive strategies will be used.[93] (The same thing appears to be true when token economies are used in institutions, when rewards for good grades are promised by parents, and for that matter, whenever pop behaviorism is in evidence: instead of taking responsibility to help and care, to teach skills and solve problems, the person in a position of power often holds out an incentive and assumes that things will sort themselves out.)[94] A compensation system is no substitute for careful management, just as a behaviorist approach is no substitute for getting to the root of problems, but it is often used that way.

13. Rewards discourage risk-taking. "People will do precisely what they are asked to do if the reward is significant," enthuses one proponent of pay-for-performance programs.[95] And here we have identified exactly what is wrong with such programs. Whenever people are led to think about what they will get for engaging in a task, they will do only what is absolutely necessary to get it. There is less inclination to take risks or explore possibilities, which helps explain why creativity declines when people are driven by rewards. Thus, as Philip Slater observes, "getting people to chase money . . . produces nothing except people chasing money. Using money as a motivator leads to a progressive degradation in the quality of everything produced."[96]

Excellence pulls in one direction; encouraging employees to think about how well they are doing (and what they will earn as a result) pulls in another. Tell people that their income will depend on their productivity, or on their performance rating, and they will focus on the numbers. "Employees may do what is necessary for scoring higher on the evaluation form rather than what is genuinely needed for doing the job correctly," one pair of analysts has pointed out.[97] This often involves manipulating the schedule for completing one's tasks — "gaming" — in order to get the reward.[98] Salespeople may delay processing an order, or conversely, promise it sooner than it can be delivered, in order to qualify for an incentive based on sales recorded in a given period of time. They may also while away the hours monitoring the numbers that determine how much they will earn.[99] And they may even engage in patently unethical and illegal behavior as a result of the pressures generated by incentive programs.[100]

In a sense, playing games with numbers or convincing customers to buy what they don't need constitutes a kind of risk-taking behavior. But the risks we want people to take — being willing to explore new possibilities in a quest to improve quality — are minimized by the presence of rewards. An extrinsic orientation, for example, makes people less likely to challenge themselves. Instead, they are apt to choose the easiest possible task to do, since this maximizes the chance of getting the reward and getting it quickly.

When employees participate in setting performance standards, such as in organizations using the "management by objectives" technique popularized by Peter Drucker, "they have an incentive to set goals at safe levels . . . to assure high ratings and rewards."[101] But the problem here is not that people are naturally lazy or that they have unwisely been given a voice in determining the standards to be used. (In fact, "employee participation in setting goals has been found to lead to higher goals than if goals are imposed.")[102] Rather, the problem is with the use of an incentive system: people set their sights lower because they have been made to think about the reward they will receive.

14. Rewards undermine interest. Possibly the most compelling reason that incentive systems fail is the phenomenon described in chapter 5: extrinsic motivators not only are less effective than intrinsic motivation but actually reduce intrinsic motivation. The more a manager gets employees to think about what they will earn for doing their jobs well, the less interested they will be in those jobs. This is both an undesirable consequence in its own right and an explanation for the finding that rewards lower performance.

In the early 1970s, Edward Deci published a paper in a journal of organizational behavior showing that rewarding people for engaging in a task tends to undermine their intrinsic motivation to do it. Because only a few other studies subsequently appeared in such publications,[103] some in the field may have assumed this finding was a fluke. But "the research has consistently shown that any contingent payment system tends to undermine intrinsic motivation,"[104] even if most of that research has been published in periodicals rarely read by people interested in management.

Deci and his colleagues believe extrinsic motivators have this effect because they are perceived as controlling. Others favor the explanation that "Do this and you'll get that" automatically devalues the "this": that is, the task comes to be perceived as a tedious prerequisite for getting a goody. McGregor, for example, noticed that the rewards given to workers are typically intended for use when they get home, the result of which is that "work is perceived as a form of punishment which is the price to be paid for various kinds of satisfaction away from the job."[105]

Whatever the reason for this effect, though, the risk of *any* incentive or pay-for-performance system is that it will make people less interested in their work and therefore less likely to approach it with enthusiasm and a commitment to excellence. Furthermore, *the more closely we tie compensation (or other rewards) to performance, the more damage we do.* (One could hardly ask for a sharper contrast between two positions than that between this one and the behaviorists' claim that we should strive for the most direct possible relation between pay and performance.) And that damage, in case the point is not sufficiently clear, is not limited to the performance of individual workers. As the political economist Robert Lane concluded, the ultimate consequence of using rewards — of emphasizing extrinsic rather than intrinsic factors in the workplace — is to erode "not only work enjoyment but also the productivity of manufacturing and commercial enterprises."[106]

One last point, which I made earlier with respect to rewards in general, applies with special force to the workplace: incentive plans do not respond to the extrinsic orientation exhibited by some workers so much as they *create* this focus on financial factors. As surveys have documented, supervisors assume that people who work for them are mostly interested in money. The management system of choice is therefore Skinnerian, with pay made contingent on performance. Since extrinsic factors eat away at intrinsic motivation, people become less interested in their work as a result and increasingly likely to require extrinsic incentives before putting out an effort. Then the supervisors point to that orientation, shake their heads, and say, "You see? If you don't offer them a reward, they won't do anything."

It is a classic self-fulfilling prophecy, and it did not escape the attention of critics like McGregor, Herzberg, and Levinson.[107] In a general sense, psychologist Barry Schwartz conceded, behavior theory may seem to provide us with a useful way of describing what goes on in American workplaces. But — and this is the critical point — "it does this not because work is a natural exemplification of behavior theory principles but because behavior theory principles . . . had a significant hand in transforming work into an exemplification of behavior theory principles."[108]

Behaviorism has made a substantial impact on the way we think about our work and the way we do it. But the specific programs it has wrought, such as incentive plans, do not and cannot bring about the results we want. Their failure is multiply determined: many different studies find that rewards simply do not get people to do a better job, and many different factors explain why. Some of the data and rationale supporting this radical critique have been around for decades; some have emerged more recently. But by now we ought to face the troubling fact that manipulating behavior by offering reinforcements may be a sound approach for training the family pet but not for bringing quality to the workplace.

~8~

LURES FOR LEARNING:
Why Behaviorism Doesn't Work
in the Classroom

[Unlike] a hundred years ago . . . the approved view to-day is that
an intrinsic interest in the activity regardless of ulterior consequences is an enormously superior means of learning.
— Edward L. Thorndike, 1935

WHEN THEY FIRST GET to school, they are endlessly fascinated
by the world. They are filled with delight by their newfound ability to
print their own names in huge, shaky letters, to count everything in
sight, to decode the signs they see around them. They sit on the floor
at story time, eyes wide and jaws slack, listening raptly as the teacher
reads. They come home bubbling with new facts and new connections
between facts. "You know what we learned today?" they say.

By the time the last bell has rung, the spell has been broken. Their
eyes have narrowed. They complain about homework. They count the
minutes until the end of the period, the days left before the weekend,
the weeks they must endure until the next vacation. "Do we have to
know this?" they ask.

I am painting with broad strokes here. In truth, the process is a little
different for each child; it may take place in a few days or a few years
or (in a few fortunate cases) not at all. It may even be worse than what
I have described: students may be left not only regarding learning as a
chore but regarding themselves as unequal to the task. In any case,
there is nothing natural about these changes. They cannot be written
off as an archetypal loss of innocence, an inevitable developmental
progression. Rather, if children's enthusiasm is smothered, it is a direct
result of something that happens in our schools. No single factor can
completely account for this dismaying transformation, but there is

one feature of American education that goes a long way toward explaining it: "Do this and you'll get that."

Two recent studies of elementary school teaching confirm what everyone already knows: rewards are used constantly in nearly every classroom to try to motivate children and improve their performance.[1] They are offered stickers and stars, edible treats and extra recess, grades and awards. New goodies are substituted as students get older, but the Skinnerian formula follows them. Often they are rewarded for getting rewards: a good set of grades means a place on the honor roll, perhaps a special ID card, a basket of freebies at local stores, and even cash from parents. One newspaper article describing such incentives begins, "Your kids won't study? Don't ground them, pay them."[2]*

When rewards don't succeed at enhancing students' interest and achievement, we offer — new rewards. (It is remarkable how often, in both our public and private lives, we react to the failure of a given strategy by doing it some more.) When this too proves ineffective, we put the blame on the students themselves, deciding that they must lack ability or are just too lazy to make an effort. Perhaps we sigh and reconcile ourselves to the idea that "it is not realistic to expect students to develop motivation to learn in classrooms."[3]

For those who look at education from a public policy perspective, issuing reports on American schooling, serving on task forces, or publishing columns, the solution to whatever is wrong with the system invariably takes the form of some combination of carrots and sticks: teachers ought to be rewarded or punished for *their* performance; schools should be threatened with lower enrollment if they do not somehow whip themselves into shape and successfully compete for students. Free-market conservatives, heaping scorn on teachers' unions for resisting such plans, argue that "nobody changes without incentives."[4] But the unions, or at least their most visible representatives, disagree only about specific policies. On the underlying philosophy, they speak the same language. "No system really works unless it operates with incentives," declares American Federation of Teachers president Albert Shanker.[5] And *The New Republic* chimes in: "People respond to incentives."[6]

This sort of doctrinal consistency is a rare and extraordinary thing to behold. Pop behaviorism informs virtually every aspect of American education and also shapes the perspective of most of its critics.

---

*Notice that the only two solutions that come to mind here are punishments and rewards, two versions of behavioral manipulation.

When so much of what happens to our children rides on a single theory, it's worth pausing to ask whether it accords with what we know of how people learn.

The Motivation to Learn

If we start from scratch, setting aside everything we think we know about grades and other motivational inducements, three facts eventually present themselves.

Fact 1: Young children don't need to be rewarded to learn. The children who arrive at school every weekday morning represent a range of interests and abilities and circumstances. Some come from homes where intellectual curiosity is encouraged, some from places where it is a challenge just to survive. But the fact that children are not equally receptive to what the teacher is doing at any given moment should not distract us from recognizing that the desire to learn itself is natural.

Martin Hoffman, a researcher who specializes in the study of empathy, once said that parents and teachers who want to help children become socially responsive are not working alone: they have an "ally within the child."[7] Exactly the same may be said of adults interested in fostering intellectual development. "Children are disposed to try to make sense out of their environments,"[8] and as nearly every parent of a preschooler or kindergartner will attest, they play with words and numbers and ideas, asking questions ceaselessly, with as purely intrinsic a motivation as can be imagined. As children progress through elementary school, though, their approach to learning becomes increasingly extrinsic (see page 91), to the point that careful observers find "little evidence of student motivation to learn in the typical [American] classroom."[9]

Fact 2: At any age, rewards are less effective than intrinsic motivation for promoting effective learning. The point here is quite simple: just as adults who love their work will invariably do a better job than those goaded with artificial incentives, so children are more likely to be optimal learners if they are interested in what they are learning.

Several studies have found a positive correlation between intrinsic motivation and academic achievement for children of different ages. Most of this work has been correlational, which means that we can't necessarily assume the child's motivation causes achievement to go up or down; indeed, there is reason to think that achievement may affect motivation, too. Still, at least one researcher has concluded there is a causal relationship: "reduced intrinsic motivation produces achievement deficits."[10]

When we look at how children view a particular assignment, the relationship is even more impressive. One group of researchers tried to sort out the factors that helped third and fourth graders remember what they had been reading. They found that how interested the students were in the passage was *thirty times* more important than how "readable" the passage was.[11] Based on the evidence reviewed in chapter 3, we would expect intrinsic interest to play an even more prominent role in the sort of learning that involves conceptual and creative thinking.

There may be some disagreement about *why* interested learners are likely to be effective learners,[12] but the fact itself is hard to dispute. As the epigraph to this chapter indicates, even Thorndike, the grandfather of behaviorism, acknowledged it. Indeed, the finding hardly seems controversial: if kids like what they're doing, they do it better; who could disagree with that? But the point is actually more subversive of the conventional educational wisdom than it may appear. For example, many teachers and parents talk about motivation as if it were a single quality, something that students have to a greater or lesser degree. The research I have just mentioned is so important because it shows that what matters is not just how motivated someone is but the source and nature of that motivation.[13] Even copious amounts of extrinsic motivation — wanting to do well in order to obtain some goody — may actually interfere with achievement.

For another thing, a number of traditionalists grumble that the trouble with our schools today is that work is made to seem like fun.[14] (Would that this were true!) If the point here is that not everything enjoyable is of educational value, it is hard to disagree.[15] But the evidence clearly refutes the dour, puritanical notion that anything important must be unpleasant — or conversely, that anything children are eager to do must be worthless. When students are enthusiastic and motivated, they may not be jumping for joy all day, Jere Brophy points out, but they will be more likely to take seriously the things they are learning, "find them meaningful and worthwhile, and try to get the intended benefit from them."[16]

Once, when I was a high school teacher in the early 1980s, I gave a ride to a fifteen-year-old girl who had no particular interest in anything she was being taught. Awkward and taciturn, she spoke only to ask if I would turn on the car radio. She then proceeded to sing along with every song that was played for the duration of the ride, displaying not only more enthusiasm than I had thought possible but also a rather remarkable memory. Relating the event to my colleagues later, I shook my head and smiled condescendingly at how this girl, a washout in the classroom, had somehow managed to learn Top Forty lyrics to perfection.

Only later did I realize that the girl had something to teach me about motivation and its relationship to achievement. If we teachers had never seen her steel-trap memory in action, or witnessed the look of total absorption I glimpsed in the car that day, that was not necessarily just a reflection of her misplaced priorities. It may have said more about what was going on in the classes she sat through — the curriculum and the motivational strategies being used. No one had to promise her an A for learning all those songs, or threaten her with an F for messing up. Her most impressive achievement did not require carrots and sticks. It may have required their absence.

For all our talk about motivation, I think we often fail to recognize a truth that is staring us in the face: if educators are able to create the conditions under which children can become engaged with academic tasks, the acquisition of intellectual skills will probably follow. We want students to become rigorous thinkers, accomplished readers and writers and problem solvers who can make connections and distinctions between ideas. But the most reliable guide to a process that is promoting these things is not grades or test scores: it is the student's level of interest. Educators and parents ought to be focusing their attention on whether students read on their own and come home chattering about what they learned that day. It is theoretically possible for a child to be highly intrinsically motivated and still perform poorly. But the number of such students, I warrant, will never be great.

Now consider the converse: performing well, jumping through the hoops, doing all the homework, studying for the tests, making the grades, grooming the transcript, pleasing the adults — and hating every minute of it. This profile fits millions of children. They are learners, yes, but reluctant, other-directed learners who have been trained to read everything that is assigned and nothing that is not assigned. They are, in Montaigne's unsettling phrase, "mules laden with books."[17] More than three decades ago, Jerome Bruner described the results of this paint-by-number approach to achievement, focusing on very successful students who are "seekers after the 'right way to do it'":

Their capacity for transforming their learning into viable thought structures tends to be lower than [that of] children merely achieving at levels predicted by intelligence tests. . . . They develop rote abilities and depend upon being able to 'give back' what is expected rather than to make it into something that relates to the rest of their cognitive life. As Maimonides would say, their learning is not their own.[18]

But now I must confess that I have another agenda as well. I do not see interest merely as a means to the end of achievement. Even if it were just as easy to be a successful learner without intrinsic motivation, I believe that the desire to wrestle with ideas, sample literature, and think like a scientist is also valuable. I think we should want children who want to learn, who not only have reading skills but actually read. As Richard Ryan and a colleague argue, it is not enough "to conceive of the central goal of 12 years of mandatory schooling as merely a cognitive outcome." Instead, we should aim for children who are "willing and even enthusiastic about achieving something in school, curious and excited by learning to the point of seeking out opportunities to follow their interests beyond the boundaries of school."[19]

Few are likely to quarrel with such a goal, yet motivation as an end, not merely a means, seems to be missing from most of the national discussion about what is wrong with our schools and how to fix them. (Indeed, it is spoken of too rarely even in terms of its contribution to achievement.) To raise the issue is, by implication, to inquire into the very purpose of an education — a disconcerting prospect, perhaps, for those whose objective is to turn out adequately skilled workers who can increase corporate profits.[20] If, like John Nicholls, we are put off by talk about "investing in education," a phrase that "seems to express a desire for skills that will pay rather than a passion to make things of value";[21] if, like Charles Silberman, we think school "should prepare people not just to earn a living but to live a life — a creative, humane, and sensitive life,"[22] then children's attitudes toward learning are at least as important as how well they perform at any given task.

The gist of Fact 2, though, is that even if what matters to us is how well children learn, we still have to focus on intrinsic motivation since it is far more effective than rewards at producing excellence. That in turn means we have to be concerned with the fact that this critical ingredient begins to evaporate after a few years of schooling. How does this happen? Go back to Bruner's description of the unimaginative overachiever. That style, "in which the child is seeking cues as to how to conform to what is expected of him . . . starts in response to the rewards of parental or teacher approval," he argues.[23] And this leads us to . . .

Fact 3: Rewards for learning undermine intrinsic motivation. It would be bad enough if high grades, stickers, and other Skinnerian inducements just weren't very good at helping children learn. The tragedy is that they also vitiate the sort of motivation that *does* help. Carole Ames and Carol Dweck, two of our most penetrating thinkers on the subject of academic motivation, have independently pointed out that we cannot explain children's lack of interest in learning simply by citing low ability, poor performance, or low self-esteem, although these factors may play some role.[24] The decisive issue, it turns out, concerns students' goals with respect to learning. If teachers — or, according to one study, parents[25] — emphasize the value of academic accomplishment in terms of the rewards it will bring, students' interest in what they are learning will almost certainly decline. "All rewards have the same effect," one writer declares. "They dilute the pure joy that comes from success itself."[26]

Because I have already laid out the arguments and evidence for this effect in chapter 5, including a number of examples and studies relevant to learning in particular, there is no need to describe again how extrinsic motivators undermine intrinsic motivation. Instead, I want to focus on two reasons for this effect, each of which has been the subject of considerable attention by education researchers: the use of controlling techniques in the classroom, and the emphasis on how well students are performing. The work on these topics doesn't always make explicit reference to rewards, but both frameworks are clearly relevant to the practice of grading and the use of other extrinsic motivators with students.*

Making Students Learn

A top corporate executive, accustomed to the exercise of power, lamented not too long ago about the decline of education in this

---

*In what follows, I will not discuss an additional reason (proposed in chapter 5) for the detrimental effect of rewards on motivation — namely, the devaluing of an activity that occurs when it comes to be seen as a prerequisite for receiving a goody. There is every reason to think that this explanation applies to what happens in the classroom; anything students are told they have to do in order to be rewarded may come to be seen for that very reason as something they wouldn't want to do if given a choice. I'm unaware of any empirical tests of this paradigm in the classroom, however, so I have chosen to focus on two other accounts where more work has been done.

country. Children, he declared, must be "made to understand the importance of learning."[27] The approach captured in this short phrase is emblematic of what is wrong with American schooling. The aggressive attempt to "make" children do things — and even more absurd, to "make" them understand why they should care about what they have been made to do — is a recipe for failure. If, to paraphrase a famous critical report, an unfriendly foreign power had attempted to impose on America a mediocre educational system, it could have devised no better plan than to establish mechanisms for tightly controlling what students do in school.

In saying this, it must immediately be noted, I am not arguing that educators ought to stop providing guidance or instruction, that children should be free of all structures so they can learn entirely on their own. In chapter 11, I will say more about what it means to provide students with a reasonable degree of autonomy. For now it should be enough to point out that we have a very long way to go before we run the risk of allowing too much freedom. At present, says William Glasser, "coercive teachers are the rule, not the exception, in our schools. . . . We pressure students to learn what they do not want to learn, and then punish them with low grades when they do not learn it." The result, he adds, is that "we lose them as learners."[28]

To control students is to force them to accommodate to a preestablished curriculum. It is to tell them not only what they have to learn but how they have to learn it and what will happen to them if they don't — or what they will get if they do.[29] Tests are used not so much to see what students need help with but to compel them to do the work that has been assigned. Rewards, of course, are only one ingredient of this bitter bouillabaisse, but the concept of control helps us understand how it is that rewards contribute to turning eager learners into antsy clock-watchers.

Every teacher, principal, and educational administrator in the country ought to take a moment each Monday morning to read aloud the following three sentences by Richard Ryan and Jerome Stiller:

The more we try to measure, control, and pressure learning from without, the more we obstruct the tendencies of students to be actively involved and to participate in their own education. Not only does this result in a failure of students to absorb the cognitive agenda imparted by educators, but it also creates deleterious consequences for the affective agendas of schools [that is, how students feel about learning]. . . . Externally imposed evaluations, goals, rewards, and pressures seem to create a style of teaching and learning that is antithetical to quality learning outcomes in school, that is, learning characterized by durability, depth, and integration.[30]

There are values lurking in this statement, to be sure; it is assumed that a deep, lasting education, and even an active role for students in it, is desirable. But Ryan and Stiller are primarily summarizing empirical findings here, findings that are not very well known. Whatever one's feelings about the intrinsic merit of controlling strategies, they have certain predictable consequences, at least within our culture, that cannot be ignored.

Telling students exactly what they have to do, or using extrinsic incentives to get them to do it, often contributes to feelings of anxiety and even helplessness.[31] Some children, instead of rebelling against coercion, simply relinquish their autonomy. In one study, ten- and eleven-year-olds who received controlling evaluations of their performance were more likely to let the experimenter pick the next task for them, as compared to children who had just heard informational feedback.[32] High school students, accustomed to a highly directive style of instruction and suddenly asked to think for themselves, have been known to insist that they have "a right to be told what to do."[33] These results, besides being troubling in their own right, have ominous implications for learning. Research has demonstrated that feelings of anxiety and helplessness are associated with lower-quality performance.[34] Moreover, children who lack a sense of autonomy are likely to pick tasks that don't offer much challenge.[35]

Then there is the matter of intrinsic interest. Controlling environments have been shown consistently to reduce people's interest in whatever they are doing, even when they are doing things that would be highly motivating in other contexts. One study of thirty-five elementary school classrooms, for example, found that children who had controlling teachers displayed lower self-esteem and intrinsic motivation than did those whose teachers supported their capacity to make choices.[36] Another study showed that a highly controlling approach used with one task reduced people's interest in a second, entirely different task. The motivation-killing features of control, in other words, can spill over to poison attitudes about new activities.[37]

An extrinsic orientation is "associated with poorer overall performance" on academic tasks, according to Ann Boggiano and Marty Barrett. But where does that orientation come from? We cannot simply call this a child's natural "learning style" or assume she lacks motivation. In part, someone's apparent need for rewards and punishments is a reflection of how much she has been controlled by rewards and punishments in the past. "Frequent and consistent use of controlling strategies . . . may well foster a shift from an intrinsic to an extrinsic orientation."[38]

In an autobiographical essay published in 1946, Albert Einstein reflected on his days as a student of physics some fifty years earlier. He recalled his teachers with affection but, referring to exams, said, "This coercion had such a deterring effect that after I had passed the final examination, I found the consideration of any scientific problems distasteful to me for an entire year."[39] In the same vein, an assessment of teaching and learning at Harvard University in 1992, based on interviews with 570 undergraduates, concluded that many students avoided taking science classes not because of the heavy workload but because of the competition for grades.[40]

Controlling structures can drive people away from exploring valuable subjects. When they are younger, students can be forced to sit through a class, but they cannot be forced to be interested in it, or to do well. It stands to reason, as I argued above, that lower intrinsic motivation translates into lower achievement. But some researchers have demonstrated this connection directly. For example, first and second graders painted less creatively when they were given controlling instructions about how they were to handle the paints.[41] College students who received controlling feedback about how well they were solving a puzzle — that is, comments that compared their performance to how they should be doing — didn't do as good a job as those who just received straightforward information about their performance.[42] And children were less likely to succeed on a range of measures of classroom achievement if their parents tended not to give them much opportunity to make decisions and feel a sense of self-determination at home.[43]

What does all this mean? The evidence strongly suggests that tighter standards, additional testing, tougher grading, or more incentives will do more harm than good. Naturally we want to make sure that students are learning, but such tactics make it more difficult for that to happen. Students are already excessively controlled, which helps explain why so many are losing (or have lost) interest in what they are doing. We can almost watch that interest drain away each time a teacher invokes a bribe ("C'mon, Ellen, you're so close to getting an A in here") or a threat ("Do you want a zero, young man?").* The same

---

*What is even more appalling, many teachers hold out the possibility of more academic work as a punishment (or the possibility of less work as a reward),[44] which drives home the lesson that learning is something a student should want to avoid.

is true of a range of other instruments of control, such as calling on students even if they have not raised their hands.[45]

So why don't teachers stop doing these things? I think there are several plausible explanations. First, some teachers cannot imagine how else they could do their jobs, particularly when they must work with children whose behavior is difficult to deal with — or for that matter, when they simply have too many children in one room. Controlling academic strategies, in other words, can be a response to nonacademic features of the classroom.

Second, it takes more time to bring students in on the process of making decisions, and many teachers already feel there are not enough hours to do what has to be done. Third, as a former teacher who found himself relying on grades to "motivate" students, I can testify that controlling approaches can also be wielded out of desperation: I lacked the skills — and, arguably, the curriculum — to help students develop a genuine interest in learning. (The controlling strategies ultimately failed, of course. You can only promise so many A's or threaten so many F's before the returns begin to diminish. And when students finally respond to someone brandishing a grade book by saying "I don't care," the teacher is out of tricks. The effect is similar to being told by a store cashier, "I'm sorry, but we don't honor U.S. currency here." One can only stammer, "But that's all I've got!")

Finally, teachers control students when they themselves are pressured to perform. This is a point lost on policymakers who, in the name of accountability, would increase the use of rewards and punishments to which teachers are subjected. Not surprisingly, teachers who feel that administrators don't listen to their views, and who have little influence over the educational program, are particularly likely to report feelings of psychological distress.[46] But it appears that when they feel powerless, or manipulated by the likes of merit pay,[47] teachers are also more likely to become impatient with students for whose performance they will have to answer. When sixth graders in one experiment were promised rewards for successfully tutoring younger children, they "devalued the younger child who was making errors," losing patience and becoming generally unpleasant (as compared with tutors who were not working for a reward).[48] When undergraduates in another study were asked to teach people how to solve a puzzle, those who were given controlling instructions that emphasized performance standards became more demanding and controlling in how they taught.[49] In short,

> when teachers feel pressured by superiors they tend to become more controlling with their students. . . . [When it is] emphasized that they

are responsible for their students' performing up to standards . . . teachers tend to . . . give children less choice and less opportunity for autonomous learning. This behavior, in turn, is likely to have deleterious effects on the children's intrinsic motivation.[50]

The effects on the quality of learning are just as pronounced. Researchers in one experiment gave fourth-grade teachers two tasks to teach their students. Some were told that their job was "simply to help the students learn how to solve the problems"; others were warned that it was their "responsibility to make sure that students perform up to standards" and do well on a test. The result: children taught by the teachers who felt pressured did not learn the tasks as well as those whose teachers were not under the gun.[51] Another fascinating study, meanwhile, found that the mere knowledge among students that their teacher was "extrinsically constrained" affected their own motivation.[52] The damage done by rewards, then, is not limited to the person who gets them.

We could probably come up with other reasons to explain why teachers and administrators use extrinsic devices and other techniques of control. The key point is that they are finally ineffective and, in fact, are likely to produce a cluster of symptoms that might be described as "burnout" if displayed by an adult. In chapter 11, I will discuss more promising approaches to tapping children's motivation and helping them to learn.

Tighter Control: The Case of Special Education

Controlling techniques in general, and rewards in particular, are most pervasively applied to children with special needs and challenges — and to those who simply carry a label that sets them apart. These children are subjected to a relentless regimen of Skinnerian manipulation, complete with elaborate charts, point systems, and reinforcement schedules. Even teachers and clinicians who would hesitate to use such methods with other children assume it is justified for those who are classified by a distinguishing set of initials.

Consider the fate of students who are said to be "learning disabled," a category so elastic that virtually all of us could be diagnosed that way in one situation or another.[53] Teachers report that they act in a more controlling way with such children than they do with other students.[54] The result is that even though learning-disabled students were no less intrinsically motivated than their peers in the early grades,[55] they come to be "more dependent on external sources of evaluation" such as grades, rewards, and teachers' judgments, "whereas regular students [feel more] capable of making decisions on their own."[56]

Achievement is one casualty of this approach. Even on very simple tasks, the use of rewards has been found — sometimes to the researchers' surprise — to have a detrimental effect on the performance of children labeled learning disabled or hyperactive.[57] Likewise, an extrinsic orientation "may decrease performance in students of lower levels of intelligence below that predicted by their mental age levels."[58]

Children with greater needs and handicaps are controlled even more tightly. Classes for them "tend to be heavily dominated by externally controlling teaching practices and extrinsic motivational incentives."[59] In a survey of programs around the country for children labeled behaviorally disordered or emotionally disturbed, one group of researchers recently found an "emphasis on behavioral management, often to the exclusion of a concern with learning." Moreover, behavioral management in practice typically meant obedience rather than helping "children become self-directed and to assume responsibility for their behavior."[60] In fact, one study showed that teachers of retarded children were so intent on reinforcing certain (adult-specified) behaviors that as a rule they tended to ignore the children's choices and expressions of preference.[61]

In judging the merits of programs geared to students with disabilities, Edward Deci and his colleagues contend that the central question is whether they "promote self-determined functioning." Their answer is that behavior modification formats, by far the most pervasive approach, have exactly the opposite result. "Pressuring them with rewards, tokens, deadlines, and prescriptions is counter to supporting autonomy," they argue. Even subtly controlling environments "can be detrimental to self-regulation" and lead, over time, to "poorer achievement and adjustment in the classroom."[62] The more they are controlled, the more they come to need control and the less they have the chance to take responsibility for their own learning and behavior.

Two writers who specialize in work with severely handicapped children have observed that behavior management systems turn teachers into technicians and students into "objects to be manipulated, shaped, or molded" — "passive agents of our actions rather than contributing members of the educational process." Students' spontaneous behaviors, which may be meaningful to them and "important to their overall development," are automatically viewed as interfering with the behavioral goals that have been established by adults.

When these tightly controlled behavioral programs fail, the blame is placed on the specific reinforcement protocol being used or on the teacher who implements it or on the child — never on the premises of behaviorism itself. When these programs succeed in altering children's behavior, it is typically at the expense of creating "instructional dependency" and preventing them from developing "the ability to choose and to have some control over [their] own destiny [which] is one of the most important skills that can be imparted to severely handicapped students, or to anyone else for that matter."[63]

Special education teachers, who have a very difficult job to do, are both underpaid and underappreciated. Most clearly want what is best for the children they work with. Unfortunately, they are trapped by a system that has them, in effect, training these children as if they were pets. In many cases, they — or the educators who trained *them* — fail to appreciate the difference between a structured environment and a controlling one. Never having been exposed to approaches that are both more respectful and more effective in the long run,[64] they may have taken on faith that extrinsic techniques are necessary for the students they work with, when in fact such approaches serve only to create a dependence on these very techniques.

"How'm I Doin'?"

Even before I had read the research, it was quite clear to me as a teacher, and before that as a student, that A's and other artificial incentives for learning are no less techniques of control than harsher measures are. Eventually it also became clear that this fact helped explain their failure. But rewards reduce the prospects of effective learning for another reason, too: they lead students to concentrate on the question that stands as the title of this section.

The work of Carole Ames, Carol S. Dweck, and John Nicholls converges on a single crucial distinction concerning how to think about what happens in schools. Variously framed as "mastery versus ability," "learning versus performance," and "task versus ego," the basic point is that there is an enormous difference between getting students to think about what they are doing, on the one hand, and about how well they are doing (and therefore how good they are at doing it), on the other. The latter orientation, in which rewards typically play a starring role, does a great deal of harm.

Students who are encouraged to think about what they are doing, assuming it is something worth doing, will likely come to find meaning in

> the processes involved in learning content, value mastery of the content itself, and exhibit pride in craftsmanship. . . . Their focus is on the processes involved in working with the content or performing the skill, and not on themselves, their abilities, how their progress will be perceived by others, or issues of success or failure or reward or punishment.[65]

This is precisely what we want to promote — partly because a student who is caught up in what he is learning is more likely to be successful in learning it.

By contrast, *students led to think mostly about how well they are doing — or even worse, how well they are doing compared to everyone else — are less likely to do well.* This may seem paradoxical, but the fact is that students overly concerned about their performance come to see learning as a means to an end, the end being the good grade or other reward they will receive. They start to think that their performance, especially when they fail, is due to innate intelligence (or its absence): "I screwed up, therefore I'm stupid." That in turn leads them to assume there isn't much point in trying harder next time, which means they are unlikely to improve. It also leads them to try to avoid difficult tasks so they can escape a negative evaluation. After all, to think about your performance is to think less about what you are doing than about how you appear to others.[66]

From this description and the research on which it is based, I think it is possible to tease out two distinct reasons that a performance orientation has unfortunate consequences. First, someone who is attending to how well he is doing has his self-concept on the line. His image of himself as smart or competent is endangered by the risk of failing to meet a certain standard of performance. The attempt to protect that image usually comes at the expense of a desire to try one's best, which can seem risky. If you don't try, you can't fail. Second, the more the student is focused on how well he's doing, the less he is absorbed in the task itself. That absorption facilitates learning, so anything that undermines it is educationally disruptive.

This is not to say that when an assignment has been completed its worth cannot be judged. I have already discussed the value of informational feedback. There is a time to think about whether what one has done is any good, and it is usually necessary to talk with others about the quality of one's work. But the extent and frequency of these evaluations can easily be overdone for adults in the workplace, let alone for children in the classroom. The research is clear: getting children to focus on their performance can interfere with their ability to remember things about the challenging tasks they just worked on.[67] It can undermine their ability to apply scientific principles to new situations.[68] It can reduce the quality of their work as measured on tests of creativity[69] and their "readiness to contemplate diverse ideas."[70]

The researchers who conduct such studies generally induce a performance orientation by what they say about the purpose of the experiment or by telling subjects what to think about. But what happens when they use traditional classroom techniques that focus students' attention on their performance — common practices such as giving grades for work or offering reminders that they'll be tested on what they're doing? The answer is that the effects are exactly the same: compared to students who are allowed to get wrapped up in the task itself, those thinking about grades or tests don't do as well on measures of creative thinking or conceptual learning. Even when they only have to learn things by rote, they are more apt to forget the material a week or so later.[71]

I will have more to say later about the disadvantages of grades. My point for the time being is that students don't learn very effectively when adults hold out the promise of rewards, compare one child's performance to another's (leading them to think in terms of winning and losing rather than learning),[72] or rely on any other practices that draw their attention to how well they are doing. Moreover, these strategies chip away at intrinsic motivation. When you tell students that how well they do on a task reveals how creative they are,[73] or when you grade them,[74] their interest in what they are doing declines.

In one intriguing experiment conducted by Israeli researcher Ruth Butler, some sixth-grade students were led to focus on how well they performed at a creative task (making pictures out of a page of preprinted circles) while others were just encouraged to be imaginative. Then each student was taken to a room that contained a pile of pictures supposedly drawn by other children in response to the same instructions. Each student also found information describing how to figure out his or her "creativity score" and compare it to those of the others. Sure enough, the children who were allowed to become immersed in the task were more interested in *what* their peers had done; those who were told to think about their performance now wanted to know *how* their peers had done relative to themselves. The famous "Wad-ja-get?" preoccupation of students — compulsively comparing their own grades to others' — is not a function of human nature but of the performance orientation that suffuses most American classrooms and stifles children's interest in what they are learning.[75]

Getting students to think about how they are performing also increases their fear of failure. Trying not to fail is, of course, very different from trying to succeed. One's efforts in the former case are geared at doing damage control, minimizing risks, getting by. In school, "the game is not to acquire knowledge but to discover what answer the teacher wants, and in what form she wants it."[76] Surveys of elementary school students reveal that they have learned they are supposed to finish the assignment, do it quickly, and if possible, get the right answer. Much more rarely does a child think he is supposed to try to understand what he is working on.[77] Students often say that "getting grades is the most important thing about school."[78] And the more emphasis teachers and parents place on performance, the more students are set back by failure. By contrast, those who are task oriented tend to be relatively resilient.[79]

Now take this pattern one step further: someone who is concerned to minimize failure is unlikely to challenge herself. Not only rewards (see page 65) but anything that makes students preoccupied with how well they are doing will lead them to choose the easiest possible tasks: the point is to do well, not to learn. Apart from all the evidence demonstrating that this is true,[80] all we have to do is wander onto a college campus and behold the Quest for the Perfect Gut — the search for the least demanding course.[81] The rule of thumb is the more intense the focus on performance, the less the interest in intellectual challenge.

The performance focus makes things even more difficult for children who, for whatever reason, have stopped trying hard or who are especially anxious about how they will do[82] — a finding that will probably not seem surprising. Less obvious, but no less true, is the fact that a performance orientation is also bad news for high achievers. In a study by Dweck and a colleague, these students too "passed up the opportunity to increase their skills on a task that entailed public mistakes" when encouraged to think about how well they could do it.[83] Similarly, Butler has found that under such conditions — and particularly when grades are emphasized — top students are relatively uninterested in self-improvement or in the quality of the work they do.[84]

Here, then, is another lens through which to look at those plodding overachievers of whom Bruner spoke. They watch their grade point averages with the eye of an emergency room technician monitoring a patient's blood pressure. Consequently, they are "less willing to take risks."[85] In their fixation on extrinsic rewards, they often don't feel very good about themselves: some preliminary research suggests that there is actually a negative relation between the grades students make in high school and how positive they feel about themselves and the world a few years later.[86] One educator concerned about gifted children remarks that "those students who are most excited by the educational possibilities before them are those we may be hurting most . . . in the process of using extrinsic rewards."[87]

Some teachers who realize this have moved away from rewards and a stress on performance. But teachers operate within significant constraints: with their students' standardized test scores published in the newspapers and scrutinized as if they were a meaningful measure of learning, teachers often feel obliged to get children obsessively concerned about how they are doing. These pressures on teachers must be eased in order for counterproductive practices in the classroom to stop.

One group of educational critics tells us, "Kids are failing to learn because we're afraid to let them know when they get something wrong for fear of injuring their self-esteem." The truth is that kids are *constantly* fearful of getting things wrong, which is why they do as little as they can get away with. Another group of critics tells us, "We need fewer punishments and more rewards; kids should be helped to stop fearing F's and to start thinking it's realistic to get A's." The truth is that the problem is not just punishments but also rewards, not bad grades but the emphasis on grading per se. Anything that gets children to think primarily about their performance will undermine their interest in learning, their desire to be challenged, and ultimately the extent of their achievement. Small wonder that rewards have precisely those effects.

9

BRIBES FOR BEHAVING:
Why Behaviorism Doesn't Help Children Become Good People

> If we want children to become able to act with personal conviction
> about what is right . . . we must reduce our adult power and avoid
> the use of rewards and punishments as much as possible.
>
> — Constance Kamii, 1984

BRIBES AND THREATS WORK. If I held up a pile of hundred-dollar bills and promised to hand them over if you learned every word on this page by heart, you would probably start committing them to memory. If I held a loaded gun to your head and told you I was going to pull the trigger unless you immediately ripped this page out of the book and ate it, you would very likely find these ideas a lot easier to swallow. If the punishment is aversive enough, or the reward appealing enough, there is no telling what you (or I) would agree to do.

This is the reason so many parents and teachers insist that punishments and rewards are effective at dealing with children. "One more word and you're grounded for the week" can produce silence. "If you put away your toys, I'll get you that Nintendo game you want" can clean up a room in a hurry. Extrinsic motivators are hard to discard, not only because many people have no idea what to do instead, but also because they get the job done.

Two simple questions, however, cast the issue in a radically different light. In response to the assertion "Rewards [or punishments] work," we need to ask, first, Work to do what? and second, At what cost? The first question by itself is enough to keep us busy for quite a while.

The Price of Obedience

I can think of no better use of fifteen minutes for any of us who are parents or teachers than pausing to think about — and even to list on paper — the long-term goals we have for our children. What would we like them to be able to do, to want to do, to feel, to be like in the years to come? Having asked people in different places to reflect on these questions, I have noticed a substantial overlap among the ideas generated by different groups. Invariably, what I hear is a desire for children to be self-reliant and responsible but also socially skilled and caring, capable of surviving and succeeding in life yet willing to question and think in a creative and critical manner, confident and possessed of an unshakable faith in their own worth while still being open to criticism and new ideas. Some people emphasize one item more than another, and some propose amendments to this list, but few of these core objectives strike anyone as outrageously controversial.

The next part of the exercise, which takes longer than fifteen minutes, is to systematically reconsider what we do with children, our day-to-day practices, in light of these long-term goals. The unsettling news is that rewards and punishments are worthless at best, and destructive at worst, for helping children develop such values and skills. What rewards and punishments do produce is *temporary compliance*. They buy us obedience. If that's what we mean when we say they "work," then yes, they work wonders.

But if we are ultimately concerned with the kind of people our children will become, there are no shortcuts. Good values have to be grown from the inside out. Praise and privileges and punishments can change behavior (for a while), but they cannot change the person who engages in the behavior — at least, not in the way we want. No behavioral manipulation ever helped a child develop a commitment to becoming a caring and responsible person. No reward for doing something we approve of ever gave a child a reason for continuing to act that way when there was no longer any reward to be gained for doing so.

Consider the issue of responsibility. A great many adults who complain that children don't act "responsibly" really mean that they don't do exactly what they're told.* Glasser noticed this a long time ago:

---

*The same trick is played with the word *respect*, which is often used to denote simple obedience; the child who thinks for herself and asks challenging questions is called disrespectful — along with other epithets that say as much about the speaker as about the individual being described.

"We teach thoughtless conformity to school rules and call the conforming child 'responsible.'"[1] If this is the sort of responsibility we wish to promote, then a ceaseless application of punishments or rewards would seem the most efficient way — possibly the only way — to go about it. But if by *responsibility* we mean the capacity to act carefully and thoughtfully, to make ethical judgments and behave in accordance with them, then, as educator Constance Kamii's comment at the head of this chapter suggests, extrinsic motivators take us in the wrong direction.

Richard Ryan has distinguished sharply between "helping a child develop certain values, such as a sense of responsibility, and getting a task done, such as taking out the garbage. Getting the task done is the easy part," he adds.[2] Behavior modification programs can accomplish *that*, but they actually "forestall rather than promote self-determination," which is a prerequisite for the sense of responsibility in which we are ultimately interested.[3] Put it this way: a child who complies in the hope of getting a reward or avoiding a punishment is not, as we sometimes say, "behaving himself." It would be more accurate to say the reward or punishment is behaving him.

So why do we rely on extrinsic motivators with our children? For starters, we tend to fall back on whatever will produce compliance. It is more convenient for us to get the garbage taken out, to get a child into bed at night (or out the door in the morning), to head off an imminent tantrum or squabble between siblings in the grocery store — regardless of how our tactics for doing this may affect the child's long-term development. Time constraints are very real, of course, and our own emotional needs, or even convenience, also count for something. But we need to be aware of the costs of these quick fixes: rather than rationalizing them as being in the child's best interest, we ought to face the fact that behavioral manipulation is ultimately detrimental. Let us be honest when we reward or punish by asking ourselves for whom we are doing it (them or us?) and for what (the development of good values or mere obedience?).

That second question forces us to examine just how committed we really are to the development of positive values and all those other long-term goals we may list in a reflective moment. When new parents gratefully exclaim to friends and relatives, "He's such a *good* baby!" they mean that their infant sleeps a lot, doesn't cry excessively, and isn't much trouble. But how many parents have in mind a similar definition of *good* when they describe an older child (or when a teacher describes a class) that way? All parents have had moments of wishing that their children would simply obey without making a fuss. The more deep-seated that wish becomes, the more a desire for a child who isn't any trouble overrides other goals, the more likely one is to resort to punishments or rewards.

Another reason we take the extrinsic route is that we have come to think that doing something about a problem means doing something *to* children. Some people, including many thoughtful, educated parents, seem to dream in black and white. They can see only two alternatives: punish or do nothing. We crack down or we let it slide; we are authoritarian or permissive. Sometimes each parent is assigned to one position: "My husband is the disciplinarian in the family: he yells at the kids and sends them to their rooms; I let 'em get away with murder."

Thinking seriously about raising children — or teaching them, for that matter[4] — begins with a challenge to this false dichotomy. Some researchers have pointed out that we need not choose between being punitive or permissive; it is also possible to set limits and exert firm control while being warm, caring, and responsive.[5] Others have observed that we need not choose between doing something punitive to children versus doing nothing; we can expand the idea of doing something to include providing rewards. These reformulations are improvements, but very limited ones. Ideally, we need to think about alternatives that move past the very idea of extrinsic control or behavioral manipulation. In chapter 12, I will present some ideas on how to do that.

While teachers' obligations are somewhat different from those of parents,[6] the social and moral goals they hold for children are substantially the same. Yet these goals are undermined by the "hidden curriculum" offered in classrooms — to wit, "Do what the teacher says, live up to teacher expectations for proper behavior, keep busy, keep quiet and don't move too much, stick to the schedule."[7]

Where do these priorities come from? First, teachers themselves are often judged on the basis of whether their students sit quietly and obey.[8] Second, teachers may take for granted that the only way two or three dozen people can learn in the same room is if one person exerts absolute control. Third, unilateral power can be pleasing (and its absence disconcerting) to some teachers. One college instructor of my acquaintance recalled threatening to punish students for coming to class late, whereupon she reported feeling that she was now "back in control again." This woman was simply more honest with herself than are many other teachers and parents who do not acknowledge that the overriding concern is to stay in charge. The implicit model is that of a zero-sum game: "If I'm not in control, the student has beat me." The point is not to solve problems and learn together but to win a power struggle.

Whatever the cause, the hidden curriculum dictates that teachers do not spend their time helping children to become caring and responsible, but on maintaining "discipline." "Most discipline schemes, euphemistically known as classroom management techniques, reek of manipulation," one writer has remarked.[9] Specifically, most are based on an admixture of exactly two ingredients: punishments and rewards. Again, relying on extrinsic motivators makes perfect sense when our long-term goals are eclipsed by short-term objectives such as bringing order and control to the classroom.

Some educators think we can, or even must, get children to be quiet and compliant first; *then* we can promote more ambitious values. This is a pact with the devil, and it doesn't work any better than the tactic I have called "bait and switch," in which extrinsic motivators are used to induce students to learn in the hope that these devices can simply be faded out once intrinsic interest develops.[10] If the classroom is established from the start as a place where children simply obey rather than help to make meaningful decisions, it is very difficult to abandon autocracy later. Indeed, educators may claim that control is only a temporary necessity, but current practice suggests that it is rarely relinquished:

> Far from helping students to develop into mature, self-reliant, self-motivated individuals, schools seem to do everything they can to keep youngsters in a state of chronic, almost infantile, dependency. The pervasive atmosphere of distrust, together with rules covering the most minute aspects of existence, teach students every day that they are not people of worth, and certainly not individuals capable of regulating their own behavior.[11]

Students get the message about what adults want. When fourth graders in a variety of classrooms (representing a range of teaching styles and socioeconomic backgrounds) were asked what their teachers most wanted them to do, they didn't say, "Ask thoughtful questions" or "Make responsible decisions" or "Help others." They said, "Be quiet, don't fool around, and get our work done on time."[12] Similarly, in interviews with second and sixth graders that probed their beliefs about what it means to "behave well," the most common single answer had to do with keeping quiet.[13]

In some classrooms, these messages accompany (and complement) a curriculum of rote learning; in others, they accompany (and clash with) a more ambitious approach to academics.[14] But one way or another, millions of children learn to shut up and do what they're told. This lesson is typically enforced by classroom management programs that are undisguised exercises in extrinsic control. The most popular of these, known as Assertive Discipline, amounts to a combination of bribes and threats to enforce rules that the teacher alone devises. Children are rewarded for mindless obedience; the names of students who fail to obey are written on the blackboard for all to see; questions or objections are dismissed as irrelevant. All problems in the classroom are attributed to the students, and punishments imposed on them are said to result from their "choices."

Even judged by relatively narrow criteria, the evidence suggests that Assertive Discipline is ineffective.[15] But if it did succeed in keeping order in the classroom, this program, like all carrot-and-stick techniques used at school or at home, fails to help children become reflective, compassionate people. As one researcher summed up the evidence, "Children do not learn to be moral by learning to obey rules that others make for them. . . . The lessons of behavioral approaches to discipline are often precisely contrary to what we wish children to learn."[16]

Punishing Children

How do we punish children? Let us count the ways. We incarcerate them: children are sent to their rooms, teenagers are "grounded" and forbidden to leave the house, students are sentenced to "detention," and all may be forcibly isolated through "time-out" procedures.[17] We use physical violence on them: corporal punishment in public schools is still permitted in most states (though long since abandoned by most of the world's developed nations)[18] and spanking is still approved (and used) by the overwhelming majority of American parents.[19] We humiliate children by yelling at or criticizing them in public. We withdraw or withhold privileges, deny them food or companionship, deliberately ignore them,[20] prevent them from doing things they enjoy. At school, we subject them to F's and zeroes, additional assignments, playground citations, trips to the principal's office, and suspensions — all of which may be threatened in advance or explicitly described on a hierarchical list of "consequences," the approved euphemism for punishment.

Here is another exercise that teachers and parents often find valuable, which I invite you to do now. Close your eyes (when you finish this paragraph), return to your childhood, and think of a time when you were accused of doing something bad. Recall the alleged misbehavior as specifically as you can, as well as what the adult in question did or said to you and how it made you feel.

What constantly impresses me when I ask people to remember such incidents is how vivid the recollections are — as if the event had happened last week instead of many years ago. Some tales are shocking in the cruelty inflicted on children. Some are stories of a brief but harsh rebuke, a refusal to believe the child's account, a minor humiliation that the adult had probably forgotten a few days later but the child carried forever. Some of these children never again trusted or respected that authority figure; some refused to participate in class for a very long time; some still carry with them a smoldering resentment fed by fantasies of revenge. I have heard people say they were more compliant for a while after the incident in question; I have never heard anyone say that a punitive response helped make him or her a better person. The only people who tell of being positively affected are those whose stories concern a parent or teacher who *didn't* punish, who responded instead with unexpected gentleness and understanding.

This is really an exercise in perspective taking — imagining the point of view of someone else — except that here the other person is oneself as a child. Once we can recapture that perspective, it is easier to put ourselves in the place of the children we raise or teach today. The idea here is to imagine on a regular basis how our reactions to their behavior may affect them more deeply than we realize, how today's careless exercise of power on our part may become tomorrow's bitter memory for them.

Consider the long-term effects of punishment. Skinner argued that when we punish someone we teach only what he is not supposed to do and offer insufficient guidance on what he should do instead.* But this criticism only scratches the surface. Punishment doesn't even teach what not to do, much less the reason not to do it: what it really teaches is the desire to avoid punishment. The emphasis is on the consequence of the action (to the actor), not the action itself. We say, "Don't let me catch you doing that again!" and the child silently responds, "Okay — next time you won't catch me."

Punishing children does teach some lasting lessons, though. Take

---

*For that matter, as other behaviorists have pointed out, "it is equally true that reinforcement procedures do not teach which particular responses should not occur."[21]

the use of violence to discipline children. Regardless of what we are trying to get across by spanking, paddling, or slapping them, the messages that actually come through are these: "Violence is an acceptable way of expressing anger" and "If you are powerful enough you can get away with hurting someone." For decades, researchers have consistently found that children subjected to physical punishment tend to be more aggressive than their peers, and will likely grow up to use violence on their own children. These effects are not confined to victims of what is legally classified as abuse: even "acceptable" levels of physical punishment may perpetuate aggression and unhappiness.[22]

So attached are some parents to physical punishment that they persist in using it when their children hurt someone else. Many of us have seen this sort of thing on display in public places: "We don't [*slap*] hit [*slap*] people [*slap*]!" In one poll, a plurality of parents (41 percent) chose physical punishment as the preferred way of dealing with a child who is aggressive,[23] apparently believing that the best way to teach that hurting is wrong is by hurting. It would be a comical juxtaposition if it weren't so tragic.

But it is not only physical punishment that proves ineffective in the long run, makes children more aggressive, and leads to other undesirable consequences. *All* punishment, by which I mean any reliance on power to make something unpleasant happen to a child as a way of trying to alter that child's behavior, teaches that when you are bigger or stronger than someone else, you can use that advantage to force the person to do what you want.

Punishment also provokes resistance and resentment, which a child may take out on other people, such as peers. It leads children to feel worse about themselves since they often assume they must be bad if someone keeps doing such bad things to them. And it spoils the relationship between the child and the adult: a parent or teacher who relies on punishment becomes, in the eyes of the child, a rule enforcer, someone who may cause unpleasant things to happen — in short, someone to be avoided. To the extent that helping children develop good values depends on establishing a caring relationship with them, the use of punishment makes that much less likely to happen. As Thomas Gordon once commented, "The more you use power to try to control people, the less real influence you'll have on their lives."[24]

The research literature leaves no doubt that punishment is counterproductive. Studies over more than half a century show that when adults use disciplinary approaches variously described as "highly controlling," "power-assertive," or just plain punitive, children become more disruptive, aggressive, and hostile. A child who is punished by his parents is more likely than other children to break rules when he is away from home.[25] One early and influential study that involved extensive interviews with hundreds of mothers of kindergarten-age children discovered that "punishment of specific acts not infrequently had just the effect the mother wanted," with the result that many of these mothers "thought they were able to get good results from punishment." The long-term results, however, were another matter:

> The unhappy effects of punishment have run like a dismal thread through our findings. Mothers who punished toilet accidents severely ended up with bed-wetting children. Mother who punished dependency to get rid of it had more dependent children than mothers who did not punish. Mothers who punished aggressive behavior severely had more aggressive children than mothers who punished lightly. They also had more dependent children. . . . Our evaluation of punishment is that it is ineffectual over the long term as a technique for eliminating the kind of behavior toward which it is directed.[26]

Some years later, Kamii, drawing from Piaget's work, argued that punishment leads to three possible outcomes: "calculation of risks" (which means children spend their time figuring out whether they can get away with something), "blind conformity" (which fails to teach responsible decision-making), or "revolt."[27]

The root of punishment is coercion. This is apparent when the punishment is particularly brutal, but it is no less true in other cases. Even "a seemingly benign and kindly form of control, to bend rather than break a child's will . . . [is] unlikely to create a genuine sense of autonomy in the child, or a sense of choice and responsibility," observes Philip Greven. "The child still [has] to accept the parent's will as the child's own."[28] Piaget put this point more succinctly: "punishment . . . renders autonomy of conscience impossible."[29]

Despite all this, punishment is certainly the dominant form of discipline in this country, and discipline, in turn, is what we seem to think children need. Asked to pick "the main fault of parents in raising children nowadays," more respondents in a Gallup poll (37 percent) chose "no discipline" than any other response. (By contrast, only 6 or 7 percent thought the major problem was that children are "not treated as persons" or are treated with a "lack of understanding.")[30] When children ask for an explanation of what we have told them to do, we commonly fall back on "Because I said so!" This answer is tempting when we have run out of patience, but really it is no answer at all. It says, in effect, "I don't have a good reason for making you do this — or I don't care enough to explain the reason to you — but you have to do it anyway because I'm more powerful than you are."* No wonder child development specialist Rheta DeVries observes, "Some people have to overcome romantic tendencies in thinking about young children. But most people have to overcome tendencies to authoritarian relations with children."[31]

When a child is bullied into acting the way we demand, he will often resist. But this is not because he is "hard to handle"; more likely it is because he has been treated as a thing to be handled. Researchers have found that the more we restrict children's choices — the more controlling and heavy-handed we are — the less likely they will comply.[32] Authoritarian parenting and teaching therefore generally fail even on their own terms: forget about such ambitious goals as helping kids become responsible, decent people; this approach ultimately doesn't even succeed at getting them to do what we tell them. And when it fails, many adults invoke the need for even stricter discipline and punish them some more.

The Consequences of "Consequences"

A number of psychologists and educators influenced by the work of Rudolf Dreikurs[33] denounce punishment as harsh and ineffective and suggest instead that children be made to suffer "consequences" — especially those described as "logical" or "natural" — for their actions. Some partisans of this view concede that it is not always easy in practice to distinguish between punishment and consequences.[34] After all, the two "are alike in [saying] . . . 'When you do this, then this will happen.'"[35]

But others insist that they reflect qualitatively different prescriptions for dealing with children. A consequence is, by Dreikurs's definition, related to the misbehavior; it is also supposed to be reasonable (that is, not excessive) and respectfully applied. Here are some examples of consequences recommended by proponents of the idea:

• A child who tips her chair back in class must stand up for the rest of the period.

• Food is taken away from children who persist in not washing up before dinner.

---

*Some parents even find it funny to display this philosophy on T-shirts and bumper stickers in the form of the slogan BECAUSE I'M THE MOMMY, THAT'S WHY. This is about as amusing as any other expression of a totalitarian sensibility.

- Anyone who repeatedly taps a pencil is told that the pencil will be taken away unless the tapping stops.
- Students who don't finish their work before recess have to stay in class to complete it. ("If teachers are concerned about children not getting enough exercise, they might require that the student do twenty-five jumping jacks. . . . This is not punishment as long as the Three Rs for Logical Consequences are remembered.")
- A child who forgets to bring her apron to home economics class is prevented from cooking.
- Students who commit various infractions are not permitted to go on field trips, are forced to eat in the classroom rather than the cafeteria, are required to sit in the principal's office, or must "write for me how you intend to stop breaking this rule."[36]

If we define *punishment* as an intervention that forces someone to do something she'd rather not do (or prevents her from doing something she wants to do) as a way of trying to change her behavior, then it is hard to see how these are not punishments.[37] More important, it is hard to see how a child could experience them as anything other than punitive, even if they are less abusive than other things that might have been done to her. What Dreikurs and his followers are offering us is just Lite Punishment.

If these writers don't see it this way, it may be because they overstate the significance of whether what we do to a child is related to what the child did. The fact of the matter is that forcing a child who misbehaves at dinner to go without food is not all that different from forcing her to miss a favorite television show; the first punishment is technically more directly related to the original act (which may be satisfying to the adult), but that doesn't make it any less a punishment.* Similarly, announcing matter-of-factly what we will do to a child who fails to comply is no less a threat than yelling the same piece of information.

If a child tips her chair back too far, she will fall over. That is a "natural consequence" — and the fact that it qualifies for that label offers no argument for letting it happen; caring adults go out of their

---

*The source of the disproportionate emphasis accorded to this relationship may be a function of Dreikurs's belief that "children retaliate [when they are punished] because they see no relationship between the punishment and the crime."[38] If this assumption is wrong, and I think it is, then the distinction between punishment and consequences melts away and we are left needing an alternative to both of them. A better account of the child's anger and desire to retaliate is that they are rooted in the adult's use of power, which "frustrates not only the act but also the child's need for autonomy."[39]

way to prevent many such consequences from occurring. If, by contrast, a child who tips her chair back is forced to stand up for the rest of the period, that is a punishment. If it seems "logical" to a teacher, this may just be a function of the teacher's inability to imagine other ways of dealing with the problem (assuming it really is a problem). The less inevitable the response comes to seem, the less the teacher is inclined to justify it as logical. And the more aware he becomes of the long-term effects of punishment, whatever we choose to call it, the less he is inclined to see it as desirable.

Some teachers and parents seem to think that consequences are acceptable as long as children have been clearly warned about what will happen if they misbehave. These warnings allow adults to pride themselves on their fairness — and to shrug off complaints — since adequate notice was given before the punishment was imposed: "Hey, I warned you what would happen, didn't I?"

But what is actually promoted by this arrangement? A list of specific rules and consequences establishes a confrontational tone; the message is not that members of a community will work together and try to help someone who stumbles, but that anyone who violates a pre-established edict is in trouble. Adults are defined principally as enforcers, obliged to prove that they follow through on their threats. Children are encouraged to focus in a legalistic way on exactly what behavior is covered by each rule, how the rule will be applied, what circumstances may create exceptions, and so forth.[40] Some will be tempted to test the limits to see what they can get away with. And as with any other punitive arrangement, children learn more about the use of coercion than about how or why to act responsibly.[41]

Some people maintain that children are taught a useful lesson by being made to suffer unpleasant consequences when they do something wrong.* After all, when an adult is caught robbing a bank, there are consequences to be paid. Children had better learn that now so they don't think they'll be able to get away with anything they want to do in life.

The first problem with this argument is that it assumes the child will derive the intended lesson from a punishment. Suppose a ten-year-old

---

*I am assuming here for the sake of the argument that the behavior would indeed be identified as wrong by most observers, even though many children are punished for doing things that offend only the adult in question. One characteristic of an approach rooted in power is that *anything* the controller deems "bad" or "inappropriate" can elicit a punitive response. The reasonableness of the demand is never questioned, only how to implement it.

taunts her younger brother and makes him cry. If her parents force her to spend the evening in her room, she will probably not devote that time to reflection on the connection between cruelty and unpleasant consequences. More likely she will spend the evening feeling victimized,[42] growing increasingly angry at her parents (and feeling less likely to talk with them about the underlying feelings of jealousy that led to the incident), resenting her brother, and perhaps resolving to be more clever when she plots her revenge.

The second problem with what might be called the "bank robber argument" is that we want children not to do unethical, hurtful things because they know these things are wrong and because they can imagine how such actions will affect other people. Punishment doesn't contribute at all to the development of such concerns; it teaches that if they are caught doing something forbidden, they will have to suffer the consequences. The reason not to be a bully is that someone may punch you back; the reason not to rob a bank is that you may go to jail. The emphasis is on what will happen to *them*. This represents the lowest level of moral reasoning, one associated with very young children, yet it is the punishing adult who seems to be thinking in these terms here.

Once again we have to ask what our ultimate goals are. Do we want only to control short-term behaviors, or do we want to help children become responsible decision-makers? To choose the latter is to say that motives matter: we care about not only what children do, but why they do it. The more we attend to these issues, the less likely we will be to defend an approach that says "If you do something bad, here's what I'll do to you." Teaching children to think about the consequences (to themselves) of doing something wrong does nothing to nurture a lasting commitment to good values. In fact, it undermines that enterprise.

This is not an academic argument. Practically speaking, getting children to focus on what will happen if they are caught misbehaving is simply not an effective way to prevent misbehavior. This is why punishment typically backfires, as the evidence cited earlier suggests. People who rob banks assume they won't get caught, which means there will be no consequences for their action, which means they have a green light to go ahead and rob.

Indeed, if an auditorium were filled with bank robbers, wife batterers, and assorted other felons, we would likely find that virtually all of them were punished as children.[43] Whether the punishments were called "consequences" is irrelevant: what matters is that these people were trained to focus not on what they were doing and whether it was right, but on what would happen to them if someone more powerful didn't like what they did. Thus, if it is argued that punishments and rewards are appropriate for children because adults act in response to these inducements, our answer is yes, some do. But are they the sort of adults we want our children to become?

"And If You're Good . . ."

Countless parents, including some who deliberately try to avoid using punishment, have gotten into the habit of buying their children's good behavior with money and treats.[44] Teachers too use privileges and good grades, parties and movies to get individual students or whole classes to act "appropriately." Both at home and at school, praise is frequently used to manipulate children's behavior. Typically the goal of rewarders is no different from what punishers have in mind: "Do what you're told."

But sometimes rewards are used in the hope of promoting undeniably worthy qualities, such as generosity and concern for others. Some schools in upstate New York, for example, try to induce such values by posting the photos of helpful children in hallways or awarding them coupons for free merchandise;[45] Good Citizenship awards are common across the country.

Unfortunately, even when the intent is to support meaningful, long-term goals rather than simple compliance, rewards are no more useful than punishments. Earlier I argued that no technique that relies on control, no gimmick that manipulates behavior, can help a child grow into a good person. Now I want to stress the disconcerting point made in previous chapters: positive incentives fit that description just as surely as do negative incentives.

Many teachers and parents would like children to be concerned about other people's welfare, to be sensitive to someone else's distress and to take steps to try to relieve it. The evidence, however, shows that anyone who is rewarded for acts of generosity will be less likely to think of himself as a caring or altruistic person; he will attribute his behavior to the reward instead. "Extrinsic incentives can, by undermining self-perceived altruism, decrease intrinsic motivation to help others," one group of researchers concluded on the basis of several studies. "A person's kindness, it seems, cannot be bought."[46] The lesson a child takes away from Skinnerian tactics is that the point of being a good person is to get rewards. It follows that when the rewards stop coming, the caring behavior may stop too:

> Children who come to believe that their prosocial behavior reflects values or dispositions in themselves have internal structures that can generate behavior across settings and without external pressures. By contrast, children who view their prosocial conduct as compliance with external authority will act prosocially only when they believe external pressures are present.[47]

They may, for example, come to act in accordance with Tom Lehrer's droll revision of the Boy Scouts' motto: "Be careful not to do / Your good deed when there's no one watching you."

Sure enough, the available research indicates that *children whose parents believe in using rewards to motivate them are less cooperative and generous than their peers.* One study found that grade school children whose mothers relied on tangible rewards were less likely than other children to care and share at home and were also less likely to be helpful in a laboratory experiment.[48] Another study found that four-year-olds who were frequently praised for prosocial acts were less likely over time to engage in them than children who did not receive verbal reinforcement.[49]

The problem, as we have seen in other contexts, is not with the item that is offered to children as a reward. There is nothing wrong with taking one's children out for pizza as a treat or throwing a popcorn party for one's class. There *is* something wrong, however, with making these things contingent on certain kinds of behavior: "Do this and you'll get that." The problem arises for the reasons outlined in chapters 4 and 5, which I'd like to revisit one last time, focusing on their application to the question of children's actions and values.*

First, rewards punish. It is no less controlling to offer goodies for a desired behavior than to threaten sanctions for its absence (or for the presence of an undesired behavior). A controlling paradigm does not help children to act responsibly. As Kamii has written, "Rewards do not make children any more autonomous than punishment. . . . [The child motivated by rewards is] governed by others just as much as the child who is 'good' only to avoid being punished."[50] What's more, the fact that rewards can be withheld or withdrawn for failure to act in a specified manner makes the whole experience seem puni-

---

*The fourth reason offered in chapter 4 to explain the failure of rewards, their tendency to undermine risk-taking, is more relevant to creative performance than to behavior and values.

tive. Most of the reasoning and evidence reviewed in this chapter about the harms of punishment apply to rewards as well.

Second, rewards rupture relationships. They open up an enormous chasm between the parent and child, now defined as the rewarder and the rewarded. Children who try to please us by doing what we require so as to obtain what we are dangling in front of them are less likely to ask for help in thinking through problems, or to do anything else that might jeopardize their chances of getting what we are offering. There is a significant difference between developing a caring alliance of openness and trust with children and offering rewards to elicit certain behaviors. The former provides the foundation for helping children reach those long-term goals identified earlier. The latter makes this less likely.

Third, rewards ignore reasons. *Why* are children acting selfishly or disrespectfully or aggressively? There is no end to the possible explanations for a given problem. And there is no beginning to solving that problem until we have investigated those explanations. It can be awfully hard for parents to resist bribing or threatening, but either is a way of manipulating behavior without looking into what is really going on. No wonder both fail to bring about meaningful change.

Finally, rewards reduce the child's desire to act in a particular way. This phenomenon is not limited to a child's motivation to learn; it extends to behavioral issues, as the research on generosity makes painfully clear. Whenever someone has been led to think of herself as doing something in order to receive a reward, regardless of whether that something is multiplying numbers, making the bed, or helping a person in distress, the task being rewarded comes to seem less appealing in its own right.

Some acts simply aren't intrinsically interesting but are nevertheless valuable and important, such as various obligations one has to others in a community. Even here, rewarding a child for doing these things (or punishing him for not doing them) reduces the chance that he will come to accept responsibility, because, by virtue of being mechanisms of control, rewards make the child feel less responsible, period. The ultimate result is that extrinsic motivators not only fail to promote but actually undermine the commitment to good values we fervently want children to acquire.

Parents and teachers would do well to think about various styles of discipline, management, or socialization in terms of what questions children are encouraged to ask in each instance. A strategy that relies on punishment or consequences prompts a child to wonder, "What am I supposed to do, and what will happen to me if I don't do it?" A strategy based on rewards leads the child to ask, "What am I supposed to do, and what will I get for doing it?"

The first thing that strikes us about these two questions is that they are at bottom not very different from each other. The second thing we realize is that neither one gets a child anywhere close to the issues with which we are ultimately concerned. What we are after, I think, is children who ask themselves, "What kind of person do I want to be?" — or even "What kind of classroom [or school, or family, or community] do *we* want to have?" Approaches that encourage children to pose these important questions will be reviewed in chapter 12. For now, my point is that a child has little cause to think in such terms if he or she is raised on a diet of pop behaviorism.

· *Part Three* ·

BEYOND REWARDS

Introduction

EVEN BEFORE WRITING THIS BOOK, I have criticized the use of rewards many times in print and in person, sometimes in a few summary sentences and sometimes at tedious length. People have reacted in a variety of ways, as you might imagine, but the most common response is neither to endorse nor to challenge the arguments and evidence I have offered. It is to utter three words: "What's your alternative?"

The question would seem to be perfectly reasonable, and yet I have found it frustrating and difficult to answer for several reasons. First of all, the alternative to rewards depends on whether we are talking about raising children, teaching students, or managing employees.

Second, how we ought to address a problem in any of these areas depends on what caused the problem. What is most alluring about pop behaviorism is its promise of one answer to all questions. It is a false promise, though, which helps explain why rewards don't work in the long run. For people accustomed to a bite-size solution ("Do this and you'll get that"), my apologetic explanation that there simply isn't one "alternative" to rewards prompts knowing smirks that seem to say, "Uh-huh. I thought so. Come back and talk to me about what's wrong with [incentive plans/grades/stickers/praise] when you're ready to tell me what to put in their place." Of course, no answer to all the complex motivational issues we find ourselves facing is both easy *and* effective. The temptation is therefore strong to pick one that is just easy.

The last and most important reason for my discomfiture when I am asked for an alternative to rewards is the fact that discussions about alternatives generally assume there is agreement on the objective. If I were to tell you that road construction will make it difficult for you to get to work tomorrow, you might ask me to suggest an alternative route and I would cheerfully give you one ("Instead of turning left at the gas station, go straight and continue past the bank . . ."). That's because neither of us questions where you are trying to go.

But when we talk about rewards, the goal is very much at issue. If what you want is to get a child, a student, or a worker to do what you say, then the answer to the question "What's the alternative to rewards?" is that there probably is no alternative (with the possible exception of punishment). To induce short-term compliance, behavioral manipulation is the best we've got.

If, however, your goal is to tap your employees' intrinsic interest in doing quality work, or to encourage your students to become lifelong, self-directed learners, or to help your child grow into a caring, responsible, decent person, then it makes no sense to ask "What's the alternative to rewards?" because rewards never moved us one millimeter toward *those* objectives. In fact, rewards actively interfere with our attempts to reach them.

The goals for parents, teachers, and managers that I have just described are the goals that interest me — and, I hope, you. But since dangling goodies in front of people doesn't help us to attain these goals, we shouldn't find ourselves in the position of having to be convinced to trade in rewards for something new. We are, in effect, starting from scratch. So what *can* help us reach these ambitious goals? Here, finally, is a meaningful question. My attempt at an answer is contained in the three chapters that follow.

~ 10 ~

THANK GOD IT'S MONDAY:
The Roots of Motivation in the Workplace

A high wage will not elicit effective work from those who feel themselves outcasts and slaves, nor a low wage preclude it from those who feel themselves an integral part of a community of free men. Thus the improvement of this element of the supply of labour is an infinitely more complex and arduous task than if it depended upon wage alone.

— D. H. Robertson, 1921

YOU CAN'T ALWAYS JUDGE a book by its cover, but you can sometimes feel justified in discarding one on the basis of its title. Anything called "How to Motivate Your Work Force," "Making People Productive," or something of the sort can safely be passed over because the enterprise it describes is wholly misconceived. "Strictly speaking," said Douglas McGregor, "the answer to the question managers so often ask of behavioral scientists — 'How do you motivate people?' — is, 'You don't.'"[1]

Of course, it is possible to get people to do something. That is what rewards, punishments, and other instruments of control are all about. But the *desire* to do something, much less to do it well, simply cannot be imposed; in this sense, it is a mistake to talk about motivating other people. All we can do is set up certain conditions that will maximize the probability of their developing an interest in what they are doing and remove the conditions that function as constraints.[2] This chapter offers a very brief review of those conditions, a summary

· 181 ·

of what research and experience suggest are useful ways of providing an environment conducive to motivation in the workplace.

Step One: Abolish Incentives

To challenge the pay-for-performance approach is to invite the question, Well, then, how *should* people be paid? What must be stressed immediately is that this question, while a reasonable one to pose, is not nearly as important as most managers seem to think. Although some alternative plan for compensation will have to be devised, nothing we come up with is going to help people become motivated.

W. Edwards Deming distills half a century's worth of experience observing and advising organizations as follows: "Pay is not a motivator." Frederick Herzberg amends this declaration by reminding us that money can nevertheless be a *de*motivator. This means that compensation systems often act as barriers to achieving productivity, quality, and intrinsic motivation, but they do not — they cannot — help us reach these goals. The implication is that books emphasizing the importance of paying people "correctly" distract us from the issues that really matter, and consultants peddling elaborate compensation schemes are selling a bill of goods.

Here are the basic principles I would propose to those responsible for setting policy: Pay people generously and equitably. Do your best to make sure they don't feel exploited. Then *do everything in your power to help them put money out of their minds.* The problem with financial incentives is not that people are offered too much money; earning a hefty salary is not incompatible with doing good work. Rather, the problem is that money is made too salient. It is pushed into people's faces. Moreover, it is offered contingently — that is, according to the principle "Do this and you'll get that."[3] To end this practice is to take the first step — but only the first step — toward fixing what is wrong with organizations.

Let me be autobiographical for a moment. Each time I address a business audience about the harms of rewards, there is always one man who, after sitting through the talk with his arms folded and a derisive look on his face, rouses himself to challenge me as follows: "I guess you won't be accepting any money for this lecture, then, huh?" This reaction tells me that I haven't been successful in explaining the relationship of money to motivation. I try to find another way to say that the trouble is not with money per se but with the way people are made to think about money and the way it is used to control them.

When someone contacts me about giving a lecture or writing an article, I ask how much money is involved and often negotiate for the maximum amount that seems to be fair and that the organization can afford to pay. Then, assuming we have come to an agreement, I do my best not to think about the money again. I do this because I fear the consequences of construing what I am doing in terms of what I am being paid: eventually I might find myself thinking, "A is paying me twice as much as B, so I'd better do twice as good a job for A." If I ever reach that point, my integrity will be gone, and my intrinsic motivation will have fled along with it.

What I attempt to do, in other words, is *decouple the task from the compensation*. Since I am self-employed, this is largely a matter of how I think about my work — what I attend to, and when, and how. But for people who do not work for themselves, it is imperative that the act of decoupling be facilitated by the organization. This is done mostly by avoiding certain practices — specifically, anything that encourages people to become preoccupied with what they will get for what they are doing.

Other than well and fairly, how should people be paid? Different organizations have experimented with different arrangements. The most ambitious try to compensate employees on the basis of need, or else they pay everyone equally. A less drastic approach is to take into account such factors as how long an individual has been with the organization, what special training and skills she has, and how time-consuming or complex her job is. If the company has had a profitable year, I see no reason those gains should not be distributed to the employees; after all, their work is what produced the profit.[4] These recommendations accord, more or less, with those of Deming[5] and, as I understand it, with the practice of most companies in Japan and elsewhere.[6] Some major U.S. corporations — a minority, to be sure — are beginning to move in this direction because of Deming's influence or because of a gradual realization that pay-for-performance is an inherently flawed concept.[7]

Step Two: Reevaluate Evaluation

After abolishing merit pay, we need to take a hard look at its first cousin, the performance appraisal. This is typically a stressful annual ritual in which employees are ranked, rated, or otherwise judged — a tradition that should have been retired long ago in light of how misleading its results are and how predictably it generates resentment and impedes cooperation.

So what do we do instead? Rather than just shopping for a new technique, we might begin by asking why people are being evaluated. So often the changes in procedure we implement have no lasting impact because we never pause to reflect on our goals and motives. In this case, some critics have suggested that the performance evaluation persists because it is "a very effective tool for controlling employees . . . [that] should not be confused . . . with motivation of employees."[8] Others argue that its appeal consists in allowing superiors to shift the responsibility for solving problems to their subordinates.[9] Whatever the accuracy of these charges, performance evaluations are most commonly defended on the grounds that they are needed to

1. determine how much each employee is paid or who will receive various awards and incentives;
2. make employees perform better for fear of receiving a negative evaluation or in the hope of getting a positive one;
3. sort employees on the basis of how good a job they are doing so we know whom to promote; or
4. provide feedback, discuss problems, and identify needs in order to help each employee do a better job.

I have already argued at some length that the first and second justifications make no sense, since pay-for-performance plans as well as a carrot-and-stick approach to motivation are counterproductive.[10] The third motive raises a host of complex questions, and I will content myself here with just two paragraphs on the subject.

In thinking about promotion, we take for granted that an organization must be shaped like a pyramid, with many people clamoring for a very few desirable and lucrative jobs at the top, as if this arrangement had been decreed by God. In fact, both how many such positions are available and how many people want them are the result of institutional decisions. We create a climate in which employees are made to feel like failures if they are not upwardly mobile,[11] and we arrange the majority of jobs so that those who hold them are given very little money and responsibility. Were these things to change, the competitive scramble for promotions might be eased and we would be obliged to rethink the whole issue of who does what in an organization.

Even within the standard hierarchical arrangement, the use of performance appraisals to decide on promotions is based on three dubious assumptions: first, that someone's achievement in his current job is a reliable predictor of how successful he will be in another, very different, position;* second, that how much someone has achieved is a more important consideration in deciding whether and how his responsibilities will change than what sort of work he prefers and finds intrinsically motivating; and third, to the extent that performance does matter, that it is best judged by the evaluation of a superior rather than by one's peers or oneself.

Clearly, much more could be said about evaluating people in order to sort them like so many potatoes. Like the first two justifications for appraisals, using them to calculate pay and to "motivate" employees, basing promotions on performance evaluations is basically a way of doing things *to* people. Consider, by contrast, the fourth rationale, which is that evaluations are useful as a way of helping employees do better work. This seems altogether legitimate, in part because it offers the possibility of working *with* people. If our overriding concern really is to foster improvement, then the contours of a program for evaluation begin to take shape:

• It is a two-way conversation, an opportunity to trade ideas and ask questions, not a series of judgments about one person pronounced by another. In effective schools, for example, evaluations of teachers exist "to find reasons for the strengths and weaknesses they identify, and they treat teachers as equals in exploring solutions."[12]

• It is a continuous process rather than an annual or quarterly event.

• It never involves any sort of relative ranking or competition.

• Most important, it is utterly divorced from decisions about compensation. Providing feedback that employees can use to do a better job† ought never to be confused or combined with controlling them

---

*It is possible that performance appraisals are used as the basis for promotion not because we think they give us information about who will do well in a new job but in order to reward someone for how well she performed in the old one. Apart from all the other weaknesses of behaviorist thinking, this sets people up for failure after they have been promoted.

†A number of writers have justified conventional performance appraisals, including those tied to rewards, on the grounds that they serve to communicate expectations to employees and to offer useful feedback about performance. If these really are our goals, we need to think about how to create the most positive context for providing this information. People are least likely to be receptive to feedback when they are fearful of being judged, when they are forced to compete against others, and when extrinsic motivators are involved.

by offering (or withholding) rewards. "Using performance appraisal of any kind as a basis for reward is a flat out catastrophic mistake," says consultant Peter Scholtes.[13] Back in the 1960s, Herbert Meyer sounded the same warning, pointing out that it is "foolish to have a manager serving in the self-conflicting role as a counselor (helping someone improve performance) when, at the same time, he or she is presiding as a judge over the same employee's salary. . . ."[14] And from yet a third source:

> By linking compensation to performance appraisal . . . the exchange between superior and subordinate is then not about performance but rather about pay, and it is only likely to produce de-motivators. . . . [A discussion about] progress and performance without the prospect that such a review must result in a penalty or an award to the employee [means that] the communication is more likely to stay open and honest.[15]

This recommendation does not amount merely to saying that supervisors should refrain from talking about money during an evaluation; it means that the entire process of providing feedback, assessing progress, and making plans ought to be completely separate from salary determinations. If such sessions are to be productive, there must be no reward or punishment hanging in the balance. The fact is that no matter how sensitively conducted and constructive an evaluation may be, it becomes a counterproductive force if how much people are paid depends on what is said there.

Step Three: Create the Conditions for Authentic Motivation

Alan S. Blinder, a Princeton University economist, recently edited a research anthology entitled *Paying for Productivity: A Look at the Evidence.* He summarized its findings as follows: "Changing the way workers are *treated* may boost productivity more than changing the way they are *paid*."[16] This makes sense because treating workers decently allows them to become motivated, and motivation in turn boosts productivity.[17] If motivation and productivity are in short supply in our workplaces, this may just have something to do with the way workers are treated there.

When employees are asked to describe the conditions they need, or when reflective and experienced managers are asked to describe the conditions they try to create, a variety of suggestions are offered. But there is substantial overlap in the ideas, a consensus that people in managerial positions ought to do these things:

Watch: Don't put employees under surveillance; look for problems that need to be solved and help people solve them.

Listen: Attend seriously and respectfully to the concerns of workers and try to imagine how various situations look from their points of view.

Talk: Provide plenty of informational feedback. People need a chance to reflect on what they are doing right, to learn what needs improvement, and to discuss how to change.

Think: If one's current managerial style consists of using extrinsic motivators, controlling people's behaviors, or simply exhorting them to work hard and become motivated,* it is worth thinking carefully about the long-term impact of these strategies. It is also worth asking where they come from. A preference for using power in one's relationships with others, or a reaction to being controlled by one's own superiors, raises issues that demand attention.

Most of all, a manager committed to making sure that people are able and willing to do their best needs to attend to three fundamental factors. These can be abbreviated as the "three C's" of motivation — to wit, the *collaboration* that defines the context of work, the *content* of the tasks, and the extent to which people have some *choice* about what they do and how they do it. The remainder of this chapter explores these three ideas; in the following chapters, I will argue that the same model is also a useful way of thinking about what happens at school and at home.

Collaboration

By now, enough has been written about teamwork that it is probably unnecessary to construct an elaborate defense of the importance of helping employees work together.[18] On most tasks, especially those that involve some degree of complexity and require some degree of ingenuity, people are able to do a better job in well-functioning groups

---

*This is sometimes done by hiring "motivational speakers" to come lecture to one's employees. At best, the result is a temporary sense of being re-energized, much like the effect of eating a doughnut. When the sugar high wears off, very little of value is left in the system.

than they can on their own. They are also more likely to be excited about their work. Both effects are due to the exchange of talent and resources that occurs as a result of cooperation — and also to the emotional sustenance provided by social support. People will typically be more enthusiastic where they feel a sense of belonging and see themselves as part of a community than they will in a workplace in which each person is left to his own devices.

Anyone who judged the status of U.S. corporations on the basis of their rhetoric would assume that cooperation was an integral feature of American business. The truth is that it's much easier to find people saying all the right things about the importance of teamwork than to find a genuine commitment to the practice. Some executives confine their efforts to issuing "Let's all pull together" memos.* Some companies actually do assign people to teams, but without providing the training needed to make teamwork work. (The inevitable failure can then be blamed on how uncooperative the individuals in question are, or how it is just "natural" to want to work alone.) Sometimes employees are given the chance to cooperate within their division or department, but nothing is done to establish the cross-functional connections required for coordination among departments. Finally, some managers undermine the value of cooperation by simultaneously perpetuating competition, either by explicitly setting one team against another or by using compensation systems that have the same effect. As usual, McGregor's observations are incisive:

> Most so-called managerial teams are not teams at all, but collections of individual relationships with the boss in which each individual is vying with every other for power, prestige, recognition, and personal autonomy. Under such conditions unity of purpose is a myth. . . . [However,] the limits on human collaboration in the organizational setting are not limits of human nature but of management's ingenuity in discovering how to realize the potential represented by its human resources.[19]

Of course, simply putting people in groups does not ensure that cooperation will take place. Considerable effort and organizational commitment are required to make that happen. Instead, though, many managers simply fall back on the usual gimmick for getting people to do things: bribery. Apart from everything else that is wrong with

---

*Even worse is the tendency to talk about being a "team player" — a phrase that seems to suggest a commitment to cooperation but actually, on closer inspection, is apt to constitute a demand for simple obedience and conformity.

rewards, they are ineffective at developing and sustaining successful collaboration. As one professor of business administration comments, "Pay should not be an active ingredient in promoting teamwork and motivating performance. . . . Telling people you are going to change the compensation system rallies them around compensation when what you want them to do is rally around making teams work."[20]

Content

Even at a workplace with the most enlightened management practices imaginable, including an emphasis on cooperation, employees will not be motivated if what they are doing all day holds no interest for them. "Idleness, indifference and irresponsibility are healthy responses to absurd work," said Herzberg.[21] Elsewhere he issued this challenge to executives: "If you want people motivated to do a good job, give them a good job to do."[22] These acid aphorisms point the way to making a revolutionary improvement in people's work lives.

What is a good job? Let us start by aiming high: at its best, it offers a chance to engage in *meaningful* work. The sense of doing something that matters is not the same as a feeling of intrinsic motivation. It isn't just that the process of working provides enjoyment, but that the product being made (or the service provided) seems worthwhile and even important, perhaps because it makes a contribution to a larger community. Mihaly Csikszentmihalyi, who has spent much of his career describing the pure pleasure of "flow" experiences, points out that beyond such enjoyment "one must still ask, 'What are the consequences of this particular activity?'"[23] The question is not just "Are we having fun yet?" but "Are we making a difference?"

If all jobs that did not meet this standard were eliminated, an awful lot of people would be thrown out of work. I offer it as a long-range consideration, a star by which to navigate as we think about the ultimate value of our activity. The meaningfulness of jobs has obvious moral implications, but it ultimately pertains to the question of motivation as well: most people who have the chance to engage in work they think of as important are profoundly committed to what they do.

Even if we set this criterion to one side, the central point remains: for people to care about their work, it is necessary to attend to what that work consists of — the content, not merely the context, of a job. Motivation is typically highest when the job offers an opportunity to learn new skills, to experience some variation in tasks, and to acquire and demonstrate competence. Different people, it goes without saying, prefer different levels of challenge and a different balance between predictability and novelty. But the basic points are essentially universal. Again, Herzberg put it well:

> Managers do not motivate employees by giving them higher wages, more benefits, or new status symbols. Rather, employees are motivated by their own inherent need to succeed at a challenging task. The manager's job, then, is not to motivate people to get them to achieve; instead, the manager should provide opportunities for people to achieve so they will become motivated.[24]

How can such opportunities be provided? The possibilities range from making relatively minor adjustments in a given organization, at one end of the continuum, to working for an overhaul of our economic system, on the other. The easiest change for a manager is, whenever possible, to let people work at the jobs that they are most likely to find interesting. That means hiring people (and reassigning them) not only on the basis of what their résumés say they are most qualified to do but also on the basis of what they *like* to do. It means giving employees a chance to sample a variety of jobs in an organization until a good fit is found, and allowing them to transfer periodically in order to keep things interesting. As management theorists Richard Hackman and Greg Oldham have noticed, "When people are well matched with their jobs, it rarely is necessary to force, coerce, bribe, or trick them into working hard and trying to perform the job well. Instead, they try to do well because it is rewarding and satisfying to do so."[25]

A more difficult, but also more meaningful, step is to restructure jobs so they become more interesting to more people. (Few employees, after all, want to be matched to tedious, unchallenging assignments.) "Work motivation often can be enhanced by increasing the levels of responsibility, meaningfulness, and feedback that are built into jobs," Hackman and Oldham argue. Their formula for doing so includes making sure that each worker has some knowledge of the results of what she is doing, experiences responsibility for these results, and sees the work as valuable (at least in the sense of offering the chance to use a variety of skills). Making such changes in the content of work is critical, they argue, because "motivation at work may actually have more to do with how tasks are designed and managed than with the personal dispositions of the people who do them" — a viewpoint that clashes directly with the tendency to blame individuals when something goes wrong.[26]

But these changes, welcome as they might be, still leave us with jobs that seem by their very nature to be devoid of interest. What can be done about inherently boring work? One answer, offered implicitly by some social reformers, is to take the content of these jobs as a given and insist that people who do them get paid more. This seems to me unsatisfactory. Our concern that people receive adequate compensation must not distract us from the question of how their day-to-day quality of life can be improved. This calls for attention to job content, which again can be tackled on two levels — changing work design in order to minimize monotony and effecting large-scale social transformation.

The moderate response is to deal with jobs more or less as they are and try to make them more palatable. In chapter 5, I reviewed Deci's three-pronged strategy for doing so, which includes acknowledging frankly that the task may not be fun, offering a meaningful rationale for doing it anyway (in terms of its indirect effects, for example),* and giving people as much choice as possible about how they perform the task (see page 90 and also Csikszentmihalyi's thoughts on the subject on page 304 note 78). Another research psychologist, Carol Sansone, has described how people "regulate their motivation to perform necessary activities over time," artificially enhancing the level of difficulty to keep things interesting, adding variety however they can, and attending to incidental task information.[27] (Here, of course, the burden is on the person doing the job to make it *seem* more appealing rather than on the supervisor to make it more appealing in reality.)

One sociologist, studying a group of garbage collectors in San Francisco, discovered that most of them were quite satisfied with their work because of the way it — and the company — was organized. Relationships among the men were highlighted, tasks and routes were "varied enough to break the monotony of the work's routine," and the company was set up as a cooperative, meaning that each worker owned a share of the business and felt a "pride of ownership." Clearly, it is premature to assume that certain categories of work are inherently distasteful and will be pursued only for extrinsic reasons.[28]

---

*Compare the use of explanation, an appeal to reason, with an approach that appeals to power, such as controlling people by the use of incentives or threats. The contrast recalls a point made by developmental psychologists (reviewed in chapter 12) to the effect that the purpose of requests can be explained to children instead of relying on the assertion of power to get them to obey.

The radical response to this problem is to question the necessity of making people do wretched work in the first place. It would seem that some tasks that are even more disagreeable than garbage collection simply cannot be avoided. But what interests me are the unpleasant jobs that do not have to be done in order for society to function, those whose existence reflects the premise of our economic system that if something sells, it has value by definition and should be produced. Should convenience foods or luxury appliances be made available if the human costs of preparing or assembling them are severe? Our answer may be yes, but the question needs to be asked. If the issue is rarely addressed, it is partly because many people are forced to choose between working at such jobs and not working at all — a choice framed not by "life" but by our economic system. These people are expected to be grateful that any employment is available, regardless of the psychic and physical toll of doing such work.

What it comes down to is this: we who benefit from someone else's mind-numbing labor — we who defrost our frozen dinners without ever considering what life is like for those invisible others who spend eight grueling, repetitive hours a day preparing them — are quick to say such work must be done. From one perspective, this reflects another facet of the sharp division between the haves and the have-nots; the latter are left with the work that lacks interest. From another perspective, it could be said that what we collectively gain as consumers we lose as producers: our shelves are full of goods, while our lives are empty of meaningful work.[29]

The central point, though, is that in any responsible discussion of intrinsic motivation, and especially of the role played by the content of tasks, we must remind ourselves of the social context. If work is to be improved, it must first be made bearable for those who endure injuries of body, mind, and spirit for our convenience.

Choice

We are most likely to become enthusiastic about what we are doing — and all else being equal, to do it well — when we are free to make decisions about the way we carry out a task. The loss of autonomy entailed by the use of rewards or punishments helps explain why they sap our motivation. But managers must do more than avoid these tactics; they need to take affirmative steps to make sure employees have real choices about how they do their jobs.

To describe much of what is wrong with our workplaces is to enumerate the effects of restricting people's sense of self-determination. This situation is more egregious the lower we are in the hierarchy. By and large, those who do the least interesting work and receive the least compensation are those who should, at a minimum, have the consolation of being able to make decisions about how they carry out their assignments. Instead, they are the most carefully controlled.

Regardless of the organizational level, though, the difference between success and failure, enthusiasm and apathy, even health and sickness, can often be traced back to this issue:

• Why do so many employees become burned out and bitter? Burnout is not a function of how much work they have to do so much as how controlled and powerless they feel.[30]

• What kind of job is associated with high levels of psychological stress and coronary heart disease? Not the "'success oriented,' managerial or professional occupations (where Type A and high incomes are most prevalent)" but those where "individuals have insufficient control over their work situation."[31]

• Which characteristic of an organization is most likely to kill creativity? Not inadequate pay or tight deadlines, but "a lack of freedom in deciding what to do or how to accomplish the task, lack of sense of control over one's own work and ideas."[32]

• Why do people so often mutter and groan when a change in policy is announced? Not because it is a change but because it is announced — that is, imposed on them. (This distinction forces us to reconsider assumptions about the alleged conservatism of "human nature." As Peter Scholtes has observed, "People don't resist change; they resist being changed.")[33]

• What makes workers look for or invent reasons to stay home from work? One answer suggests itself when we notice much lower rates of absenteeism in workplaces where employees are able to participate in making substantive decisions.[34]

• Which middle managers are most likely to act in an autocratic fashion toward those below them in the hierarchy? Very likely those who are restricted and controlled themselves.[35]

People are most motivated when they are able to participate in making decisions about organizational goals (and, of course, are given the necessary information and resources to do so). Even when those goals are determined by others, it is critical that employees be able to decide how best to reach them, that they hear from a supervisor, "Here's where we need to get; you decide how we get there." For example, jobholders can be given discretion in setting schedules, determining work methods, and deciding when and how to check on the quality of the work produced. Employees can make their own decisions about when to start and stop work, when to take breaks, and how to assign priorities. They can be encouraged to seek solutions to problems on their own, consulting with other organization members as necessary, rather than calling immediately for the supervisor when problems arise.[36]

To give employees the chance to make decisions is not to manage by inaction. Like parents who cannot see an alternative to harsh, punitive control on the one hand and total permissiveness on the other, some organizational theorists assume that supervisors are either making all the decisions or else doing nothing. The truth of the matter is that creating structures that support worker autonomy is itself a challenging job.[37]

When managers become aware of a problem, either one arising within the organization or an external challenge to it, their first impulse should be to bring every employee into the process of working out a solution. As McGregor says, nothing "can justify excluding the individual from . . . active and responsible participation . . . in decisions affecting his career."[38] That commitment extends to devising ways of coping with hard times and searching for alternatives to laying people off.[39]

The importance of choice has a direct bearing on the sorts of changes described throughout this chapter. It informs the decision to eliminate incentives, since rewards and punishments are methods of control. It guides our attempt to reconfigure performance appraisals.[40] It is an integral part of any effort to change the content of jobs.[41] And it must accompany the use of cooperation, since teams will not function effectively if they are denied any real authority over what they do and how they do it.[42]

But it would be more than a little ironic if we simply imposed such changes on workers by fiat. The principle of self-determination that lies behind the content and motive of these reforms must also inform the method of implementing them. If we try to force a new idea, even a very good idea, down people's throats, they will cough it back up. Besides being more respectful and consistent, working collaboratively with employees can also be justified on purely pragmatic terms.

When implemented as a systematic program, increased choice sometimes goes by the name of "participative management."[43] A number of case studies suggest that when such plans are adopted by companies, both in the United States[44] and in other countries, such as Japan and Sweden,[45] they are successful by several measures. At a recent conference in which economists reported on research pertaining to profit-sharing programs, the most striking and "totally unexpected" finding to emerge from the various presentations was that worker participation both enhances the success of such programs and "also has beneficial effects of its own."[46] And a review of forty-seven studies that quantified the extent to which participation in decision-making affected productivity or job satisfaction found a positive effect on both, regardless of the kind of work people did. The effect was stronger in real-world research than in laboratory simulation studies.[47]

This is not to say that every participative management program ever attempted has been successful. But where such plans have failed, it has typically been because there wasn't *enough* participation: too few employees were included, the program didn't last long enough to do any good, the decisions workers were permitted to make were relatively inconsequential, or the recommendations made by employees were essentially ignored by upper management.[48]

Such limitations on employee participation programs may well be the rule rather than the exception in U.S. corporations. One large survey found that such systems were in place at about half of the organizations polled, but the median proportion of employees actually involved in these programs was less than 15 percent. Even if they were not formally excluded, most workers stayed away because they were "skeptical of the real importance of the program to the organization."[49]

Is such skepticism justified? William Foote Whyte recalls the days when it first became fashionable to talk of humanizing the workplace. Quite a few managers were

> willing to listen to information and ideas that might give them some new gimmicks. The question that they frequently asked revealed the nature of their interest: "How can we make the workers *feel* that they are participating?" We sought to explain that, in the long run, workers would not *feel* that they were participating unless they had some real impact upon decisions important to management as well as to workers. This generally ended the conversations.[50]

Trying to create a subjective sense of control, or to avoid the appearance of manipulation, amounts to an effort to deceive, not to make real change of the kind that helps people become excited about their jobs. Besides being unethical, it ultimately doesn't work: people figure out pretty quickly when they are being manipulated.[51]

Even managers who are sincere about providing genuine choice to employees may handicap such programs by hanging on to the premises and practices of behaviorism. This residual commitment manifests itself in two ways: offering employees the chance to make decisions as a reward for doing something else, and offering some other inducement for taking part in a participative management program.[52] Until the theory of motivation advances, the new management techniques cannot take hold.

Taking choice seriously also requires us to question the hierarchical nature of organizations. "So-called participative programs that merely make employees feel good but don't actually change the power relationships in the workplace probably have not actually increased the amount of the employees' responsibility."[53] To put this another way, giving people responsibility for, and control of, their own work is tantamount to introducing democracy to the workplace, and democracy in any arena is profoundly threatening to those who exert undemocratic control.[54] To this extent, it makes perfect sense that executives would typically implement participative management programs in a halfhearted, temporary, or partial fashion, if at all.

Americans love to talk about democracy. Even in the economic realm, where it is conspicuously absent, few repudiate the concept explicitly. Instead, the preferred justification for depriving people of control over their work is to argue (without evidence) that an organization cannot be run efficiently without top-down management — or to claim that most workers don't really want to make decisions. The latter is sometimes said to be the reason that participative management plans often fail: the majority of employees would rather take orders.[55]

Show me an employee who has to do what she is told, who has learned to distrust smiling assurances that the boss's door is always open for someone with a suggestion or complaint, whose intrinsic motivation has evaporated in the face of a regimen of rewards and punishments, and I will show you an employee who may well shrug off an invitation to participate in a brand-new, memo-driven Worker Involvement Program. To say that such workers are uninterested in having a say over what they do all day is, to put it gently, a contrived conclusion. When management earns their trust, when it provides the time and resources necessary to make informed decisions, they are generally only too happy to take steps to manage themselves and begin to take control of their lives.

To talk about people taking control of their lives, though, raises larger questions about our ultimate goals. Are we principally concerned to increase the return on investment for the owners of a company or to provide a better quality of life, including meaningful tasks, a sense of empowerment, and healthy, supportive relationships, for everyone who works there? Obviously the latter goals are consistent with — indeed, are powerful contributors to — better performance. But at some point we may have to decide what matters most. Any number of managers and consultants have made it clear that, in their view, the psychological well-being and motivation of the vast majority of people who go to work in the morning are important only insofar as they contribute to higher productivity for the organization.* Most research on "worker satisfaction," for example, is conducted only because of, and only in terms of, its status as a contributor to performance.

Such questions, of course, invite a fresh examination not only of the practices at some companies but of the foundations on which our economic system rests. The man who reacted to a criticism of incentive plans by blurting out "Well, isn't that communism?" undoubtedly sensed that something deeper than merit pay is at issue here. In the United States, to associate something with communism or socialism is generally just a way of discrediting it; the terms are epithets with emotional resonance rather than references to alternative systems. Nevertheless, to open an investigation into the practices associated with behaviorism is to find ourselves grappling with the much broader issue of democracy. And if we are committed to the latter, we may find ourselves calling into question our most fundamental (and least examined) institutions.

---

*I would include in this category the relatively daring thinkers who urge managers to abolish incentive plans, stop thinking about market share, and emphasize teamwork, but whose objective is simply to improve customer satisfaction and, ultimately, profits. Such reformers call to mind the sports coaches and consultants who urge athletes to focus on excellence rather than victory — in order to win.

~11~

HOOKED ON
LEARNING:
The Roots of Motivation in
the Classroom

> If there is not an inherent attracting power in the material,
> then . . . the teacher will either attempt to surround the material with
> foreign attractiveness, making a bid or offering a bribe for atten-
> tion by "making the lesson interesting"; or else will resort to . . .
> low marks, threats of non-promotion, staying after school. . . .
> But the attention thus gained . . . always remains dependent upon
> something external. . . . True, reflective attention, on the other
> hand, always involves judging, reasoning, deliberation; it means
> that the child has a *question of his own* and is actively engaged in
> seeking and selecting relevant material with which to answer it.
> — John Dewey, 1915

THERE ARE PROFOUND DIFFERENCES between managing
employees and teaching children, between bringing quality to the
workplace and to the classroom.[1] But there are also striking parallels,
not only because of the Skinnerian framework they currently share,
but also with respect to prescriptions for meaningful change. The
steps I outline here for moving beyond behaviorism resemble those
offered in the previous chapter; the three components of motivation — collaboration, content, and choice — will seem particularly
familiar.

One specific similarity between work and school is that the same
misconceived question is regularly posed in both places. Douglas
McGregor reminded us that "How do you motivate people?" is not
what managers should be asking. Nor should educators: children do
not need to be motivated. From the beginning they are hungry to

make sense of their world. Given an environment in which they don't feel controlled and in which they are encouraged to think about what they are doing (rather than how well they are doing it), students of any age will generally exhibit an abundance of motivation and a healthy appetite for challenge.

"How do I get these kids motivated?" is a question that not only misreads the nature of motivation but also operates within a paradigm of control, the very thing that is death to motivation. "I never use the expression 'motivate a child,' " says Raymond Wlodkowski, who specializes in the topic. "That takes away their choice. All we can do is influence how they motivate themselves."[2]

But influence them we can — and must. The job of educators is neither to make students motivated nor to sit passively; it is to set up the conditions that make learning possible. The challenge, as two psychologists put it, is not to wait "until an individual is interested . . . [but to offer] a stimulating environment that can be perceived by students as [presenting] vivid and valued options which can lead to successful learning and performance."[3] This chapter sketches some of the features of such an environment.

Remove the Rewards

Let there be no misunderstanding: if a teacher stops using extrinsic motivators tomorrow, dumps the stickers and stars and certificates in the garbage can and puts the grade book away, students are not going to leap out of their seats cheering, "Hooray! Now we can be intrinsically motivated!"

There are at least three reasons they will not do so. First, they were not consulted about the change. A teacher who makes unilateral decisions, regardless of their merit, is in effect saying that the classroom does not belong to the students but only to her; their preferences do not matter. People do not usually cheer when things are done *to* them. That is why teachers contemplating a new way of doing things ought to bring the children in on the process — in this case, by opening up a discussion with them (at a level appropriate to their age) about why people learn and what impact rewards really have.

Second, abandoning behaviorist tactics by no means guarantees that real learning will take place. The structures that thwart motivation must be removed, but it is also necessary to establish the conditions that facilitate motivation, to create the right curriculum and the right school climate. The second half of this chapter is concerned with this process.

Finally, if students have spent years being told that the reason to read and write and think is because of the goodies they will get for doing so, and if the goodies themselves are appealing to them, they may resist the sudden withdrawal of rewards. Without pressing the metaphor too far, it might be said that students can become addicted to A's and other incentives, unwilling to complete assignments without them and also dependent on them for their very identity.

The signs of such dependence are questions such as "Do we have to know this?" or "Is this going to be on the test?" Every educator ought to recognize these questions for what they are: distress calls. The student who offers them is saying, "My love of learning has been kicked out of me by well-meaning people who used bribes or threats to get me to do schoolwork. Now all I want to know is whether I have to do it — and what you'll give me if I do."

The teacher who hears this message may not have caused the extrinsic orientation it bespeaks. He may also be limited in his ability to deal with the problem. But at least he should understand that it is a problem. The fact that students have come to see themselves as learning in order to get rewards means that the transition back to intrinsic interest can be a slow and arduous journey. But the more difficult it is to wean students off gold stars and candy bars, the more urgent it is to do so. The *teacher's* distress call — which can sometimes sound more smug than distressed — is the insistence that students won't bother to learn anything that isn't going to be graded. It would be absurd to respond to this by saying, "Oh, then, by all means — keep feeding them extrinsic motivators." The only sensible reply is "If they're that far gone, we haven't got a minute to waste in trying to undo the damage that rewards have done!"

Need We Grade?

For teachers and parents who are convinced by the evidence that rewards for learning are counterproductive, it is difficult enough to discard the stickers and stars, edible treats, and other incentives that have been dangled in front of students for so long. Getting rid of grades, however, presents a challenge of a different order of magnitude. Even if they had the power to do so, many people are likely to be more reluctant about giving up something so integral to our educational system that it is hard to imagine life without it. That very reluctance suggests that we need to challenge ourselves with hard questions about the necessity and value of grading children.

To begin with, we might ask *why* grades are given. The answers that are typically offered mirror the reasons cited for the use of performance appraisals in the workplace. Grades are justified as follows:

1. They make students perform better for fear of receiving a bad grade or in the hope of getting a good one.
2. They sort students on the basis of their performance, which is useful for college admission and job placement.
3. They provide feedback to students about how good a job they are doing and where they need improvement.

Let's take these in order. I have spent the last 200 pages arguing that the first rationale is fatally flawed. The carrot-and-stick approach in general is unsuccessful; grades in particular undermine intrinsic motivation and learning, which only serves to increase our reliance on them. The significance of these effects is underscored by the fact that, in practice, grades are routinely used not merely to evaluate but also to motivate. In fact, they are powerful demotivators regardless of the reason given for their use.

Grades do serve a purpose of sorts: they "enable administrators to rate and sort children, to categorize them so rigidly that they can rarely escape."[4] Most of the criticism one hears of this process is limited to how well we are dividing students up, whether we are correctly dumping the right ones into the right piles. Some people contend that the major problem with our high schools and colleges is that they don't keep enough students off the Excellent pile. (These critics don't put it quite this way, of course; they talk about "grade inflation.") Others argue that the categories are too rigid, the criteria too subjective, the tests on which grades are based too superficial. Thus, it is alleged, grades do not provide much useful information to businesses hiring workers or colleges admitting students on that basis.[5]

I think the latter criticism is on the mark. Studies show that any particular teacher may well give two different grades to a single piece of work submitted at two different times; the variation is naturally even greater when the work is evaluated by more than one teacher.[6] What grades offer is spurious precision, a subjective rating masquerading as an objective assessment. One writer wryly proposed that "a grade can be regarded only as an inadequate report of an inaccurate judgment by a biased and variable judge of the extent to which a student has attained an undefined level of mastery of an unknown proportion of an indefinite amount of material."[7]

But this criticism of grading is far too tame. The trouble is not that we are sorting students badly — a problem that logically should be addressed by trying to do it better. The trouble is that we spend so much time sorting them at all. In certain circumstances, it may make sense to ascertain the skill level of each student in order to facilitate teaching or placement. But as a rule the goal of sorting is simply not commensurate with the goal of helping students learn. "Faculties seem not to know that their chief instructional role is to promote learning and not to serve as personnel selection agents for society," as one group of critics put it.[8] In a highly stratified society — one composed, in turn, of highly hierarchical organizations — some people undoubtedly find it convenient to have students arrive having already been stamped PRIME, CHOICE, SELECT, or STANDARD. But if the sorting process makes it more difficult to educate, then we need to make up our minds about the central purpose of our schools.

The third justification for grades is that they let students know how they are doing. Indeed, students are currently led to rely on grades for information about their ability and competence, and that reliance increases as they get older.[9]

There is nothing objectionable about wanting to get a sense, at least periodically, of how things are going. In fact, informational feedback is an important part of the educational process. But if our goal is really to provide such feedback, rather than just to rationalize the practice of giving grades for other reasons, then reducing someone's work to a letter or number is unnecessary and not terribly helpful. A B+ at the top of a paper tells a student nothing about what was impressive about the paper or how it could be improved. A substantive comment that does offer such information, meanwhile, gains nothing from the addition of the B+. In fact, one study suggests that the destructive impact of grades is not mitigated by the addition of a comment;[10] the implication is that comments should replace rather than supplement grades.

If students want to know where they stand, then, grades do not provide them with usable information. But again we need to dig even deeper in assessing what is wrong with the status quo. The problem is not just that grades don't say enough about people's performance; it's that the process of grading fixes their attention *on* their performance. Teachers concerned with helping students learn, as I argued in chapter 8, will try to free them from a preoccupation with how well they are doing. At a minimum, such teachers will not intensify that preoccupation by taking students' academic temperature every day — or even worse, telling them how they rank relative to one another.

Grades are often based on tests, and tests are sometimes justified as a way for teachers to know how well their students are doing.[11] While I'm not prepared to urge the abolition of all tests, I do think that there are usually other ways, less punitive and more informative, to meet this goal. (My premise here is that the reason we want to know how well students are doing is to help them learn more effectively in the future — the only legitimate purpose for evaluation.) Assuming that classes are kept at a reasonable size, a competent teacher has a pretty good sense of how each student is doing. Anyone who requires a formal test to know what is going on may need to reconsider the approach to instruction being used and whether he or she is talking too much and listening too little.[12] Indeed, a series of interviews with fifty teachers identified as being superlative at their craft turned up a strikingly consistent lack of emphasis on testing, if not a deliberate decision to minimize the practice.[13]

In particular, a classroom that feels safe to students is one in which they are free to admit when they don't understand something and are able to ask for help. Ironically, grades and tests, punishments and rewards, are the enemies of safety; they therefore reduce the probability that students will speak up and that truly productive evaluation can take place.*

To summarize, grades cannot be justified on the grounds that they motivate students, because they actually undermine the sort of motivation that leads to excellence. Using them to sort students undercuts our efforts to educate. And to the extent we want to offer students feedback about their performance — a goal that demands a certain amount of caution lest their involvement in the task itself be sacrificed — there are better ways to do this than by giving grades.

The Straight-A Student: A Cautionary Tale

The advantages cited to justify grading students do not seem terribly compelling on close inspection. But the disadvantages only become

---

*Actually, some students — the most self-confident — *will* speak up in grade-oriented classrooms, but they will speak up to impress the teacher and improve their standing. This has nothing to do with speaking up to try out new ideas about which they may feel tentative, to ask a question in order to learn, or to let teachers know when they are struggling.[14]

more pronounced the more familiar one is with the research[15] and the more experience one has in real classrooms. In chapter 8 I cited evidence showing that students who are motivated by grades or other rewards typically don't learn as well, think as deeply, care as much about what they're doing, or choose to challenge themselves to the same extent as students who are not grade oriented.

But the damage doesn't stop there. Grades dilute the pleasure that a student experiences on successfully completing a task.[16] They encourage cheating[17] and strain the relationship between teacher and student.[18] They reduce a student's sense of control over his own fate and can induce a blind conformity to others' wishes — sometimes to the point that students are alienated from their own preferences and don't even know who they are.[19] Again, notice that it is not only those punished by F's but also those rewarded by A's who bear the cost of grades.

A few years ago I had the opportunity to address the entire student body and faculty of one of the country's most elite prep schools. I spoke, by coincidence, during the cruelest week in April, when the seniors were receiving their college acceptances and rejections. I talked to them about the desperate race they were joining. Already, I knew, they had learned to put aside books that appealed to them so they could prepare for the college boards. They were joining clubs that held no interest for them because they thought their membership would look good on transcripts. They were finding their friendships strained by the struggle for scarce slots in the Ivy League.

This they knew. What some of them failed to realize was that none of this ends when they finally get to college. It starts all over again: they will scan the catalogue for courses that promise easy A's, sign up for new extracurriculars to round out their résumés, and react with gratitude rather than outrage when professors tell them exactly what they need to know for exams so they can ignore everything else. They will define themselves as premed, prelaw, prebusiness — the prefix *pre-* indicating that everything they are doing now is irrelevant except insofar as it contributes to what they will be doing later.

Nor does this mode of existence end at college graduation. The horizon never comes any closer. Now they must struggle for the next set of rewards so they can snag the best residencies, the choicest clerkships, the fast-track positions in the corporate world. Then come the most prestigious appointments, partnerships, vice presidencies, and so on, working harder, nose stuck into the future, ever more frantic. And then, well into middle age, they will wake up suddenly in the middle of the night and wonder what happened to their lives. (If the feeling persists, the graduate of a good medical school will write out a prescription for them.)

To be sure, a fate even more dismal probably awaits those who must struggle to keep their heads above water financially as well as psychologically. But a treadmill appears under any student's feet when the first grade appears on something she has done. This treadmill produces motion without movement for those who struggle for rewards as well as for those who struggle to avoid punishments: either way, it is a race that cannot be won.

All of these things I said to this prep school audience, sweating profusely by now and sounding, I began to fear, like an evangelist. But I felt I also needed to offer a message for the teachers and parents present. If you know from experience what I am talking about, I said, then your job is to tell these students what you know and help them understand the terrible costs of this pursuit — not to propel them along faster. They need from you a sense of perspective about what is taking over their lives far more than they need another tip about how to burnish a college application or another reminder about the importance of a final exam.

Where do children learn to be grade-grubbers? From this: "You'd better listen up, folks, because this is going to be on the test." And from this: "A B-minus? What happened, Deborah?" And from this: "I take pride in the fact that I'm a hard grader. You're going to have to *work* in here." The fact is that

faculty members have it within their power to reduce this pernicious and distorting aspect of educational practice that often seems to work against learning. If faculty would relax their emphasis on grades, this might serve not to lower standards but to encourage an orientation toward learning.[20]

But teachers have not created this sensibility single-handedly. I have seen students desperate to get into the most selective universities since before they were born. I have followed that urgency back to its source. I have watched entire childhoods turned into one continuous attempt to prepare for Harvard (a process I eventually came to call "Preparation H"). I have met parents who did all this with the best of intentions — and also parents whose real objective was to derive vicarious pleasure from the successes of their children, to trump their friends when the talk turned to whose kids had made good. In both cases, I have seen the desiccated lives that result.

When I had finally finished speaking, I looked out into the audience and saw a well-dressed boy of about sixteen signaling me from the balcony. "You're telling us not to just get in a race for the traditional rewards," he said. "But what else is there?"

It takes a lot to render me speechless, but I stood on that stage clutching my microphone for a few moments and just stared. This was probably the most depressing question I have ever been asked. Here, I guessed, was a teenager who was enviably successful by conventional standards, headed for even greater glories, and there was a large hole where his soul should have been. It was not a question to be answered (although I fumbled my way through a response) so much as an indictment of grades, of the endless quest for rewards, of the resulting attenuation of values, that was far more scathing than any argument I could have offered.

From Degrading to De-Grading

When something is wrong with the present system, you move on two tracks at once. You do what you can within the confines of the current structure, trying to minimize its harm. You also work with others to try to change that structure, conscious that nothing dramatic may happen for a very long time. If we move exclusively on the latter track, such as by mobilizing people to dismantle grading systems, we may not be doing enough to protect our students, our children, from the destructive effects of the grades and other rewards with which they are going to be controlled in the meantime. But — and this point can be more difficult to recognize — if we simply reconcile ourselves to the status quo and spend all our time getting our children to accommodate themselves to it and play the game, then nothing will change and they will have to do the same with *their* children. As someone once said, realism corrupts; absolute realism corrupts absolutely.

If there is no reason to grade students, students should not be graded. But until we can make the grades disappear (at least from our own schools), we can take small and, yes, realistic steps in the right direction. Here is the way to do that, reduced to its essence: *teachers and parents who care about learning need to do everything in their power to help students forget that grades exist.*

Following this advice requires a revolution in the way we think about school and deal with students. We will have to reconsider what learning is about, where it comes from, and whether we are serious about promoting it. But the changes it requires, and the practical difficulties it may create, need to be weighed against the current emphasis on grades, which, however comfortably familiar, has been documented to be destructive. (Sometimes in evaluating a proposal for change, we weigh its risks and flaws as if the alternative, the way things are at present, were flawless.)

However radical are its implications, this is advice we can put into effect immediately. For parents, it means first of all thinking carefully about one's motives for pushing children to get better grades. After reading the evidence and weighing the arguments, it makes sense for parents to consider putting aside grades and scores as indicators of success and to look instead at the child's *interest* in learning. This is the primary criterion by which schools (and our own actions) should be judged.

Concretely, I would suggest that parents stop asking what a child got on a paper and stop making a fuss over report cards. This doesn't mean we don't care: it means we care enough about learning to stop doing what gets in its way. It means we care enough about our children to think about the subtler implications of what we are doing to them. The social psychologist Morton Deutsch argues that when a father offers his daughter ten dollars if she gets an A on a math test, this

> communicates a variety of possible messages to the girl . . . about her own motivation (for example, "I am not strongly motivated by my own desires to do well in math; I need external incentives"), about math ("It is not the sort of subject that people like me would find interesting to study"), about her father ("It's important to *him* that I get a good grade; does he care about what is important to *me*?"), and so on. Further, the incentive will tend to focus attention on the potential reward (the ten dollars) and the most pleasant, direct, and assured means of obtaining it. Thus, attention will be focused on getting the A rather than on studying and learning math; this may lead to cheating or to special methods of study oriented toward test performance rather than acquisition of enduring knowledge.[21]

In general, parents might replace conversation about grades with other sorts of questions: "What did you do in school today that was really fun?" "Did you hear or read something that surprised you?" "What does it feel like when you finally solve a tough math problem?" "Why do *you* think the Civil War started?" Keep in mind, though, that what we say (or don't say) isn't enough: if good grades still fill us with delight, and bad grades with despair or rage, our reactions will give us away.

For teachers, the effort to minimize the salience of grades is more challenging. Here are seven suggestions:

1. Even if you must come up with a grade at the end of the term, **limit the number of assignments for which you give a letter or number grade, or better yet, stop the practice altogether.** Offer substantive comments instead, in writing or in person. Make sure the effect of abolishing grades isn't to create suspense about what students are going to get on their report cards, which would defeat the whole purpose. Some students will experience, especially at first, a sense of existential vertigo: a steady supply of grades has defined them, and now their bearings are gone. Offer to discuss privately with any such student the grade he or she would probably receive if report cards were handed out that day. With luck and skill, the requests for such information will decrease as students get involved in what is being taught.

2. If you feel you must not only comment on certain assignments but also give them a mark, at least **limit the number of gradations.** For example, switch from A/B/C/D/F to check-plus/check/check-minus. Or . . .

3. **Reduce the number of possible grades to two: A and Incomplete.** The theory here is that any work that does not merit an A isn't finished yet. Anyone concerned about educational excellence should adopt this suggestion enthusiastically because its premise is that students should be doing their very best. It has the additional advantage of neutralizing the effect of grades. Most significant, it restores proper priorities: helping students improve becomes more important than evaluating them; learning takes precedence over sorting.[22]

4. **Never grade students while they are still learning something;** even more important, do not reward them for their performance at that point.[23] Pop quizzes and the like smother the process of coming to understand. They do not give students "time to be tentative."[24] If you're not sure whether students feel ready to show you what they know, there is an easy way to find out: ask them.

5. **Never grade for effort.** Grades by their very nature make students less inclined to challenge themselves (see chapter 8). The result, a school full of students indifferent to what they are being asked to learn, sometimes prompts educators to respond with the very strategy that helped cause the problem — specifically, by grading children's effort in an attempt to coerce them to try

harder. The fatal paradox, though, is that while coercion can sometimes elicit resentful obedience, it can never create desire. A low grade for effort is more likely to be read as "You're a failure even at trying." On the other hand, a high grade for effort combined with a low grade for achievement says "You're just too dumb to succeed." Most of all, rewarding or punishing the *child's* effort conveniently allows educators to ignore the possibility that the curriculum or learning environment may just have something to do with his or her lack of enthusiasm.

6. **Never grade on a curve.** Under no circumstances should the number of good grades be artificially limited so that one student's success makes another's less likely. "It is not a symbol of rigor to have grades fall into a 'normal' distribution; rather, it is a symbol of failure — failure to teach well, failure to test well, and failure to have any influence at all on the intellectual lives of students."[25]

7. **Bring students in on the evaluation process** to the fullest possible extent. This doesn't mean having them mark their own quizzes while you read off the correct answers. It means working with them to determine the criteria by which their learning can be assessed, and then having them do as much of the actual assessment as is practical. This achieves several things at once: it makes grading feel less punitive, gives students more control over their own education, and provides an important learning experience in itself. Students can derive enormous intellectual benefits from thinking about what makes a story interesting, a mathematical proof elegant, or an argument convincing. Mark Lepper and a colleague have noted that to a considerable extent one's "perception of competence at an activity will depend [on] . . . whether one has to succeed by his or her own standards or by someone else's."[26]

Just as students should be brought in on the evaluation process, so should they be included in a discussion about all these changes. The rationale for moving away from grades should be explained, and students' suggestions for what to do instead and how to manage the transitional period should be solicited.

Finally, a few words for school administrators. Asking teachers to reduce the salience of grades by changing their daily classroom practices is a stopgap measure. Ideally, end-of-term grades can and should be dispensed with as well. Moreover, when teachers are left to de-emphasize grades on their own, and only a few attempt to do so, students may be left with the message that the nongraded subject or class is less important than others where they are still marked. As with most other kinds of educational reform, change must be made at a schoolwide (if not district-wide) level.

The abolition of grades may upset some parents, but one reason so many seem obsessed with their children's grades and test scores is that this may be their only window into what happens at school. If you want them to accept, much less actively support, the move away from grades, these parents must be offered alternative sources of information about how their children are faring. Plenty of elementary schools function without any grades, at least until children are ten or eleven. One way to implement such a change is to phase out letter grades one grade level at a time, starting with the youngest classes.

It is more ambitious, but by no means impossible, to free high school students (and teachers) from the burden of grades.* Probably the major impediment to doing so is the fear of spoiling students' chances of getting into college. Contrary to popular belief, however, admissions officers at the best universities are not eighty-year-old fuddy-duddies, peering over their spectacles and muttering about "highly irregular" applications. Often the people charged with making these decisions are just a few years out of college themselves and, after making their way through a pile of interchangeable applications from 3.8-GPA, student-council-vice-president, musically accomplished hopefuls from high-powered traditional suburban high schools, they are desperate for something unconventional. Given that the most selective colleges have been known to accept home-schooled children who have never set foot in a classroom, it is difficult to believe that qualified applicants would be rejected if, instead of the usual transcript, their schools sent along several thoughtful qualitative assessments from some of the students' teachers, together with a form letter explaining how the school prefers to stress learning rather than sorting, tries to cultivate intrinsic motivation rather than a performance orientation, and is consequently confident that its graduates are exquisitely prepared for the rigors of college life. Indeed, admissions officers for two of the country's most prestigious universities confirm that they do receive, and seriously consider, applications that contain no grades.[27]

---

*Even short of abolishing grades altogether, the most egregious related practices, such as using them to rank students against each other, can certainly be eliminated.

Learning as Discovery

One of the reasons extrinsic motivators such as grades are so destructive of interest and achievement is that they focus students' attention on their performance. If we don't do things to students that compel them to think constantly about how well they are doing, we have taken the first step toward helping them learn. To take the next step, we need to think about instruction in terms of affirmatively helping them become engaged with tasks.

The available research shows that encouraging children to become fully involved with what they're working on and to stop worrying about their performance contributes to "a motivational pattern likely to promote long-term and high-quality involvement in learning."[28] This strategy does wonders for students who are anxious about schoolwork or who have stopped trying.[29] But it also seems to help those who are high achievers: a survey of students attending an academically advanced high school found that the more they described a class as one in which the teacher emphasized understanding, improvement, trying new things, and risking mistakes (as opposed to emphasizing grades and competition), the more they liked the class, the more learning strategies they reported using, and the more they preferred challenging tasks.[30]

Bruner likes to talk about the teacher's role as helping students approach what they are doing with a mind to "discovering something rather than 'learning about' it." The benefit of that, he continues, is that "the child is now in a position to experience success and failure not as reward and punishment, but as information." This is a critical distinction. Feedback indicating that a student "is on the right track . . . [or] the wrong one" is what produces improvement, and teachers need to make sure students get plenty of it. But the capacity to see success and failure *as* feedback is even more important, and that requires teachers (and parents) to stress the task itself, not the performance.[31]

How do we tap children's motivation and create that sense of discovery? Several writers have addressed the topic at length, and their work should be consulted for a more detailed discussion.[32] In the meantime, here are five suggestions:

• **Allow for active learning.** Not only small children but also adults generally learn most effectively when they can see and touch and do, not just sit at a desk and listen. Active, hands-on activities are not just breaks between the real lessons; done correctly, these *are* the real lessons.

• **Give the reason for an assignment.** If a task isn't heuristically valuable, it probably shouldn't be assigned. (Unhappily, teachers don't always get to make that judgment.) If a task *is* valuable, its value should be explained to those being asked to do it. One study found that "a major reason for the students' low quality of engagement in assignments was teacher failure to call attention to their purposes and meanings."[33] If we expect children to want to learn something, we have to give them a clue as to why they should be motivated. Besides, it is a simple matter of respect to offer such explanations.

• **Elicit their curiosity.** People are naturally curious about things whose outcome they can't guess or, once the outcome is known, about things that didn't turn out as expected.[34] Adults who read stories to young children often have an intuitive understanding of this principle: they stop in the middle and ask, "What do you think is going to happen next?" or "Why do you think she did that?" This is the heart of intrinsic motivation, and the skillful exploitation of this fact pulls older students too into tasks. Why would a character in a story who seems so normal not be able to remember when his mother died? How can something that seems so much like water stay at temperatures this low without freezing? What do you think happened when these people refused to back down but also refused to use violence?

• **Set an example.** A teacher ought to let children hear her talk about what she finds enjoyable about teaching and let them see her reading or engaging in other intellectual pursuits for pleasure. (Parents too can set an example by how they describe their own work. Kids who hear Mom or Dad groaning about having to get back to the grind on Monday learn something about motivation.)[35] Teachers can also set an example by admitting when they don't know something, by demonstrating tenacity in the face of failure,[36] by questioning the conventional wisdom, and by showing how they make sense of a piece of writing that is hard to understand.

• **Welcome mistakes.** MISTAKES ARE OUR FRIENDS, announces a sign seen on some classroom walls. Experienced teachers watch and listen closely for when students get things wrong. They don't become defensive, because they know mistakes don't necessarily reflect poor teaching. They don't become angry, because they know mistakes don't necessarily reflect sloppiness or laziness. (If they do, the challenge is to figure out why a student is being sloppy or lazy and work together to solve the problem.) Mistakes offer information about how a student thinks. Correcting them quickly and efficiently doesn't do much to facilitate the learning process.[37] More important, students who are afraid of making mistakes are unlikely to ask for help when they need it, unlikely to feel safe enough to take intellectual risks, and unlikely to be intrinsically motivated.

The Three C's Again

One of the most disquieting things about American education is the emphasis placed on being quiet. If we attend to all that is *not* being said by students, we realize that the absence of children's voices occurs by design and is laboriously enforced. Talking is called "misbehaving," an indication of lack of self-control or self-discipline, except under highly circumscribed circumstances, such as when a pupil is recognized by the teacher for the purpose of giving a short answer to a factual question.[38] Most of the time students are supposed to sit quietly and listen. Teachers who depart from this norm by letting them talk more freely are said to have lost control of their classrooms (a marvelously revealing phrase).

Like most features of our schools, the demand for silence issues from a theory of learning that is largely invisible, despite the scope of its influence. That theory sees the teacher (or book) as a repository of information that is poured, a little bit at a time, into the empty vessel known as the student. The student's job is to passively retain this information — and now and then, to regurgitate some of it on command so we can be sure enough of it got in. To facilitate the process we employ rewards for success, punishments for failure, and an elaborate scoring system to keep track of the transfer. Glasser put it well:

Teachers are required to stuff students with fragments of measurable knowledge as if the students had no needs — almost as if they were things. Education is defined as how many fragments of information these "student-things" can retain long enough to be measured on standardized achievement tests.[39]

It is all of a piece, really — the sort of curriculum that lends itself to being poured or stuffed into students' heads, the fact that students themselves have very little to say about the process, the discipline required to keep them silent and separate, the view of learning as a transmission of information, and the view of children (and ultimately all organisms) as inert objects that must be motivated to learn from the outside with the use of reinforcements and threats.[40]

At the risk of sounding melodramatic, I believe we will never know what real education is until we have shaken off this sterile, discredited model. To do so, to help students learn, we have to do more than avoid using rewards. The foundation of an alternative approach can be described, once again, in terms of the three C's of motivation introduced in the previous chapter.

Collaboration: Learning Together

American schools offer two basic modes of instruction. In the first, children are set against each other, competing for artificially scarce grades and prizes, struggling to be the first with the right answer. The subliminal lesson is that everyone else should be regarded as potential obstacles to one's own success. In the second, children are seated at separate desks, taught to ignore everyone else, reminded not to talk, told that the teacher wants to see "what you can do, not what your neighbor can do," given solitary seatwork assignments followed by solitary homework assignments followed by solitary tests. The subliminal lesson is "how to be alone in a crowd."[41]

This is the extent of most teachers' repertoires: pit students against each other or pry them apart from each other. The only problem with these arrangements is that neither is particularly conducive to learning. As thinkers such as Piaget and Dewey have explained, learning at its best is a result of sharing information and ideas, challenging someone else's interpretation and having to rethink your own, working on problems in a climate of social support. (Note that all these things usually require talking.) Understanding and intellectual growth are derived not only from the relationship between student and teacher, or between student and text, but also from the relationship between one student and another.

One of the most exciting developments in modern education goes by the name of cooperative (or collaborative) learning and has children working in pairs or small groups. An impressive collection of studies has shown that participation in well-functioning cooperative groups leads students to feel more positive about themselves, about each other, and about the subject they're studying. Students also learn more effectively on a variety of measures when they can learn with each other instead of against each other or apart from each other. Cooperative learning works with kindergartners and graduate students, with students who struggle to understand and students who pick things up instantly; it works for math and science, language skills and social studies, fine arts and foreign languages.[42]

This is not the place for an exegesis of the research on cooperative learning, for explaining why the practice works and under what conditions and how to implement it, or for describing the different versions of classroom teamwork and how they differ. My purpose here is mostly just to affirm that anyone thinking about learning and motivation, anyone interested in educational reform, must attend to the relationships among students in the classroom and consider the importance of collaboration.[43]

The opportunity to collaborate ought to be the default condition in the classroom — the arrangement that is used most of the day except when there is good reason to do things another way. (On occasion, for example, teachers will want to make some time for individualized study.) Clustered around tables rather than seated at separate desks, students should be helped to get in the habit of turning to each other to check out an idea or answer a question.

David and Roger Johnson, two of the country's leading proponents of cooperative learning, have offered a delicious suggestion for turning customary practice on its head: principals might wander through the halls of their schools, listening at each classroom door. Whenever they hear nothing, they ought to make a point of asking the teacher, "Why isn't any learning going on in here?" Indeed, a classroom where collaboration is taken seriously is a place where a visitor has trouble finding the teacher (since he is usually wandering around the room, serving as a resource for teams, rather than stationed behind a desk) and also has trouble hearing him (since his voice rarely rises above and overpowers the voices of students).

The evidence of real classroom experience converges with the evidence of rigorous research to support the use of cooperative learning. However, as vital as it is to break out of the traditional individualistic and competitive frameworks, I have come to believe that it is even more important to move past the behaviorist model of instruction. If we do the former without the latter, we remain shackled to the same theories of learning and motivation currently in effect — and also committed to most of the same practices. The single exception is that we are now bribing groups rather than individuals to learn. In particular, the use of certificates, grades, and other extrinsic motivators to induce children to work together has the effect of taking away with one hand (for all the reasons described in this book) what we have just given with the other (by letting children work together).[44] Fortunately, I believe an increasing number of people within the cooperative learning movement are coming to recognize this.

Content: Things Worth Knowing

Even an elementary school student could tell you that how much work people do, or how long they do it, is less important than what they are doing. ("It is not enough to be busy; the question is, what are we busy about?" is how Thoreau put it.)[45] This point, however, seems to be lost on critics who think the most important way to improve our educational system is to increase the length of the school year (or the school day) or to pile on more homework. What they fail to grasp, what a ten-year-old might tell them, is that their efforts would be better spent trying to improve the content of the curriculum that fills those hours and notebooks.

Right now, a good deal of what students are required to do in school is, to be blunt, not worth doing. The tasks they are assigned involve very little creative thought and very much rote learning. These tasks have no apparent connection to children's lives and interests. In fact, there is no apparent connection between any two sentences on a worksheet, between any two tasks, between any two courses.* As Mark Lepper and a colleague have observed,

> Information is presented in an abstract form, dissociated from the con-
> texts in which it might be of obvious, everyday use to children. Topics
> are presented when the schedule calls for them, not when particular
> children are especially interested or "ready" to learn about them.[46]

In a word, learning is decontextualized. We break ideas down into tiny pieces that bear no relation to the whole. We give students a brick of information, followed by another brick, followed by another brick, followed by another brick, until they are graduated, at which point we assume they have a house. What they have is a pile of bricks, and they don't have it for long.

Students are instructed to fill in the missing letters or words on a concatenation of sentences, to work one multiplication problem after another, to learn the chief exports of Peru, to memorize the difference

---

*The American high school schedule, in which students spend forty or fifty minutes on a subject before the bell rings (at which point they salivate and move on), is a remnant of a century-old model used with factory workers. It has little use on the assembly line today, yet we still seem to think that teaching and learning can take place in such a system.

between a metaphor and a simile, to read chapter 11 and answer the even-numbered questions that follow, to keep busy until the bell sets them free. After school they must trudge to the library to copy down some facts from the encyclopedia about Dickens or the division of labor or the digestive system, facts that will be recopied more neatly and handed in as a report. The result of such requirements is not, contrary to claims of traditionalists, intellectual rigor; it is closer to rigor mortis. We lose children as learners because they are turned off by the whole process. Even the best students do what they have to do only because they have to do it — and then they put it out of their minds.

Why do schools coerce children to learn things of such little value? Setting aside the fact that there is room for disagreement about what is valuable, I think there are several reasons:

• For generations, students have been drilled until their minds went to sleep; it is easiest to keep doing what has always been done. It is easier yet to avoid even questioning its value.

• Interesting lessons often take more work to prepare and to teach.[47] "Read chapter 3" requires only that a teacher read chapter 3. Multiple-choice tests can be graded quickly.

• A curriculum geared to the needs of learners requires of the teacher an enormous amount of flexibility, a high tolerance for unpredictability, and a willingness to give up absolute control of the classroom. Control is easier to maintain when teaching becomes a simple transfer of disconnected facts and skills. Indeed, "many teachers . . . maintain discipline by the ways they present course content."[48]

• The current curriculum lends itself nicely to standardized testing and sorting of students. Instead of figuring out what is worth teaching and then devising an appropriate means of assessment, we start with the imperative to evaluate.

Whatever the explanation, it is in the context of an unappealing, if not intellectually bankrupt, curriculum that we wonder why our students are not motivated, why they drop out of school, why they underachieve. We become angry when they daydream or create distractions to amuse themselves* or fail to finish their work on (our)

---

*One of my epiphanies as a teacher came with the realization that students' disruptive acts were less a sign of malice than of a simple desire to make the time pass faster. No strategy for classroom management can hope to be effective in the long term if it ignores the fact that misbehavior often reflects students' lack of interest in much of what we are teaching. They can't get out, so they act out. Ironically, the very strategy that is intended to keep a tighter grip on the classroom is often responsible for behavior problems. The connection between the two, however, is not always obvious.[49]

schedule. We wave the grade book out of desperation, write children's names on the blackboard to warn them, send them to study hall. In short, we place the responsibility squarely on the children instead of on a curriculum that few members of our species would find intrinsically motivating. As Brophy and Kher put it, "Many of the tasks that students are asked to do seem pointless or unnecessarily boring, so that in these cases, finding better tasks is a more sensible response to low motivation than attempting to stimulate interest in such tasks."[50] When a teacher complains that students are "off-task" — a favorite bit of educational jargon — the behaviorist will leap to the rescue with a program to get them back "on" again. The more reasonable response to this complaint is to ask, *What's the task?*[51]

Not surprisingly, this way of framing the problem meets with considerable resistance on the part of many educators. More than once I have been huffily informed that life isn't always interesting, and kids had better learn to deal with this fact. The implication here seems to be that the central purpose of school is not to get children excited about learning but to get them acclimated to doing mind-numbing chores. Thus is the desire to control children, or the unwillingness to create a worthwhile curriculum, rationalized as being in the best interests of students.

Another response to these ideas is to turn them into a caricature, the better to wave them away. "Let kids do only what they find interesting? Why don't we just let them read comic books instead of literature?" We can respond to this by affirming that an engaging, relevant curriculum is not one that is watered down to win over students. Reading literature is a terrific idea; the problem is that too many children are forced to make their way through workbooks instead. Educational excellence comes from motivation, and "the goals toward which activities [are] directed must have some meaning for students in order for them to find the challenge of reaching that goal intrinsically motivating."[52]

Does this mean we abandon basic skills? No. It means that these skills are nested in real-life concerns. The learner's interest is the focal point. Children are curious about how fast they are growing: here is the context for a lesson on addition or decimals. They want to write a story about how a spaceship carries them away: here is where we introduce the basics of punctuation they'll need. They ask to hear about the Vietnam War: here is our reference point for bringing in earlier historical events. Contrast this approach with having to convert a set of twenty decimals into fractions, answer the questions about semicolons in the textbook, listen to a lecture on something called the Progressive Era.

When things are taught in isolation, they are harder to understand and harder to care about. Thus, our question is not merely, What's the task? but, How does the task connect to the world that the students actually inhabit? As Dewey put it, "the number 12 is uninteresting when it is a bare, external fact," but the solution is not "to offer a child a bribe" to manipulate naked numbers. Rather, we take our cue from the fact that a number already

> has interest . . . when it presents itself as an instrument of carrying into effect some dawning energy or desire — making a box, measuring one's height, etc. . . . The mistake, once more, consists in overlooking the activities in which the child is already engaged, or in assuming that they are so trivial or so irrelevant that they have no significance for education.[53]

The premise of this entire discussion is that children are people who have lives and interests outside of school, who walk into the classroom with their own perspectives, points of view, ways of making sense of things and formulating meaning. What we teach and how we teach must take account of these realities. This is the basis for a school of thought known as "constructivism," derived largely from the work of Dewey and Piaget, which stands in crisp relief to the premises of behaviorism. It holds that

> people learn by actively constructing knowledge, weighing new information against their previous understanding, thinking about and working through discrepancies (on their own and with others), and coming to a new understanding. In a classroom faithful to constructivist views, students are afforded numerous opportunities to explore phenomena or ideas, conjecture, share hypotheses with others, and revise their original thinking. Such a classroom differs sharply from one in which the teacher lectures exclusively, explains the "right way" to solve a problem without allowing students to make some sense of their own, or denies the importance of students' own experiences or prior knowledge.[54]

This approach provides the framework for the growing movement to teach children to read by starting them out with things worth reading, as well as for hands-on mathematics lessons and other curricular innovations that are billed as "learner-centered."[55] It stands behind the injunction that the teacher should be "the guide on the side, not the sage on the stage."

Even apart from that radical reconstruction of the teacher's role, there are features of educational content that should be considered by anyone concerned about whether learning takes place in a classroom. For one thing, we need to think about the difficulty level of what children are assigned. At least one social scientist has built a career on the observation that people do their best when the tasks they are working on are neither so easy as to be boring nor so difficult as to cause anxiety and feelings of helplessness.

The point should be self-evident, but apparently it isn't. Some teachers, wanting to help students feel good about themselves, give them easy assignments and plenty of positive reinforcement on successful completion. The strategy fails to create a desire for more challenging work.[56] Other teachers, scornful of "dumbing down" the curriculum, pride themselves on giving students assignments that are way beyond their reach. This is a good way of making students feel stupid. Something in the middle makes a lot more sense. In fact, students not only react well to moderate challenge but actually seek it out: experimental work has shown that children "appeared to be intrinsically motivated to engage in those tasks which were within their reach but developmentally just beyond their current level."[57]

Intrinsic motivation also flourishes when students are not always doing the same thing. Moreover, a variety of *kinds* of tasks, each requiring different skills, has an additional advantage: it helps to reduce the glaring disparities in status in the classroom. If, by contrast, all assignments demand verbal fluency, children may come to look down on their peers who lack this one particular facility.[58]

Tasks can be varied not only from one day to the next but also from one student (or team) to the next at any given time. Give students "several alternative assignments from which they can choose," and competition in the classroom will likely decline. After all, if not everyone in the room is doing the same thing, the social comparison that can degenerate into competition is less likely to occur.[59]

When these two suggestions are combined — that is, when teachers use a variety of assignments that offer the right amount of challenge — students are given the opportunity to feel a sense of accomplishment. That feeling of having worked at something and mastered it, of being competent, is an essential ingredient of successful learning. And, as one researcher notes, "classrooms that provide a variety of concrete activities for many ability levels do not need reward stickers or praise to encourage learning."[60]

Finally, learning tasks can sometimes be embellished and embedded in a context that heightens their appeal. Many educators are concerned about "sugar-coating" activities — a justifiable concern in some cases, since these efforts may lack intellectual nourishment. But carefully designed programs, such as fantasy contexts in computer-based learning, have been shown to lead to "increased learning and retention of the material, greater generalization of that learning, heightened subsequent interest in the subject matter, enhanced confidence in the learner, and improvements in the actual process of learning."[61] As long as these efforts do not distract us from the more important task of making sure the primary subject matter is meaningful and connected to children's real-life experiences,[62] they can play a role in enhancing the motivation to learn.

Choice: Autonomy in the Classroom

Every teacher who is told what material to cover, when to cover it, and how to evaluate children's performance is a teacher who knows that enthusiasm for one's work quickly evaporates in the face of control. Not every teacher, however, realizes that exactly the same is true of students: deprive children of self-determination and you deprive them of motivation. If learning is a matter of following orders, students simply will not take to it in the way they would if they had some say about what they were doing.

The rationale for giving children choice is threefold. First, it is intrinsically desirable because it is a more respectful way of dealing with others. Second, it offers benefits for teachers. Their job becomes a good deal more interesting when it involves collaborating with students to decide what is going to happen. As one fifth-grade teacher in upstate New York says,

> I've been teaching for more than 30 years, and I would have been burned out long ago but for the fact that I involve my kids in designing the curriculum. I'll say to them, "What's the *most* exciting way we could study this next unit?" If we decide their first suggestion isn't feasible, I'll say, "Okay, what's the *next* most exciting way we could study this?" They always come up with good proposals, they're motivated because I'm using their ideas, and I never do the unit in the same way twice.[63]

Teachers also benefit in other ways from allowing students to be active participants in their learning. One group of researchers notes that in this situation, the teacher is "freed from the chore of constantly monitoring and supervising the children's activity and [is] able to give her full attention to . . . interacting with the children" as they work.[64]

The third reason to make sure that students have some say over what they do all day — the reason that will be my primary focus here — is that it works better:

• When second graders in Pittsburgh were given some choice about their learning, including the chance to decide which tasks they would work on at any given time, they tended to "complete more learning tasks in less time."[65]

• When high school seniors in Minneapolis worked on chemistry problems without clear-cut directions — that is, with the opportunity to decide for themselves how to find solutions — they "consistently produced better write-ups of experiments" and remembered the material better than those who had been told exactly what to do. They put in more time than they had to, spending "extra laboratory periods checking results that could have been accepted without extra work." Some of the students initially resisted having to make decisions about how to proceed, but these grumblers later "took great pride in being able to carry through an experiment on their own."[66]

• When preschool-age children in Massachusetts were allowed to select the materials they used for making a collage, their work was judged more creative than the work of children who used exactly the same materials but did not get to choose them.[67]

• When college students in New York had the chance to decide which of several puzzles they wanted to work on, and how to allot their time to each of them, they were a lot more interested in working on such puzzles later than were students who were told what to do.[68]

• When teachers of inner-city black children were trained in a program designed to promote a sense of self-determination, the children in these classes missed less school and scored better on a national test of basic skills than those in conventional classrooms.[69]

• Fourth-, fifth-, and sixth-grade students who felt they were given personal responsibility for their studies had "significantly higher self-esteem and perceived academic competence" than children who felt controlled in their classrooms.[70]

• When second graders who spent the year in a constructivist math classroom, one where textbooks and rewards were discarded in favor of an emphasis on "intellectual autonomy" — that is, where children, working in groups, took an active role in figuring out their own solutions to problems and were free to move around the classroom on their own initiative to get the materials they needed — they developed more sophisticated higher-level reasoning skills without falling behind on basic conceptual tasks.[71]

The evidence goes on and on. At least one study has found that children given more "opportunity to participate in decisions about schoolwork" score higher on standardized tests.[72] They are more likely than those deprived of autonomy to continue working even on relatively uninteresting tasks.[73] They are apt to select assignments of the ideal difficulty level so they will be properly challenged (assuming there are no rewards involved).[74] There is no question about it: choice works.

The different versions of choice represented in these studies remind us that there is more than one way to put the idea into effect. Some are more modest in scope than others, but all involve substantive decisions about learning. I am not talking here about perfunctory matters such as letting older students choose which of three essay questions they will address in their final papers; I am talking about giving students of all ages considerable discretion about things that matter in the classroom.[75]

Every day ought to include at least one block of time in which children can decide what to do: get a head start on homework, write in their journals, work on art projects, or read library books. Creative writing assignments offer plenty of opportunity for decisions to be made by the writers themselves. The same is true of selecting stories — not only for individual reading but when the class reads together. ("Here are five books that the supply store has in stock," a fourth-grade teacher may say to the class. "Why don't you flip through them during your free time this week and we'll decide together on Friday which one we'll read next.") In expressing an idea or responding to a lesson, children sometimes can be allowed to decide what medium or genre they will use — whether they want to write a poem, an essay, or a play, make a collage, a painting, or a sculpture. Mathematics lessons can be guided by quantitative issues of interest to students. In fact, the entire constructivist tradition described in the last section is predicated on the idea of student autonomy. The same can be said about some (but by no means all) versions of cooperative learning.[76]

Notice that in each of these examples the teacher offers guidelines or broad parameters within which children can choose. It is not necessary for a teacher to turn over all pedagogical responsibilities to students in order for them to be involved in their education — nor, as Dewey pointed out, is it desirable for teachers to do so.[77] Different teachers will find a different balance between telling students what to do (or limiting their choices) and letting them decide; this will depend on the age of the students, constraints placed on the teacher,* and the teacher's need for control, among other factors.

In any case, the teacher will need to help students learn the skills with which they can make the best use of their freedom. "Opportunities to develop self-management and self-regulatory strategies must accompany the assignment of responsibility," says Carole Ames.[78] We want to avoid situations in which a teacher lets children decide what to do and how to do it, discovers that the children are unable to plan a major project over a period of time, and reverts to a controlling approach.

> I have heard teachers give it up after a single attempt, saying, "Children cannot behave responsibly," then remove all further opportunity for students to practice and grow in their responsible behavior. I have also heard teachers say, "Children cannot think for themselves," and proceed thereafter to do children's thinking for them. But these same teachers would *never* say, "These children cannot read by themselves," and thereafter remove any opportunity for them to learn to read.[79]

One last point: the idea of choice appears to many of us as a dichotomous affair — "Either you make it or I do"; either students get to decide something, or it's determined by the teacher. This perspective overlooks various possibilities, all of which should have a place in an educator's repertoire. Sometimes a decision about what to read, say, or how to spend time is made by each student individually; sometimes it is made by each cooperative learning group; sometimes it is made by the whole class. Moreover, the responsibility to choose does not have to be thought of as turned over to students *or* kept by the teacher: some choices can be negotiated together. The emphasis here is on shared responsibility for deciding what gets learned and how the learning takes place. That negotiation can become a lesson in itself — an opportunity to make arguments, solve problems, anticipate consequences, and take other people's needs into account — as well as a powerful contribution to motivation.

•   •   •

---

*If teachers are compelled to teach a certain lesson, they might open up a discussion with students, asking them to try to figure out why someone thought the subject was important enough to be required and then working with them to devise a connection to their real-world concerns and interests.

Children start out enthusiastic and skillful learners. Helping them to stay that way through school is partly a matter of what we give them to learn. In the section on content, I argued that boring assignments ought to be scrutinized and those that cannot be justified should be discarded. Unlike tedious jobs, at least some of which have to be done, there is no reason that anyone should have to do something that doesn't contribute to a meaningful education.

Still, not everything we think children ought to learn is highly motivating in itself. I want to make clear that the suggestions offered in this chapter do not presume that every lesson plan will hook children on its own. Thus, when students do successfully learn material that is not immediately appealing to them,[80] it is worth attending to the factors that help that happen.

I offer a modest example from my own days as a student. When I was in high school, I memorized every element on the periodic table, from actinium to zirconium. This is not an inherently interesting thing to do, so the circumstances in which I did it may be relevant here. First, the decision to learn them was my own; no one told me I had to or rewarded me when I succeeded. Second, I roped a couple of friends into doing it with me; apart from the help people can offer each other to facilitate learning, most tasks are simply more pleasant with social support. Third, the challenge became less tedious (and to be frank, less difficult) because what we actually did was memorize a song: the satirist Tom Lehrer had already set the names of the elements to music. This made the task seem rather like a game. I'm not sure which of these factors was the most decisive, but I do know that a couple of decades later I can still recite the entire periodic table. By contrast, all I remember from an entire year of advanced placement European history is the phrase "warm-water ports."

No one ought to be required to memorize the elements — or for that matter, the state capitals. But there are aspects of learning that require hard work, and it is here that talented teachers really shine. They arrange for students to be part of a community of learners who help each other do their best. They embed the task in a question or context to which students resonate, and they help make the connections to the questions clear. They give students choice about how they will approach a task and a reasonable rationale for what they are being asked to do.

And, to bring this discussion back full circle, skilled teachers remove obstacles to interest, such as rewards. For critics of our educational system who despair that we can ever get past behavioral manipulation, I close with a few hopeful findings. In chapter 7, I noted that while many employees have been battered with extrinsic motivators to the point of becoming dependent on them, most people still say they are more concerned about doing interesting work than about how much money (and how many rewards) they can collect. The same thing may be true of students. When about 350 high schoolers were asked about their objectives, "reaching a personal goal" was ranked number one, whereas extrinsic rewards, such as being publicly recognized for an achievement, were seen as much less important. "Winning a contest," in particular, showed up at the very bottom of the list. In a striking parallel to the data on employee goals, teachers who were asked what motivated students incorrectly assumed that extrinsic motivators were more important to students than they actually were.[81]

As for teachers' beliefs about learning, there is obviously a wide range of assumptions and practices to be found. It is impossible to wish away the pervasiveness of Skinnerian techniques in American schools. But a recent national survey of elementary school teachers found fairly widespread understanding that rewards are not particularly effective at getting or keeping students motivated. Such strategies as awarding special privileges to those who do well or publicly comparing children's achievement were seen as less successful than giving students more choice about how to learn or letting them work together.[82] The fact that extrinsic tactics are frequently used despite this knowledge may reflect pressure to raise standardized test scores or to keep control of the class. If teachers understand that rewards are not helpful for promoting motivation to learn, perhaps this is not the overriding goal of educators. If so, then a renewed call to emphasize the importance of motivation is what we need. We *can* get children hooked on learning — if that is really what we are determined to do.

Questions for Review

1. Compare and contrast performance appraisals and report cards.

2. What are the three reasons that abolishing rewards will not cause students to cheer, "Hooray! Now we can be intrinsically motivated!"? Can you think of a fourth?

3. The author's argument that much of our curriculum is intellectually "bankrupt" appears in Chapter 11. Do you think this is a coincidence?

4. What *are* the chief exports of Peru?

   Extra credit: What do you think the author would say about extra credit?

~12~

GOOD KIDS
WITHOUT GOODIES

The best way out is always through.
— Robert Frost,
"A Servant to Servants"

AS LONG AS PEOPLE have children to raise and doubts about how to raise them, there will be other people who make their living by offering advice. The disagreement among these advisers about what parents should do is somewhat disconcerting. Even more disturbing, though, are some of the points where their approaches overlap.

The great majority of books and seminars on bringing up children share three features, all of which are generally taken for granted. First, more talk is devoted to eliminating unwanted behaviors than to promoting positive values and skills; second, step-by-step plans are provided for parents to implement; and third, copious use is made of punishments ("consequences") and/or rewards ("positive reinforcements"). These same characteristics describe most programs intended to help teachers with the nonacademic aspects of school life.

Each of these three features is connected to the other two. Someone who chooses to focus on stopping bad behaviors is apt to prefer a program that describes exactly what to do and say, and conversely, someone who wants to follow a recipe is apt to think in terms of day-by-day challenges rather than long-term values. Both orientations, meanwhile, seem consistent with tactics that emphasize extrinsic control.

This chapter, which does not presume to offer anything like a comprehensive guide to raising children, takes a different tack on all three issues. There is nothing wrong with trying to deal with troublesome behavior, and some of what follows addresses this matter directly. But an approach that focuses on coping with problems does little to help children grow into good people, and may actually interfere with that goal. On the other hand, if we are effective in promoting positive values and skills, we may reduce the number of problems requiring intervention on a daily basis. To concentrate on those values and skills may be a way of feeding two birds from one feeder, so to speak.*

The second characteristic of most how-to-parent guides, their recipe approach, is even more difficult to defend. Anyone who purports to tell a parent or teacher exactly what to say and do to children in a range of situations is selling a modern version of snake oil. While it is appealing to imagine we can simply memorize some magic words to insert into (or delete from) our sentences, the right tone to use, and the correct way to respond to resistance, the truth is that it is impossible to reduce the awesome complexity of human interaction to a few scientific-sounding formulas. Such an approach cannot possibly be effective at reaching any but the most superficial objectives. Besides, presenting a set of easy-to-follow, foolproof instructions is disrespectful to parents in the same way that the techniques being peddled are often disrespectful to children.

Parenting guides also share a reliance on punishments and rewards, and I want to begin by urging that we dispense with these tactics or at least drastically reduce their use. The reason to do so has already been presented at some length in this book, which means we might now move on to reframing the way we think about our relationships with children.

Beyond Control

There comes a point in a child's second year when a baby who is carried around and fed and put to sleep — who basically has things done to it — becomes a person with a point of view. Quite a lot has been written about a toddler's quest for autonomy, about the formation of identity and the exercise of will. Much of the advice offered to parents, however, amounts to a series of new and cleverer strategies for doing things to a child who now may loudly resist requests. I propose that this period be seen instead as an opportunity to shift from doing things *to* an infant to doing things *with* a child.

To make sense of this distinction, we need to think about the rules and restrictions placed on children. There is nothing inherently objec-

---

*I prefer this expression to the more familiar one that depicts two birds being stoned to death.

tionable about "structures" or "limits" that speak to such matters as when they should go to bed, what they should eat, which items are not to be played with, and where they must not go. Whether any given limit is reasonable, however, is another matter. That is something that can be determined by considering such questions as the purpose of the limit, how confining it is, and who came up with it.

Combining these three criteria, we might say that limits and structures can be endorsed most readily when the purpose is defensible (for example, protecting a child from injuring himself), their restrictiveness is minimized (for example, preventing access to certain cabinets rather than forcing a toddler to stay in one small space), and the child has contributed to the arrangement to the fullest possible extent (for example, in helping come up with a plan for getting homework done).

It is also important to look at how limits and structures are maintained. This raises the idea of *control*, a word that generally implies the use of coercion or pressure to impose one's will on a child. Edward Deci and Richard Ryan have distinguished an environment for children that is structured or limited from one that is controlling. Their objection is to the latter.[1] Even the most ardent opponent of control would hesitate to rule out all such interventions, particularly with young children. Sometimes it is necessary to insist, to put one's foot down. Still, it seems reasonable to propose that parents and teachers try to use the least intrusive or coercive strategy necessary to achieve a reasonable end. Don't move a child roughly if you can move her gently; don't move her gently if you can tell her to move; don't tell her if you can ask her.

If we pay attention to the degree of control used by a parent who is trying to get a child to do something, we can usually predict quite a bit about how that child will act in other situations. Researchers keep finding that a heavy-handed approach is not only less effective but also more likely to be associated with disruptive and aggressive behavior patterns when the child is away from home. In an early experiment, Martin Hoffman noticed that an even better way to predict those behavior patterns was to keep watching to see how parents reacted if their children didn't do what they were told. The outcomes were worse when a parent hollered, hit, threatened, punished, or otherwise turned up the heat in an effort to regain the upper hand after initial noncompliance.[2]

If many of us act this way, it is not only because we lose our tempers, but also because it may seem to us the only alternative. We convince ourselves that we are not just imposing our will but teaching the child what happens when he misbehaves, and that this will prevent future misbehavior. Moreover, we see ourselves as administering an elemental sort of justice: having broken a rule, the child must now be punished.

In chapter 9 I argued that the first rationale is fatally flawed; punishment teaches about the use of power, not about how or why to behave properly. The second rationale, reflecting as it does a value about what *should* be done, cannot be disproved by evidence. But it makes sense to probe this belief to see what it rests on. My impression is that the commitment to punishing children typically reflects a fear that the failure to respond this way will mean that they "got away with something."

If we dig still further, we find that this perception upsets us for two reasons. First, it implies that the child has "won." Our authority has been challenged, and the more we construe a relationship as a battle for power, the more wildly we will lash out to preserve that power. Second, we are concerned the child will come away thinking he can repeat whatever it was he did. This concern, in turn, betrays a particular assumption about children's motives, namely that a child is inclined to do what he can get away with and will keep doing it until forcibly restrained. Ultimately, our need to punish (or dread of not punishing) is predicated on a tacit theory of human nature.

Each of these beliefs and motives that underlie the practice of punishment can be held up to the light for inspection. Do we really want to pursue an adversarial relationship with a child? If not, then it makes no sense to choose our response with an eye to preventing him from winning a contest for power, because there is no contest for power. Likewise, we need to ask why we believe children "naturally" revel in nasty, selfish, antisocial behavior and desist only because they fear what will happen to them. The evidence says otherwise.[3]

In my view, there are two fundamentally different ways one can respond to a child who does something wrong. One is to impose a punitive consequence. Another is to see the situation as a "teachable moment," an opportunity to educate or to solve a problem together. The response here is not "You've misbehaved; now here's what I'm going to do to you" but "Something has gone wrong; what can we do about it?"

The latter represents a different way of seeing as much as a different way of reacting, and there are plenty of reasons to favor this perspective. Using power to make unpleasant things happen to someone is an intrinsically objectionable way of interacting with people, especially

232 / BEYOND REWARDS

children. If there is any way to avoid this, it seems virtually self-evident that we should do so. Moreover, working together to solve problems offers a vote of confidence, a statement of trust, to a child. It says, "I believe that when you understand the moral issues involved, and when you have the necessary skills, you will act responsibly." This belief sets into motion what we might call an "auspicious" circle: the more we trust, the more likely a child is to live up to that trust.

But does this work in the real world? Actually, the more apt question is, Does punishment work in the real world? Experience and research teach us that troublesome behavior increases when children are punished, that underlying problems aren't solved, that dubious values are modeled. Almost anything would represent an improvement over this. An atmosphere of respect rather than coercion, a commitment to work with children on developing the capacity to behave well, a willingness to figure out what has gone wrong and to fix it together — these add up to an approach that is not only nicer but far more likely to produce lasting results.

Sure, replies the skeptic. This orientation is fine initially, or for minor infractions. But what about repeated or very serious wrongdoing? Don't we have to impose a punishment (or "consequence") at some point?* Let us respond to this question first by exposing its premise, which is that adults haven't really taken action (or gotten serious) until they have caused something unpleasant to happen to a child. This assumption reflects a widespread tendency, described earlier, to think in dualistic terms: either we punish or let it go. (The problem-solving approach recommended here would thus be construed as a fancy version of letting it go.) Another belief that may implicitly inform this perspective is that until a child has suffered, nothing meaningful has taken place. No pain, no gain.

The fact of the matter is that everything we know about the futility of punishment doesn't stop being true just because the child's behavior is especially disturbing or has continued over time. Punishing a child for a truly destructive act is no more sensible than punishing her for a trifle; one could argue it makes even less sense because the stakes are higher. By contrast, trying to get to the heart of the problem and work

---

*Teachers who take this position sometimes adopt a utilitarian standard that says, in effect, "I've got a lot of children to worry about, and it may be worth punishing or removing a difficult child so that everyone else can benefit." One problem with this line of reasoning is that the example of power and coercion set by punishment also affects the very people who are supposed to benefit from it — that is, the students who watch a teacher deal with a problem by relying on controlling strategies.

it out *is* a meaningful response even if — in fact, partly because — it is not painful or humiliating.

The temptation to punish grows as the act persists, not because punishment becomes inherently more sensible but because we become more desperate. This is what might be called the blue-in-the-face syndrome — as in "I've talked and talked to the kid and nothing has changed." Apart from the fact that a punitive strategy is even less likely to work (except, of course, to secure temporary, resentful obedience), this posture makes about as much sense as saying, "I've typed and typed and I *still* haven't produced a good book; clearly, typing doesn't work." When one approach to solving problems together doesn't produce results, it makes sense to modify the approach, not to abandon the idea of solving problems in favor of using threats and coercion.

It would be an exaggeration to say that even a single application of the latter is an unredeemable tragedy. The occasional mildly punitive response or Skinnerian incentive that we deliver when we can't think of anything else to do is not going to permanently rupture a child's emotional health — at least, not if the environment is generally warm, loving, and respectful. But it is vital that we keep in mind the desirability of avoiding punishment and reward whenever we can. There is a difference between forgiving ourselves an occasional blunder and refusing to admit that certain approaches *are* blunders.

Doesn't it take enormous reservoirs of patience and self-restraint to work through a problem (repeatedly, in some cases) rather than falling back on extrinsic short-cuts? Isn't it unrealistic to expect parents and teachers to do this? The answers are yes to the first question and no to the second. When we put down the book and return to the exigencies of everyday life, where time and patience are limited, where children sometimes seem to present us with a steady stream of repetitive demands and even infuriating provocations, the research and analysis concerning punishment can seem impossibly remote. The urge to punish and yell and even hit — or to rely on the tactic of control by seduction (that is, rewards) — can be difficult to resist. Every parent knows this, and it makes no sense to hold out a standard for our own behavior that can never be reached.

All the same, we ought not and need not dispense with standards and goals. Nor should we underestimate what we are capable of doing. It takes time to develop confidence in a child's capacity to function in the absence of bribes or threats. More to the point, it takes time to develop confidence in our own ability to manage without them. A friend of mine said to me not long ago, "The reason I never

spanked my second kid is simple: I got better at being a mom."
Another mother of my acquaintance once confessed, "I tell my daughter 'Here's what I'll give you if you clean your room' because I don't
have the skills to reach her any other way."

These parents are viewing their own behavior in a manner that
strikes me as enormously promising and constructive. Even though
they have used punishment and reward, they don't just dismiss criticism of these techniques as "unrealistic." (Perhaps they realize that all
fundamental change seems impractical at first.) They don't insist defensively that children will respond to nothing except extrinsic manipulation (an insistence that usually means it's the parents who know
nothing else). Rather, these mothers are able to see themselves as
learners, as people in the process of getting better at what they do.
They may need time and assistance to shake free of old habits and give
up the quick fixes of pop behaviorism, but they know intuitively that
this is the right direction in which to move.

Solving Problems: Return of the Three C's

The alternative to using control with children can be usefully described in terms of the issues I have referred to as the "three C's":
content, collaboration, and choice. In this section, I will briefly discuss
the role played by each in our responses to problematic behavior;
later, I will return to some of these themes in considering the long-
term enterprise of helping children grow into good people.

Content. When people at work do a poor job, it is necessary to
look at what they are being asked to do — that is, the nature of the
work. When students fail to learn, the first question to ask is what
they are expected to learn and whether it is worth learning. Likewise,
when we are concerned that a child does not comply with a request,
we must begin by considering the nature of that request.

This perspective can be highly threatening to people whose premise
is that others should simply do what they are told. Their preferred
question is "How can I make them?" — a question whose answer is
invariably couched in behavioristic terms. Parents may feel this way
even more acutely than managers or teachers do because in no other
arena do we take for granted so asymmetrical a relationship as that
between parent and child. Some managers will have another look at
job design when problems develop at work; some teachers will try to
improve the curriculum when their students don't successfully com-

plete assignments. But few parents react to a child's disobedience by wondering whether they should rethink what it was they told the child to do. If they seek advice, it is typically only to figure out how to change the *child's* behavior.

The suggestion that parents (and, with regard to classroom management issues, teachers) ought to question how reasonable their demands are is not a terribly sophisticated point. It does not seem to call for extensive support by argument or evidence. One either regards it as an idea with obvious validity, however challenging it may be to put into practice, or dismisses the whole discussion as inconsistent with one's basic beliefs about raising children. My purpose here is not to convince those who think a parent has the right to expect unquestioning obedience to any command, but to remind everyone else that dealing with a child's misbehavior starts with asking serious questions about our expectations and demands.

One can engage in that questioning in a very general way: Are we setting up rules "that conflict with basic needs, drives or tendencies [that] will, necessarily, create conflict" such as regularly trying to prevent children from making noise, moving around, or expressing emotion?[4] Are we asking them to react in a way that doesn't make sense given their capacities at a particular stage of development, such as demanding that they think about the long-range consequences of their behavior before they are able to do so?

One can also question specific requests in terms of their necessity and desirability. We say that a three-year-old cannot play with a knife; the child is unhappy with the restriction; we think about it some more but decide that it really is too dangerous (and we explain that to her). We tell a six-year-old to stop playing with an ice cube at the dinner table; the child is unhappy with the restriction; we think about it some more and decide that there is really no harm in doing so. (Reconsidering one's original prohibition is, of course, completely different from relenting out of exhaustion: "Oh, all right, go ahead.")

Some rules and requests are obviously justified; some are obviously cruel and unnecessary. Most fall somewhere in between, requiring us to weigh, say, a child's desire to explore his environment with the possibility that he will hurt himself, or the pleasure he takes in boisterous play with the rights of those around him. Good parenting is not defined by which decision one makes in each instance so much as by the willingness to think about these decisions — as opposed to the tendency to say no habitually and to demand mindless obedience to mindless restrictions.

Collaboration. The process of making decisions about what children ought to do, and what they can reasonably be expected to do, is not something the parent does alone. The older the child, the more she should be brought into the process: we explain to her, listen to her, consult with her, plan with her. The best way to characterize the alternative to punishment and rewards is as "mutual problem solving," the heart of which is collaboration.

Explanation is the most limited version of collaboration, and it is the very least we owe a child. Even when the child is too young to participate in deciding, or when we have determined that a rule is simply nonnegotiable, simple decency requires us to replace "Because I said so" (an appeal to power) with "Here's why . . ." (an appeal to reason). Such an approach is also more likely to be effective: research backs up the commonsense precept that a child is more likely to respond positively to a request when a rationale for it has been provided.[5]

Although explanations obviously should be fitted to the child's ability to understand, the form they take will vary depending on the situation. Sometimes they will resemble what Martin Hoffman calls "induction," in which the child is led to see how her actions affect other people.[6] Sometimes they will be charged with emotion: reason need not exclude passion, such as when a parent is explaining why we do not punch people. (The trick is to make sure that the passion does not overshadow the message itself.) The explanation should always be part of a conversation in which the child's reaction is welcomed, not a speech to which the child must silently listen.

Ideally, however, collaboration will not be limited to an adult's explaining to a child why the latter has to (or cannot) do something. It is instead a process of making a decision together. In the case of what is usually referred to as a disciplinary matter, the first stage is to talk about whether the act in question really is a problem, and if so, why. Typically parents make this determination on their own and announce that the child's behavior must change. The child, however, may not understand why it should change — other than because a powerful person, with rewards and punishments at his command, decrees it. (Such changes are therefore usually superficial and temporary.)

Is it really wrong for children to keep their rooms messy? Must they stop grabbing toys that belong to friends? Do students in the classroom really have to raise their hands before speaking? Sometimes the parent or teacher has made up her mind about the answer, in which case the objective is, through conversation, to help the child understand the reason. Sometimes — too rarely, I believe — adults are willing to arrive at a mutual understanding with children of what constitutes inappropriate behavior.*

In either case, thinking out loud together about what is wrong (and why) is integral to the promotion of children's moral development. "When significant discipline problems do occur," says John Nicholls, "they can be transformed into intellectual challenges that make every child a legislator — a moral philosopher. Instead of exercises in the control of behavior, there are adventures in ethics."[7]

Assuming that a child's behavior has been clearly identified as problematic, the next task is to figure out its source, particularly if this is not the first time it has occurred. As I have argued, rewards and punishment are deficient partly because they attempt to control behavior without regard to its cause. Different schools of thought will tend to identify different reasons for behavior, emphasizing, for example, the child's need for attention, the example that has been set for him (he may be aggressive with his friend because his parent is aggressive with him), the network of relationships in the family or classroom, and so on. Theories aside, different circumstances will lend different meanings to the same sort of behavior.

So how do we ascertain the cause? The obvious answer is to ask the child. Often the parent doesn't stop to do this, either because it is assumed the reason for the behavior is clear or because the question isn't seen as important. Sometimes the question is posed, but in a harsh, threatening tone ("Why are you late getting ready for school again? Huh? Why? Answer me!"), so the child understands full well that he is not really being asked to speculate about possible reasons; he is being asked to drop his head, look penitent, mumble something, and hope to avoid punishment.

Younger children cannot always identify and verbalize their motives. Five-year-olds do not pause reflectively and say, "Well, Daddy, I guess I slugged Zachary because I'm displacing my emotional turmoil caused by hearing you and Mommy yell at each other so much." They are more likely to shrug and mutter, "I dunno." (Older children, too, may do this, but the chance of eliciting a more meaningful response is

---

*Many adults have adopted the strategy of trial lawyers during cross examination, which is never to ask a question to which they do not already know the answer. This approach helps them to maintain a sense of power, avoid any feeling of vulnerability, and head off real collaboration.

enhanced by creating a nonpunitive, collaborative atmosphere so children feel safe talking about what they do know.) When the child cannot be forthcoming, parents and teachers have to become detectives, looking for clues as to possible causes and trying out hypotheses tentatively in the process of working out a solution.

The next step is to come up with a plan together: "How do you think we can solve this problem?" "What do you think we should do now?" Some people favor drawing up formal contracts to codify the agreement, but whether a plan is put into writing is not nearly so important as how the agreement was reached: jointly or by the adult alone? freely or under duress? based on some understanding about the act's moral status or as a way of avoiding a punishment (or obtaining a reward)? One good way to figure out whether a contract will be helpful is to ask the child. Sometimes a reasonable follow-up to a destructive action is to try to restore, replace, repair, clean up, or apologize, as the situation may dictate. "When children are not afraid of being punished, they are willing to come forward and make restitution."[8]

Finally, it is often useful to arrange to check back later to see whether the problem got solved, how the plan worked, whether additional or entirely new strategies may be needed — or perhaps just to allow the child to feel proud of herself for the resolution. Such discussions also let the participants reflect on the process and decide whether it seemed fair and constructive. This is especially important when students meet as a class to solve a problem.

Choice. A discussion of collaborative problem solving shades into the issue of choice or autonomy for children. When adults are unsure about why something happened or what should be done about it, the slogan to keep in mind is "Bring the kid(s) in on it." The more a child feels part of the process, the more his point of view is solicited and taken seriously, the fewer problems there will be to deal with.

Later in this chapter I will deal with the issue of autonomy in some detail, not as a technique for responding to misbehavior but as a fundamental component of raising or teaching children and helping them develop positive values and skills. The only point I want to make for the time being is that we need to be wary of how the concept of choice has been distorted by some people who offer advice on discipline. Parents and teachers are sometimes encouraged to impose punitive "consequences" on a child while verbally attributing the punishment to the child's own choice — for example, saying to a child who plays tennis in the house, "I see you've chosen to spend the evening in your room." The appeal of this tactic is no mystery: it appears to relieve the adult of responsibility for what he is about to do to the child. But it is a fundamentally dishonest attribution. The child may have chosen to play with her toy indoors when she was told not to,* but she certainly didn't choose to be confined to her bedroom; it was her father who did that to her. To the injury of punishment is added the insult of a kind of mind game whereby reality is redefined and the child is told, in effect, that she asked to be punished. This gimmick uses the word *choice* as a bludgeon rather than giving children what they need, which is the opportunity to participate in making real decisions about what happens to them.[9]

Caring Kids

Responding to, or even preventing, irresponsible behavior is not enough. We want to emphasize the positive, to help a child act responsibly and develop prosocial values over the long run. But how? The elimination of rewards and punishments may be necessary for that purpose, but clearly it is not sufficient. Fortunately, a fair amount of research exists that addresses this more ambitious agenda. There are, of course, no sure-fire instructions to follow, but there are some general guidelines worth reviewing.

   Caring.   Children are more likely to grow into caring people if they know they themselves are cared about. A warm, nurturing environment is the sine qua non of positive development. (It also turns out to be useful for the more limited goal of getting children to do what we ask.)[10] If children feel safe, they can take risks, ask questions, make mistakes, learn to trust, share their feelings, and grow.[11] If they are taken seriously, they can respect others.† If their emotional needs are met, they have the luxury of being able to meet other people's needs.[12] Deprived of these things, however, they may spend their lives doing psychological damage control. Their own needs may echo so loudly in

---

*Even this assumption needs to be questioned, since the child may lack the capacity for rational decision-making or impulse control that is implicit in suggesting she made a choice. If so, the child needs help in developing these faculties, not punishment accompanied by blame.

†A discouraging proportion of adults who demand that children treat them with respect — or complain loudly about how kids today fail to do so — think nothing of behaving toward their children with an utter lack of respect.

their ears that they will be unable to hear, much less respond to, the cries of others.

In order to be a caring person, a parent or teacher must first be a person. Many of us are inclined instead to hide behind the mannerisms of a constantly competent, smoothly controlling, crisply authoritative Parent or Teacher. To do so is to play a role, and even if the script calls for nurturance, this is not the same as being fully human in front of a child. A person (as opposed to a parent or teacher figure) sometimes gets flustered or distracted or tired, says things without thinking and later regrets them, asks children for their opinions, maintains interests outside of parenting or teaching and doesn't mind discussing them. Also, a person avoids distancing maneuvers such as referring to him- or herself in the third person (as in "Mr. Kohn has a special surprise for you today, boys and girls").

For the most part, the position that caretakers should be caring is not particularly controversial. However, vestiges of an opposing point of view from another era still turn up from time to time. One still hears, for example, the old chestnut that crying infants must not be picked up and comforted too often lest they become spoiled, a view that is consistent with pop behaviorism in its prediction that responsiveness will just reinforce the baby's crying.[13] (It is also a view vigorously rejected by virtually everyone who is knowledgeable about infant development.)[14]

Among educators, meanwhile, there is still some credence given to the slogan that a teacher must not let down her guard and smile at her students until after Christmas. (One hopes whoever came up with that bit of advice is no longer in a position where he or she can continue doing harm to children.) Other teachers defensively insist that they are "not here to be liked," which is usually a rationalization for their inability or unwillingness to express care for their students. The available research "clearly demonstrates that nice teachers are highly effective . . . [and refutes] the myth that students learn more from cold, stern, distant teachers."[15]

Modeling. Even before children are steady on their feet, and even after they adopt a pose of impermeable indifference, they are learning how to be a person by watching the kind of people we are. Almost everyone knows that adults teach by example. What is often forgotten is that we do so constantly, whether we mean to or not. We may, for example, do something in front of a child with a mind to modeling a particular attitude or behavior, but the unsettling truth is that the child was also learning from how we acted ten minutes earlier, when we weren't thinking about what we were doing.

If children see us walk past people in distress, they learn that other people's pain isn't our concern. If they hear us talk about the world in "Us versus Them" terms, they learn that people from different backgrounds don't have to be treated the same as people who are like us. If they are subject to power-based, controlling forms of discipline, they learn that this is how you act toward people who are weaker than you. But if they grow up around love and fairness and respect and compassion, these are the lessons they learn instead. Indeed, studies show that children are more likely to act generously when they see an adult act that way, and they are more likely to grow into concerned, helpful adults themselves when their parents show the way.[16]

We model when we listen respectfully, when we try to help people we don't know, and when we admit our mistakes. Outside of providing love, few things we can do with children are as important, or as difficult, as apologizing to them for something we regret having done. Adults who take this idea one step further and tell children, "If I ever say something to you that embarrasses you or hurts your feelings (which I may do sometimes because I'm not perfect), please let me know" are setting an example of courage as well as concern.

By caring for children we demonstrate by force of example the importance of caring (in addition to simply providing something they need). However, this impulse has to be balanced against the desire to let them help themselves and discover their competence at solving problems on their own. Equally important, but more often overlooked, rushing in to help may preclude their getting assistance from friends or siblings or classmates. We want to model helping, but we don't want to teach, in effect, that there is no need to come to the aid of a peer because an adult will take care of everything.

Explaining. "Show and tell" is more than an elementary school activity. The two concepts, modeling and explaining, are natural counterparts. To leave out the former is to ignore a bit of common-sense wisdom that is supported by research: actions really do speak louder than words. To leave out the latter is to deprive children of a chance to think and talk about the importance of what they have seen so as to more fully incorporate it into their repertoires.

I have argued that solving problems requires us to talk with children, to offer explanations and interpretations. But this is not just a strategy for dealing with trouble; it is part of how, day by day, a child comes to be a moral person. Researchers have found that people whose parents tended to reason with them when they were children, rather than punish them or otherwise demand simple obedience, were more likely to act altruistically (in one study) and to become involved in social service activities and political activism (in another).[17] The use of induction in place of power-based tactics by middle-class mothers was found in other research to be "consistently associated with advanced moral development" on the part of their children.[18] One experiment even suggested that explanations can reduce aggression.[19]

Of course, beyond a commitment to talking with children, what we choose to explain, and how we do so, are terribly important. Explanations should not be limited to pointing out the effects of negative behaviors: just as children should be helped to understand why hitting is bad, so they must be encouraged to think about why helping is good, beyond being told that it is. Moreover, the reason offered should not simply invoke self-interest but call their attention to how other people feel when they are helped.[20]

Sometimes we will want to discuss with children what it means to act responsibly and compassionately — not lecture to them so their eyes glaze over but explore together how one might deal with difficult situations. What can we do when we see a homeless person in the street, for example, or a big kid picking on a small kid, or someone we know in tears? How do we act around a friend whose grandmother has just died? What do we do when someone tries to help *us* and we don't want the help? If adults often seem clueless in such circumstances, this may reflect how little opportunity they have had to talk over these issues.

Attributing positive motives. It is worth attending not only to what we say and do but to what we believe — about "human nature," about children, about this particular child, and about why this particular child did what he did this afternoon. Assuming the worst in each case can become a self-fulfilling prophecy. Consider the view that morality basically has to be forced down the throats of unwilling children, that socialization amounts to taming wild impulses, that selfishness and aggression are more natural than cooperation and caring. Parents who take this position are likely to be authoritarian in the way they deal with their children,[21] and so too, we can assume, are teachers. Controlling, punitive tactics, in turn, produce exactly the sort of antisocial behavior that is expected, confirming the view that such tactics are needed.

Conversely, the belief that children are actually quite anxious to please adults, that they may simply lack the skills to get what they need, that they will generally respond positively to a caring environment — this can create a very different reality. And so it is for our assumptions about specific children and why they do what they do.

Attributing to a child the best possible motive that is consistent with the facts[22] may set in motion another of those "auspicious" circles. We help children develop good values by assuming whenever possible that they are already motivated by these values, rather than by explaining an ambiguous action in terms of a sinister desire to make our lives miserable.

Offering opportunities to care. People learn by doing, and adults who want children to learn about caring will provide an array of opportunities for them to experience the practice firsthand: caring for pets, looking out for younger siblings, tutoring other children, working with classmates to make decisions and solve problems, and so on.[23] The story may be apocryphal, but it is said that the coats worn by Chinese children some years ago buttoned up the back so as to require each child to turn to another for help in getting dressed. This is just the sort of opportunity we should be providing for children to balance our otherwise relentless campaign to make them self-sufficient. Independence is useful, but caring attitudes and behaviors shrivel up in a culture where each person is responsible only for himself.

Collaboration, previously framed as something that happens between an adult and a child, must take place on a regular basis among children too, particularly at school. Learning and playing should routinely be set up so as to promote cooperation and interdependence. For example, elementary school activities in which children write or draw something about themselves can be modified so that each child writes about or draws someone else's experiences and ideas. Similarly, each student (of any age) ought to have a permanent partner who is responsible for making sure she has the assignments in case of absence. If we are serious about raising children to be caring people, we must move away from environments that require them to defeat each other in order to be successful — or at best, to ignore each other — and establish structures where they come to take responsibility for one another instead.[24]

Emphasizing perspective taking. All of us want children to grow up to be helpful and caring. But I think we want even more than that. First, we want them not merely to do good things in order to obtain rewards or avoid punishments (even of the psychological variety), but because they see themselves as helpful, caring people. It is acceptable, even desirable, to take pleasure from helping and to feel distressed by other people's pain, but we hope that our children sometimes will reach out to others just because those others need the help, without

244 / BEYOND REWARDS

any thought of personal gain. (This is a reasonable definition of altruism, and it defines some, but not all, prosocial acts.)

Second, we want children's actions to come from the head as well as from the heart; they should develop both a rational understanding of ethical principles and an emotional connection to other people. Many programs of moral development emphasize one of these to the exclusion of the other.

Finally, we want children to develop what Ervin Staub has called a "prosocial orientation"[25] — a generalized inclination to care, share, and help across different situations and with different people, including those they don't know, don't like, and don't look like. Lending a hand to a close friend is one thing; going out of one's way for a stranger is something else.

All three of these goals can be met by promoting the practice of trying to imagine the way other people think, feel, and look at the world. This is what psychologists call "perspective taking." It is first cousin to the practice of feeling our way into someone else's emotional life, which is called "empathy." When children are encouraged and helped to engage in these practices, they are well on the way to becoming caring people.[26]

The failure to adopt other people's points of view, to take an imaginative leap out of oneself, is one way to account for much of the behavior we find troublesome, from littering to murder. (Kafka once referred to war as "a monstrous failure of imagination.") Perspective taking helps us at once to see others as fundamentally similar to ourselves despite superficial differences (in that we share a common humanity) and as importantly different from ourselves despite apparent similarities. Children first come to see that they mustn't treat people in a way they themselves wouldn't want to be treated. But then, we hope, they become even more sophisticated and realize that George Bernard Shaw was right when he cautioned us not to "do unto others as you would have them do unto you [because] they may have different tastes" — to say nothing of different needs, backgrounds, and worldviews.

In short, perspective taking is a focal point for raising or teaching children to be ethical and compassionate. While empathy is probably a natural capacity for almost all of us,[27] perspective taking needs to be, and can be, taught. For example, we can:

• *Model it:* We set a powerful example if, after encountering someone rude, we say to a child something like, "Boy, I guess that man must have had a pretty bad day to yell at us like that, huh?" If we react to unpleasantness by trying to understand, we show children that there are alternatives to anger. More to the point, we get them accustomed to trying to look at a situation from someone else's point of view — and trying to figure out where that point of view came from.

• *Use it to solve problems:* Teachers who find that two students are perpetually criticizing or fighting with each other might sit them down together and ask each to interview the other, to learn as much as possible about that person's interests and beliefs and background. Such information helps turn someone from an object into a subject, to make the person's humanity come alive. That, in turn, makes it nearly impossible to act cruelly toward him or her.

• *Use the arts:* The stories assigned by a teacher or suggested by a parent can be chosen specifically for their emphasis on different (and sometimes conflicting) points of view. Perspective taking, moreover, can provide a way of exploring virtually any book or movie: children can be asked to describe events as they might appear to another character, rewrite an episode to highlight another point of view, engage in role-playing, or otherwise imagine things from a different direction.

• *Teach it directly:* Various activities have been designed to help children notice and attend to others' feelings and points of view,[28] and more exercises of this kind can be devised for that purpose by teachers and parents.

The Role of the Schools

A growing number of observers, in surveying the moral state of our society, are concluding that professional educators have a role to play alongside parents in contributing to children's moral, social, and behavioral development. To some extent this is because many children simply are not exposed to positive values at home, and it falls to the schools to take up the burden. To some extent it is because educators already play a role in teaching values whether they mean to or not: every element of classroom life is unavoidably saturated in values. One way or another, a teacher's responsibility (and opportunity) is to help children become not only good learners but good people.[29]

The process of doing so cannot be reduced to simply teaching a set of social skills to each student. It is not a matter of what the teacher does for (or, better, with) this child and that one but rather how a caring classroom and school community can be created to serve as the context in which children acquire positive attitudes and skills. Prosocial values are learned in a community, and part of what is learned is the value *of* community.

My own thinking on this question has been shaped by one particular educational program that was designed in the early 1980s to help elementary school–age children become more caring and responsible. The staff of the Child Development Project (CDP), based in Oakland, California, has designed (and continues to refine) a program to this end and has rigorously monitored its impact. Its premise, which I share, is that if children are to internalize prosocial values, they must be helped to become part of a caring community, which the CDP defines as

> a community where care and trust are emphasized above restrictions and threats, where unity and pride (of accomplishment and in purpose) replace winning and losing, and where each person is asked, helped, and inspired to live up to such ideals and values as kindness, fairness, and responsibility. [Such] a classroom community seeks to meet each student's need to feel competent, connected to others, and autonomous. . . . Students are not only exposed to basic human values, they also have many opportunities to think about, discuss, and act on those values, while gaining experiences that promote empathy and understanding of others.[30]

To call this a tall order understates the case. But it is one that can be filled partly by doing what I have already described: caring, modeling, explaining, and so on. The CDP, along with other researchers and educators, has added to these gerunds a number of programmatic components that really do seem to work. Among them are a version of cooperative learning uncontaminated by grades or other extrinsic motivators, an approach to disciplinary matters very much like what I have been calling mutual problem solving, and also the following:

• **Class meetings.** Students of any age need to have time set aside to sit down together and make decisions, share news, review what has happened during the preceding day (or week or year), plan events, and solve problems. The process of doing so can take time and patience, but the process is the point — an idea difficult for some efficiency-minded teachers and students to grasp. From such sessions, facilitated by a teacher who must decide at each moment whether to sit back or step in, students come to believe their decisions matter. They feel as if they belong to a community, and they come to know what it takes to make a community function. They develop a commitment to the values they have helped to define. And they learn the skills of listening, taking other people's perspectives, thinking through a problem, and resolving conflicts.[31] Few contrasts are as striking as that between students participating in such meetings, taking responsibility for deciding how they want their classroom to be, and students sitting in rows, being bribed or threatened to conform to the teacher's rules.

• **Unity-building activities.** The idea here is to learn about each other as individuals and slowly come to feel part of an "us." The class may decide on a class name or logo; they may work together on a class play, mural, quilt, song, newspaper, or book. They may publish a class directory, post their photos on the bulletin board, and work together on service projects or other activities around the school and outside of school.

• **Schoolwide programs.** Two classes representing different age levels can be paired in order to extend the ideas of unity and community and provide for regular cross-age interaction, something conspicuously absent from most American schools. When an older child looks out for and works with a younger "buddy," the one has an opportunity to learn caring by practicing it, and the other feels cared about and has caring modeled by, of all things, someone who isn't even a grownup. Other activities can involve the whole school, including something like a town meeting. Alternatively, cross sections of the school, with a few children from each grade level and staff members (including custodians and secretaries) may meet together on a regular basis.

• **Prosocial literature.** Here is a splendid example of feeding two birds from one feeder: the stories from which children learn language skills from spelling to symbolism can be chosen not only for their usefulness in this respect but also for the way they illustrate important values (such as kindness, fairness, tolerance, and so forth), elicit empathy, and generate discussion about issues relevant to children's own real-life concerns. The key point here is that, as with modeling, the stories teachers choose are *always* teaching values even if they are not used for that purpose and even if the lesson may not be noticed by teacher or student. (Children may be learning, for example, that males solve problems while females look on, that violence is effective, or that people usually do important things on their own rather than collaboratively.)

Each of these school-based programs has a role to play in helping children develop positive values, just as each of the approaches described in the preceding section offers something that parents and teachers alike can use in support of the same goal. But there is one issue, one way of framing the alternative to rewards and punishments, that must take precedence. That issue, choice, was raised briefly in the context of dealing with behavioral problems. We return to it now to explore its essential contribution to children's long-term development.

The Chance to Choose

Many different fields of research have converged on the finding that it is desirable for people to experience a sense of control over their lives. In the last two chapters I tried to show that this is a key variable in predicting people's interest in, and success at, work and school. But the benefits reach into every corner of human existence, starting with our physical health and survival.

"The most significant factor in an individual's ability to remain in good health may be a sense of control over the events of life," one psychologist has remarked.[32] Indeed, research has found that people who rarely become ill despite having to deal with considerable stress tend to be those who feel more control over what happens to them.[33] In a well-known experiment, nursing home residents who were able to make decisions about their environment not only became happier and more active but were also more likely to be alive a year and a half later than were other residents.[34] And when patients who require medication for pain (either just after surgery or on an ongoing basis) are able to choose when to administer it themselves, they typically need smaller doses, experience fewer side effects, report being less anxious, and (in the case of postsurgical patients) may even recover more quickly than those who are given the medication by someone else.[35]

The psychological benefits of control are, if anything, even more pronounced. Our emotional adjustment is better over time if we experience a sense of self-determination; by contrast, few things lead more reliably to depression and other forms of psychological distress than a feeling of helplessness.[36] Whereas rewards are notably ineffective at maintaining behavior change (see chapter 3), we are likely to persist at doing constructive things, such as exercising, quitting smoking, or fighting cavities, when we have some choice about the specifics of such programs.[37] Laboratory experiments have also shown that we are better able to tolerate unpleasant sensations like noise, cold, or electric shock when we know we have the power to end them.[38]

Children are no exception to these rules, the studies show. Year-old infants had fun with a noisy mechanical toy when they could make it start; it was less interesting, and sometimes even frightening, if they had no control over its action.[39] Elementary school students had higher self-esteem and a greater feeling of academic competence when their teachers bolstered their sense of self-determination in the classroom.[40]

More relevant to our concerns here is the importance of autonomy in fostering children's social and moral growth. One is repeatedly struck by the absurd spectacle of adults who talk passionately about the need for kids to become "self-disciplined" and to "take responsibility for their own behavior" — all the while ordering children around. The truth is that if we want children to take responsibility for their own behavior, we must first give them responsibility, and plenty of it. The way a child learns how to make decisions is by making decisions, not by following directions. As Kamii has written,

> We cannot expect children to accept ready-made values and truths all the way through school, and then suddenly make choices in adulthood. Likewise, we cannot expect them to be manipulated with reward and punishment in school, and to have the courage of a Martin Luther King in adulthood.[41]

In fact, an emphasis on following directions, respecting authority (regardless of whether that respect has been earned), and obeying the rules (regardless of whether they are reasonable) teaches a disturbing lesson. Stanley Milgram's famous experiment, in which ordinary people gave what they thought were terribly painful shocks to hapless strangers merely because they were told to do so, is not just a comment about "society." It is a cautionary tale about certain ways of bringing up children. The point is that an emphasis on obedience "is not only not enough; it may be dangerous."[42]

Morality and courage are not the only values at issue here. To talk about the importance of choice is also to talk about democracy. At present, as Shelley Berman, a former president of Educators for Social Responsibility, has drily noted, "We teach reading, writing, and math by [having students do] them, but we teach democracy by lecture."[43] At best, we have children vote for one proposal, or student council candidate, over another. William Glasser has said, "Children who attend a school in which they are asked to take some responsibility for the curriculum and rules discover democracy."[44] That concept in its fullest sense goes well beyond (and ideally may even exclude) voting:[45] it involves talking and listening, looking for alternatives and trying to reach consensus, solving problems together and making meaningful choices. It is a vital lesson for children if we hope to prepare them to participate in a democratic culture — or to work toward transforming a culture *into* a democracy.

Degrees of Freedom

In light of the importance of choice, it may be useful to return once more to the question of what our objectives really are as parents or teachers. To this point I have distinguished only between short-term compliance and long-term promotion of values. When we look more closely, though, we find a somewhat more complicated array of alternatives.

The first, and least ambitious, goal is to get children to do what they are told. Even here, letting children make some decisions increases the likelihood of compliance with a request: a two-year-old is more likely to sit down for lunch if she gets to choose which cereal to eat and the bowl out of which she will eat it. (Of course, rewards and punishments too can get children to comply for the time being.)

Beyond compliance is the desire to induce children to keep following our rules even when there is no immediate reward to be obtained or punishment to be avoided — that is, to get them to "internalize" these rules. Here it is even more important to provide children with opportunities to make decisions. After all, if explaining the reason for a rule increases the probability that a child will follow it, inviting him to help devise the rule and figure out how to implement it is likely to be even more effective. Now he feels some commitment to the rule. (This is why the most important question to ask teachers whose classroom wall features a list of rules for behavior is, Who made them up? The teacher alone or the class as a whole?)

Many people who write about child development and education stop at this point, contenting themselves with the observation that it is better for children to internalize a rule than to obey only in the face of external control. But Ryan and Deci have made what I think is a critically important distinction between two versions of internalization. In one, which they call "introjection" (borrowing from psychoanalytic theory), children swallow the rule whole. It is inside them but essentially unprocessed. Unhappily, it is possible to feel controlled from the inside as well as from the outside; people sometimes "pressure themselves in much the same way that they can be pressured by external events."[46]

Internalization by itself — even the kind identified as introjection — satisfies someone whose chief concern is to get a child to do something without the adult's having to stand around prodding him with bribes and threats. Like a wind-up toy, a child who has introjected a particular value will stay in motion after the controller has left the scene. No wonder those who direct and profit from a particular economic system prefer "a self-controlled — not just controlled — work force."[47] And no wonder the concept of internalization, so far from representing a clear alternative to behaviorism, is implicitly embraced by Skinner:

> Let the individual be free to adjust himself to more rewarding features of the world about him. In the end, let his teachers and counselors "wither away," like the Marxist state. I not only agree with this as a useful ideal, I have constructed [in *Walden Two*] a fanciful world to demonstrate its advantages.[48]

Ryan and Deci argue persuasively that we should aim higher than this. To say we want children to internalize a value is not enough because frequently that process takes the form of introjection. The alternative they propose, integration, involves helping a child make the value her own, understand its rationale, and experience a sense of self-determination in acting in accordance with it. The objective here is a deeper experience of choice, one understood not just as a selection of Option A over Option B but as something "anchored in the sense of a fuller, more integrated functioning."[49] Adults can help children reach this goal by supporting their autonomy, giving them chances to solve their own problems (both alone and with their peers), inviting them to participate in making meaningful decisions, and engaging them in discussion about all of the above.[50]

Even integration, however, is not the last word on the subject. Ultimately, I think, we want children not only to be deeply committed to our values and rules but to be capable of making their own decisions about which values and rules to embrace. Here too the best preparation for making decisions is practice at making decisions. But we adults will also have to think in terms of helping children acquire the social, ethical, and cognitive skills necessary for reflection about which ends are worth pursuing and how best to pursue them.[51] Moreover, we will have to trust children at some point, resisting the temptation to judge our efforts on the basis of how closely the values children choose correspond to our own. This, of course, is a far cry from trying to implant a piece of ourselves in a child so he or she "voluntarily" makes all the same decisions we would make.

Autonomy is not simply one value among many that children should acquire, nor is it simply one technique for helping them grow into good people. In the final analysis, none of the virtues, including generosity and caring, can be successfully promoted in the absence of choice. A jarring reminder of that fact was provided by the following declaration made by a man whose name is (or should be) familiar to most of us: he recalled being "taught that my highest duty was to help those in need" but added that he learned this lesson in the context of the importance of "obey[ing] promptly the wishes and commands of my parents, teachers, and priests, and indeed of all adults. . . . Whatever they said was always right."

The man who said this was Rudolf Höss, the infamous commandant of Auschwitz.[52] Prosocial values are important, but if the environment in which they are taught emphasizes obedience rather than autonomy, all may be lost.

Barriers to Choice

If we are serious about the value of self-determination, then a number of issues have to be reframed in light of this commitment. For example, it is a truism that children need and secretly want limits, that we are actually doing them a service by imposing restrictions regardless of how they may complain about them. While it is true that rules and structures have their place, "the critical question," as Thomas Gordon has remarked, "is not *whether* limits and rules are needed in families and schools, but rather *who* sets them: the adults alone or the adults and kids — together?"[53] For the parent or teacher to unilaterally devise structures and impose them on a child becomes progressively more objectionable the older the child is.

Consider another example: some people insist that two parents must always present a united front by taking the same position in front of a child. True, two wildly different approaches to parenting in the same family will lead to problems, but there is something rigid and inauthentic about trying to deny that Mom and Dad don't always see things the same way. More to the point, if the child is deprived of any opportunity to decide what happens to her, the parents' unity amounts to an alliance of them against her.[54] Again, choice is the decisive issue.

"A child must have a voice in determining what goes into his stomach, what he wears, what he does with his free time and what he is answerable for in his class," writes Nancy Samalin, an adviser on parenting issues.[55] But how much of a voice? At what age, and on what issues, should children be deciding things for themselves (or in concert with an adult)? The answer is that no precise formula can be specified in advance. Struggling to figure out the right balance day by day is a major part of a parent's job description.

Adults need to check a child's capacity to make decisions, to make sure he has the requisite skills. But they also must be prepared for problematic responses from children who are not used to exercising choice. These responses are most common when a teacher provides the opportunity to make decisions to students who are accustomed to being controlled. First, children may simply resist, indignantly contending that questions about curriculum and rules are not their responsibility. This attempt to "escape from freedom," as Erich Fromm has put it, offers the teacher an invitation to talk about whose classroom it is, what it feels like to be ordered around, and some of the other themes discussed in this chapter.

Second, children may be skeptical about the offer and test the adult by making obviously inappropriate suggestions to see if she reasserts her authority and confirms their suspicions that the offer wasn't made in good faith. While there may be some proposals that simply cannot be put into effect, the teacher will often have to go along with decisions he knows aren't sensible, suggesting that the class try them out for a while and then reconvene to assess whether they seem to be working.

Third, children may say what they assume the adult wants to hear (or what they have heard other adults say). For example, asked to propose some guidelines for class behavior, a third grader may recite, "We should keep our hands to ourselves." This can happen because children are anxious to please us, or because they don't fully trust that the teacher wants to hear what they have to say, or because no one has helped them to think through the decision-making process.[56] It is tempting for the teacher to accept the child's offering gratefully, figuring that she has let children choose *and* gotten the rule she wants — the best of both worlds. Unfortunately, an echo is not a choice. She needs to stop the process at this point and talk with the children about the difference between "saying what you think somebody wants to hear" and "saying something even when you're not sure how somebody is going to react," emphasizing that the latter is what she is looking for here.

Some of these same responses may turn up at home, too, particularly if a parent switches from an autocratic to a more democratic style.* But children's resistance is not the only problem that adults need to consider. Even more fundamental is the question of their own capacity to relinquish control. Some may be unprepared for the transformation of the adult/child relationship that is entailed by letting the child make choices, and they may react by snatching away the decision-making power just given to the child on the grounds that he or she has failed to make the "right" decision (that is, the one they prefer). This not only fails to support children's autonomy but can also generate considerable resentment.

Other adults, meanwhile, grant to children the right to make choices that are severely constrained or even illusory from the beginning. I have heard a number of parents and teachers proudly announce their willingness to turn over to children the opportunity to decide things where the adult doesn't much care what the outcome is. This, of course, leaves the adult comfortably in control and constitutes only the first step in promoting autonomy. Far more meaningful is the willingness to let children make decisions about the things that matter, where we *do* care what they come up with but are willing to give up power anyway. As one educator says, "Much of the control we exercise as teachers" — and, we might add, as parents — "belongs properly to the children and it is fear that keeps us from giving it to them."[58]

Finally, and most insidiously, there is the practice of letting children *think* they are making a decision when they have no real power to do so. (This tactic has already been discussed in the context of manipulation by employers to create a purely subjective sense of control among workers; see page 195.) I recently heard a well-known national advocate for children and education reminisce about her experiences as a teacher. Recalling a student who constantly and articulately challenged her authority, she commented with a smile, "I had to be a better negotiator than she was." This remark suggests that what had taken place was not negotiation at all but manipulation. After all, an adult has to be on her toes to be clever enough to disguise what is really going on.

Some parents take pride in letting their children think they are making a decision when the game is actually rigged. The "engineering of consent," as it has been called, seems to offer autonomy while providing "the assurance of order and conformity — a most seductive

---

*Happily, there is some reason to think that, over the years, more parents in our culture have come to value autonomy as opposed to obedience[57] and therefore may be less likely to use an autocratic style of parenting.

combination. Yet its appearance and its means should be understood for what they really are: a method of securing and solidifying the interests of those in power."[59] This description by educator James Beane might have been inspired by the behavior of politicians, but it is no less applicable to the province of parents. If we want children to learn how to choose, they must have the opportunity to make real choices.

Freedom from Rewards

Not long ago, a high school Spanish teacher in Wisconsin told me a story about a problem that developed in one of her classes. In an effort to promote social skills as well as academic excellence, she had paired up her students for the term so they could help each other learn. One girl who had an impressive facility with the language begged to be reassigned to someone else since her partner was having trouble keeping up. The teacher denied the girl's request but eventually decided to do something more drastic: she stopped giving grades to her students.

At the end of the term, when it was time to switch partners, the high-achieving girl surprised the teacher by asking if she could continue to work with the same student. Freed from the pressure of grades, she had come to enjoy helping him and watching his progress. Her inclination to care was no longer smothered by the presence of extrinsic motivators; these had led her to look on her peers mostly in terms of how they would affect her chances of getting an A.

The moral of this story, I think, is that if we want children to act in a caring fashion — or for that matter, to become part of a community, to learn to take responsibility and make choices — we are obliged to set up the structures that will facilitate movement in this direction and also to remove the barriers. Rewards and punishments actively interfere with what we are trying to do at home and at school. They defeat our best efforts to promote positive values, and they undermine the strategies described throughout this chapter (and the two preceding chapters).

The most compelling case for abandoning extrinsic control is made every day by parents and teachers who have done so. They (and their children) are living proof that it is not only realistic to stop bribing children to behave but infinitely preferable. For example, teachers who have moved toward creating a caring community in the classroom, a place where children work together to make decisions, sometimes say they would quit rather than go back to a program of behavior modification and rule enforcement.

I realize that people who use rewards as a matter of course may find the evidence reviewed in this book deeply disturbing. In fact, I hope they do. "Does this mean I'm a bad teacher (or parent)?" is a question that may reasonably cross the mind of anyone who has relied faithfully on behavioristic assumptions and practices. My answer is that anyone willing to challenge him- or herself with that concern thereby demonstrates exactly the courage and flexibility that children need to be around. (It is tempting to respond instead, "I don't care what your studies say: rewards work, and that's that.") The capacity to call into question one's long-standing ways of thinking and acting, to reconsider an approach so ingrained as to be second nature, belongs at the top of any list of what makes a good parent or teacher. And Skinnerian dogma belongs at the top of any list of what needs careful reexamination. The bad news is that we have paid an enormous price for having accepted it for so long. The good news is that we can do better.

APPENDIXES

NOTES

REFERENCES

INDEX

Appendix A

A CONVERSATION WITH B. F. SKINNER

Long before he became this country's most influential psychologist, Burrhus Frederic Skinner (1904–90) decided to become a writer. He graduated from Hamilton College with a degree in English and spent a miserable year with his parents, trying to figure out what to do with his life and struggling with what other people would call an identity crisis.

Then he found behaviorism. "I did not consider actual suicide," he later wrote in his autobiography. "Behaviorism offered me another way out: it was not I but my history that had failed. . . . I have learned to accept my mistakes by referring them to a personal history which was not of my making and could not be changed."[1]

He had found himself by abandoning his self. A doctorate from Harvard followed, academic appointments in Minnesota and Indiana, and a triumphant return to Cambridge in 1948. When I met him in 1983, he was still there, living in the fashionable part of the city, socializing now and then with the likes of Julia Child, and getting a ride from his wife each morning to his office on the seventh floor of Harvard's William James Hall. Just across the corridor were walls of circuitry boards, clicking and flashing their red lights, connected by wires to closed, numbered boxes with tiny peepholes. Inside of each was a pigeon, pecking away in order to be fed.

"I've lived long enough to pick up some reputation," he told me modestly. "Eighty years will do it." He talked with an air of amused detachment about drawing crowds wherever he went, about being approached on the street for autographs. "I'm always surprised that people recognize me or come to hear me talk," he said. "I don't know why I should be; I've been getting surprising audiences for nearly thirty years. But I don't get any bang out of it at all. I get much more pleasure out of a good two hours at my desk in the morning."

Once, he said, a man came up to him on the street and asked whether he was a preacher. This gave him a good laugh since he didn't believe in God. But the man on the street wasn't altogether wrong. In a sense, Skinner *was* a preacher, a proselytizer by temperament, his writings an extended sermon about the folly of "mentalism" — that is, the assumption that what we do can be explained by appealing to anything other than observable behaviors and the environmental contingencies that reinforce them.

In his autobiography, every one of his critics is taken to task for failing to grasp his ideas. "Behaviorism is very badly misunderstood everywhere," he complained to me. "*I'm* very badly misunderstood." To him, I began to realize, a criticism implied a misreading since it was impossible both to understand his theory and reject it.

Despite his conviction and his fame, I, like others who met him over the years, found Skinner disarmingly gracious. In my case, he agreed to come speak to my class even though he didn't know me and, the following year, to put up with several hours of cross-examination that went well beyond what I needed to write a profile of him for a magazine. Each question he answered courteously, and yet as if from a great distance. I sensed that he was no less reserved with people he knew better.

The one real insight about Skinner that came to me after talking with him for a while was that he was less a theorist than a technician. The man was fascinated — indeed, almost obsessed — with practical problems of design. He talked about the challenge of designing a more efficient hearing aid. Years before, he had taken considerable pleasure in inventing a more comfortable, enclosed bassinet for his infant daughters (which gave rise to a cruel rumor that he was confining them in "Skinner boxes" of the sort used for lab animals). He devoted himself to the design of "teaching machines" for children that foreshadowed today's educational computer programs. (His pride in this — "I was thirty years ahead of my time" — is matched by bitterness that most educators weren't interested in his idea.) He collected practical suggestions for how to make one's last years a little easier, eventually coauthoring a self-help book for senior citizens. Even the question of when to get up in the morning was an engineering problem: by rising at 4:00 A.M. he could not only get in a few hours of work before the phone started ringing but could travel to England (where one of his daughters lives) and adjust to a standard business schedule without suffering jet lag.

Everything, as Skinner saw it, was a problem to be solved, and his most famous and infamous pronouncements can be understood in that context. "Designing a culture is like designing an experiment," he once wrote. In recalling how, during World War II, he trained pigeons to steer missiles (leading again to bitter disappointment when his proposal did not excite enough interest), he became ingenuously enthusiastic: "What a fascinating thing! Total control of a living organism!"

It may, therefore, be something other than modesty that led him to muse, "I don't think I'm a classical picture of a great thinker, or anything of that sort. I don't believe that I have a very high IQ. I think I've done very well with what I've got. There are skills I just don't have. Fortunately I got into a field where I could use the ones I do have — largely practical skills."

I asked him later about death and he shrugged, claiming he didn't dwell on the topic. "I never think much about dying. I have no fear of death. My family is well taken care of. The only thing I fear is not finishing my work. There are things I still want to say." In fact, he continued, working up an enthusiasm for the topic, "I don't know *why* people fear death. Of course religious people do because they're not at all sure whether they're going to go to hell or not, but there are those who don't believe in that who still can't face annihilation."

The belief that there is no self, which served him so well as a young man, also helped him in his last years to deal with the prospect of ceasing to be. "I can now take all of my faults and all of my achievements and turn them over to my history, and the point I make is that when I die personally, it won't make a bit of difference. Because there's nothing here, you see, that matters. [With this view] you don't fear death at all."

Excerpts from Our Conversations:

[**On behavior therapy's rejection of behaviorism**]:   I think it's quite wrong, but it's inevitable. People who are face to face with patients, clients, across the table, they're not going to work on external, controllable variables. They're going to ask people, "How do you feel?" and they're going to take that as evidence of what probably happened, but they're not going to find out what happened. And they're going to say, "What do you plan to do?" — they're not going to take careful measurements of potentialities of behavior.

Q. Well, why? What does that say about the theory?

A. Too much trouble! They make money by the number of people they see, and you can't expect anyone facing a client to do more than use behavioral principles to interpret what is happening. It's very easy just to go back on what's been in the genius of the language for thousands of years — the whole notion that people do things because of their attitudes and feelings, their thoughts. I want to find out where all those came from, but you don't need to bother if you're just consulting with someone. . . . I think the cognitive psychologist is a Johnny-come-lately. The cognitive people have never been practical. And psychoanalysis, while it is a practice, isn't practical. I can't imagine psychoanalysis really dealing with serious illnesses in the world today.

Q. And yet you're surrounded by pigeons in this office, while the cognitivists and the psychoanalysts are seeing real people. They're on the front lines, so to speak. If *they* find it impractical or unwieldy or not useful to employ your language and your model, might that not indicate something about the deficiency of the model?

A. No, no, not at all. If I were talking to a group of children about astronomy and the night sky and so on, I wouldn't really go into the Big Bang and millions of light-years and whatnot. I'd talk about the Big Bear and the Big Dipper.

Q. So talking with children is analogous to having therapy with clients?

A. Yes. Well, you can't use technical terms with the ordinary client. You can't teach him behaviorism in order to talk to him that way. What you can do, and what I think a good behavior therapist does, is to spot the nature of the problem and deal with it indirectly. A very good example of that, I think, is what Dr. Vaughan and I did in our book *Enjoy Old Age*, where the word *behavior* doesn't occur in that text. Nor does *reinforcement* or *discriminative stimulus*. We didn't use any technical terms at all because we're not writing for people who know anything about the science of behavior. At the end, just to reassure our colleagues, we have a little glossary explaining what we mean when we say "what you like to do and enjoy doing." You could do that with a book on astronomy. You could say "the sun rises" — and then, in a footnote: "Well, actually, it doesn't; the world turns."

Q. I wonder, though, if the fact that when we have a conversation about human beings we find ourselves calling on those concepts might not suggest that these are very real kinds of things.

A. I don't think it suggests they're real. I think it suggests that they are the immediate things. [*He reads from* A Matter of Consequences, *pages 191–92, where he has translated La Rochefoucauld's* Maxims *into the language of behaviorism.*]

Q. And you're satisfied that your translation misses nothing of the original — it only makes it more precise.

A. Yes, it isn't reducing it to anything, either, you see. . . . If you are a completely nonverbal organism, and if people with whom you associate simply dealt with you nonverbally — that is, fight you or make love with you — they wouldn't ask you "What are you doing?" You would never have any of these concepts. You would never look at yourself and say, "Am I happy?" You never would look at yourself and say, "What do I intend to do?" . . . You would be just like any nonverbal organism, and that's the stuff that the cognitive people don't even touch. They're talking about what happens when a verbal environment arises and induces individuals to report about themselves. [In a community] someone wants to know [whether] you see that. Well, they say, "Do you see that?" Up till that point, you've seen it — you'd reach for it if you wanted it, and so on. But now something else happens. You *see* that you're seeing it. But you wouldn't without that question. . . .

Q. Do you still hold to [your original] account of love?

A. We are disposed to do nice things to some people and harmful things to others. Love and hate are extreme cases of that. . . . In mutual interaction, two people who meet, one of them is nice to the other and that predisposes the other to be nice to him, and that makes him even more likely to be nice. It goes back and forth, and it may reach the point at which they are very highly disposed to do nice things to the other and not to hurt. And I suppose that is what would be called "being in love."

Q. If I introspect and, on the basis of my life, find that love and freedom are concepts whose depths aren't touched by a behavioristic analysis, aren't you in fact asking me to accept on faith the adequacy or the superiority of your model? Isn't it a faith that's even grander than the faith in which I'm asked to believe that there's a God?

A. Oh, I don't think there's any faith involved here. It's either useful or it isn't useful. I don't think physics is asking you to take on faith [its] interpretation of high-energy physics and so on. . . . It's as good as we can do at the moment.

Q. Yes, but it has to do with me, today; it doesn't have to do with subatomic particles or nebulae out there. You're saying, "Your sense of yourself is imprecise if not downright incorrect. Believe my model instead." Why isn't that precisely analogous to "You think that you're deciding what to do, but in fact God has predetermined your actions"? Both violate my experience.

A. I don't think I say quite that. I would say I believe we have discovered relations between what a person does and the natural selection of the species and the history of the individual and the resulting effect of the current setting. If you understand that, you can very often solve problems — personal problems of your own, designing conditions that will solve problems of other people, instruction or therapy or incentive systems or penology, and so on. And it's based upon rather rigorous research, of which there is nothing comparable in, let us say, Freud or someone like William James. They had very plausible accounts, of course. It's lots of fun to use a Freudian system to interpret everybody. . . . It's much easier to use Freud or James because it came out of daily life and you can put it back in quite easily, whereas the other came out of laboratory research and it isn't easy to see it in an instance in daily life. But it is there if you look for it. And it is exactly like the way in which a skilled craftsman deals with — let us say, a tinsmith — the way in which he bends metal and applies solder and shapes things and so on. He has a very good science of working with metal, but it has nothing to do, practically, with actual metallurgy and with what a real engineer would do. It's easier for him and it would be a great mistake to try to get him to look at the atomic structure of metals and why some of them fuse better than others and so on.

Q. But the person who examines the chemistry of a metal, for example, doesn't deny, as you do, the other reality. He doesn't attempt to say that it's based on a misconception —

A. It isn't the reality he denies. He doesn't deny the other way of talking about the same reality. I don't object to novels written in everyday lay psychology. Of course! I tried my hand at translating a few passages from George Eliot. You can't do it. For example, "feelings" — it's a shorthand way of talking about histories. With my friends I will talk about my "ideas," my "feelings," my "plans" and "intentions" and whatnot. Young behaviorists are often embarrassed when they use these words. I was too, at one time, but I wouldn't be now. Nor do I object, really, to a social worker or a therapist using that in dealing with clients. I think it's probably the best way to do it. . . .

Q. What if one were to argue that all of science can only go so far in providing a plausible account of the reality that I face as a human being?

A. Oh, I accept that.

Q. The limits of science?

A. Yes. [*Pause.*] The current limits — they change in time.

Q. No, I mean that science, some have argued, has a kind of arrogance about it. What it can't explain now, it will be able to explain eventually.

A. The history of science simply indicates that, doesn't it? Not that I don't think for a moment that astronomy will ever do a complete account of the universe. But they certainly make progress.

Q. But certain human realities, it's argued, are not analogous with metal or even pigeons. And to that extent, humans are qualitatively different from other things that the physical sciences —

A. Again, people differ because they belong to verbal communities which give them reasons for looking at themselves. And they're looking at their bodies in a way that pigeons never do. And it proves to be very useful to others and themselves. I don't deny that. It also leads to science, mathematics, and so on.

Q. But humans, except for that verbal ability and what flows from that, and except for greater complexity, are quantitatively rather than qualitatively different from lower organisms?

A. I think that the human being is nothing more than a member of an evolved species.

Q. But I'm not asking about the evolution, the past. I mean, one can claim that we are evolved rather than created out of nothing and still believe that the current state of human beings is different in kind from the current state of lower organisms.

A. Whether it's kind or quantity I don't know, but I would say that people do things that animals do not do. And it comes about because of the emergence of the operant control of the vocal musculature, which made verbal behavior possible — or made it much more likely. . . .

Q. One of the things that you find fault with in conventional views of human beings is the idea that we actually choose our behavior. . . . [But] when you write a book and attempt to argue a position, it seems like a pointless gesture because you were simply determined to have written it, I was determined to have read it; whether I find it plausible or not also is determined. Now doesn't that run against the idea of writing and reading a book or attempting to persuade me of something? Aren't you implicitly appealing to me to believe you, to choose to believe you?

A. No. No. I've said many times that my rats and pigeons have taught me more than I've taught them. The behavior of the scientist is shaped by his subject matter, and it is a continuing evolutionary

266 / APPENDIX A

process. Now what it's all about, whither we are drifting, I don't know. Where we came from I don't know either. These are questions — whether they are meaningful or not is itself a question. But we do what we can and we stop there.

Q. But you're suggesting that there's something flawed about Chomsky's view or about a religious conception of life or about psychoanalysis. You're saying that yours in some sense is a more scientific, a more useful, and ultimately — when you begin to get grander about humans in *Beyond Freedom and Dignity* — you begin to take on almost an apocalyptic tone, that if we don't accept this view and the consequences of behavioristic analysis, we're in real trouble. Now aren't you appealing to a free human to believe and then put into effect your recommendations?

A. No, I'm creating a new environment which I would hope would lead individuals to act in different ways about the problems. The therapist doesn't change the person; the therapist adds to the person's history.

Q. So your book becomes part of that environment in the same way that a sudden rain shower would affect my behavior by causing me to seek shelter.

A. That's right. That's right.

Q. When we talk about setting up a whole new environment, à la Walden Two, how does an individual like Frazier appear to step out of the controlling environment, if he himself is controlled, in order to control others or to set up an environment that controls others?

A. You see, he doesn't control others. He designs a world that controls others.

Q. But how does he even do that if he himself is controlled? Doesn't it seem to exempt him temporarily from —

A. Oh, no, all the way through he's a specialist at controlling himself, and you control yourself as you control others. You change your own environment to control yourself and you change the environment of others to control them. . . . There is no one in control in Walden Two; no one's passing out the M&M's. There's some contractual arrangements about number of hours, but that's just bookkeeping. It's a world that reinforces the behavior needed to keep the world going.

Q. There may not be anyone in control anymore, but somebody had set up a system and got it going, sort of like a deistic model of the universe —

A. That's right. And the man who invented the governor on steam engines is dead; he's not controlling all the steam engines.

Q. But there's a system of cause and effect in place that governs people's behavior. You've been asked a hundred times how *Walden Two* is different from the anti-utopian novels of Orwell and Huxley. But I'm still not sure I get it. I'm still not sure I don't see the possibility for totalitarianism.

A. Oh, it could have been designed that way, but it was designed so it couldn't be. The planners move off and can't be reappointed, and the managers are just jobs, and so on. . . . The question is not whether someone can take it over, but whether it's possible to have such a situation at all, and if it might then be so good that people would defend it. . . .

Q. Let me ask you about value judgments for a moment. I want to read you a quotation from Bertrand Russell and get your reaction —

A. By the way . . . [I met Russell at a dinner once and said to him,] "You may be interested to know that you were responsible for my becoming a behaviorist when I read your book *Philosophy*," and he said, "Good heavens! I thought that book demolished behaviorism." Well, it did, but I didn't read that part. . . .

Q. Here's what Russell said: "I can't see how to refute the arguments for the subjectivity of ethical values, but I find myself incapable of believing that all that is wrong with wanton cruelty is that I don't like it." [*Skinner chuckles.*] Do you have a similar kind of dilemma or do you —

A. Oh, well, yes, obviously wanton cruelty is wrong for two reasons: it is wrong in the sense that a culture that tolerates it would be a weak culture. That has to do with the survival of the culture, not with what people feel. But in order to prevent it, the culture teaches people it's wrong and that they should feel guilty about it. It punishes them for it and that gives you the feeling it's wrong. That's very different from the reason why the culture does all of this.

Q. So in every case values reduce to two things — one is cultural survival —

A. There are three levels. There are the values of natural selection: salt is good, sugar is good — now they're no longer good because we get too much of them. Then there's the personal: what is reinforcing to you, for your own reasons. And the culture: what is good for others, what cultures reinforce in individuals because it's good for the culture and the survival of the culture, not just what people like. . . . A world that's designed in such a way that most of the time you're doing what you want to do, which is positively reinforced behavior, is an effective world. However, it won't be judged by that in the long run. Happiness is not the ultimate good. It's the ultimate good for the individual, but it's not the ultimate good for the society.

Q. But all these are instrumental uses of the word *good;* it's what philosophers would call a "nonmoral" sense, exclusively. So you've wiped the moral sense out of existence.

A. If you mean the word *sense* there, a moral *sense,* then there's the distinction again as whether this is the consequence that's selecting it or the mode of promoting which has to do with using measures which the individual reports, make him *feel* guilty, and so on.

Q. Let us take a hypothetical instance of a behavior — let's take sacrificing virgins in a primitive culture. It's not maladaptive for the culture, let us say, and the persons in it have no qualms about it. Now, what can you say about it other than "Yuck, I don't like it," just as you don't like broccoli?

A. Well, what *can* I say? I mean, I don't know the conditions at the time, how this came about. . . . Since I don't know the survival value it may have had for the culture, I can't say it's wrong in that sense. If I then say, if this were in my culture, my culture has taught me to say that it's wrong, so I say it's wrong. . . .

[*On creativity and the self*]:   When I finished *Beyond Freedom and Dignity,* I had a very strange feeling that I hadn't even written the book. Now I don't mean this in the sense in which people have claimed that alter egos have written books for them and so on, but this just naturally came out of my behavior and not because of anything called a "me" or an "I" inside. . . .

Man is not a creator. . . . That doesn't mean there haven't been great books or great music. Of course! The individual is very important. The question is what is actually happening when it happens, you see. If you think that Beethoven was someone who possessed a special kind of genius which enabled him right out of nothing to write nine great symphonies, then you're just wrong and you won't do much as a teacher of music. If you think instead that Beethoven was someone who, when he was very young, acquired all the available music at the time and then, because of things that happened to him personally, as accidents and variations, he introduced new things which paid off beautifully so he went on doing them, and he wrote because he was highly reinforced for writing, then that's a different view and he's still a great man.

Q. Don't you think there might be some part of human behavior that can't be explained this way?

A. Well, you can always say that maybe there's something about human behavior that hasn't been explained or can't be explained, but that's like saying to Newton that there are a few bodies that don't obey the law of gravity. Where are they? . . .

Samuel Butler . . . said that a hen is simply an egg's way of making another egg. Today the geneticists will say the same thing: the organism is . . . just something that is temporarily involved so that genes can survive. Now I think the same thing can be said of cultures. I gave a paper once in the Poetry Center of New York on "Having a Poem." I compared having a poem to having a baby. The audience didn't like my analysis of having a baby because I said that . . . a mother is simply a fertilized egg's way of making more fertilized eggs.

When I was in high school, I was very much impressed by a botany book which described the life of a radish. I've been accused of regarding myself as a radish, and I think that's probably correct. The first year, this radish stores up this great big root. The next year, it puts out branches and flowers and seeds and finally the little thing down there is all gone; moreover, the whole plant is dead when the seeds are ripe. So a radish plant is just a way radish seeds make more radish seeds. Now I argued that's true of a poet, too: a poet is simply a way in which a literary tradition makes more of a literary tradition. Now things happen to a poet, these are the variations in genetics, and something new comes out — but it isn't due to the poet. It's the poet's personal life, the poems he's read, the criticism he's received, and so on — all of this is responsible for what he's done. Should you then give him credit? Well, we do give credit, because that's how we get people to do things, but scientifically it's not deserved. If the question is how much the individual contributes, I think the answer to that is: nothing.

Appendix B
WHAT IS INTRINSIC
MOTIVATION?

For the purpose of analyzing the effects of rewards, it may be enough to define intrinsic motivation as the desire to engage in an activity for its own sake — that is, just because of the satisfaction it provides.[1] This offers a nice, crisp contrast to extrinsic motivation, which means that one takes part in the activity because of some other benefit that doing so will bring. However, if we look at the question more closely, things become a good deal more problematic and, for some of us anyway, more interesting. I want to explore a few of the questions, disputes, and complications that arise in thinking about intrinsic motivation (IM).

The very idea of IM is controversial in some quarters because of its implicit affirmation that what people do isn't always initiated by forces outside the self. While such forces can explain some of our behavior, it's also possible, and even necessary, to appeal to other motivational systems, which focus on what is inside of us. Behaviorists, not surprisingly, have not looked kindly on discussions of IM because its premise challenges the core of their belief system. They have reacted either by denying its existence or, what comes to the same thing, trying to collapse it into their own framework. If something looks intrinsic, they insist, it's just because we haven't yet figured out the real (extrinsic) causes. (For more on the behaviorists' responses, see Appendix C.)[2]

Apart from this dispute, there are quite a few controversies among those who take the concept of IM seriously but can't seem to agree on exactly what it means. To begin with, we need to decide whether it is to be defined negatively (specifically, as that which is present when an individual does something without expecting a reward), positively, or both. The negative definition is convenient for conducting experiments, and it is used explicitly or implicitly by a number of researchers: they record how often or how long subjects engage in an activity when no extrinsic benefits from doing so are expected. This technique, as I will explain later, has raised a number of troubling issues.

Defining IM positively, which is favored by more theorists, opens up a Pandora's box (not to say a Skinner box) of difficulties. The major question is whether we understand the concept in terms of a desire to engage in a particular task or in terms of certain qualities and more general motivations that define human beings. If the latter is chosen, we naturally will want to know what those qualities are. The nominees include a desire "to feel good,"[3] "an orientation toward learning and mastery,"[4] and a need for competence and self-determination[5] as well as, perhaps, to relate to and be engaged with others.[6]

Whether any or all of these needs can be shown to be innate or universal, and if so, whether they are indeed the most fundamental human motivators are questions for another day. What interests me now is the relation between any such characteristics and the topic of intrinsic motivation. It would seem that the connection depends largely on the question we are asking. If we want to know what it means to say that humans are intrinsically motivated organisms, or why they want to do so many things, it might indeed be useful to try to identify some primary drives or needs. But if all we want to know is what it means to say that people are (or this person is) intrinsically motivated to pursue this particular task, then it may be enough to answer in terms of the appeal that this task holds. The definition offered in the first sentence of this essay, which doesn't bother to postulate, say, a basic need for humans to be challenged, might be sufficient for this purpose.

Once our definition of IM goes beyond someone's desire to perform a particular activity, we begin to run into other problems. One is that the wider human goals designated as intrinsic (such as exploring the environment or expressing oneself) may actually interfere with an individual's focus on a specific task. I may have to choose between satisfying my basic curiosity and attending to the job I'm doing at the moment. The two approaches to understanding IM may, in other words, tug in opposite directions.[7]

Another problem is that it is sometimes unclear whether a given characteristic defines IM or is only empirically associated with it. Either intrinsically motivated people turn out to be autonomous (or vice versa), or else autonomy is part of what we mean by the phrase *intrinsically motivated.* If we try to have it both ways, our argument becomes circular. Even people who have written extensively about the topic occasionally seem confused about whether IM entails task involvement by definition or whether IM (defined some other way) promotes task involvement.

Finally, we will have to decide whether to build situational elements into our understanding of IM. To take a concrete example, people often lose interest in a task when they keep doing it over a period of time.[8] Does this mean that someone was not really intrinsically motivated to work on that task after all? Or is IM itself partly a function of novelty? Since interest is so variable, must we avoid attributing motivational properties to activities? And what about attributing the motivation to perform an activity to individuals, since that too depends on the circumstances?

Let us put these conceptual problems aside and look at a very practical issue: how IM in its task-specific sense is measured. Beginning with Deci's early experiments, there have basically been two techniques: asking people how they feel about the activity and watching to see how much time they spend on it (in the absence of extrinsic factors) when given a choice. These are two appealingly straightforward ways of getting at the idea of IM — or so it would seem.

In fact, neither technique is without problems. Self-report measures, while undeniably useful, raise the question of whether people are describing their feelings accurately — or in some cases, whether they even know what they feel (which unleashes a host of philosophical questions). Do experimental subjects exaggerate how much they enjoyed what they were asked to do because this is the answer they think the researcher wants to hear? Do some kinds of people do this more often than others, raising the possibility that a measure of IM is actually gauging something else entirely?

The "free choice" measure — secretly observing people to see whether they return to an activity when they're not obliged to do so — carries its own difficulties. The length or proportion of time spent on the target task varies depending on a range of situational and dispositional factors, including how appealing the available alternative activities happen to be to the individual. The researcher wants to know whether you will continue to play a game when left alone with it for five minutes or whether you will read a magazine. But the answer may say as much about which magazines are in the room as it does about your interest in the game.[9] In experiments where subjects are not left alone, moreover, they may be inclined to keep playing the game partly out of a desire to please the experimenter.

As if to emphasize the risk of putting our faith in either or both of these techniques for quantifying IM, one study after another has found that the two may not point in the same direction: the correlation between self-report and behavioral measures is often negligible.[10] This fact led Ryan and Deci to reflect on what is implied by a situation where someone keeps working on an activity in the absence of extrinsic inducements. Is this in itself a valid indicator of IM? The answer, they decided, is probably not, and with this conclusion comes a bundle of new questions about motivation.

All of us are familiar with people who drive themselves mercilessly to achieve, who approach their work with a compulsiveness that led to the introduction of the term *workaholic*. What is interesting for our purposes about this style of task engagement is that it does not depend on the anticipation of receiving rewards or punishments from the environment. The pressure is internally generated and yet devoid of "the genuine interest, enjoyment, and excitement that phenomenologically define intrinsic motivation."[11] Could this description fit some of the experimental subjects who report low interest in an activity while nevertheless continuing to work at it on their own time?

Ryan and his colleagues set out to answer that question. They told some subjects that the task they were being given to do would reveal how intelligent they were; others were just encouraged to become involved in the task without feeling that their egos were on the line. It turned out that there was no match between the self-report and behavioral measures of interest (what they said about the activity and whether they continued working on it) for the former group. If people felt anxious about whether they were any good at the task, they were more likely to keep at it, presumably more to "preserve their self-worth" than because it was intrinsically motivating. "Although free-choice behavior is a reflection of intrinsic motivation" when people are encouraged just to explore the activity, "it is more of a reflection of internally controlling regulation in conditions of ego involvement," they concluded.[12] *Internal* does not always imply *intrinsic*.

This conclusion offers a direct challenge to psychological theories that distinguish only between what is inside a person and what is outside. It forces us to reconsider not only how we measure IM but what the concept really means. And it raises questions, as I suggested in chapter 12, about whether it is enough just to get children to "internalize" norms and values. After all, feeling controlled from the inside isn't much of an improvement over feeling controlled from the outside.

This last point reminds us that IM, for all its importance, is sometimes irrelevant to the questions that matter to us as parents and teachers. We want children to put their own needs aside sometimes and do what is in the interest of a larger group of people, to respect the rights of others even when this involves inconveniencing themselves. Such behavior is not really analogous to, say, reading, since it is not something in which one develops or maintains an intrinsic interest (although it is sometimes described as intrinsically valuable). In his description of life in an American classroom, Philip Jackson observed that "it is hard to imagine that the students will ever find anything intrinsically satisfying about being silent when they wish to talk," a fact that suggests "the notion of intrinsic motivation begins to lose some of its power"[13] — or at least its pertinence to nonacademic issues.

If, however, we see the world only in terms of intrinsic versus extrinsic motivation, we will be inclined to think that whatever is not described by the former must be described by the latter. Practically speaking, that means we may resort to extrinsic motivators to induce children to act responsibly. But this dichotomous view overlooks the possibility of helping them internalize a commitment to such actions, and doing so in such a way that they come to feel a sense of self-determination about the matter and ultimately are able to decide for themselves what kind of people they want to be.[14]

The need to introduce a concept such as internalization implies that the intrinsic/extrinsic dichotomy is not exhaustive. In fact, we can come up with other real-life situations that can't readily be classified as one or the other. Consider a scientist whose prime motive is to contribute to her field, or a labor organizer who is interested in fighting injustice and helping working people. Or imagine a student in a classroom where learning often takes place in cooperative groups: he finds the activity extremely engaging, but mostly because of the pleasure derived from working with others.

In these examples, people are not seeking what we would ordinarily call extrinsic rewards, yet neither are they motivated by the tasks themselves. The scientist may not particularly enjoy the laboratory work, the organizer may not be enthusiastic about making phone calls and attending meetings, and the student may not be delighted with the math assignment per se.

I think what explains our frustration in deciding how to categorize these people is a quality of intrinsic motivation that has gone largely unnoticed by psychologists: it is a concept that exists only in the context of the individual. The scientist, the organizer, and the student are all motivated by social concerns, and these don't easily fit into such a paradigm. Forced to choose, we would have to say that these motives are extrinsic to their tasks rather than intrinsic. But the fact that we have to lump such motives with the quest for money or grades reveals a limitation in the idea of IM. It is an idea that was never intended to apply to something beyond the needs of separate selves. That this point has rarely even been raised among researchers and theorists may say something about the pervasiveness of an individualistic framework in psychology.[15]

On the other hand, I am not convinced that we ought to discourage people from being intrinsically interested in what they are doing. For example, writers who love the act of writing are not necessarily being self-indulgent and oblivious to larger social concerns. Even less does it follow from the importance of living in a world with others that we should promote the use of extrinsic motivators. We depend on each other for emotional support and for feedback about what we have done, but neither of these has to take the form of rewards.

Very similar to the concern about IM's focus on the individual is the idea that someone intrinsically motivated is caught up only in the process of what he is doing, to the exclusion of the product. To be sure, our society encourages a preoccupation with the product, the bottom line, the practical result. Thus, Csikszentmihalyi finds it refreshing "when experience is intrinsically rewarding [because then] life is justified in the present, instead of being held hostage to a hypothetical future gain."[16] However, it was also Csikszentmihalyi whom I quoted in chapter 10 offering the reminder that "intrinsic rewards are not an ultimate standard to strive for. One still must ask: What are the consequences of this particular activity?"[17] It is important to consider the content of our work, what it means beyond the pleasure it may provide.

The relative emphasis we ought to give to process and product considerations is a topic too ambitious for this discussion. My question is limited to whether encouraging an intrinsic orientation threatens to exclude product concerns. The answer depends on whether we equate intrinsic with process, and extrinsic with product. I am not sure this equation is warranted. Clearly that which pertains to the process of doing something is not always intrinsic to the task: the student who loves cooperating is an example of that. Conversely, it may be possible for one's purely intrinsic motivation as an artist to be geared as much to the product that results as from the creative act that preceded it.[18] Satisfaction in the doing is different from satisfaction in having done, but both might reasonably be classified as intrinsic. The latter is more similar to the former than it is to doing something for a reward.

Here again, of course, everything depends on how we define our terms. My point is that it is not at all obvious what is meant by the phrase *intrinsic motivation*. What appears at first blush an uncomplicated idea reveals itself as a tangle of possibilities, all of which have substantive implications for what we counterpose to the use of rewards.

Appendix C
THE BEHAVIORISTS TALK BACK

For more than two decades, published research has raised questions about the use of rewards. Other objections, of course, based on first-hand experience or moral considerations, have been voiced for even longer than that. Anyone familiar with this literature might be curious to know how these arguments have been received by individuals with a long-standing professional (and sometimes personal) commitment to rewarding people.

If you look through recent psychology textbooks, articles in journals with a behaviorist orientation, or practical guides to behavior modification, you will soon discover that the principal response to these challenges is silence. Even the two researchers best known to social and developmental psychologists for their work demonstrating the detrimental effects of rewards, Edward Deci and Mark Lepper, are simply not cited in most writings by behaviorists. Whether that is because they are unaware of this line of research or because they find it unworthy of mention or inconvenient to contend with is not clear.

Several writers in the behaviorist camp, however, have taken note of at least some of this work and discussed it in tones ranging from genuine concern over its implications to outright contempt. I think it is worth reviewing the arguments they offer in defense of their field. While I don't pretend to a posture of disinterested objectivity — indeed, I will attempt to respond to each of their points — I don't want to give the impression that everyone who has read arguments similar to those offered in this book has found them persuasive. Readers can judge for themselves the merits of the various claims and, of course, will be better able to do so after reading some of the original research cited in the preceding pages as well as the responses from the behaviorist perspective.[1]

The arguments in support of rewards — or more accurately, the arguments against the criticisms of rewards — fall into four general categories. First, the motives of critics are questioned. Second, rewards are said to be necessary or inevitable. Third, they are said to be effective. Finally, they are said to be harmless.

What Are the Critics' Motives?

Some writers have accused those who criticize the use of rewards of doing so "on ideological grounds"[2] or, in the case of those who have done "most of the . . . well over 100 studies" on the topic, of being "theory driven."[3] If the implication here is that values inform the work of those who don't like rewards, this is absolutely true — and no less true of those who do like them. If the implication is that empirical investigations are best conducted in the absence of theory, this is a debatable proposition, to say the least. And if the implication is that a (hypothetical) perfectly unbiased observer, someone untroubled about ethical issues and interested only in the effect of rewards on achievement or on continuing motivation, would find little cause for concern in the research literature, I believe this conclusion is simply insupportable. The number of studies conducted by researchers who expected rewards to be effective and found the reverse is a fairly decisive refutation of this charge, as is the sheer number of replications of the work showing that intrinsic motivation declines in the presence of extrinsic motivators.

Second, at least three behaviorists have accused their critics of wanting children to be intrinsically motivated to learn even though the interest that these critics (and other adults) have in their own work presumably "depends heavily upon the weekly pay checks they receive."[4] This is said to represent "a double standard,"[5] and it is hinted that people opposed to extrinsically driven learning are trying to deny something to children that they themselves enjoy — or perhaps, that they are trying to cheat children by getting them to learn something "only" because it is interesting.

To begin with, the belief that all adults are motivated by money would seem to be most informative for what it reveals about the person who holds it. As suggested by the evidence reviewed in chapter 7, this is not true of most people, and certainly not of most writers and academics. More to the point, behaviorist strategies in the workplace tend to backfire — a fact worth keeping in mind when we read that "only the academic work of students is said to be put at risk by extrinsic rewards," implying that because these rewards work so well everywhere else they must really be effective in the classroom after all.[6] To someone who says "We use money as a carrot for adults, so why not do the same with grades for children?" the proper response is not to accept the latter but to question the former.

But even if pay-for-performance plans *were* beneficial, this would not begin to justify the use of something similar with children. The activities are different (learning to read is simply not commensurate with doing a job), the people are different (treating children like adults overlooks a number of relevant developmental considerations), and our goals in each case are different (we are particularly concerned about the enduring attitudes toward learning that children develop). Finally, while adults generally must earn money to live, the same cannot be said of grades or other extrinsic motivators used with students; the latter are unnecessary and therefore not analogous.

Rewards Are Necessary

Behaviorists in the field of education have been most inclined to argue that rewards are indispensable, since students will not do what is necessary to learn "without some kind of reward, such as praise, grades, or recognition."[7] Or as another writer puts it, "if a student is asked to add 3 + 7, what is the intrinsic reward for answering correctly? . . . The teacher must supplement intrinsic rewards with extrinsic rewards."[8] (This is said to be particularly true in the case of "a child who has had difficulty learning"[9] or a task that has no immediate appeal.)

I have already addressed these objections, with respect to the alleged need to use rewards to get people to do things that are uninteresting in general (chapter 5) and the operative assumptions about children's motivation to learn in particular (chapter 8). The case for extrinsic motivators is often made by setting up false dichotomies: either we praise, or we are grimly silent[10] (overlooking the possibility of providing informational feedback); either we hand out reinforcements, or we just have students repeat something by rote in the hope that their performance will improve automatically[11] (overlooking any number of nonbehavioristic approaches to teaching).

Similarly misleading is the contention that abstract math problems can be made palatable by, in effect, bribing students to do them: the hidden assumption here is that this is how math must be taught, overlooking the educational traditions that take their cue from the way each child actively constructs meaning and makes sense of the world rather than treating students as passive responders to environmental stimuli (see chapter 11 and, in particular, Dewey's comment about teaching numbers). There are many ways of dealing with pedagogical difficulties, such as inquiring into what we're asking children to learn, and how, and with whom. Dangling a reward for successful performance isn't necessary to solve the problem. More to the point, it is not really a solution at all, but a way of circumventing the issue.

Rewards Work

Very rarely have behaviorists addressed the research indicating that performance tends to decline on a range of tasks, particularly those requiring some degree of creativity, when people are expecting to be rewarded. Instead, relying on early laboratory research showing an increase in the number of operant behaviors or an improvement in the performance of mechanical tasks, they often simply assert that rewards work — even, in one case, going so far as to claim that "no one disputes [their] effectiveness."[12] I am aware of only one direct response to a study showing that rewards undermined children's performance on a straightforward task: the answer was that more rewards would have turned things around.[13]

As for the finding that behavior modification programs rarely lead to changes that are maintained and generalized to other settings, the usual response is that the practitioners or researchers in question didn't correctly understand the principles of Skinnerian theory or didn't successfully implement them. In some cases, it is argued that the rewards being used in the studies weren't truly reinforcing.[14] In other cases, it is said that by simply tinkering with the schedule of reinforcement or attending to unintended effects caused by other aspects of the environment, it is possible to "program for maintenance." One wonders how long it is possible to continue accounting for the lack of meaningful results by insisting that a basically sound approach is poorly implemented in every case.

Rewards Are Harmless

Finally, there is the attempt among behaviorists to challenge various arguments about the undesirability of rewards. Against the charge that pop behaviorism is controlling it is contended, first, that everything is controlling, whether we realize it or not, and second, that behavioral technologies are neutral in themselves since they can be used in the service of any end (and are therefore unobjectionable). I discussed these arguments in chapter 2.

To the empirically based contention that the use of extrinsic motivators leads to a decline in intrinsic motivation, some behaviorists have replied that plenty of people continue to engage successfully in various activities despite having been rewarded for doing so, which proves that rewards do not always undermine interest. "Outstanding achievement always produces extrinsic rewards of some kind . . . [so how] do outstanding achievers maintain their motivation?"[15]

In fact, both halves of this sentence are open to question. The nature and degree of the extrinsic reward that is "always" produced for achievement is actually quite variable. To be paid for one's work is quite different from having that pay conditioned on one's achievement. To receive some unexpected recognition after the fact is quite different from being promised an award if one does a good job. In both contrasts, the latter offers a salient reward that probably feels more controlling and emphasizes the means-ends contingency involved, in which case we would indeed expect to see a reduction in intrinsic motivation. Where rewards (especially money, which may not be perceived as a reward for achievement at all) are less significant and can be decoupled from the work, there is no reason to predict a decline in motivation. To that extent, its failure to appear is not an argument against the general principle.

The second half of the statement assumes that persisting at some activity implies the existence of intrinsic motivation for it. As I tried to explain in Appendix B, this is not a fair assumption. Many people continue to do something, and may even do it competently, without finding it gratifying in its own right. Perhaps they work only because they are still receiving extrinsic motivators, and will continue only as long as that remains true. Alternatively, they may persist out of an anxious, almost compulsive, need to prove their worth. The latter might suffice for getting the job done, but it is not an ideal way to live, it is not what we want for our children, and it is not evidence that intrinsic motivation is unaffected by rewards.

Having said all this, I don't think this objection can be dismissed entirely. Some people undoubtedly remain intrinsically interested in what they do despite the attempts of others to control their performance or task engagement with incentives. It is worth remembering that psychological principles do not operate mechanistically and invariantly. If some people can smoke two packs of cigarettes a day over many years and live long, healthy lives, then surely some individuals can endure a regimen of extrinsic motivators and survive with their interest in an activity intact. It happens. But in thinking about how to treat students or employees or anyone else, we need to consider the odds involved. I believe our obligation is to avoid doing something that has a high probability of adversely affecting intrinsic motivation.

Behaviorists have also responded to the argument about the effect of rewards on motivation by challenging the claim's accuracy in several ways. In chapter 5 I considered three of these challenges: that the effect occurs only with task-contingent, not performance-contingent, rewards; that it can be mitigated by letting people administer rewards to themselves; and that it occurs only when rewards are used for too long instead of being faded out. (Ironically, some behaviorists have also argued that research showing a detrimental effect of rewards is flawed because subjects were not rewarded over a long enough period.)

In addition, five other responses to this research have been offered:

1. The effects on motivation are sometimes said to be "transient and limited."[16] On this point, see page 299 note 13, or walk into any high school or college classroom and listen to students asking whether a given fact or idea is going to be on the test and therefore needs to be learned.

2. Some have said that only tangible reinforcers, like money, toys, or food, are potentially destructive: symbolic rewards, such as gold stars or plaques to recognize performance, are not only believed to be more "natural" and easy to administer, but harmless almost by definition. Emphasizing that a certificate presented to students for working well as a team is worth only two cents, one researcher argues that it just communicates "the teacher's pride and satisfaction with their cooperative efforts. Is that so terrible?"[17]

The answer is that while one study did find symbolic rewards were less detrimental to young children's intrinsic motivation than tangible rewards were,[18] quite a bit of research has shown that either kind can be counted on to undermine interest. The toxicity of an extrinsic motivator, after all, is not due to its exchange value or practical usefulness but to its status as an extrinsic motivator (see chapter 5). And those factors are present when we give someone a plaque just as surely as when we present a pizza or a pile of money.

It is useful to keep in mind in this discussion that if behaviorists fall back on symbolic rewards when the tangible variety are shown to be particularly destructive (or simply prove impractical to use over time), it is probably because their theoretical framework dictates that the best we can hope for is the substitution of one kind of reinforcer for another, the premise being that some form of control will always be · necessary.[19] Those of us who reject that premise will not need to try to rescue one version of reward by insisting it is less destructive than another.

3. Behaviorists often reject the possibility that intrinsic motivation is endangered by the use of rewards because they reject the existence of intrinsic motivation itself. The more doctrinaire of their number make a point of cordoning off the phrase within quotation marks as if to demonstrate that the very concept is dubious. It is axiomatic to them that all behavior depends on environmental contingencies, so what seems to be intrinsic is simply that for which we have not yet discovered the external reinforcement.

Thus, one writer insists that "very little is actually known about this form of 'intrinsic' motivation largely because it is difficult to characterize"[20] — meaning that it is difficult to understand from within the conceptual framework of behaviorism. Others try to force it into that framework, redefining intrinsic motivation as "a simple form of conditioned reinforcement, in which the stimuli associated with the task have been correlated with approval, praise, or some other form of reinforcement" or the behavior has been "controlled by infrequent extrinsic rewards."[21]

Here it becomes clear that we are dealing with an unchallengeable dogma: if one enters the discussion already convinced that "all behavior is ultimately initiated by the external environment,"[22] no argument or data could ever suffice to show the existence of motivation that is truly intrinsic. (Notice that this is quite different from arguing that intrinsic and extrinsic motivation are not always easy to separate in practice, a point that can be readily conceded but that does not deny the effect that a clear example of the latter has on a clear example of the former.)

4. Some behaviorists have offered very specific methodological criticisms of the research concerned with the impact of rewards on motivation. The points at issue include the value of comparing one group of subjects to another as opposed to monitoring the motivation of each individual subject, the extent to which a subject's initial interest in the task is known, and the difference between the effect of a reward that is promised and one that is delivered.[23] Readers will have to judge the weight of these criticisms for themselves; I will point out only that

a variety of experimental designs over two decades have repeatedly corroborated the basic finding.

5. Finally, behaviorists have conducted some studies of their own, predicting that extrinsic motivators would not have any detrimental effect and finding exactly that. (It is curious that some of the same theorists who challenge the existence of intrinsic motivation purport to show that it is uncompromised by the administration of rewards.) I have found four such studies conducted with children, but it is hard to give them much credence since the number of subjects involved are five, six, nine, and three, respectively.[24] As best as I can ascertain, only two studies have failed to find a detrimental effect of rewards with adult populations (college students), and one of these involved only three subjects.[25] Various other objections can be offered to the experimental designs used in these studies,[26] but the fact is that chance alone would predict that some of a very large number of studies will not replicate even a very robust finding. I think the research, viewed in its totality, makes it very difficult for an open-minded individual to deny that promising people rewards runs the risk of reducing their interest in what they have been rewarded to do.

Very few disputes in the social sciences can be settled once and for all to the satisfaction of everyone. Even with more than a hundred studies already published, there continue to be disagreements about how key words are defined and what would constitute a decisive proof. Not many behaviorists will read this book, or any other that challenges the use of rewards (and the paradigm that leads people to use them), and announce that it is time they found a new line of work. Nor will most teachers, parents, or managers accustomed to saying "Do this and you'll get that" suddenly resolve to change their ways. My hope, though, is that even the reader who doesn't accept every argument offered here, or who has doubts about the import of one or another piece of research, may nonetheless decide that there is enough evidence to justify calling into question a set of beliefs and practices that affects us deeply every day of our lives.

NOTES

1. SKINNER-BOXED

1. Thorndike ultimately formulated the Law of Effect as follows: "Of several responses made to the same situation, those which are accompanied or closely followed by satisfaction to the animal will, other things being equal, be more firmly connected with the situation, so that, when it recurs, they will be more likely to recur; those which are accompanied or closely followed by discomfort to the animal will, other things being equal, have their connections with that situation weakened, so that, when it recurs, they will be less likely to occur. The greater the satisfaction or discomfort, the greater the strengthening or weakening of the bond" (1911, p. 244).

2. "It is absolutely necessary, then, when workmen are daily given a task which calls for a high rate of speed on their part, that they should also be insured the necessary high rate of pay whenever they are successful. This involves not only fixing for each man his daily task, but also paying him a large bonus, or premium, each time that he succeeds in doing his task in the given time" (Taylor, 1911/1947, p. 121).

3. See Ravitch, 1974, p. 16.

4. While a reward may or may not produce certain effects, a reinforcement by definition strengthens the behavior for which it is given. This is one reason that Skinner preferred the latter term, and it is the reason I avoid it: an effect on behavior must be shown empirically rather than assumed a priori. Whether rewards produce the consequences we expect of them is, after all, an open question. (For discussions of the concept of reinforcement, see McCullers, 1978, pp. 12–14; Schwartz et al., 1978, pp. 248–49; Breger and McGaugh, 1965, pp. 345–46.)

5. Watson, 1930, p. v. Another behaviorist put it a bit differently in a recent book on the subject: what distinguishes human behavior from rat behavior is the fact that the "environmental events controlling human behavior" take place over a longer period of time (Rachlin, 1991, p. 265). This is rather like saying the main difference between a living person and a corpse is that the former is less likely to be found underground.

6. Skinner, 1974, p. 168.

7. Skinner, 1983, pp. 400, 412.

8. "No one thinks before he acts except in the sense of acting covertly before acting overtly" (Skinner, 1974, p. 235).

9. More succinctly: "What is love . . . except another name for the use of positive reinforcement?" (Skinner, 1962, p. 300).

10. Skinner, 1972, pp. 99, 102, 107. Similarly, two well-known practitioners of behavior modification talk only of "maladaptive behavior," which they define as "behavior that is considered inappropriate by those key people in a person's life who control reinforcers" (Ullmann and Krasner, 1965, p. 20).

11. Any number of critics have argued that there is a fatal inconsistency in trying to convince someone to accept this repudiation of selfhood and freedom. When an author argues for the validity of his model or exhorts us to do something — Skinner in particular was a scold who filled his books with prescriptions — he is necessarily appealing to a free reader, someone who has the ability to weigh the arguments and act on the recommendations (see, for example, Chomsky, 1971). Moreover, if all actions, including verbal actions, are just driven by reinforcers, why should we accept any statement, including this argument by Skinner, as true? There is no reason, after all, to expect that only true statements are reinforcing for those who make them. The very idea of truth is finally consigned to the same fate as moral value in the Skinnerian universe.

12. Watson, 1930, pp. 5, 2.

13. Thorndike put it this way: "If a thing exists, it exists in some amount, and if it exists in some amount, it can be measured" (quoted in Fiske, 1979, p. 156). This sort of reasoning, a remnant of the philosophical movement known as positivism, has long since been repudiated by most serious thinkers, but it retains a certain intuitive appeal among pop behaviorists.

14. Whitaker and Moses, 1989.

15. Skinner, 1990, p. 1209. As he had for many years, Skinner conceded in this paper that behaviorists, like everyone else, were obliged to speak in the vernacular to make themselves understood, using expressions such as "I feel . . ." and "I need . . ." But although such "references to an initiating self are unavoidable" in everyday conversation, there is "no support for [their] use in a science" (ibid.).

16. "Dumping the Gold Card," 1991.

17. Alexander, 1992; Tousignant, 1992.

18. Gingrich quoted in Solomon, 1991, p. 206. The strength of such a program, according to this article, is that "it takes human nature as it is" — a telling reflection of the sort of assumptions that drive pop behaviorism. See also Clymer, 1992, p. 47.

19. "Let's Do Lunch, Billy," 1991.

20. Quick, 1990.

21. Zaslowsky, 1989. Subsequently, the program has been considered or adopted in areas of California and Maryland as well. See also Raspberry, 1990.

22. Annual incentive plans for managers were offered in 92 percent of manufacturing companies, according to an article published in 1986 (cited in Halachmi and Holtzer, 1987, p. 80); 90 percent of Fortune 500 companies had short-term incentive plans in 1980 (Posner, 1986, p. 57); 94 percent of 179 corporations polled had some kind of reward and recognition program in a survey reported in the *Total Quality Newsletter* (cited in Stuart, 1992, p. 102); three quarters of the 1,600 organizations whose representatives were questioned by the American Productivity Center had some form of incentive plan as of 1987 (O'Dell, 1987, p. 8); and more than 80 percent of companies in still another survey claimed in 1984 that they "gave salary increases only in the form of merit pay" (Nash, 1985, p. 170).

23. This quotation appears in a book called *Teaching the Elephant to Dance* (Belasco, 1990, p. 166), which I selected virtually at random from a bookstore business shelf.
24. Francella, 1983.
25. Lawson, 1984; this quotation and the preceding comment by Skinner both appear on p. 86.
26. The sentence "Psychologists know that people (and most other living organisms) respond to incentives" sets up a discussion about economic decision-making in Lipsey et al., 1987, p. 9. Conversely, within social psychology, the school of thought known as "equity theory" offers the most blatant example of incorporating the assumptions of neoclassical economics. The more general tendency to apply these assumptions in all contexts — to assume that any human activity can be explained in terms of a model based on narrowly self-interested, rational consumer behavior — has been called "economic imperialism" by the psychologist Barry Schwartz (1986, chaps. 9–10). Traditional assumptions about the role of rationality in economics have been questioned by such writers as Amitai Etzioni, Amartya Sen, and to a more limited extent, Robert H. Frank. For challenges to the belief that human motivation, or even a reasonable understanding of rationality, must always be based on self-interest, see the anthology edited by Jane Mansbridge, *Beyond Self-Interest* (1990); and also my book *The Brighter Side of Human Nature* (Kohn, 1990a).
27. Herzberg, 1966, p. 89.
28. From watching adults use rewards, "the child may then attempt to 'buy' his or her own friends" (Balsam and Bondy, 1983, p. 292). Preschool children whose behavior was controlled by reinforcements have been observed "hiring the services of one another" (O'Leary et al., 1972, p. 4).
29. Boggiano et al., 1987; Barrett and Boggiano, 1988. Another investigator found that the much-replicated effect by which people who are rewarded become less interested in the task in question (which is the subject of chapter 5) was not predicted by students or adults (Hom and Riche, 1988).
30. As an English psychologist, Susan Isaacs, remarked in 1932, "When we ask children *not* to move, we should have excellent reasons for doing so. It is stillness we have to justify, not movement" (quoted in Silberman, 1970, p. 128).
31. One study found that supervisors tend to "demonstrate relatively less leadership" when incentives are in place (Rothe, 1970, p. 550). And a huge survey of American corporations discovered an unusually low rate of programs encouraging active employee involvement in those organizations that used small-group incentive plans (O'Dell, 1987, p. 52). On the general point that it is temptingly easy for supervisors to rely on compensation programs to do their managing for them, see Herzberg, 1966, p. 172; Meyer, 1975, p. 46.
32. McGregor, 1960, p. 96.
33. See Boggiano et al., 1987, p. 875.
34. That behaviorism "proves" itself true in this way is a theme that runs through the work of Barry Schwartz. "Reinforcement-maximizing people are . . . made, not born," he points out. We often assume that a system of rewards simply takes advantage of "a fundamental feature of the human character" when it actually "*turns people into* reinforcement-maximizing economic actors" (1990b, p. 199). Ultimately, he has written elsewhere, "it

may be that as more components of the natural environment are subjected to modification by applied reinforcement theory, and more components of human behavior are thus controlled by reinforcement contingencies, a point will be reached at which virtually all human behavior will look like operant behavior. If this point is reached, it will tell us not that reinforcement theory has captured something general and essential about human nature, but that [it] has produced something general in human nature" (1982b, p. 58).

2. IS IT RIGHT TO REWARD?

1. This comment is quoted in Miller, 1984, p. 158. For more on the "just world" phenomenon, see Rubin and Peplau, 1973, 1975; Lerner, 1970.
2. See, for example, Ehrenreich, 1989, pp. 68–72, 84–91, 168–95.
3. Lerner, 1974, p. 539. Likewise, Morton Deutsch emphasizes that "equity is only one of many values that underlie systems of distributive justice." For example, he continues, "'need' may be the predominant value of distributive justice in the family or other caring institutions . . . [and] 'equality' may be the predominating value in friendships and other solidarity relationships" (1985, pp. 29–30).
4. Deutsch, 1985, p. 30.
5. Ibid. See also Barry Schwartz's discussion of "economic imperialism," mentioned in n. 26 of the preceding chapter.
6. Studies reported in Lerner (1974) demonstrate that this is true with children. Research with undergraduates likewise finds that when two subjects work on a puzzle and each must decide how to divide a five-dollar payment between them, those who don't know each other are likely to make their decision based on how well each did at the task. When the two are roommates, however, most choose to apportion the money equally (Austin, 1980).
7. See Bond et al., 1982, p. 188.
8. Ibid., p. 187.
9. Sampson, 1975, pp. 54–57.
10. Swap and Rubin's research on personality is cited in Leung and Bond, 1984, p. 794.
11. Sampson, 1975, p. 58.
12. Patton, 1972, pp. 58, 62.
13. Schwartz, 1990b, pp. 196–97.
14. Goldstein (1988, p. 12) uses this phrase in a somewhat different context.
15. For example, "How to Handle Your Kids with Praise" is the subtitle of one article for parents (Lawson, 1984).
16. Thus, "the unconscious assumption behind the reward-punishment model is that one is dealing with jackasses, that people are jackasses to be manipulated and controlled." The relationship between the controller and the controlled is therefore "inevitably one of condescending contempt whose most blatant mask is paternalism" (Levinson, 1973, pp. 10–11).
17. For example, Douglas McGregor wrote that "management appears to have concluded that the average human being is permanently arrested in his development in early adolescence." Citing the work of Chris Argyris, he observes that "managerial strategies . . . are admirably suited to the capacities and characteristics of the child rather than the adult." If managers evaluate workers in the same way that teachers grade their students, "we

should not be surprised if the reactions to an objective appraisal are sometimes immature" (1960, pp. 43, 86).

18. Whyte, 1955, p. 3. Of course, the tendency to reduce people to the status of
"human assets" or "human capital" cannot be blamed entirely on behaviorism. But this reduction does not occur only in a business context, and
Whyte was not the only one to notice it. Arthur Koestler described behaviorism as "the twentieth-century postscript to the nineteenth century's
mechanistic materialism, its belated and most consistent attempt to describe
living organisms in terms of machine theory" (1967, p. 557).

19. Particularly in his early writings, Skinner made much of how operant theory
differed from the stimulus-response model that is associated with classical
conditioning theory. The original behavior that is reinforced, in his view, is
"emitted" rather than evoked by a prior stimulus, which may seem to
suggest that organisms can initiate action. But this is an awfully thin version
of initiation if all subsequent behavior is controlled by the expectation of
reinforcement. The Skinnerian position that behavior "can be fully explained by appeal to relations between it and a small set of environmental
factors, both past and present, and that it is typically controlled by these
environmental factors, so that by manipulating the environment one can
manipulate behavior in lawful, predictable ways is radically incompatible
with our everyday inclination to assign a fair measure of autonomy and
responsibility to human agents" (Schwartz and Lacey, 1988, p. 29).

20. Deci and Ryan, 1985, p. 70.

21. Deci and Ryan, 1987, p. 1026.

22. I am aware that the word *control* can also be used in a stronger sense, to
denote the application of physical force to overpower someone. Neither the
threat of punishment nor the promise of reward is controlling, according to
this narrower definition, because strictly speaking one is free to resist the
positive or negative consequences imposed for acting, or failing to act, in a
particular way. First of all, though, this freedom may be severely constrained by a sufficiently onerous punishment: one may not be literally
"controlled" by a command to "hand over your wallet or die" (in that one
could choose the latter option), but the practical difference is not very great.
Second, the freedom to resist is a relative matter, dependent on, in the case
of a reward, one's perceived need. A desperately poor individual is more
controlled by the offer of a substantial sum of money in exchange for
performing some behavior than is someone affluent because he is less free
to decline it. Finally, there is a more meaningful difference, again in a
practical context, between the use of persuasion and the use of tactics
intended to control (such as punishments and rewards) than there is between these tactics and the application of absolute control.

23. Bachrach et al., 1984, p. 22.

24. Meyer, 1975, p. 41. Harry Levinson notes that supervisors and consultants
typically ask, "'How can the employee *be* motivated?' Often the implication is that by doing something to the person or his environment, he can be
made to do, by someone else, what is either desired or expected of him"
(1973, p. 19).

25. "The token economy, as a motivating environment for psychiatric patients,
is an example of the direct application of principles derived in the experimental animal laboratory to complex human behavior." This is the first
sentence of an article written by psychologists who are generally supportive
of the idea (Carlson et al., 1972, p. 192; see also Kazdin, 1976, p. 98).

26. See Glynn, 1990, esp. pp. 383–84, 392–95.
27. For examples of critical reviews of token economy programs in psychiatric hospitals — all published the same year in different journals — see Biklen, 1976; Hersen, 1976; Zeldow, 1976. Questions about the efficacy of such programs have been raised even by enthusiastic supporters of the concept (see Kazdin, 1976, p. 105).
28. Drabman and Tucker, 1974; the quotations are taken from pp. 181, 183, 182, 187, and 184, respectively.
29. Condry and Chambers, 1978, p. 76.
30. Of all the controversial elements of Skinner's worldview, one of the least credible and most distasteful was his attempt to deny this fact by insisting that "the relation between the controller and the controlled is reciprocal. . . . In a very real sense, then, the slave controls the slave driver" (1972, p. 161). This perplexing refusal to acknowledge the reality of oppression, to attribute symmetry even to the most egregious example of subjugation, proceeds from a failure to acknowledge that controllers typically have a lot more alternatives available to them than do the controlled. Specifically, controllers have the capacity to set the agenda by deciding what must be done in order for the reward to be received, and can change this agenda at will (on this point, see Lacey, 1979, pp. 13–14).
31. Quoted in Hemp, 1992, p. 41.
32. Kirsch, 1974, p. 314. Likewise, another psychologist (who, incidentally, describes himself as an "avowed behavior modifier") remarks that a token economy in a hospital "would appear to serve as an effective system of ward management rather than as a proposed treatment regimen" (Hersen, 1976, p. 209).
33. Winett and Winkler, 1972, pp. 501–502. Even more pointedly, they declare that "behavior modifiers have been instruments of the status quo, unquestioning servants of a system which thrives on a petty reign of 'law and order' to the apparent detriment of the educational process itself" (p. 501). Likewise, Samuel Bowles and Herbert Gintis, in the course of analyzing the political and economic objectives furthered by American education, observe that "the reward system of the school inhibits those manifestations of personal capacity which threaten hierarchical authority" (1976, p. 42).
34. Watson, 1930, p. 21.
35. Csikszentmihalyi, 1978, p. 210.
36. One of Watson's most famous passages highlights this supposed malleability of our species: "Give me a dozen healthy infants, well-formed, and my own specified world to bring them up in and I'll guarantee to take any one at random and train him to become any type of specialist I might select — doctor, lawyer, artist, merchant-chief and yes, even beggar-man and thief, regardless of his talents, penchants, tendencies, abilities, vocations, and race of his ancestors" (1930, p. 104).
37. James Beane (1990, p. 74) makes this point. Richard Ryan and a colleague also argue that when, instead of controlling children with rewards or punishments, we give them responsibility for making choices, they are more likely to grow into "interested, active, and empowered citizens" of the sort best able to participate in a democracy (Ryan and Stiller, 1991, p. 118).
38. Audre Lorde, quoted in Brown and Gilligan, 1992, p. 10.
39. Andrews and Karlins, 1972; the quotations are taken from pp. 6–8. The

claim that behavior modification programs and other attempts to control what people do is "value-neutral" is commonly made by behaviorists.
40. Lacey and Schwartz, 1987, p. 175.

3. IS IT EFFECTIVE TO REWARD?

1. Rachlin, 1991, p. 132.
2. Hackman and Oldham, 1980, p. 38. The same point was made by McCullers, 1978, pp. 14–15.
3. Thorne, 1990.
4. "Getting a student to internalize a behavior (i.e., to engage in a behavior without necessarily receiving any extrinsic reward) should be the goal of every behavior modification program," declares one supporter of such programs (Kaplan, 1991, p. 21). And from two others: "The *sine qua non* of successful therapy is that behavior be generalized to situations other than the therapeutic one" (Balsam and Bondy, 1983, p. 290).
5. Kazdin and Bootzin, 1972, pp. 359–60.
6. Kazdin, 1982, pp. 435–37.
7. Greene et al., 1976, p. 1229. Similar results were reported in a comparable study involving children's choice of different art media (Colvin, 1972). If the effects of behavioral programs like these don't "transfer to new situations," another researcher has observed, "it seems reasonable to assert that so long as the locus of control is tied to people and procedures that are external to the learner, there is no reason to expect such transfer to occur" (Thomas, 1980, p. 218).
8. With behavior modification programs for children, most studies have yielded "no evidence of positive generalization," one group of behaviorists concludes. In fact, the researchers point out a few pages later, "there is little reason to expect" it (Johnson et al., 1976, pp. 161, 185). From another pair of reviewers: "When appropriate measures of subsequent task engagement have been obtained in situations where rewards were clearly no longer available, decreases in task engagement . . . have been obtained, in some cases, following the withdrawal of reasonably long-term token-economy programs" (Lepper and Greene, 1978b, pp. 142–43). And as recently as 1990, another writer claims that it still "has not been fully determined" whether such programs produce any long-term changes (Glynn, 1990, p. 401).
9. See Lepper and Greene, 1978a, p. 226. To an avid behaviorist, it is only logical that if rewards don't produce lasting changes, the solution is to give more of them. "To avoid backsliding," says Kazdin, we need to provide more rewards in more settings or shift from one reward to another (1976, p. 105; see also O'Leary et al., 1972, pp. 3–4). From another source: "Children who have difficulty in school and home settings should probably receive simultaneous treatment in both settings. If positive generalization across settings is desired, active programming of such generalization appears to be required" (Johnson et al., 1976, pp. 185–86).
10. For a general critique of the use of behavioral techniques by health educators, see Green et al., 1986, pp. 517–19.
11. Dienstbier and Leak, 1976.
12. Kramer et al., 1986.
13. Curry et al., 1991; the quotation appears on p. 323. Corroborating the

results of this experiment is an earlier study by the same researchers indicating that when two people smoke the same amount and have an equally strong desire to stop, the one whose reason for quitting is extrinsic (e.g., to save money, to avoid being nagged, to receive a financial incentive) is much less likely to kick the habit than someone motivated by concerns about health or self-control (Curry et al., 1990).

14. Geller et al., 1987; the quotation appears on p. 14. When a commitment to a theory is strong enough, however, facts can be conveniently brushed aside. Two years later, in another journal, the same author declared that "incentive strategies have been particularly promising as a method of increasing safety belt use," and then cited the very research review just described — apparently hoping no one would look it up and discover what had actually been found (Geller et al., 1989, p. 4).

15. Kazdin, 1976, p. 102.

16. Deci and Ryan, 1985, p. 286. If the goal is for behavior change to continue once rewards are no longer forthcoming, and for it to transfer to new situations, Deci and Ryan argue that there is no reason to expect these things to happen on the basis of operant theories of learning; the reinforced behavior can be prolonged using various techniques, but eventually it should extinguish (p. 285).

17. Miller and Estes, 1961; the quotation appears on p. 503.

18. Glucksberg, 1962. There was no statistically significant difference in solution time when the subjects got the boxes already emptied of their contents. In a second study, a different group of subjects were required to recognize a word — either a simple one like *church* or an unusual one like *percipience* — when it was flashed on a screen. Once again, those working for a reward didn't do as well when the task was difficult. And two years later, Glucksberg (1964) published yet another report showing that a financial incentive undermined the capacity of undergraduates to perform another task, this one involving constructing an electrical circuit, when the solution wasn't obvious. Those promised a reward took more than twice as much time to solve the problem.

19. Spence, 1970, 1971; the quotation appears on p. 1469 of the second article.

20. Viesti, 1971; the quotations appear on pp. 181–82.

21. Deci, 1971, Experiment 2.

22. McCullers and Martin, 1971; the quotation appears on p. 836.

23. Kruglanski et al., 1971.

24. Lepper et al., 1973, p. 135; Greene and Lepper, 1974, p. 1144. The primary finding of these studies was that the rewards reduced children's interest in drawing, a topic to which we shall return.

25. One creativity experiment found that a monetary reward boosted the number of ideas children came up with but had no effect on the quality of those ideas (Ward et al., 1972). Another study found that children who particularly liked to draw tended to produce more drawings but did a sloppier job when they were trying to get an award (Loveland and Olley, 1979). In the workplace, as we will see later, financial incentives regularly produce short-term quantitative gains in performance (how many, how fast, etc.) if the tasks are simple; those gains disappear, however, if we look at the effects on quality. A reviewer summarized the research this way: "One of the effects of anticipated rewards on task performance is to increase activity but to lower the quality of that activity" (Condry, 1977, p. 469).

26. McGraw and McCullers, 1979.
27. Garbarino, 1975. A later study of 1,330 college students who had signed up to tutor disadvantaged children found that those who admitted to volunteering for extrinsic reasons (such as getting academic credit or better dormitory rooms) tended to report that their tutees didn't benefit as much as the tutees of students whose motives were less oriented to what they would get out of the experience (Fresko, 1988). The strength of this study is that it was based on real-life experiences rather than a contrived laboratory task; it also sampled a large number of people. Unfortunately, the students themselves provided the only assessment of how much their tutees were benefiting, and those who saw themselves as more altruistic (or who would like others to see them that way) might have been inclined to exaggerate the value of their work.
28. Fabes et al., 1981.
29. Fabes et al., 1986.
30. Schwartz, 1982b, 1988.
31. Amabile, 1985. Creativity was judged by having a dozen professional writers evaluate the writing samples independently without knowing what the study was about.
32. Amabile et al., 1986.
33. Unpublished data by Teresa Amabile, Brandeis University, 1992. The study was conducted with professional artists, each of whom was invited to submit a batch of commissioned and noncommissioned works. Without knowing what distinguished the two piles, ten other professional artists independently judged the commissioned art to be significantly less creative than the noncommissioned art ($p = .014$). The artists who had done the work felt the same way, incidentally, and also reported feeling more constrained when working for commissions. In fact, the more an artist perceived a commission for a given work as constraining or controlling, the less creative it was judged to be.
34. An unpublished report of this research, Diana I. Cordova and Mark R. Lepper, "The Effects of Intrinsic versus Extrinsic Rewards on the Learning Process," is described in Lepper and Cordova, 1992, pp. 201–202; the quotation is on p. 202. Their study was partly intended to determine whether making the task more fun by embedding it in a fantasy scenario would improve the children's performance, which it did. But the promise of a reward dragged down the performance even of the children in the fantasy condition.
35. Deutsch, 1985, p. 157.
36. Boggiano and Barrett, 1991.
37. Deutsch, 1985, p. 162.
38. Danner and Lonky, 1981, p. 1049.
39. McGraw, 1978, p. 34.
40. In combing the research on this topic, I have come across a handful of early studies purporting to show that creativity *can* be operantly conditioned. This work leaves a great deal to be desired, however, in terms of experimental rigor. Typically the studies are conducted with only a handful of subjects, or they fail to include a control group to assess the creativity of subjects who receive no reward, or they overlook the possibility that subjects are scoring better on creativity tests after a reward is offered (compared to before) simply because by then they have had some practice doing the task.

Moreover, the measures of creativity that are used, while familiar to those who study the subject, are more than a little unsatisfying. Borrowing from a distinction offered by McGraw, Amabile has noted that the tasks used in behavior modification studies are almost always "algorithmic," meaning that it is pretty clear from the beginning what has to be done in order to be judged creative, and meeting the criteria is a matter of applying a familiar formula. By contrast, people working for a reward do not do better at truly "heuristic" tasks, where new ground must be broken and cutting-edge approaches invented; in fact, they usually do worse (see Amabile, 1979, pp. 230–31). Finally, although some gains may be observed in these studies, there is no evidence that reinforced individuals are more creative on the next task they attempt. With this in mind, and in light of all the research demonstrating a reduction in genuine creativity when rewards are used, we are less likely to be impressed with the sort of experimental result proudly cited by behaviorists. The study they mention most often consists of an intervention with a grand total of three four-year-old girls showing that they were more likely to arrange blocks in new patterns when praised for doing so (Goetz and Baer, 1973). Read the other creativity studies by behaviorists (e.g., Glover and Gary, 1976; Halpin and Halpin, 1973; Raina, 1968; Johnson, 1974; Ward et al., 1972) and you will find little to challenge the conclusion that while it is possible to provide conditions that facilitate creativity, it is simply not possible to bribe people to be creative.

41. Condry, 1977, pp. 471–72.

4. THE TROUBLE WITH CARROTS

1. For example, see Spence, 1970, p. 110; McCullers and Martin, 1971, p. 837; Reiss and Sushinsky, 1975, passim.
2. See the second experiment reported in Ross, 1975; Smith and Pittman, 1978. The latter study showed that the reduction in interest caused by a reward did not weaken as the task was repeatedly performed, which is what the distraction hypothesis predicts.
3. The last locution, offered by the philosopher W. V. Quine, is quoted in Kagan, 1984, p. 125.
4. Lewin, 1935, p. 153. Of course, Lewin also recognized distinctions between rewards and punishments.
5. Newby, 1991, p. 197.
6. Sears et al., 1957, p. 324.
7. An early and very small study of after-school clubs that had been set up for ten-year-old boys found that "both praise and criticism were especially characteristic of our autocratic [adult] leaders"; democratic leaders used less praise — probably, according to the researchers, because "both praise and criticism . . . suggest an emphasis on *personal evaluation from the leader's standpoint* . . . a status-hierarchy . . . [in which] the leader is setting himself up as chief judge of the status and achievement of the members of the group" (White and Lippit, 1960, pp. 531–32). More recently, a study in which undergraduates were asked to take the role of teachers discovered that those who were pressured to extract maximum performance from their pupils were both more critical and controlling, on the one hand, and more likely to praise, on the other (Deci et al., 1982, p. 856).
8. Just because something is unpleasant, of course, does not mean that we should expect that everyone will actively resent this and rebel. (Alice Miller

[1984] has persuasively described how even people who were victims of physical punishment as children may convince themselves that it must have been for their own good; once grown, they may then victimize their own children, as if to remove any traces of doubt.) Instead of complaining when they are punished by rewards, some people will react by coming to see themselves, their motives, and the tasks they work on each day in a different light. If, as I will argue later, the use of rewards drains the joy out of much of what we do, this result can fairly be described as punitive whether or not people are up in arms over the fact.

9. Ohanian, 1982, p. 19.
10. Deci and Ryan, 1985, p. 301.
11. Pearce, 1987, p. 171.
12. The research literature supporting the achievement-enhancing effects of cooperative learning is immense. David and Roger Johnson (whose favorite motto is quoted in the text), Robert Slavin, Shlomo Sharan, and others have published reviews of studies on the topic. I summarize their work and others', while trying to account for the demonstrated superiority of cooperative learning, in Kohn, 1992a, chap. 10.
13. Zeldow, 1976, p. 319.
14. I discuss this issue at length in chapters 6 and 7 of my book *No Contest* (Kohn, 1992a).
15. Jordan, 1986, p. 409.
16. Several studies have corroborated this; see, for example, Haines and Mc-Keachie, 1967.
17. This dynamic was noticed by a researcher as early as 1932: "Generally, the usual classroom incentives call forth a response for maximum exertion only from the few very able pupils, while the majority of the pupils, knowing that their chances for excelling are limited, fail to be motivated to do their very best" (Zubin, 1932, p. 50). The same, of course, is true of workplace incentives.
18. For example, see Ames, 1978, 1981.
19. "If a group contingency is used, some members of the group may be aggressive in order to ensure that the group as a whole fulfills the reinforcement contingency" (Balsam and Bondy, 1983, p. 291).
20. Theodore H. Cohn, a compensation specialist, is quoted in Kanter, 1987, p. 66. Sometimes safety rather than performance is the criterion on which bonuses are based: everyone in the department is rewarded if and only if there are no injuries. The result, according to occupational health and safety specialist Philip Korman (personal communication, December 1992), is that an incentive is created to avoid reporting injuries. Moreover, such programs effectively shift responsibility away from the employer, whose legal responsibility it is to maintain a safe workplace, and to the employees.
21. Garbarino, 1975, p. 427.
22. Seligman et al., 1980.
23. Some schools present high-achieving students with cards good for discounts at local restaurants and stores. One major impact of this reward is the relative status it provides recipients. One high school senior is quoted as saying the card is "fun to have because a lot of people don't have one" (Tousignant, 1991, p. A1). The point is that it isn't necessary to set up an incentive program as a competition — that is, with an artificial limit on the number of prizes available — in order to sabotage relationships among students.

24. Posner, 1986, p. 59.
25. A dissertation experiment found some time ago that subordinates were more likely to ask for help when their supervisors were not also charged with enforcing a certain level of performance (Ross, 1957). The same point has been made in a study of merit pay for teachers, which provides them with "a strong incentive not to bring problems to their principal's attention and to be selective about the information they do provide to a principal" — a situation that not only makes life more difficult for both principals and teachers but also, ultimately, for students (Bachrach et al., 1984, p. 23).
26. Glasser, 1990, p. 29.
27. This policy, which goes by the name of "Learnfare" in Wisconsin, unfairly singles out for pressure those who depend on public assistance. Presumably, policymakers would like to see all children stay in school, but they apply coercion selectively to the neediest students because with them they have some leverage. As one mother and activist put it, "class status, not truancy alone, determined who would be abused by Learnfare" (Gowens, 1991, p. 90). When parents' subsistence payments are cut, the policy is doubly unfair; it penalizes people for lacking absolute control over the behavior of their teenage children. (The latter point is made by an observer who, however, then goes on to distinguish between the use of penalties, which he opposes, and rewards, which he sees as likely to "uplift and encourage" [Besharov, 1992, p. 19] — thereby overlooking the fundamental similarity of these two forms of control.)
28. Baron, 1988, p. 117.
29. This is a theme that runs through the work of Barry Schwartz; see especially Schwartz, 1982b.
30. Several studies of this kind are reviewed in McGraw, 1978, pp. 37–40, 55.
31. Pittman et al., 1982, p. 790.
32. This is the title of an article by the late John Condry published in 1977. Elsewhere, he and a colleague have remarked that "periods of exploration in which the goal seems to be shunted to the side may not only be natural but may also be facilitative" — that is, useful for learning and solving problems (Condry and Koslowski, 1979, p. 254).
33. Amabile, 1988, pp. 144, 143.
34. See Schwartz, 1982a, 1988.
35. Schwartz and Lacey, 1982, p. 247.
36. Schwartz, 1988, p. 129.
37. Lewin, 1935, p. 156; McGraw and Fiala, 1982. The Zeigarnik effect, discovered in the 1920s, refers to the fact that people are generally inclined to return to tasks from which they have been interrupted. But Kenneth McGraw and Jirina Fiala found that when subjects have already received a reward for working on a task (in this case, a jigsaw puzzle), they were more likely than nonrewarded subjects to leave it unfinished when given the chance.
38. Drabman and Tucker, 1974, p. 181.
39. See Condry and Chambers, 1978; Harter, 1978; Pearlman, 1984; Shapira, 1976; Fabes et al., 1988; and the five studies cited in the next three notes.
40. Two studies on this point are described in Locke, 1968, pp. 181–83.
41. Pittman et al., 1982. Another study found, to the contrary, that subjects went back to more difficult tasks when the reward was withdrawn, but the researchers conceded that this may have been due to a peculiarity of the

task they used, a computer game whose difficulty level was easily adjusted (Newby and Alter, 1989). Even this finding, of course, corroborates the central point that rewards lead people to avoid challenging themselves; the only disagreement concerns the permanence of that effect.

42. Boggiano et al., 1991, p. 517.

43. The fact that we see the task as an obstacle to getting a reward is closely related to the idea that interest in the task tends to decline under these conditions, which is the subject of the following chapter. Other theorists prefer to think of it this way: "attention is focused on the easiest route" to the reward because rewards "create a 'performance' context" in which we care more about how we are doing than what we are doing (Condry and Chambers, 1978, p. 67). I will return to this idea too in the context of exploring the effects of rewards on education. Yet another explanation for the tendency to pick easier tasks was proposed by Fabes et al. (1986): the promise of a reward for a job well done may seem to imply that the job is more difficult than we thought — to difficult to enjoy, perhaps. These researchers reported that third-grade children offered a toy for working on a maze game thought it was harder to solve than did those who weren't offered a toy.

44. Pearlman, 1984, p. 541.

45. Children have been found to be "intrinsically motivated to engage in those tasks which were within their reach but developmentally just beyond their current level" (Danner and Lonky, 1981, p. 1046). The entire tradition of "constructivism" in educational theory, based in part on the work of Jean Piaget, affirms the child's fundamental desire to make sense of the world. (I discuss this movement in chapter 11.) Even apart from educational questions, a number of theorists and researchers concerned with human motivation have persuasively challenged "tension reduction" or homeostatic models, which hold that organisms always seek a state of rest. Gordon Allport made that challenge explicit, and all of the work showing that we are motivated by a need to attain a sense of competence (Robert White), to be self-determining (Richard deCharms, Edward Deci, and others), to satisfy our curiosity (D. E. Berlyne), or to "actualize" our potential in various ways (Abraham Maslow) implicitly refutes the idea that it is natural to do as little as possible.

46. Two behaviorists seem to concede this when they note that "it is possible when a reward such as candy is given following successful math work, candy-getting is the operant strengthened, with math work being only one member of that operant class" (Balsam and Bondy, 1983, p. 291).

5. CUTTING THE INTEREST RATE

1. Surprisingly, research in the workplace has not always found a significant relationship between workers' reported satisfaction with their jobs and the quality of their performance. In the mid-1980s, one review of the available studies found that the two variables were "only slightly related" (Iaffaldano and Muchinsky, 1985), which echoed the results of previous reviews. Another analysis, however, turned up a more impressive correlation between satisfaction and performance (Petty et al., 1984), and the two also seem to be closely related when we look at organizations as a whole rather than at individuals (Ostroff, 1992). (Other studies [e.g., Guzzo and Katzell, 1987,

p. 109] have found that job satisfaction *is* pretty clearly related to whether an employee will stay with an organization.) That there should be anything but a consistent and strong relationship between how satisfied people are with their work and how well they do it is rather puzzling. It is hard to imagine, for example, that, everything else being equal, someone's productivity would not drop if she came to detest what she was doing. A low overall correlation does not necessarily mean that this isn't true, of course. It might be that above a certain threshold level of satisfaction, other factors are more relevant to performance. Conversely, it might be the case that people who do very good work may nevertheless be unhappy because of other aspects of their environment, even though *low* satisfaction and performance nearly always go hand in hand. Also, we would need to know more about whether the relationship is stronger with certain kinds of jobs and certain kinds of measures of how well people are doing their work. The most important point to be made about this research, though, is that an employee who reports being satisfied on a questionnaire is not necessarily enamored of the work itself. "If a task is dull . . . people may be more satisfied and may enjoy the experience more if they are paid for it. But that does not mean that they are more intrinsically motivated for it. . . . The satisfaction and enjoyment are extrinsic" in this case (Deci and Ryan, 1985, p. 83). Thus, the absence of a correlation between satisfaction and performance does not challenge the contribution that intrinsic motivation makes to quality work.

2. Researchers have found that extrinsic incentives can sometimes reduce the quality of people's work even when these incentives don't seem to have an effect on interest in the task (e.g., see McGraw and McCullers, 1979). The preceding chapter, after all, offered four other explanations for the detrimental effect of rewards on quality.
3. Koestner et al., 1987, p. 389.
4. Deci, 1971, Experiment 1; the quotation appears on p. 114. The results of this very first study were not overwhelming: there were only twenty-four subjects, with the result that the difference between the two groups (in terms of how much time was spent on the puzzle during the last session, after one group had been rewarded, corrected for how much time each group had spent on it initially) did not reach conventional levels of statistical significance ($p < .10$). Moreover, there was no difference in interest at all as measured by a questionnaire. Subsequent studies not only replicated the basic effect, however, but demonstrated it more convincingly.
5. Personal communication, September 1992. He also describes this experience in Lepper, 1983, pp. 308–309.
6. Lepper et al., 1973.
7. When studies of how other controlling factors affect intrinsic interest are added to those looking at rewards, the total exceeds one hundred, according to a recent paper on the subject (Ryan and Stiller, 1991, p. 120).
8. At least one researcher has had a similar experience. Harry Hom (in press) found that undergraduates generally could not predict that rewards would reduce intrinsic interest but were not surprised when the effect was explained to them, with some saying "I knew it all along."
9. Birch et al., 1984.
10. Personal communication, September 1989.
11. Wallack, 1992.

12. Schwartz, 1982b, p. 53n5.
13. Obviously, just because people do less creative work when a reward is at stake does not mean that their creativity will be permanently damaged. But research exploring what happens to interest in particular tasks confirms an enduring negative effect. Lepper, remember, found that preschoolers were still less interested in drawing with Magic Markers up to two weeks after they had been rewarded for doing so. Another study found that children who were promised a prize for playing with a drum were less interested in it four to five weeks later (Ross, 1975, Experiment 1). Two other researchers, meanwhile, found such an effect a week after the reward was presented but not after seven weeks had passed. Still, they pointed out, for children's reduced interest in drawing to persist even one week after being rewarded "represents a rather powerful and lasting change in behavior associated with a seemingly small reward" (Loveland and Olley, 1979, p. 1209). Another reviewer was similarly impressed: "Given that studies typically involve only a single reward, the persistence of the effect is remarkable and is one of its strongest claims to importance. In the usual classroom [or, we might add, workplace] setting where rewards are dispersed continually over long periods, one might expect the effect to be even longer lasting" (Morgan, 1984, p. 24).
14. "The subsequent behavioral effects of manipulations of extrinsic incentives do not depend upon the immediate effects of these manipulations on behavior during the experimental sessions" (Lepper and Greene, 1978b, p. 122).
15. "The key question is whether . . . the undermining of people's intrinsic motivation for an activity simply means that they won't choose that activity as a means to intrinsic satisfaction or whether it means that their overall intrinsic motivation will tend to decrease in addition to their decreased interest in the one activity," as Deci and a colleague put it. Already, they continued, preliminary evidence supported the latter view (Deci and Porac, 1978, p. 174). In the early 1990s, a Canadian study confirmed that rewards do indeed tend to "subvert intrinsic motivation to pursue other activities that were never intended to fall under the influence of the extrinsic constraint" (Enzle and Wright, 1992, p. 33).
16. Morgan, 1983. "The undermining effect among observers was not persistent because the opportunity was quickly presented to try out the activity" — in this case, a jigsaw puzzle — and discover that it really was enjoyable. "In other circumstances such opportunities might not be present" (p. 644).
17. Gottfried, 1986, p. 91. A recent survey of working adults did find that older people were slightly less extrinsically motivated than younger people on average (Amabile et al., 1991). It is possible, though, that the older people in this study were also more experienced at their jobs or were earning more money; motivational orientation may actually be related to one of these factors rather than to age itself.
18. One exception is a study that offered colorful stickers to kindergartners for working on a maze. Different ways of presenting the reward had different effects on how long the boys spent playing with the maze on their own time, whereas any sort of reward reduced the girls' apparent interest in it. However, nonrewarded girls seemed more interested than nonrewarded boys, which complicates the picture (Boggiano et al., 1985).
19. Tenth-grade girls scored higher than boys on a measure of intrinsic intellec-

tual orientation in one survey (Lloyd and Barenblatt, 1984). In another, elementary school–aged girls too were less likely than boys to give pressure from the teacher as their reason for doing homework or classwork (Grolnick and Ryan, 1990, p. 180). In a third study, female undergraduates described themselves in ways suggesting a more intrinsic orientation toward academics than males had (Vallerand and Bissonnette, 1992, pp. 609–10; other research pointing to the same conclusion is mentioned on p. 615). On the other hand, another survey of children in elementary school found the girls to be more motivated by extrinsic factors than the boys were (Boggiano et al., 1991, Experiment 1). Typically, the measures used in such studies assume that orientation exists on a single continuum, with extreme extrinsic on one side and extreme intrinsic on another. This, as more recent research indicates, may be a mistake: the two possibilities operate independently of each other such that one person could be high or low on both (e.g., see Harter and Jackson, 1992).

20. For example, see Terrell et al., 1959; and the studies cited in Spence, 1970, p. 104.

21. Condry, 1978, p. 183n2.

22. Spence, 1971 (and see the discussion of previous research on pp. 1462–64); Ward et al., 1972; Sewell and Walker, 1982.

23. Lloyd and Barenblatt, 1984; Gottfried, 1985, 1990.

24. McGregor, 1960, p. 41. Since jobs that are highly regimented are typically jobs that also don't pay very well, it is hard to figure out whether a greater concern with extrinsic rewards is due to the absence of power or of money. But there is no doubt that people at the bottom of the totem pole do have such a concern (see Kovach, 1987; Jurgensen, 1978; Lawler, *Pay and Organizational Effectiveness,* cited in Guzzo and Katzell, 1987, p. 107; Shapiro, 1977; Hackman and Oldham, 1980, p. 11). One study also suggests that black workers are more concerned about extrinsic factors than are white workers (Shapiro, 1977). This disparity persists even when social class and income level are statistically controlled. But as the researcher concedes, "black workers may receive lower levels of extrinsic rewards, other than income, than white workers" (p. 28) and therefore may be more concerned about them. Also, the only intrinsic factor examined in this study was the self-reported concern with having a job that provides a feeling of accomplishment; other factors might well be equally important to blacks and whites.

25. One of the first explanations offered for the effect of rewards on intrinsic motivation went like this: when we see ourselves doing something and getting rewarded for it, we infer that we must have been motivated by the reward rather than by interest in what we were doing. External pressures act to displace, or cause us to "discount," the internal explanation for our behavior. We conform to that self-perception and become less interested in the task. Lepper, who derived this model from the work of social psychologists Daryl Bem and Harold Kelley, called this the "overjustification" hypothesis. Of the several problems with it that have been identified, two stand out as particularly troublesome. The first is that the account is based on a theory that assumes we have no privileged access to our own motives and must figure out why we act in the way we do, just as we figure out why others act in the way *they* do, by relying on observable behavior and circumstantial clues. This, of course, is itself a remnant of behaviorism, and it is an assumption difficult to reconcile with our experience of ourselves.

The second problem is that young children are unable to make the sort of sophisticated inferences about the relationship among multiple motives that the theory describes. Since rewards clearly do have an effect on the attitudes of small children, there must be some other explanation for how it happens. (For a discussion of this issue, see Lepper et al., 1982, pp. 52–53; Morgan, 1984, pp. 18–19; Boggiano and Main, 1986, p. 1120.)

A second theory proposes that when people seem less interested in a task for which they have gotten a reward, what is really going on is not a change in the way the task is regarded but a tendency to feel bad as a result of being rewarded. Lower intrinsic motivation just means more negative affect. Thus, if something else makes you feel good (or bad), that will have much more bearing than a reward on how interested you are in the activity (see Pretty and Seligman, 1984; Fabes et al., 1988). This theory seems difficult to defend since it is certainly very common for people to feel happy to receive a desired reward but nevertheless become less interested in whatever they are rewarded to do. Even if it is true that only feelings are involved, moreover, the theory doesn't explain *why* rewards make people feel bad.

Still another explanation argues that instead of assuming that we don't perform as well on tasks as a result of having lost interest in them, the truth might be the other way around: we lose interest in them because we do them badly. (Any of the four reasons in the previous chapter, and particularly the last one, might explain why it is that we do a poorer job.) It does seem to be true, after all, that better school performance *causes* children to become more motivated just as surely as it *results* from being more motivated (Gottfried, 1990, p. 536). Several theorists, noting that our creativity can decline even when we seem just as interested in what we are doing (McGraw and McCullers, 1979), have speculated that rewards affect performance directly, which in turn affects motivation (McCullers et al., 1987, p. 1032). Weighed against this speculation, however, is some solid evidence to the contrary. Sometimes rewards undermine interest without dragging performance down along with it (Lepper, 1982, p. 60; see also the discussion on this point in Lepper and Greene, 1982b, pp. 114–15; Morgan, 1984, pp. 19–20) — or these performance effects, if they do occur, are only temporary, whereas the effects on interest linger (Loveland and Olley, 1979, p. 1209). While lower interest can help explain lower performance, the best guess is that rewards "disrupt both performance and interest in a somewhat independent manner" (Fabes et al., 1986, p. 25).

Because none of these three explanations for how extrinsic motivators lower intrinsic motivation seems entirely satisfactory, then, I incline to two others, which follow in the text.

26. Neill, the author of *Summerhill,* is quoted in Morgan, 1984, p. 5.
27. Lepper et al., 1982, Experiment 3. In the same paper the researchers report having told another group of preschoolers a story about a child who was given two new foods, "hupe" and "hule" (both of which, of course, are nonsense words), and told that s/he had to finish one before getting to eat the other. The children listening to this said that they would rather eat whichever of the fictitious foods had been set up as the end, as opposed to the means (Experiment 1).
28. Freedman et al., 1992.
29. Playing for toys: Boggiano et al., 1986; playing for cookies: Pittman et al., 1992, pp. 47–48; talking for money: Pittman et al., 1992, pp. 40–43.
30. Newman and Taylor, 1992.

31. Rotter, 1982. Rotter was a student of Leann Lipps Birch and a coauthor of the kefir study.
32. Boggiano and Main, 1986.
33. See especially Deci and Ryan, 1985.
34. See deCharms, 1968.
35. Deci and Ryan, 1990, p. 253.
36. Ryan et al., 1983, p. 748.
37. Reduced intrinsic motivation is "the result of the imposition of superfluous extrinsic constraints . . . not a specific function of the use of tangible rewards per se" (Lepper et al., 1982, p. 62).
38. For example, see Fisher, 1978; Fabes, 1987.
39. An unpublished study by Deci and Cascio is described in Deci and Porac, 1978, pp. 157–58.
40. Lepper and Greene, 1975; Pittman et al., 1980.
41. Enzle and Anderson, 1993. Additionally, surveillance may undermine intrinsic motivation to the extent that it fosters self-consciousness and, thus, "internally controlling regulation" (Plant and Ryan, 1985).
42. Strickland, 1958.
.43. "Evaluative contingencies constrain behavior and exert performance pressure, leading to decrements in intrinsic interest" (Harackiewicz et al., 1984, p. 298). See also Butler, 1987.
44. This effect has been found when subjects are asked to generate ideas (Bartis et al., 1988) or make collages (Amabile, 1979). Judith Harackiewicz and her colleagues discovered that performance dropped even on a pinball game when people knew they were going to be evaluated (see previous note).
45. Koestner et al. (1987), for example, found that this was true with adults. Many more studies, which I will report later, have shown that inducing children to think about the quality of their performance (as opposed to what they were learning) undermines interest, impedes achievement, and has a host of other undesirable effects.
46. Amabile et al., 1976; Reader and Dollinger, 1982.
47. Deci, Driver, et al., 1993.
48. Mossholder, 1980.
49. Deci and Ryan, 1985, pp. 325, 85. Among the research supporting this finding is Deci, Betley, et al., 1981. See also Nicholls's various reports (e.g., 1989) of the perils of instilling in children an "ego orientation" — that is, a concern about doing better than others — and my own analysis of competition (Kohn, 1992a). Of course, competition is unlikely to undermine intrinsic motivation until a child is old enough to understand the meaning of mutually exclusive goal attainment (R. Butler, 1989).
50. On the use of tangible reward plus surveillance, see Lepper and Greene, 1975; on verbal reward plus surveillance, Pittman et al., 1980.
51. Swann and Pittman, 1977.
52. Management guru Tom Peters is a good example. In the best-selling book *In Search of Excellence,* he and his coauthor dropped Deci's name and briefly mentioned the importance of intrinsic motivation, but they also spent several pages extolling the usefulness of Skinnerian positive reinforcement as if there were no incompatibility in championing both (1982, pp. 67–72). Several years later, Peters stressed the need for workers to experience a sense of "involvement and the opportunity to influence the outcome" of decisions, but he also asserted, "There is, I earnestly believe, no down-

side" to a plan (which now fills an entire chapter) that calls for managers to "provide bold financial incentives for everyone" (1987, pp. 341, 332). In another forum he declared that "business problem number one is the almost total absence of positive reinforcement" (1988, p. 80). In his view, things are wonderfully simple: positive reinforcement is good; negative reinforcement (a term he uses interchangeably with *punishment*) is bad. He even invokes the name of W. Edwards Deming to support this dichotomy, although Deming in fact opposes the use of pay-for-performance and other incentive plans on the grounds that they are inimical to quality.

53. DeCharms, 1983, p. 396. DeCharms offers this observation by way of correcting his own formulation of fifteen years earlier in which he, like many others, "separate[d] action sequences into observable elements like task plus reward" (p. 397). Ultimately, he implies later, it is necessary to question the application of a natural science model to human beings. We need to begin with the experience of the subject, and to shift from an analysis that reduces who we are into fragmentary behaviors toward a more comprehensive account of the whole. As usual, Kurt Lewin understood this decades before other theorists: "Both threat of punishment and the prospect of reward may in definite instances and to a certain degree lead to a transformation in valence of the thing itself. . . . Reward may lead the child to regard the thing not at first wanted as something to be valued for its own sake" (1935, p. 169). Also on this point, see Condry and Chambers, 1978, pp. 69–70, 75.

54. Schwartz, 1988, p. 131.

55. Deci, 1978, p. 202. This dynamic is rarely mentioned in discussions of the topic intended for general readers. A welcome exception was a parenting column in the *New York Times:* "One problem with bribery is that instead of acting as a transition to these internal motivations, it can become the primary focus of the child's efforts. The natural rewards that come with doing a job well or being part of a group are overshadowed and go unnoticed, making it less likely that the child will do the job again without another bribe" (Kutner, 1991). The same columnist, however, subsequently urged parents to "pay extra attention to your child when he acts the way you wish" (Kutner, 1992), effectively bribing the child to comply by selectively withholding something that surely ought not to be offered conditionally.

56. Elsewhere, borrowing from the work of a pair of sports psychologists, I have used this analogy to describe the process of trying to feel better about ourselves by taking part in competition. It seems even more apt with respect to the use of rewards, in part because the practice is even more common.

57. "*Self-control* is actually a misnomer for self-induced change, for although some patterns of behavior may come from within ourselves in the sense that they were acquired before birth or soon thereafter, whatever causes a behavior to appear at a given time must come from interaction with the environment. Thus *self*-control really refers to the control of behavior by certain aspects of the environment" (Rachlin, 1991, p. 264).

58. For example, see the summary of T. F. McLaughlin's work in Thomas, 1980, p. 220.

59. Johnson et al., 1976, p. 185.

60. Deci and Ryan, 1987, p. 1031.

61. Dollinger and Thelen, 1978. Another researcher, however, argues that this

result was due to the fact that the standards for what constituted successful completion of the task were not clear to the children (Enzle et al., 1991).

62. Ryan, 1982.

63. Brophy and Kher, 1986, p. 264.

64. Again, Tom Peters comes to mind: "The solution . . . is not to abandon incentives, but to base them on nonvolumetric factors as well. . . . You can keep score on quality, customer service, responsiveness, innovativeness, even customer listening. Moreover, the sheer act of keeping score will provide a positive stimulant to improvement" (Peters, 1988, p. 81).

65. For example, see Dickinson, 1989, pp. 8–9; and, borrowing from her analysis, Chance, 1992, pp. 203–204. Interestingly, of the studies cited by Dickinson in support of the claim that there is no problem with rewards that are given to people because of good performance, two don't address that claim at all and one (Weiner and Mander, 1978) shows precisely the reverse — that performance-contingent rewards *are* detrimental.

66. See, for example, Greene et al., 1976, p. 1221; Luyten and Lens, 1981, esp. p. 29.

67. Karniol and Ross, 1977; Arkes, 1979; Rosenfield et al., 1980; Zimmerman, 1985, pp. 144–52. In another study, performance-contingent rewards undermined the interest of preschool-age children but not that of older children (Boggiano and Ruble, 1979).

68. Boggiano et al., 1985.

69. Harackiewicz and Manderlink, 1984.

70. See Harackiewicz et al., 1984, for a discussion of the relative impact of competence and evaluation.

71. Ryan et al., 1983.

72. For example, see Deci, 1971, Experiment 1; Greene and Lepper, 1974; Garbarino, 1975; Smith and Pittman, 1978; Orlick and Mosher, 1978; Harackiewicz, 1979; Fabes, 1987; Lepper and Cordova, 1992, pp. 201–202. See also the studies cited in, and conclusions offered by, McGraw, 1978, p. 40; Lepper, 1983, pp. 304–305; Deci and Ryan, 1985, p. 78.

73. Weiner and Mander, 1978.

74. Personal communication, June 1992.

75. For example, see Boggiano et al., 1982; and the brief discussion in Barrett and Boggiano, 1988, p. 295. But see the following note for a study that failed to find this. Also, whether short-term interest in pursuing a task is equivalent to true intrinsic motivation is not clear.

76. Danner and Lonky, 1981, Experiment 2; the quotation appears on p. 1049.

77. Mark Lepper's more recent work concerns the promotion of students' intrinsic motivation, and the use of fantasy scenarios is one of the techniques he describes. See, for example, Lepper and Hodell, 1989, pp. 92–93; Lepper and Cordova, 1992.

78. "Can the speed at which I mow the yard or a part of it provide feedback to my actions? Can I tell how neatly I do this job in comparison to other times? Is it possible to develop rules about how to proceed — for instance by following a circular path, or a zigzag pattern? Or do I rather want to develop rules for my physical movements as I walk behind the machine? . . . Supposing I decide I want to cut parallel swaths in the grass, making a U-turn at the end of each run without overlapping any of the runs, getting as close to the trees as possible without nicking the bark. As soon as I set up these tacit rules, they define what stimuli will be relevant for me to

watch for. They also define what will be negative and positive feedback un- der the rules. When this is done, I am ready to go; and mowing grass be- comes a moderately enjoyable activity with its own set of intrinsic rewards" (Csikszentmihalyi, 1978, p. 214).

79. The relevance of children's interest in a task to their responsiveness to rewards was demonstrated by Loveland and Olley, 1979. But Lepper's original study found that rewards had to be presented after the task was completed if there was any hope of boosting the interest even of children who were bored; everyone lost interest when they were promised in advance (Lepper et al., 1973, p. 135).

80. See Arnold, 1976; Phillips and Freedman, 1985. Interestingly, both of these papers were written by people who specialize in workplace management.

81. Condry and Chambers, 1978, p. 64.

82. "It is conceivable . . . that the perception of choice is affected by the interest level of the activity that subjects are requested to perform. If asked to perform an interesting activity, subjects may have the experience of choice because they are being asked to do what they would freely choose to do. If asked to perform a dull task, subjects may experience constraint because they are being asked to do what they ordinarily would choose not to do" (Quattrone, 1985, p. 32).

83. "In situations in which an entire classroom is organized around reinforce- ment contingencies, it is extremely difficult to individualize contingencies sufficiently so that each child's interests and abilities are taken into account. Without such individualization, it will surely be the case that reinforcement is sometimes available, for some children, for some activities they would eagerly engage in without it" (Schwartz, 1982b, pp. 53–54).

84. Deci, Eghrari, et al., in press.

85. At least with respect to children in school, about half of the students in one recent study do not seem to show a consistent intrinsic or extrinsic orienta- tion over time or across different school subjects (Harter and Jackson, 1992). On the latter sort of consistency, see also Gottfried, 1985. However, Amabile and her colleagues (1991) have shown some stability over time of adults' intrinsic and extrinsic orientation on their Work Preference Inven- tory.

86. Ryan et al., 1992, p. 168.

87. Deci, Nezlek, and Sheinman, 1981.

88. Harter, 1981. One scale on Harter's questionnaire, filled out by more than 1,600 students in three states, measures the extent to which they are trying to satisfy their own curiosity as opposed to doing schoolwork for grades or the teacher's approval. Her graph of the results shows a steady and signifi- cant shift from the former to the latter motive as they get older, from third to eighth grade, before the curiosity motive rebounds slightly in ninth grade (p. 307). She replicated this trend in a later study (Harter and Jackson, 1992, p. 224).

89. Switzky and Schultz, 1988, pp. 10–11.

90. Ross, 1975.

91. Lepper and Greene, 1978b, p. 111. This account, however, is premised on an explanation for the effects of rewards on intrinsic motivation that is itself open to question — namely, that these effects are due to forming conclusions about our own motives solely on the basis of our behavior (see note 25).

92. For example, see Lepper et al., 1973; Greene and Lepper, 1974; Harackiewicz et al., 1984. However, see also Orlick and Mosher, 1978; Kruglanski et al., 1972. In the last study, some subjects received a reward without prior notice but were falsely told that it *had* been announced earlier that a prize would be given. Some of these people experienced a drop in interest, as if they really did remember being told this before engaging in the task.

93. For example, see Deci, Betley, et al., 1981; Pritchard et al., 1977; and the research reviewed in Kohn, 1992a. Some of the studies that have documented a detrimental effect of rewards on motivation actually set up competitions for the rewards.

94. On the commonly heard justification that it is necessary to "recognize excellence," see chapter 6.

95. See Kruglanski, 1978, esp. pp. 96–100.

96. Even choice with respect to a peripheral aspect of the activity may keep interest in it high, at least temporarily (Enzle and Wright, 1992, Experiment 1).

97. Pittman et al., 1977. Telling students that a physiological test indicates they are either intrinsically or extrinsically oriented toward a task affected the way they responded to it later. Unfortunately, an extrinsic induction was much more likely to reduce their interest than an intrinsic induction was to enhance it.

98. Fazio, 1981. In this study, a reward did not undermine children's interest in an activity when they were shown a photo of themselves voluntarily engaging in it earlier.

99. In a series of studies with elementary school students, listening to another child talk about how learning can be fun (and how this is more important than grades or parental approval) seemed to have some effect on the students' own motivation in that their creativity was not impeded when they were promised rewards. The results of this research were somewhat equivocal, however, and did not produce a lasting effect (Hennessey et al., 1989; Hennessey and Zbikowski, in press).

100. Csikszentmihalyi, 1990, p. 47.

101. Deci and Porac, 1978, p. 153; Ryan et al., 1985, pp. 44–45.

102. Boggiano and Barrett, 1992; Boggiano et al., 1992. "In contrast, because intrinsically motivated children pursue activities for the satisfaction inherent in the activities, particularly highly challenging ones, the desired outcome for intrinsic children is in large part tied to the effort expended in performing the activity. Moreover, because intrinsically motivated children rely only partly on external evaluation of their performance and have internal criteria for success and failure, the role of their own effort in producing a given outcome should be highly salient" (Boggiano et al., 1992, p. 276).

6. THE PRAISE PROBLEM

1. Farson, 1977, p. 66. This is the only article I could find devoted exclusively to the effects of praise in a work setting. Farson's point that praise may mostly benefit the person who gives it is echoed and applied to the classroom by Bennett, 1988, p. 23.

2. Brophy, 1981, p. 15.

3. The summary of a review by W. K. Esler published in 1983 appears in Hitz and Driscoll, 1988, p. 9.

4. Butler, 1987. The results were the same regardless of how well the student actually performed on the task.
5. Baumeister et al., 1990; the quotation appears on p. 145.
6. Meyer et al., 1979; the quotation appears on p. 268. See also replications by Barker and Graham, 1987; Miller et al., 1992. Such inferences are not generally made by younger children, however.
7. For a defense of praising ability rather than effort (as if these were the only two alternatives), see Koestner et al., 1987, 1989. For descriptions of the perils of encouraging children to focus on ability, see the various publications of Carole Ames, Carol Dweck, and John Nicholls, which are discussed in chapter 8.
8. Sylvia Plath's journal entry is quoted by Amabile et al., 1991, ms. p. 5.
9. Quoted in "Wyeth Feared Public Reaction," 1986.
10. See the account of a study by D. E. Kanouse and E. Pullan (in Kanouse et al., 1981, pp. 112–13), which found that "subjects who received praise implying continued good performance subsequently produced drawings of lower quality than either specific-praise subjects or controls . . . and they rated themselves as significantly more anxious" (p. 113). See also Kast and Connor, 1988.
11. Skinner is quoted in Lawson, 1984, p. 86.
12. Rowe, 1974, p. 302.
13. Madden, 1988, p. 143. See also Hitz and Driscoll, 1988, p. 7.
14. This point was made by Koestner et al., 1987, pp. 382–83. See also Butler, 1987, p. 475.
15. Anderson et al., 1976; Harackiewicz, 1979. Another survey found a significant correlation between the motivation and achievement of nine-year-old children and their mothers' tendency to say they praised their children for doing well and encouraged their efforts when the children did poorly (Gottfried, 1991a). It is not clear from this study whether it was praise or encouragement that mattered more, whether the mothers were accurately reporting their own behavior, and whether use of praise might be just a marker for other characteristics of these families that more directly affected the children.
16. Deci (1971, Experiment 3) found that interest neither increased nor decreased when people received verbal reinforcement for their performance; by contrast, the control group subjects' interest declined markedly for some reason as they continued working on puzzles that were generally seen as intrinsically motivating. William Swann and Thane Pittman (1977) found that "the addition of verbal reward can neutralize or eliminate the effects of contingent physical reward" (a stick-on star), but interest was no higher than it was for children who received no reward at all. See also Dollinger and Thelen, 1978.
17. This argument is offered by Pittman et al., 1983, p. 322; Lepper and Greene, 1978b, p. 130*n*.
18. Interestingly, though, in one small study, children who watched a videotape of someone being praised for what they themselves were about to do showed more interest in the task later than those who were praised unexpectedly (Pallak et al., 1982).
19. "Verbal rewards that acquire a salience of their own . . . should be experienced in much the same way as are other types of extrinsic rewards that can lead to [a decline in interest]" (Kanouse et al., 1981, p. 110).
20. Danner and Lonky, 1981, Experiment 2.

21. Smith, 1976.
22. Pittman et al., 1980; Ryan, 1982; Boggiano et al., 1988, Study 2.
23. Morgan, 1984, p. 16. Since Deci's early work is often quoted by other psychologists in support of the idea that praise isn't as bad as other extrinsic motivators, it is worth noting that he says, "I don't think fundamentally it's any different" (personal communication, February 1992). His early studies, he points out, involved not praise but informational feedback, which generally does not undermine intrinsic motivation and may even enhance it. Outside the laboratory, Deci adds, "we find praise can be very controlling. If you're trying to get [someone] to do something, that [fact will] come through."
24. Mills and Grusec, 1989, p. 299.
25. Grusec, 1991.
26. Farson, 1977, p. 67.
27. A similar point is made in Wolfgang and Brudenell, 1982, p. 238; Chandler, 1981, p. 11. By contrast, a behaviorist faced with a child's resistance can only speculate that, "due to poor learning experiences or perhaps biological deficiencies, praise and affection do not acquire reinforcing value for some people" (O'Leary et al., 1972, p. 7).
28. Kanouse et al., 1981, pp. 101, 106, 107. See also the work of Thomas Gordon.
29. Chandler, 1981, p. 12. On this point, see also Wolfgang and Brudenell, 1982, p. 237; Farson, 1977, p. 66.
30. Dreikurs, 1957, p. 43. Elsewhere, he has noted that "flattery may promote insecurity since the child may become frightened of the possibility of not being able to live up to expectations or may not be certain he will get the same kind of praise again. The child has the mistaken idea that *unless he is praised, he has no value* and therefore he is a failure" (Dreikurs et al., 1982, p. 109). The same theme can also be found in other discussions of praise, such as Chandler, 1981, p. 11; Wolfgang and Brudenell, 1982, p. 241; Madden, 1988, p. 143; Hitz and Driscoll, 1988, p. 8.
31. Rowe, 1974, pp. 301–303.
32. Cannella, 1986, p. 298. See also Kanouse et al., 1981, p. 100.
33. "Young students in the early grades are likely to find praise reinforcing. . . . Also, at any grade level, but perhaps especially in the earlier grades, students who are low in ability, who came from low-SES backgrounds, or who come from minority groups may be especially responsive to praise and encouragement from teachers. Finally, introverts apparently are more responsive than extroverts" (Brophy, 1981, p. 20). These specific conclusions should be viewed with some caution, given that the studies on which they are based may be outdated. Remember that earlier findings that children of low socioeconomic status respond more readily to tangible rewards did not prove terribly robust. Another source suggests that praise is less likely to undermine achievement when used with children of *high* socioeconomic status (Cannella, 1986, p. 298). Consistent with Brophy's assertion regarding the greater responsiveness of younger children, a later study showed that "older children give more weight to the controlling component of the [positive feedback] message than do younger children" (Kast and Connor, 1988, p. 521), which should increase the probability of a negative reaction.
34. Brophy, 1981, pp. 10–15. "Certain students (most of whom are boys) seem to get more praise and more criticism simply because they are more initia-

tory and active within the classroom: They have more of every kind of interaction with the teacher. . . . [Certain] students also tended to reward teachers for their praise by responding very positively to it — smiling, beaming proudly, and so forth. In effect, they were conditioning the teachers to praise them" (pp. 11, 12).

35. Deci et al., 1975, pp. 83–84; Koestner et al., 1987.
36. Kast and Connor, 1988.
37. Mills and Grusec, 1989, pp. 322, 303. The gender difference here, of course, refers to *what* girls as opposed to boys are praised for rather than how children of each sex interpret praise. The implication is that if boys were praised for altruistic acts, they too would be unlikely to develop an internal commitment to altruism.
38. Brophy, 1981, p. 21. To "praise" someone, for Brophy, means "to commend the worth of or to express approval or admiration" — not merely to provide feedback but to express "positive affect" (pp. 5–6).
39. Harackiewicz, 1979; Harackiewicz, Abrahams, and Wageman, 1987; Boggiano et al., 1982; Butler and Nissan, 1986; Butler, 1987.
40. When subjects in one experiment were constantly made aware of their success at solving interesting puzzles, they reported *less* interest in the task (Crino and White, 1982). Another study found that informational feedback didn't increase intrinsic motivation very much, even though controlling feedback decreased it significantly (Kast and Connor, 1988).
41. "Negative feedback — whether self-administered or administered verbally by the experimenter — adversely affected the intrinsic motivation of both male and female subjects" (Deci and Porac, 1978, p. 160). Other research has shown this is more true of people who are extrinsically oriented (Boggiano and Barrett, 1991, ms. pp. 29, 32). Occasional negative feedback can sometimes be helpful if it serves to make the positive feedback offered at other times (and, by extension, the person providing it) seem more credible. Whether criticism is welcomed depends on a number of factors, including the tone with which it is offered, the (in)security of the person hearing it, the nature of the relationship between the two individuals, the presence or absence of rewards and other controlling factors, and so on. All things being equal, negative feedback is probably less threatening when it flows from an individual in a less powerful position to someone in a more powerful position (for example, from student to teacher) than the other way around.
42. Deci and Chandler, 1986, p. 591. Lepper and his colleagues, meanwhile, have discovered that successful tutors "generally provide students with extremely little in the way of overt diagnoses concerning their errors or explicit corrective feedback." Instead, they "offer students *hints* — questions or remarks that indirectly imply the inaccuracy of their prior response, suggest the direction in which they might proceed, or highlight the section of the problem that appears to be causing them difficulty" (Lepper et al., 1990, pp. 228–29).
43. Boggiano et al., 1992, p. 286.
44. The view of Michael Lewis is described in Karen, 1992, p. 62. Also on this point, see Kanouse et al., 1981, pp. 109–10; Chandler, 1981, p. 11. On the other hand, when we are trying to promote altruism, Joan Grusec argues that "dispositional praise," whereby we attribute the characteristic to children ("I guess you're the kind of person who likes to help others"), is more

likely to help them come to develop a sense of themselves as altruistic —
and therefore act that way in the future — than is simply complimenting
them on their behavior. Some early research supported this approach with
older children, although not with four- and five-year-olds (Grusec and
Redler, 1980), but a later study raised some doubts about those findings,
yielding a much murkier set of results (Mills and Grusec, 1989).

45. Kanouse et al., 1981, p. 104. More generally, see pp. 101–109 of this article
and also Hitz and Driscoll, 1988, p. 10.

46. "General, information-free positive feedback tends to increase productivity,
but decrease interest. . . . Once attention is withdrawn, many kids won't
touch the activity again. . . . My advice is, keep the volume of feedback low,
but when you give it, make the commentary specific" (Katz, 1988, p. 16).

47. Koestner et al., 1990. See also Butler, 1987; Harackiewicz, Abrahams, and
Wageman, 1987.

48. For more on the destructive consequences of competition, see Kohn, 1992a.

49. This point is made by Bennett, 1988, p. 23.

50. For example, see Ames, 1992a, p. 337 (borrowing in this instance from the
work of Martin Covington); Hitz and Driscoll, 1988, p. 11. Even a behaviorist concedes that "older children do not as a rule favour public praise
and prefer praise to be delivered in a more private manner" (Burland, 1984,
p. 122). Brophy remarks that "an attempt to motivate other students by
vicarious reinforcement effects" may backfire. "Unless the students singled
out for such 'praise' are very immature and teacher dependent, they are
likely to feel manipulated rather than rewarded by it" (1981, pp. 15, 17).

51. Dreikurs's distinction between praise and encouragement is discussed in
Hitz and Driscoll, 1988, pp. 10–12; Nelsen, 1987, pp. 103–105; and other
books and articles on discipline.

52. The Kpelle of Liberia and the Gusii of Kenya are mentioned by one well-
known anthropologist as examples of peoples whose cultures allow children
to "grow up without experiencing praise from their parents or others for
behaving in a socially approved way or for learning a desirable skill. In
contrast with the familiar American sequence of a child's performing well,
calling the performance to adult attention, and being praised by the adult,
the African child learns through another sequence: observe the approved
task (as performed by an older sibling), imitate it spontaneously, and receive
corrective feedback only for inadequate performance. There is no expectation of recognition for good performance in learning or for carrying out a
task, yet tasks are learned and performed with skill" (LeVine, 1989, p. 63).

53. Rosemond, 1990.

54. Hagood, 1989. This article begins with an apt warning that children can
become hooked on rewards rather than on what we are trying to get them
to do. But it soon becomes clear that the author is chiefly concerned about
finding the best way we adults can "reach *our* objectives" (my emphasis)
and "maintain order in the classroom," suggesting an agenda potentially
different from what children need. It is a small step from here to the
argument that children should learn above all that "they must *earn* the
coupon or ticket" provided as a reward (her emphasis). "It is not a gift."

55. O'Brien, 1990, p. 249.

56. Adler, 1992, p. 49; the quotation is attributed to Nancy E. Curry, a psychoanalyst.

57. Laird, 1986.

7. PAY FOR PERFORMANCE

1. See n. 22 in chapter 1 for a review of recent surveys.
2. Ellig, 1982, p. 26. Ellig continues: "Not to vary compensation in relation to an objective assessment of performance is de facto to reward mediocrity and to penalize the better performing executive" (p. 28).
3. Kearney, 1979, p. 5.
4. Guzzo and Katzell, 1987, p. 110.
5. Sometimes these perfunctory defenses of the idea of paying for performance are justified by a quick nod in the direction of Thorndike's Law of Effect, equity theory, or expectancy theory, all of which are interpreted to mean that people act when they think they'll get something; the bigger the goody, the harder they'll work. If one chooses to define one's terms (for example, "get something") very broadly, such a theory would seem to be tautological or at best rather uninformative; defined more narrowly (for example, in terms of extrinsic incentives), it is simply false. Expectancy theory also predicts that intrinsic and extrinsic motivation are additive — exactly what the studies cited in chapter 5 disprove — and thus inclines its adherents to support the use of a variety of merit pay systems.
6. "At the core of any theory of the management of human resources are assumptions about human motivation," McGregor noted (1960, p. 35; see also Whyte, 1955, p. 7). A few years later, McGregor went on to suggest that management practices may also reflect an implicit position on what philosophers refer to as the mind-body problem: There is "a tacit belief that motivating people *to work* is a 'mechanical' problem . . . man has been perceived to be like a physical body at rest. It requires the application of external force to set him in motion — to motivate him to work" (1966, p. 205).
7. In an undeservedly obscure collection of essays entitled *The Great Jackass Fallacy* — the fallacy in question being that people can be motivated through the use of carrots and sticks — Harry Levinson pointed out, "Since the turn of the century, half a dozen different philosophies of management have appeared . . . each advocating a new set of techniques. Though they differ from each other in many respects, all are based on reward-punishment psychology" (1973, p. 11).
8. Eimers et al., 1979, p. A3.
9. Most writers never even raise the underlying motivational issues. Others do take the time to emphasize the importance of intrinsic motivation or even mention that extrinsic incentives are problematic — but then proceed to offer recommendations that take no account of these arguments, as if they fail to understand the significance of what they just wrote. For example, the only one of thirty chapters in an anthology on compensation to ask whether money really motivates people is sprinkled with comments that have the effect of challenging the behaviorist premise of its suggestions for fine-tuning reward systems, although the author seems not to see this (McLaughlin, 1991). Two other writers remind us that what really allows people to become motivated is a workplace characterized by mutual respect, attentive listening, and cooperative effort. But a few pages earlier, they approvingly cite "a basic lesson in psychology" — that "if you want a desirable pattern of behavior, reward it" (Mower and Wilemon, 1989, pp. 28, 24).

10. Pearce and Perry, 1983, p. 324. Interestingly, one of these authors has elsewhere remarked pointedly that "it is a rare author who does not end the list of 'merit pay problems' with upbeat suggestions for the successful implementation of such programs" (Pearce, 1987, p. 169).
11. Meyer, 1975, p. 40.
12. McGregor, 1960, pp. 33–35, 91. "Theory X is not a straw man for purposes of demolition, but is in fact a theory which materially influences managerial strategy in a wide sector of American industry today" (p. 35). The same point was made emphatically by William Foote Whyte concerning a similar set of assumptions: "Does anybody really believe in this theory of motivation any more? The answer seems to be that most people will deny that they hold such a belief and yet will then have difficulty in abandoning the belief" (1955, p. 6).
13. Peters and Waterman, 1982, p. 43.
14. Brennan, 1985, p. 73.
15. Lawler is quoted in Braham, 1989, p. 16. For others who uncritically adopt the position that extrinsic motivators must be given to encourage cooperation, see Mower and Wilemon, 1989; Rosen, 1989, p. 145.
16. Susan Leddick, a consultant, is quoted in Olson, 1992.
17. See the section contributed by Donald Berwick in Ehrenfeld, 1992, p. 18. Berwick, who is a former judge of the Baldridge Award, goes on to talk about the need for "intrinsic motivators," examples of which, as he sees it, include "putting employee photos on the walls [and] giving gifts" (p. 20).
18. For example, Monroe Haegele writes, "There is little incentive for the manager to eliminate positions [that is, throw people out of work] or radically change compensation when his or her own compensation is not affected by this behavior" (1991, p. 358).
19. McGregor, 1960, pp. 9–10.
20. A former director of sales compensation at IBM offers a similar view: "We used to give bonuses and awards for every imaginable action by the sales force. But the more complex it got, the more difficult it was to administer, and the results were not convincing. When we began to ask ourselves why Digital Equipment had salespeople, who are tough competitors, on straight salary, we decided perhaps we'd gone overboard a bit" (quoted in Kanter, 1987, p. 63). More managers might offer anecdotal corroboration of the failure of incentives except for the fact that they persist in seeing problems of attitude and performance as existing in spite of, rather than precisely because of, these systems.
21. See "Bosses' Pay," 1992, p. 20; Deming, 1986, p. 72. Furthermore, "Japanese firms almost never make use of individual work incentives, such as piecework or even individual performance appraisal tied to salary increases" (Ouchi, 1982, p. 41). "Japanese organizations do not rank employees or force 'win-lose' situations"; "only 25 percent of the companies surveyed use a performance appraisal" (Schultz, 1990, pp. 88, 86).
22. "Bosses' Pay," 1992, p. 20.
23. If two recent surveys of satisfaction are any indication, the results can vary widely. About three-quarters of the compensation and human resources specialists at almost 1,600 organizations said they approved of their incentive plans, according to a survey conducted in 1987. By contrast, only 30 percent of those using recognition awards thought that these were effective (O'Dell, 1987, p. 14). But a few years later, a study conducted by Towers

Perrin and the American Productivity and Quality Center found that only about 40 percent of senior executives were satisfied with reward or pay-for-performance systems. Interestingly, those in line positions, who are closer to the action, were even less happy with them than were respondents in staff positions (American Productivity and Quality Center et al., 1991, pp. 10, F-2). But these surveys, like most conducted on the subject, suffer from a major limitation: the people conducting them didn't bother to check with those on the receiving end of incentive plans. In his exhaustive review of evidence on the psychological dimensions of work, Robert Lane notes that "most workers do not like PBR [payment by results] and instead of being drawn to work by it, they are more likely than those paid by time to be absent from work. By definition, the rewards themselves are not aversive, but the PBR reward system is" (1991, p. 354).

24. "The incentive research literature is limited but strongly supports the conclusion that incentive plans make people productive, improving their performance" (Nash, 1985, p. 171). For someone who has found that the research literature points unmistakably to the opposite conclusion, such a statement is intriguing, to say the least. The author cites three studies to support it — or more exactly, makes three specific empirical claims, only one of which contains a citation. First, "small daily bonuses paid for coming to work on time are effective in reducing chronic tardiness." Second, "employees who are paid incentives perceive a higher linkage between performance and pay than those paid only salaries." Third, people were more likely to enlist in the navy when given a sign-up bonus or free tuition than when they weren't (although, interestingly, the size of that bonus did not affect enlistment rates). Of course, none of these three findings offers any support, much less strong support, for the idea that incentives improve performance.

25. Jenkins, 1986, p. 167.
26. For example, see Kearney, 1979, p. 8; Redling, 1981; Pearce, 1987, pp. 172–75; "Bosses' Pay," 1992.
27. Rich and Larson, 1987.
28. Jenkins, 1986.
29. Whyte, 1955, pp. 4–5.
30. Locke, 1968, pp. 174–75, 181.
31. Rothe, 1970.
32. See Guzzo et al., 1985; Guzzo and Katzell, 1987.
33. Silverman, 1983. "The merit pay system put a previously stable employee compensation system in shambles" (p. 294).
34. Pearce et al., 1985, p. 274.
35. Pearce and Perry, 1983. To assess general attitudes toward financial incentives, people were asked to react to the statement "I would probably work harder on my job performance if I thought I would then receive a cash reward or unscheduled pay increase" on a seven-point scale, with 1 meaning "strongly disagree," 4 meaning "undecided," and 7 meaning "strongly agree." The average response over the four periods ranged from 3.92 to 4.47. The average response to the statement "It is difficult to document the average performance differences among managers and supervisors" ranged from 4.58 to 4.95. Finally, and most revealingly, the response to "All in all, current merit pay provisions encourage me to perform my job well" dropped from 3.52 to 2.75 as the system was actually implemented.

36. Bachrach et al., 1984, p. 22.
37. Writing in a conservative policy journal, two analysts report with seeming disappointment that none of the teachers they interviewed "told us that merit pay itself improved teachers' classroom work. Several teachers said that the plans discussed here affected instruction, but it was the evaluation, as much or more than the raises, to which they pointed. And even these teachers saw only marginal changes. . . . Money is important to teachers, but the largest rewards come from student achievement. . . . Teachers would like higher salaries, but few say that their teaching would improve if they were paid more." Moreover, "few administrators claimed that merit pay improved teachers' work in classrooms, even though they had the strongest reason to make such claims." Overall, these writers concluded, "there is no evidence that the money had an appreciable or consistent positive effect on teachers' classroom work." The only success to which they could point was the fact that some teachers did more work outside the classroom. But this result was (1) limited to small, affluent districts, and (2) apparently due to paying teachers more when their jobs expanded to include more extracurricular responsibilities, which is not really merit pay at all (Cohen and Murnane, 1985; the quotations are from pp. 20–22). A report published the same year by the Urban Institute concluded that "there is little convincing evidence — one way or the other — on whether teacher merit pay . . . [has] substantially affected student achievement, teacher retention rates, or the ability to attract new quality teachers" (Hatry and Greiner, 1985, pp. 111–12). For a critical investigation of the specific effects of merit pay, see Bachrach et al., 1984.
38. Petty et al., 1992. In any case, the evidence of enhanced performance in this study was based on a single measure conducted immediately after the intervention. For more on the demonstrated benefits of increasing employee participation, see chapter 10.
39. On this point, see Swanson, 1992, p. 2.
40. Those at the top of the corporate hierarchy are often munificently rewarded — sometimes with multiple incentive plans — even as the company is posting losses and, worse, laying off workers by the thousands. Between 1977 and 1987, U.S. corporate profits inched up by only 5 percent, while salaries and bonuses for CEOs rose by 220 percent (Naylor, 1990, p. 568). To take but one example, in 1990 the chief executive of General Dynamics was awarded a new $4 million stock option package while the company lost half a billion dollars and fired 27,000 employees (Linden, 1991, p. 208). This becomes a practical as well as an ethical issue as soon as we begin to consider the more valuable uses to which these gargantuan sums could be put.

    John Kenneth Galbraith has observed that "the salary of the chief executive of the large corporation is not a market reward for achievement. It is much more in the nature of a thoughtful personal gesture by the individual to himself." After quoting this comment, psychologist Paul Wachtel suggests that perhaps the problem is not that modest incentives are too small for executives but rather that their salaries are much too large. "If they have become so bloated with their present accumulations that it takes hundreds of thousands of dollars to make them even notice they are getting paid for their work, we could tax their present wealth to bring it closer to the level of everyone else. They could then experience the same needs as the rest of the population and be relieved of the ennui that today robs them of the ability to respond to ordinary incentives" (Wachtel, 1983, pp. 280n, 281).

In the middle of 1992, however, top executives finally began to respond to the problem: they took decisive steps to prevent the release of any more information about how much money they were making (Cowan, 1992).

41. For example, see Guzzo and Katzell, 1987, p. 111; McGregor, 1960, p. 95.

42. Apart from the ultimate futility of substituting one form of extrinsic motivator for another, the tendency of some organizations to offer incentives chiefly as an excuse to cut compensation costs has been all too apparent to the people who work there. Bonuses in lieu of annual raises often leave employees with less take-home pay, which hardly amounts to a morale booster (Uchitelle, 1987). The use of money substitutes can be even worse: the proud recipient of a brand-new M.B.A. degree took charge of a clinic in Seattle and promptly began stamping the cute image of a froggy on the timecards of the (underpaid) nurses who had performed well. Predictably, this added insult to financial injury.

43. The size-of-incentives dilemma is identified by Kearney, 1979, p. 10; Luce, 1983, p. 21; Halachmi and Holzer, 1987, p. 88.

44. One analysis argues that efforts to improve on most performance measures to which executives' incentives are tied, such as return on equity, sales growth, or market share, do in fact tend to run counter to the company's long-term interests ("Bosses' Pay," 1992, p. 22).

45. See Halachmi and Holzer, 1987, p. 86. To those who, unaware that there is a dilemma, simply tell us to measure everything and reward on an objective basis (e.g., Eimers et al., 1979, p. A4), we can respond not only by pointing out the perils of inflexibility but also by noting that this is really an impossibility. Evaluation is unavoidably subjective. Regardless of how scientific an appraisal system may appear, two supervisors are likely to rate the same individual's work differently. "For some reason, compensation experts always try to design precise rules for processes that are inherently subjective" (McLaughlin, 1991, p. 74).

46. Scholtes, 1990, p. 51. Scholtes is a management consultant who is well known and highly regarded in the Total Quality movement.

47. Winstanley, 1982, p. 38.

48. See Thompson and Dalton, 1970, p. 154.

49. See McGregor, 1960, p. 82.

50. For example, see Scholtes, 1990, pp. 30–31.

51. McGregor, 1960, p. 83.

52. "Almost nothing is accomplished by an individual operating alone. Most work is obviously a collective effort. Yet even workers who seem quite independent depend on others for ideas, stimulation, feedback, moral support, and administrative services. When an individual makes some heroic effort and accomplishes an extraordinary task, often he or she can take the time to do that work only because others have filled in on the less heroic parts of the job. When someone is credited with a success, he or she is individually honored for what was most likely the work of many" (Scholtes, 1990, p. 27).

53. McGregor, 1960, p. 87.

54. Deming is quoted in Mullen, 1990, p. 89.

55. Deming, 1986, p. 102.

56. Deming, 1991, p. 24.
57. See the evidence reviewed on p. 76 and p. 300n24.
58. It needs to be emphasized that a critical examination of extrinsic motivation is not tantamount to telling someone who is struggling to make ends meet that he should get his mind off the subject. In fact, few things are more insulting than lofty pronouncements to the effect that the best things in life are free — spoken by people who have more than enough of the things in life that are not free. One thinks of wealthy lyricists who put such sentiments as "Nothin's plenty for me" in the mouths of poor folks.
59. Kovach, 1987.
60. Jurgensen, 1978.
61. These surveys are discussed in Csikszentmihalyi, 1990, pp. 160–61. The finding replicates a discovery made in surveys dating back at least to the 1930s. These earlier surveys also confirmed the relative importance to workers of job characteristics other than money (Watson, 1939).
62. Gruenberg, 1980; the quotation appears on pp. 267–68.
63. Greenberg and Greenberg, 1991, p. 10. The writers citing this poll continue, "In fact, we believe that one of the biggest management fallacies is that salespeople can be motivated by external factors" (ibid.).
64. See the chapters on the idea of work in Robert E. Lane's monumental scholarly work, *The Market Experience* (1991), which effectively challenges the traditional criteria by which we judge the success or failure of an economic system. For his part, Schwartz argues that "work as pure means, as purely operant behavior, is a relatively recent human invention" (1990, p. 10).
65. For a good example of this kind of thinking, see Fein, 1976.
66. Various surveys have shown that "better than 80 percent of the work force consistently report being 'satisfied' with their jobs" (Hackman and Oldham, 1980, p. 10). For example, when fifteen studies conducted during the 1970s were summed, they revealed that 52 percent of U.S. workers pronounced themselves "very satisfied" with their jobs and another 36 percent said they were "somewhat satisfied" (these figures, from Michael Argyle's *The Psychology of Happiness,* are cited in Csikszentmihalyi, 1990, p. 255n68). It is worth asking just what "satisfaction" consists in, whether self-reports on the subject are valid measures, and who the respondents are in these surveys. But such numbers offer a point of departure for a discussion of the topic that contradicts the widespread belief that most people can barely stand their jobs.
67. A survey of nearly six hundred lottery winners revealed that, of those who had been working, 60 percent of those who had won more than $1 million neither retired nor quit their jobs in the year after winning. (Those who won less were, of course, even more likely to keep working.) Moreover, many of those who did quit "later *returned* to the labor force in different types of jobs" (Kaplan, 1985; the quotation appears on p. 94).
68. To study what he calls the "flow" experience, which consists of feeling active, challenged, and fully engaged, the psychologist Mihaly Csikszentmihalyi likes to give people beepers and questionnaires to carry around with them. When they are beeped at various times during the day and evening, subjects describe what they are doing and how they are feeling. It turns out that, despite their stated beliefs that they would prefer not to be working, people actually report more flow experiences while at work than at any other time. (This was true of workers on assembly lines, too.) Despite

declarations that they hate work, people are often absorbed in it and happy at it on a moment-by-moment basis. This Csikszentmihalyi calls the "paradox of work": "People do not heed the evidence of their senses. They disregard the quality of immediate experience, and base their motivation instead on the strongly rooted cultural stereotype of what work is *supposed* to be like" (Csikszentmihalyi, 1990, pp. 157–62; the quotation appears on p. 160). In one of his studies, it turned out that "flowlike situations occurred more than three times as often in work as in leisure" (Csikszentmihalyi and LeFevre, 1989, p. 818). Nor is this the only research project to produce such results. A more conventional survey, in which participants were asked to rate the enjoyment they derived from over two dozen common activities, found that "the *intrinsic* rewards from work are, on average, higher than the intrinsic rewards from leisure." Samples in the mid-1970s and the early 1980s rated their jobs more enjoyable than all but a few leisure activities (Juster, 1985; the quotation appears on p. 340). This finding "upsets the rationale of the market [economy] as the best device for satisfying human wants and thus for maximizing human happiness" (Lane, 1991, p. 337). The rationale being challenged is that while work is unpleasant, it nevertheless provides us with the money to buy things we use at home and from which we derive our primary satisfactions.

69. Slater, 1980, p. 25. "What distinguishes wealth addicts from other addicts," he continues, "is that they have been largely successful in selling this delusion to the general public" (p. 27).

70. This point has been made by many writers; see, for example, Meyer, 1975, p. 40; Slater, 1980, p. 161. McGregor adds the important observation that there is no reason to assume that intrinsic motivation must be "associated exclusively with human activities of the kind that are defined as recreational. . . . It is not human nature that excludes the pursuit of goals yielding intrinsic rewards from the job environment" (1966, p. 210).

71. For provocative essays on these topics, see Wachtel, 1983; Slater, 1980. From the latter: "When we 'go shopping' without a clear goal in mind, means and ends have become reversed. Instead of acquiring money to help us get something we need, we buy something we don't need to help spend the money we acquired. Money, then, twists our thinking and puts us out of touch with our fundamental goals and desires. Instead of using money to serve ourselves, we use ourselves to serve money" (p. 11). Various writings by Karl Marx (especially his *Economic and Philosophic Manuscripts of 1844*) and Erich Fromm are also pertinent to the general subject.

72. Kasser and Ryan, 1993. We cannot be sure, however, that the choice to focus on financial matters causes these psychological problems. It may be that anxious, depressed people are more likely to adopt material goals, or that another variable is responsible both for this psychological profile and an emphasis on money.

73. John Kotter, quoted in "Bosses' Pay," 1992, p. 19.

74. See, for example, Herzberg, 1966, chap. 6.

75. For example, see Lerner, 1982.

76. Referring to the things that we require in order to avoid dissatisfaction as "hygiene factors" (as opposed to the things we need to become truly motivated), Herzberg writes, "There is nothing wrong with providing the maximum of hygienic benefits to the employee. The benefits should be as great as the society can afford. . . . What is in error is the summation of human needs in totally hygienic terms" (1966, p. 174).

77. The quotation, from *Motivation and Productivity* (1963), by Saul W. Gellerman, is cited in Kovach, 1987, p. 65.
78. This comment is quoted in Labich and Ballen, 1989, p. 84.
79. Gabor, 1992, p. F-1.
80. Ellig, 1982, p. 28.
81. O'Reilly and Puffer, 1989, p. 48. The case for "negative sanctions" offered in this article relies on an implicit contrast between punishing people and doing nothing when a problem arises. If the latter doesn't solve problems, the authors seem to say, we must turn to the former.
82. Herzberg, 1968, p. 54.
83. Ibid.
84. The best-known research in this regard was conducted by Herbert Meyer and his colleagues at General Electric (Meyer, 1975, pp. 42–45). More recently, people's commitment to an organization was found to decline if they received only a "satisfactory" rating (Pearce and Porter, 1986). Other reports include such comments from supervisors as these: "After we tell a man his [performance] score is below 40, he won't do anything for a month. He stews over his low rating, and he may even take a few days' sick leave, even though he's not physically sick"; and "A few men will work harder if you lower their ratings, but most will give up." Nor is it the case that only the lowest performers leave the company: "An analysis of the ratings of 60 engineers who had left over a four-year period revealed that almost all of them had above-average ratings or ratings just a few points below average," suggesting that maximum discouragement may be found when reasonably high-achieving employees are given ratings lower than what they expect or think they deserve (Thompson and Dalton, 1970, pp. 152, 153). "The more able and mobile employees often are those who leave first," another management specialist remarks, noting that the choice for supervisors who refuse to abandon a merit pay system amounts to watching employees become demoralized (with the result that they leave or become bitter and unproductive) or lowering the standards required for getting more money (Kearney, 1979, p. 10). The real issue, of course, is not how high the standards are set — the issue on which so many managers focus — but the Skinnerian system of rating and rewarding performance.
85. Halachmi and Holzer, 1987, p. 88. The use of merit pay for teachers has been found to have exactly this effect: "Those who do not receive the merit increment will experience a relative decline in their rewards, and commensurately lower their performance" (Bachrach et al., 1984, p. 20).
86. The executive is quoted in Kanter, 1987, p. 66. The result of incentive plans, says Peter Scholtes, is as follows: "Everyone is pressuring the system for individual gain. No one is improving the system for collective gain. The system will inevitably crash" (1990, p. 32).
87. Of nine companies whose representatives attended a conference in 1983, six said they used forced rankings: Exxon, Amoco, Philip Morris, Procter & Gamble, Kodak, and Goodyear (see Haller and Whittaker, 1990, pp. 131–32).
88. Thompson and Dalton, 1970, p. 156. Organizations employing a total of nine million people were surveyed in 1987 for information on the use of various incentive programs; recognition systems were viewed as the least successful, judged "positive" or "effective" by only 30 percent of respondents. On average, only 4–5 percent of employees in a given organization are winners in such programs (O'Dell, 1987, pp. 14, 71).

89. For example, the use of merit pay for teachers, "according to most studies, stimulates a competitive spirit (dissension, misunderstanding, suspicion, lowered morale) among teachers — a group which needs cooperation and a low pressure, high quality atmosphere to work best. It emphasizes individual performance at the expense of cooperative teamwork" (Weissman, 1969, p. 16).

90. A situation in which "the superior is in the role of a judge is the poorest possible one for counseling," McGregor (1960, p. 86) points out. See also Pearce, 1987, pp. 172–73.

91. "Rewards reinforce conflict avoidance, which we are discovering over and over again is very harmful for organizations. The irony is that people who are not interested in promotions and such rewards are more prepared to contribute to productive discussions. Indeed, their boss may see them as more disinterested and more credible because they are not vying for his favor" (personal communication, June 1992, from Tjosvold, a specialist in organizational behavior at Simon Fraser University).

92. One consultant, for example, notes that incentive schemes specifically designed to reduce the rate of absences are unlikely to be successful because problems like absenteeism "are merely manifestations of a person's deep dissatisfaction with his or her work — a problem that gift merchandise and travel, no matter how valuable, will hardly solve for long" (Walters, 1979, p. A5). On this point, see also Levinson, 1973, p. 30.

93. The study mentioned above (Rothe, 1970) that found the elimination of an incentive plan did not reduce welders' productivity over the long haul also noted that supervisors tend to "demonstrate relatively less leadership" when incentives are in place (p. 550). And the 1987 survey of 1,600 organizations discovered relatively little by way of active employee involvement in organizations that used small-group incentive plans (O'Dell, 1987, p. 52). Yet another researcher notes that pay for performance "impedes the ability of managers to manage" (Pearce, 1987, p. 172).

94. "Human problems were reduced to administrative problems and channeled through committees into oblivion" when a behavior modification system was implemented in a psychiatric hospital (Zeldow, 1976, p. 322). A motivation specialist, meanwhile, remarks that promising children money for every A on their report cards "relieves those parents of responsibility until the grades come out" (Peter A. Spevak, quoted in Kutner, 1991).

95. Haegele, 1991, p. 357.

96. Slater, 1980, p. 127.

97. Halachmi and Holzer, 1987, p. 86.

98. Pearce and Perry, 1983, p. 321.

99. See Rollins, 1987, p. 106: "The end result is an employee population so intent upon measuring itself that it has much less time left to perform the jobs at hand."

100. In 1992, state agencies in California and New Jersey found that employees at Sears Auto Centers were selling parts and services that customers didn't need, a practice that the company itself later seemed to acknowledge was connected to the incentive plan it had instituted two years earlier. (An advertisement responding to these allegations appeared on June 25, 1992, in major newspapers across the country.)

101. Mohrman, 1990, p. 10. See also Marlow and Schilhavy, 1991, p. 31. As far back as 1931, research on Taylor's "scientific management" made the related point that "time studies and incentive schemes could actually encour-

age workers to restrict their output. Workers knew from bitter experience that if they consistently produced more than 30 or 40 percent above the level at which bonuses began to be paid, their job would be rerated and they would have to work harder to make the same wage" (Gillespie, 1991, p. 162).

102. Mohrman, 1990, p. 10. Moreover, interest tends to drop when goals are assigned, at least on reasonably interesting tasks (Mossholder, 1980).

103. For example, see Pinder, 1976 ("Our data suggest that individuals who are paid under a noncontingent schedule may derive a more intrinsic orientation toward the work, greater work satisfaction, and higher degrees of intrinsic motivation than people paid according to a more contingent pay schedule" [p. 699]); and Jordan, 1986 (which found that health care technicians who were put on a group incentive plan became less intrinsically motivated by their work).

104. Deci and Ryan, 1985, p. 299.

105. McGregor, 1960, p. 40; emphasis omitted.

106. Lane, 1991, p. 403.

107. "People *will* make insistent demands for more money" when management has focused on money. They will "behave exactly as we might predict — with indolence, passivity, unwillingness to accept responsibility, resistance to change, willingness to follow the demagogue, unreasonable demands for economic benefits. It would seem that we may be caught in a web of our own weaving" (McGregor, 1960, pp. 41–42). "Naturally, [the manager] takes the evidence provided by their behavior as proof of his views of human nature" (McGregor, 1966, p. 215). See also Levinson, 1973, pp. 10, 30; Herzberg, 1968, p. 55. The only recognition of this phenomenon I could find in the last two decades appeared as a passing comment in an obscure journal: companies where "money rewards . . . have become traditional . . . risk 'conditioning' their technical people to value only extrinsic rewards" (Mower and Wilemon, 1989, p. 26).

108. Schwartz, 1986, p. 233. Robert Lane makes essentially the same point: an emphasis on how much money people will make shifts "the locus of causality from disposition to circumstance, from internal to external; it alters the task from chosen to unchosen. . . . Strangely, it *creates* Skinnerian man where he was missing earlier" (1991, p. 379).

8. Lures for Learning

1. "The majority of [motivational] strategies were based on supplying or restricting extrinsic satisfiers," according to one study (Newby, 1991, p. 198). Another found that 94 percent of the elementary school teachers surveyed reported using rewards to "improve classroom conduct and homework behavior." Eighty-one percent used them to improve reading behavior (Fantuzzo et al., 1991, p. 178).

2. Alexander, 1992, p. B1.

3. Brophy and Kher, 1986, p. 285. The authors contend that many teachers say as much, and "most of the rest appear to act as if they hold this belief even if they have never articulated it consciously" (ibid.). A researcher who spent time observing several teachers discusses the comments offered by one who relied on controlling techniques: "Since rewards and threats did not always result in work production, however, she seemed to want to

show the observer that it was not her fault if the students did not learn. For example, on several occasions, she spontaneously commented to the observer (in the presence of the students) that students' poor performance was due to laziness or poor work habits" (Marshall, 1987, p. 137).

4. Abigail Thernstrom, author of "School Choice in Massachusetts," published by the right-wing Pioneer Institute in Boston, is quoted in Palmer, 1992.

5. Shanker, 1990, p. 20. In 1992, Shanker devoted two of his weekly newspaper columns within a three-month period to making a case for incentives.

6. "School Haze," 1991, p. 7. The author also calls for more standards and testing that "would instill competitive pressure throughout school systems" (p. 8).

7. Personal communication, 1986.

8. Condry and Koslowski, 1979, p. 255. See also Lepper and Hodell, 1989, p. 73. Scores of other sources could be cited as well.

9. Brophy and Kher, 1986, pp. 282–83. "Apparently," they continue, "students start school with enthusiasm but gradually settle into a dull routine in which interest centers on being able to meet demands." This is exactly what John Goodlad (1984) found in his mammoth survey of over a thousand representative classrooms across the country (see esp. pp. 232–35).

10. The quotation is from Boggiano et al., 1989, p. 24. "Children who adopted an extrinsic rather than an intrinsic orientation toward schoolwork were more likely to do poorly on overall achievement, as indexed by national test scores, even when controlling for achievement scores from the previous year" (p. 23). For more evidence on this point, see Gottfried, 1985, 1990; Lloyd and Barenblatt, 1984; Harter and Jackson, 1992; Boggiano and Barrett, 1991; and the review of still other research in Sansone and Morgan, 1992, p. 266.

11. Anderson et al., 1987, p. 288. See also the work of Steven R. Asher (e.g., 1980).

12. Among the theories: intrinsically motivated learners pay more attention to what they are learning, become more deeply involved in thinking about it, or are in a happier frame of mind and therefore are more apt to succeed (see, for example, Lepper, 1985, p. 6). Boggiano and her colleagues (1992) argue that intrinsically motivated learners are also more likely to respond to feedback about their performance in a way conducive to higher achievement over the long haul: they are relatively unlikely to feel controlled by it and more given to attributing their failure to lack of effort rather than lack of ability.

13. On this point, see Ryan and Stiller, 1991, esp. p. 124.

14. For example, in a speech entitled "Why We're at Risk," former Procter & Gamble chairman Owen B. Butler (1989) talked about how "we" decided at some point that "school should be fun and not work."

15. "It is distressingly easy to design educational programs that may prove highly motivating, but instructionally useless" (Lepper and Hodell, 1989, p. 98; see also Jackson, 1968/1990, p. 111).

16. Brophy, 1983, p. 200. Education critic Frank Smith offers a useful perspective on the subject: "The underlying implication of 'learning should be fun' is that learning *will be* a painful and tedious activity unless it is primped up as entertainment. Learning is never aversive — usually we are not aware of it at all. It is failure to learn that is frustrating and boring, and so is having

to attend to nonsensical activities. . . . It is meaningless teaching, not learning, that demands irrelevant incentives" (1986, pp. 82–83).

17. Montaigne is quoted in Lepper, 1988, p. 305.
18. Bruner, 1961, p. 26. Another education researcher describes a set of "high-ability students . . . [who] are docile and compliant compared to their peers, and they seem to find school a rewarding place to be. Yet many of these high achievers learn shortcuts to achievement rewards and learn to regard out-of-class learning as unrewarding: two very dysfunctional instructional outcomes" (Thomas, 1980, p. 215).
19. Ryan and Powelson, 1991, p. 62. Carole Ames put it this way: "Motivation is too often equated with quantitative changes in behavior (e.g., higher achievement, more time on task) rather than qualitative changes in the way students view themselves in relation to the task, engage in the process of learning, and then respond to the learning activities and situation" (1992, p. 268).
20. It is unsettling to reflect on the fact that our educational system functions within a particular economic system and that the latter's interests may conflict with the goals of thoughtful educators. For example, it is reasonable to suppose that the functioning of large, undemocratic corporations requires a supply of workers who possess not only a set of skills but also a set of values. Ideally (from the perspective of those who own or run these enterprises), job applicants would appear having already been trained to accept as natural such things as competition, hierarchical control, and extrinsic motivation. By what may not be an astonishing coincidence, these are just the values that schools seek to instill. "The motivational system of the school, involving as it does grades and other external rewards and the threat of failure rather than the intrinsic social benefits of the process of education (learning) or its tangible outcomes (knowledge), mirrors closely the role of wages and the specter of unemployment in the motivation of workers" (Bowles and Gintis, 1976, p. 12).
21. Nicholls, 1989, p. 192. See also Schwartz, 1990a, p. 13.
22. Silberman, 1970, p. 114.
23. Bruner, 1961, p. 26.
24. Ames, 1992b, p. 268; Heyman and Dweck, 1992, pp. 232–33.
25. When the mothers of more than one hundred nine-year-olds were asked whether, or how often, they relied on "extrinsic reward strategies" in response to the children's school performance, it turned out that these rewards were "consistently and negatively related to motivation and achievement. These strategies were also associated with more school behavior problems and less effective learning" (Gottfried and Gottfried, 1991a, pp. 3–4).
26. Roemer, 1992, p. 58.
27. O. Butler, 1989.
28. Glasser, 1990, pp. 8, 118–119.
29. Such an approach was perceived by Frederick Taylor to be so obviously necessary that he used it as an analogy to justify the use of a similarly controlling format in the factory. "No efficient teacher would think of giving a class of students an indefinite lesson to learn. Each day a definite, clear-cut task is set by the teacher before each scholar, stating that he must learn just so much of the subject; and it is only by this means that proper, systematic progress can be made by the students. The average boy would go very slowly if, instead of being given a task, he were told to do as much

as he could. All of us are grown-up children, and it is equally true that the average workman will work with the greatest satisfaction, both to himself and to his employer, when he is given each day a definite task which he is to perform in a given time, and which constitutes a proper day's work for a good workman" (1911/1947, p. 120). Most workplaces long ago discarded Taylor's stultifying "scientific management;" but most classrooms are still run on the same basic principle.

30. Ryan and Stiller, 1991, pp. 117, 143. Ryan's colleague Ed Deci is more pithy: "Initiatives that establish stronger controls in education will result in poorer education" (1985, p. 52).

31. See, for example, Boggiano et al., 1989.

32. Haddad, 1982.

33. Research by Davis and McKnight is summarized in Doyle, 1983, p. 185.

34. See, for example, the research described in Stipek and Kowalski, 1989, pp. 384–85. "We may not be able to assure that each individual becomes 'competent,' given the difficulty of attaining this goal; but at the very least, we should not make people *helpless* by the use of well-intentioned procedures designed to motivate them" (Condry, 1978, pp. 190–91).

35. Boggiano et al., 1988.

36. Deci, Nezlek, and Sheinman, 1981; Deci, Schwartz, et al., 1981.

37. Enzle and Wright, 1992.

38. Boggiano and Barrett, 1991, ms. pp. 21, 34.

39. Einstein is quoted in Bernstein, 1973, p. 88.

40. Light, 1992, pp. 64–65. The science courses that students rated highest and lowest in overall quality had almost identical workloads. What distinguished the lowest-rated courses was more intense competition for grades.

41. Koestner et al., 1984.

42. Ryan, 1982, p. 457. Another group of researchers comments: "If such a seemingly simple manipulation as saying 'should' can have such dramatic effects, one can only begin to surmise how children may be significantly affected by their daily interactions with teachers and parents in the area of achievement" (Boggiano et al., 1991, p. 519). An earlier study with college students offered course credit for taking part in a psychology experiment that involved a study of problem solving. Half of them were informed when they showed up that they would not be receiving credit after all and were asked to participate anyway. Almost all decided to do so, and these students, deprived of compensation for their work, tried harder and performed more effectively on a range of measures than those who worked at the same task for course credit (Weick, 1964).

43. Grolnick and Ryan, 1989. One interpretation of this finding is that "excess control at home may prevent children from taking on or internalizing the regulation for their own school-related behavior" (p. 151). See also Grolnick et al., 1991.

44. Brophy and Kher list some fairly typical comments of this kind that they have heard teachers make: "If you get done by 10 o'clock, you can go outside"; "Your scores will tell me whether we need to stay with multiplication for another week"; "This penmanship assignment means that sometimes in life you just can't do what you want to do. The next time you have to do something you don't want to do, just think 'Well, that's just part of life'"; "Get your nose in the book, otherwise I'll give you a writing assignment"; "You've been working real hard today, so let's stop early"; "My

talkers are going to get a third page to do during lunch" (1986, p. 284; see also the comments offered by Teacher Y in Marshall, 1987).

45. At a conference in California, one administrator urged teachers to do this as a way of forcing students to think. The administrator himself might have benefited from an opportunity to think about the circumstances in which thinking occurs, and whether learning is more likely to be promoted by creating an atmosphere of fear or of safety.

46. Tuettemann and Punch, 1992. This was found to be particularly true of female teachers.

47. "Teachers will tend to see students as a means to an end under merit pay. Student performance in classes or tests will be the main barrier between a teacher and a merit increment," which means that "poor students would no longer pose challenges, they would pose threats" (Bachrach et al., 1984, pp. 16–17).

48. Garbarino, 1975; the quotation is on p. 427.

49. Deci et al., 1982. The comparison here is to subjects who were explicitly told that there were no performance requirements.

50. Ibid., p. 858. For more on the effects of a controlling school structure, see McNeil, 1986. A similar dynamic appears in the corporate workplace: people who feel controlled from above are more likely to try to control others down below (see Kanter, 1977, pp. 189–90).

51. Flink et al., 1990; the quotations are on p. 918.

52. Undergraduates who took a piano lesson from someone they believed was financially motivated reacted differently to the experience than those who thought the teacher was intrinsically motivated, even though teachers in the two conditions taught the identical lesson (and, indeed, didn't know what the students had been told). Those assuming their teacher was extrinsically oriented enjoyed the lesson less, thought it was less innovative, expressed less desire to play the piano again, and were less likely to try something new on the keyboard when they had the chance (Wild et al., 1992). Conversely, teachers' beliefs about students' motives for learning can be important, too. When teachers were told that certain students were extrinsically oriented, those students did, in fact, show less interest in a task after a lesson, presumably because of how the teachers' expectations changed the interaction (Pelletier and Vallerand, 1989).

53. For a penetrating critique of the concept of learning disabilities — the way the concept is formulated and applied, the way allegedly learning-disabled children are treated, and the way a neurological basis for the phenomenon has been postulated without good evidence — see Coles, 1987.

54. Grolnick and Ryan, 1990, p. 182.

55. Das et al., 1985, p. 309.

56. Lincoln and Chazan, 1979, p. 215.

57. In one experiment, rewards given to hyperactive children made them respond more impulsively (Firestone and Douglas, 1975). In another, any beneficial effects of rewards (on reaction times) disappeared as soon as the rewards stopped coming, and sometimes the use of rewards had the consequence of undermining performance from the beginning (Douglas and Parry, 1983). In yet a third study, this one with children who had short attention spans but were not hyperactive, rewards did not improve reaction times, as the experimenters had predicted; rather, it caused the children to make more mistakes (Kistner, 1985).

58. Switzky and Schultz, 1988, p. 10.
59. Ibid., p. 7. The same is true of programs for mentally retarded adults (Haywood and Switzky, 1985, p. 157).
60. Knitzer et al., 1990, pp. 34–35.
61. Houghton et al., 1987.
62. Deci and Chandler, 1986, pp. 589, 590; Deci et al., 1992, p. 470.
63. Guess and Siegel-Causey, 1985; the quotations appear on pp. 241, 233, 237, and 236, respectively.
64. Deci suggests "using as little control as possible; encouraging children to think through their own problems rather than giving them solutions; permitting them to try out their own plans and ideas; and allowing them to work at their own speed" (Deci and Chandler, 1986, p. 590). A more elaborate set of practical strategies for enhancing the intrinsic motivation of learning-disabled children is offered in Adelman and Taylor, 1983. A book-length treatment of these issues — a decisive rejoinder to the claim that behavioral manipulation is necessary with people who are severely retarded or otherwise limited in their capacity to function — has been written by a psychologist with extensive experience in the field (Lovett, 1985). For a discussion of how children with profound handicaps can and should be helped to make choices, see Peck (1985). Peck found "substantial increases in the social/communicative behavior" of severely retarded and autistic children by giving them "more opportunities for student initiation and control of social interactions" (p. 191); see also Shevin and Klein (1984). A lengthy compendium of resources on inclusive education is available from the Institute of Community Integration, College of Education, University of Minnesota, 6 Pattee Hall, 150 Pillsbury Drive S.E., Minneapolis, MN 55455. The Council for Children with Behavior Disorders (CEC, 1920 Association Drive, Reston, VA 22091) publishes a journal called *Beyond Behavior* that challenges some of the common assumptions of the field. Finally, interested educators might look at the work being done at the Inclusive Education Project at Syracuse University's School of Education.
65. Brophy and Kher, 1986, p. 264.
66. See Dweck, 1986; Ames, 1992b; Nicholls, 1989; and virtually anything else written by these three researchers. On the more general point that children's conceptions of ability are shaped by particular classroom practices, see Rosenholtz and Simpson, 1984. Dweck in particular (see Dweck and Leggett, 1988) sees a child's focus on performance as a reflection of the extent to which he or she has come to believe that intelligence is a fixed trait, although I have suggested that this belief can also follow from a preoccupation with performance resulting from other factors.
67. Graham and Golan, 1991. See also Nolen, 1988.
68. A study done in 1985 by Farrell and Dweck is described in Dweck, 1986.
69. Butler, 1992.
70. Nicholls, 1989, p. 130.
71. Grolnick and Ryan, 1987; Butler and Nisan, 1986; Butler, 1988. See also Benware and Deci, 1984.
72. Even when students are encouraged to think about the task itself, an environment that emphasizes how well they are doing compared to others may create a performance focus, or what Nicholls calls an ego orientation (Jagacinski and Nicholls, 1987). More broadly, see Nicholls, 1989; Kohn, 1992a (esp. pp. 41–43 for a discussion of social comparison).

73. Ryan, 1982, pp. 456–58.
74. Butler and Nisan, 1986; Butler, 1987. A study of junior high school students in Japan also found that those told a history test would count toward their final grade were less interested in the subject and less likely to prefer answering difficult questions than those told the test was just to monitor their progress. The same researcher found that undergraduates' interest in an intelligence test was higher when they evaluated their own work than when the experimenter evaluated it (Kage, 1991).
75. Butler, 1992. On the last point, see also Boggiano and Barrett, 1991.
76. Silberman, 1970, p. 148.
77. Research by M. Rohrkemper and B. Bershon is summarized in Brophy and Kher, 1986, p. 267; see also Blumenfeld et al., 1986, p. 102.
78. LeCompte, 1978, p. 34.
79. Heyman and Dweck, 1992. The same is true with respect to extrinsically oriented students; see Boggiano and Barrett, 1991.
80. For example, see Maehr and Stallings, 1972; Harter, 1978; Pearlman, 1984; Elliott and Dweck, 1988; and the research cited in Dweck, 1986, pp. 1041–42. Some of this research, as well as classroom observations (e.g., Marshall, 1987, p. 145), demonstrates that children who are able to focus on the task instead of on their performance do not try to avoid work; they ask for more assignments, and more difficult ones. By contrast, one study found that mothers who were especially concerned about how well their children did in school were more likely to say they preferred that their children be given projects that ensured success as opposed to projects "where they'll learn a lot of new things but also make a lot of mistakes" (Ames and Archer, 1987; the quotation appears on p. 410).
81. On this point, see Milton et al., 1986, p. 145.
82. Stipek and Kowalski, 1989; a summary of Seymour Sarason's research on anxious students appears on pp. 384–85. Two other researchers make a related point: "The teacher who emphasizes 'back to basics' in order to raise the performance level of previous low achievers thereby narrows the definition of legitimate academic performance, thus stratifying performance expectations in the classroom, with the ironic outcome that previous low performers are likely to consolidate their low academic self-concepts" (Rosenholtz and Simpson, 1984, p. 57).
83. Elliot and Dweck, 1988, p. 10.
84. Butler, 1988, pp. 12–13; 1992, p. 942.
85. Kirschenbaum et al., 1971, p. 201.
86. Unpublished data by Ray Wolfe, State University of New York at Geneseo, 1991. The correlation between average grade earned in high school and self-esteem in college for one sample of students was $-.27$. For another sample, high school grades correlated $-.27$ with "optimism" and $-.28$ with "well-being." (All three correlations are significant at $p < .01$.)
87. Rogers, 1985, p. 259. The author adds, "It is no wonder that the under-achieving gifted child is a problem of great concern — we are helping to produce them."

9. BRIBES FOR BEHAVING

1. Glasser, 1969, p. 22.
2. Ryan is quoted in Kutner, 1990.

3. Deci and Ryan, 1985, p. 263. The social critic Edgar Z. Friedenberg similarly observed that "behavior modification is planned to mold desirable behavior directly, without rooting it in ethical purposes. It seeks to operate at [the] lowest level of moral judgment: behavior is good because it is rewarded" (quoted in Ohanian, 1982, p. 19).
4. It is often implied that "teachers must choose between putting up with behavior problems and being the boss and stamping them out" (Nicholls and Hazzard, 1993, p. 56). Indeed, one behaviorist frames the choice exactly this way: "Given a disruptive class, should [behavioral consultants] try to reduce disruptive behaviors in the classroom [by means of a Skinnerian regimen] or should they ignore such problems and try to improve academic performance?" (Peterson, 1976, p. 341).
5. For example, Diana Baumrind (1971), in her influential work on child development, introduces another parental approach, an alternative to authoritarian and permissive parenting that she calls "authoritative," characterized by a combination of warmth and firm control. In a reanalysis of her data, however, Catherine Lewis argues that what "actually fosters competence or responsibility in children" is warmth and absence of punishment; parental control actually may "result in *less* internalization of behavioral norms by the child" (1981, pp. 560, 562).
6. Some of the differences between what is expected of parents and teachers are discussed in Katz, 1980.
7. The phrase "hidden curriculum" appears in Jackson, 1968/1990, p. 33. The five elements mentioned here are described in LeCompte, 1978, p. 29; see also Winett and Winkler, 1972.
8. "If teachers are obsessed with silence and lack of movement, therefore, it is in large part because it is the chief means by which their competence is judged. . . . Thus, the vows of silence and stillness are often imposed on teachers who might prefer a more open, lively classroom" (Silberman, 1970, p. 144).
9. Ohanian, 1982, p. 18.
10. See page 82.
11. Silberman, 1970, p. 134.
12. LeCompte, 1978, p. 30.
13. Blumenfeld et al., 1986, p. 98. To behave well, the students also said, is to obey the teacher, stay out of trouble, work continually, and avoid fighting.
14. In a penetrating article entitled "Compliant Cognition," educational researchers Mary McCaslin and Thomas Good observed that "behavior modification systems of student management are compatible with a curriculum of basic skill acquisition. In both systems, concern is with the identification, sequencing, and reinforcement of discrete skills" (McCaslin and Good, 1992, p. 12). Another educator puts it this way: if the mission of teachers is primarily to impart "to students a body of academic knowledge and techniques . . . [then they] must have a controlled classroom" (Watson, 1982, p. 76). In short, Skinnerian approaches to discipline are a good match for Skinnerian approaches to learning. (Not by coincidence are both included as elements of the "back to basics" movement, in which "the role of the student is to pay attention and follow directions, the role of the teacher is to effect a controlled, structured environment within which direct instruction [e.g., drill and practice] is the dominant activity, and the principal outcomes of interest are the skills and items of knowledge that comprise the

subject matter" [Thomas, 1980, p. 213].) There are some teachers, however, who experiment with innovative, "learner-centered" lessons while
continuing to rely on manipulative behavior control. This is more than a
paradox, as McCaslin and Good see it — it's "an oxymoron: a curriculum
that urges problem solving and critical thinking, and a management system
that requires compliance and narrow obedience. The management system
at least dilutes, if not obstructs, the potential power of the curriculum for
many of our students. Students are asked to think and understand, but in
too many classrooms they are asked to think noiselessly, without peer
communication or social exchange. And the problems they are asked to
think about must be solved, neatly, within (at most) 45-minute intervals. In
the problem-solving curriculum, in too many cases, the teacher sets the
performance goals, identifies relevant resources, establishes criteria for evaluation, and eventually announces winners and losers. Students generally
gain recognition and approval by paying close attention to recommended
procedures and by taking few academic risks" (1992, p. 12).

15. When various approaches to classroom management are examined empirically, some studies typically show positive effects and some show no effects.
It is rare to discover that a program has negative effects, but this is actually
what has turned up in some studies of Assertive Discipline. Overall, most
researchers have found the technique to be detrimental or to have no impact
at all (Emmer and Aussiker, 1990; Render et al., 1989). For other criticisms
of Assertive Discipline, see Crockenberg, 1982; Watson, 1982; Gartrell,
1987.

16. Covaleskie, 1992, pp. 173, 179.

17. It seems reasonable, when people's tempers are flaring, to take a few minutes to cool off before resuming a discussion. But "time out" (originally
short for "time out from positive reinforcement") is more often used as a
punitive strategy, something forcibly imposed on a child, complete, in some
cases, with a formula for calculating the number of minutes the child must
remain in solitary confinement. "There is evidence to support the notion
that timeout serves as an aversive consequence," one group of behaviorists
wrote, after noting that "some of the earliest demonstrations of timeout as
a decelerating consequence come from animal studies" (White et al., 1972,
p. 111).

18. As of 1990, corporal punishment was "still legal in 30 states, where at least
1 million schoolchildren ages 6 to 18 are paddled each year — some suffering severe bruises, broken bones, and concussions" (Hembree, 1990, p. 69).
For a list of countries that have abolished the practice, see Gordon, 1989,
p. xxi.

19. Eighty-four percent of U.S. parents said they "agreed" or "strongly agreed"
that "it is sometimes necessary to discipline a child with a good, hard
spanking," according to a 1986 poll (reported in Lehman, 1989, p. 29). In
a survey of 679 college freshmen, 93 percent of the students reported having
been spanked, leading the psychologists who conducted the study to reflect
that "although anger, physical attack, and pain are involved between two
people of vastly different size, weight, and strength, such behavior is commonly accepted as a proper exercise of adult authority over children" in our
culture and that no other interactions "carry such clear social supports for
the unilateral use of physical punishment by one party on another" (Graziano and Namaste, 1990, p. 450). It would seem that doctors play a role

in that social support: two out of three primary care physicians in a recent survey approved of the use of physical punishment (McCormick, 1992).

20. Ignoring children, on the theory that they will stop doing something if they no longer receive the reinforcement of our attention, is a particularly demeaning and shortsighted strategy. Behaviorists frequently urge parents and teachers to withhold their attention deliberately (while taking care to assure us that this doesn't constitute a punishment): in a typical passage, one psychologist asserts that "behavior such as temper tantrums in children or incoherent talk in mental patients will often disappear if it is ignored" (Kazdin, 1976, p. 102). In fact, the real message this sends is, "We don't know why you do this and we don't care" (Lovett, 1985, p. 36). To say that children who act out are just doing it for the attention, Lovett continues, seems to imply that "wanting to be noticed [is] a mysterious or stupid need. . . . [It's] a little like saying, 'You only talk to your friends because you're lonely'" (pp. 69, 104–105). To ignore a child who acts inappropriately is ultimately ineffective because it neither addresses the underlying cause of that behavior nor teaches "more sophisticated ways of confronting and satisfying a basic social need" (p. 69). Most of all, it is cruel and punitive.

21. Balsam and Bondy, 1983, p. 293.

22. Research documenting the detrimental effects of physical punishment has been published at least since the 1940s. One interesting study found a clear-cut relationship between the severity of the punishment received by eight-year-olds and how aggressive their peers judged them to be. More than two decades later, the researchers tracked down some of these same subjects and found that the aggressive children had grown into aggressive adults, many of whom were now using physical punishment on their own children (Eron et al., 1987). Even more recent research has found that alcoholics and people suffering from depression are much more likely than other individuals to have been beaten when they were children (Holmes and Robins, 1988), that toddlers who are hit by their mothers are in fact less likely than their peers to do what they are told (Power and Chapieski, 1986), and that three- to five-year-olds who are spanked by their parents are more likely than other children to be aggressive while playing at a day care center (Watson and Peng, in press). For other references on this topic, see Kohn, 1990b, pp. 135–38, 217–18. For more comprehensive discussions of physical punishment, including its social, religious, and psychological roots, see Miller, 1984; Greven, 1992.

23. Lehman, 1989, p. 29. Among primary care physicians as well there is "considerable support for use of corporal punishment in response to an aggressive misbehavior in all children's age groups" (McCormick, 1992, p. 3163). One elementary school principal, stressing her intolerance of violence, assured me a few years ago that her students "know if they hurt somebody physically, they're going to get it."

24. Gordon, 1989, p. 7.

25. Some boys who were part of an after-school club with an authoritarian leader became aggressive toward their peers immediately; others became apathetic but then exploded into violence when the leader was away (Lewin et al., 1939). Other studies have found a significant relationship between mothers' use of power-assertive techniques and their children's level of hostility with peers (Hoffman, 1960) as well as a tendency to show "weak

moral development" (Hoffman and Saltzstein, 1967). More recently, controlling parental discipline of preschoolers was related to the disruptiveness of the children's playground behavior (Hart et al., 1992). Projective tests have also suggested that students whose teachers were more controlling entertained more aggressive thoughts than other students did (Ryan and Grolnick, 1986). The point about children breaking more rules away from home when subjected to punitive discipline is attributed to a review of the research by Martin Hoffman (cited in Toner, 1986, p. 31).

26. Sears et al., 1957, pp. 485, 486, 484.
27. Kamii, 1984, p. 12; 1991, p. 383.
28. Greven, 1992, p. 88.
29. Piaget, 1965, p. 339.
30. "Main Fault," 1984, p. 28.
31. DeVries, 1987, p. 377.
32. When seven-year-olds were told by an adult that he would be "very upset and very angry" if they played with a toy when he left the room, they were *more* likely to play with it — and were also more likely to break the rules set down by another adult three weeks later — as compared with children who were initially told their disobedience would lead the adult to be "a little bit annoyed" (Lepper, 1973). In a naturalistic study, children whose mothers used controlling, punitive, or restrictive techniques were less likely than others to comply with their requests at home or in a laboratory situation (Crockenberg and Litman, 1990).
33. For example, see Dreikurs et al., 1982, chap. 12.
34. "The line between punishment and logical consequences is thin at times" (Dinkmeyer and McKay, 1989, p. 85).
35. Albert, 1989, p. 79.
36. The examples are taken from, respectively, Albert, 1989, p. 78; Dinkmeyer and McKay, 1989, pp. 84–85; Nelsen, 1987, pp. 72, 81; Dreikurs et al., 1982, p. 119; Curwin and Mendler, 1988, pp. 72, 81.
37. Strict behaviorists would describe some of these interventions as "response costs," which consist of the removal of something pleasant rather than the application of something unpleasant, but this distinction too is rather academic. For our purposes, both may be described as punishment. Thomas Gordon has observed that "Dreikurs's concept of 'logical consequences' is simply another name for the more straightforward term *punishment*" (1989, p. 31).
38. Dreikurs et al., 1982, p. 117.
39. Hoffman and Saltzstein, 1967, p. 54.
40. The same orientation may be promoted by a contract with a child that calls for rewards: these often "generate what one parent called 'the lawyer syndrome': looking for loopholes in a contract which will fulfill its literal but not intended meaning" (Balsam and Bondy, 1983, p. 291). It is perfectly reasonable for a child to think along these lines; the problem rests with the use of rewards.
41. I owe much of this analysis to Marilyn Watson, program director of the Child Development Project.
42. "Punishment is always ineffective," Alfred Adler wrote many years ago. "It can do nothing but confirm the opinion, 'Others are against me'" (1956, p. 370).
43. "Clearly, it is not permissive parents who produce the antisocials, delin-

quents, and criminals in our society. It is strict, authoritarian, punitive parents. Kids who get into serious trouble are invariably those who are reacting to, rebelling against, or escaping from being neglected or mistreated at home. The unhappy, resentful, rebellious, angry, and retaliatory young people in our society have not had too much *freedom;* quite the contrary, they have had too much control, too much discipline, too much pain and deprivation" (Gordon, 1989, p. 215). Of course, this doesn't mean that everyone who was raised by punitive parents is destined to grow into a criminal; numerous other factors, only some of them familial, are relevant to that outcome.

44. While a few studies (e.g., Boggiano et al., 1987; Barrett and Boggiano, 1988) have asked small numbers of adults to react to hypothetical scenarios in order to elicit their beliefs about the use of rewards with children, there are very few good data on just how many parents actually use rewards at home, and most of the research that does exist is quite dated by now and entirely dependent on self-reports. Interviews with 379 mothers of kindergartners in the 1950s indicated that 30 percent never or rarely used rewards, 43 percent used them "sometimes" or "fairly often," and 25 percent used them "frequently" or "regularly." As for praise, the breakdown was 7 percent for no use or rare use, 48 percent for occasional or moderate use, and 44 percent for fairly frequent, very frequent, or regular use (Sears et al., 1957, pp. 321–22). This study turned up two other interesting findings: there was a significant correlation between those who relied heavily on the use of rewards and those who relied heavily on physical punishment (p. 324), and there was no difference among social classes with respect to the use of rewards (pp. 431–32), even though quite a bit of research has shown that parents classified as lower socioeconomic status are relatively more likely to use punishment. A somewhat larger study involving one group of parents in 1953 and another group in 1971 asked how they would respond if their child did something good. Between two-thirds and three-quarters said they would use praise, and between one-quarter and one-third (including some of the same people) said they would offer a material reward. Very few respondents talked about encouraging the child to feel proud of what he or she had done (Duncan et al., 1973, p. 37).

45. Daley, 1990.

46. Batson et al., 1978, p. 90. The study found that adults who were offered money for agreeing to help a researcher rated themselves as less altruistic than those who didn't expect to be paid. Another study discovered that children who received rewards for donating something to another child (or who were fined for not donating) were less likely to explain their own behavior in words suggesting an intrinsic motivation to help than were children who received no rewards or punishments (Smith et al., 1979). Other experiments have shown that rewarding people for donating blood (Upton, 1974) or helping a blind student (Kunda and Schwartz, 1983) undermines people's motivation to help for altruistic reasons. For other relevant research, see Kohn, 1990a, pp. 202–203.

47. Grusec and Dix, 1986, p. 220.

48. Fabes et al., 1989.

49. Grusec, 1991.

50. Kamii, 1991, p. 383.

10. THANK GOD IT'S MONDAY

1. McGregor, 1966, p. 208. On this point, see also Levinson, 1973, p. 19.
2. See McGregor, 1960, p. 41; 1966, p. 204.
3. In a broader sense, virtually all paid work might be thought of as contingent in that the worker is paid for doing something. But there is an important difference between what Robert Lane calls "*molar contingency,* as in earning a living, and *molecular contingency,* as in working for pay. . . . A person required to work for a living has many choices of just how to go about it; a person required to turn out so many units of an identical product or rewarded by tokens for a specified behavior has no discretion left" (1991, pp. 360–61). Sales commissions, piece work, and bonuses are salient rewards, intended to function as motivators on a daily basis, and are therefore not really comparable to the concept of work per se.
4. In a very large survey of American organizations, "not one respondent reported that gain sharing has a negative impact on performance" (O'Dell, 1987, p. 15).
5. "Deming would pay every employee — right up through the chief executive — a straight salary or wages. Those in the same job would be paid roughly the same; some differences would be created by seniority, since everyone would get annual raises. Those raises would be uniform, not based on merit. Such a system, he argues, would encourage teamwork rather than encourage superstars. The one acceptable bonus plan to Deming is profit-sharing. But every employee would get an equal share. The chief executive getting the same bonus as a factory worker? 'Well, why not? Certainly,' says Deming, looking astonished by the question" (Linden, 1991, p. 211).
6. See p. 312*n*21.
7. "Companies as diverse as the General Motors Corporation and Eastman Kodak are . . . gradually being won over to the notion that rewarding a handful of 'winners' and holding them up as the keys to corporate innovation and success brands the majority of employees as losers, hurting morale and cooperation. . . . [Some divisions of GM have] tied compensation not to annual appraisals, but to a 'maturity curve' that consider[s] an individual's seniority, level of expertise and the overall market for his or her services" (Gabor, 1992, pp. F1, F6).
8. Halachmi and Holzer, 1987, p. 87. One useful diagnostic question, Lane suggests, is "For whose use is the feedback on performance desired? If for the performer, self-determination is protected. . . . If for a paymaster . . . control passes to others" (1991, p. 387).
9. The latter point is made by Haller and Whittaker, 1990, p. 133.
10. While performance appraisals sometimes use fear to motivate employees, one writer points out that abolishing them will not automatically improve things; the evaluation process may just be a symptom of a more general reliance on fear in the organization (see Gabor, 1990, p. 124).
11. "In some companies, the environment of attitude and practice is such that the individual who is not promotable is considered to be a failure. It is said of him that he 'lacks potential,' or that he 'has reached his ceiling.' Not only is this attitude in itself punishing, but the rewards for further growth — salary, status, recognition, etc. — are lacking (the formal machinery cannot encompass such exceptions). This, despite the probability that he could, if adequate rewards were available, continue to grow and to increase his contribution to the organization at his present level. Can the individual

who for personal reasons does not want to climb higher on the organizational ladder, but instead wishes to make his contribution to the enterprise an outstanding one at his present level, remain there without being punished in a variety of subtle ways for having made this choice?" (McGregor, 1960, p. 196; see also Scholtes, 1990, p. 48).

12. Bachrach et al., 1984, p. 25. See also Thomas Gordon's proposed alternative to the performance appraisal, which he calls a "periodic planning conference." His detailed description appears in Gordon, 1977, chap. 11.

13. Scholtes, 1990, p. 46.

14. Meyer et al., 1965/1989.

15. Halachmi and Holzer, 1987, pp. 87, 89.

16. Blinder, 1990, p. 13.

17. This view, more or less, is the gist of Theory Y. In contrast to the assumption that people have to be bribed or coerced into doing anything, Theory Y holds that "the average human being does not inherently dislike work," and that when people's basic needs are taken care of, they actively seek responsibility (McGregor, 1960, pp. 47–48).

18. See, in this connection, Tjosvold, 1986; Scholtes, 1988, esp. chaps. 6 and 7; Kohn, 1992a; much of the work of W. Edwards Deming; and many other sources.

19. McGregor, 1960, pp. 228, 48.

20. Michael Beer, quoted in Ehrenfeld, 1992, pp. 23, 22.

21. Herzberg is quoted in Bosquet, 1973, p. 25.

22. Herzberg, 1987, p. 30.

23. Csikszentmihalyi, 1978, p. 215. Robert Lane warns that an exclusive concern with intrinsic work satisfaction might be described as "self-centered" (1991, p. 403).

24. Herzberg, 1987, p. 87. Also see Levinson, 1973, p. 13. In the area of psychology concerned with motivation, an entire subspecialty has grown up around the idea that human beings have a basic need to feel competent.

25. Hackman and Oldham, 1980, p. 71.

26. Ibid., pp. 66–68, 71–82; the quotations appear on pp. 66, 76–77. The premise here is that management *wants* to make work interesting, and it may well be argued that this is not always true. "At present, however, whether work is enjoyable or not ranks quite low among the concerns of those who have the power to influence the nature of a given job" (Csikszentmihalyi, 1990, p. 154). In what may be a related point, two social scientists contend that those with power may themselves lack intrinsic motivation: "The vast majority of workers in higher levels of the hierarchy of production are by no means autonomous, self-actualizing, and creatively self-directed. Rather, they are probably supersocialized so as to internalize authority and act without direct and continuous supervision to implement goals and objectives relatively alienated from their own personal needs" (Bowles and Gintis, 1976, p. 145).

27. Sansone, 1992; the quotation appears on p. 379. She offers several concrete examples: first, an inspector in a potato chip factory might try to "discover meaningful shapes — such as the image of Elvis Presley — in the nonuniform chips" and try to build "a collection of celebrated chips"; second, people doing tasks that don't require their full attention could use the opportunity to listen to music or try to beat their previous speed record (pp. 380, 389).

28. Perry, 1978; the quotations appear on pp. 111, 119.

29. For a lucid essay on this point and, more generally, on the self-defeating, never-ending quest for more, see Wachtel, 1983.
30. For an interesting discussion of how this syndrome describes workers in the United States and the (former) Soviet Union for the same reason — that is, the inability to make decisions — see Naylor, 1990. The effects of being controlled are predictable and pervasive. For example, not long ago the top management of a big-city post office, pointing to problems with several employees, sharply curtailed the capacity of all workers to make decisions for themselves: precise job assignments were emphasized, and enforcement was tightened. The reaction on the part of the employees was to stop doing all the things they had taken upon themselves to do in order to make the facility run more smoothly, such as catch mistakes and solve problems they happened to notice, help out an inexperienced worker who was having trouble sorting mail, and so forth. Their attitude was, "If you're going to monitor and control us, we're going to do exactly what we're required to do and nothing else" (personal communication, 1990).
31. This was the finding of a major study of U.S. and Swedish workers in a range of occupations (Karasek et al., 1988; the quotations appear on pp. 915, 910). "Type A" refers to people who are impatient, competitive, and hostile.
32. Amabile, 1988; the quotation appears on p. 147. The research here consisted of surveying research and development scientists as well as people in the marketing, development, and sales departments of large organizations. When they were asked to relate an event from their work experience that exemplified high creativity, the most common single characteristic of that event was freedom. When asked to relate an instance of low creativity, the most common single factor was lack of freedom. Performance on less creative tasks in laboratory experiments is also enhanced as a rule when subjects believe they have some choice about which tasks they will work on (see a review of some of this research in Perlmuter and Monty, 1977).
33. Scholtes, 1988, p. 1:21.
34. For example, whereas "absenteeism of 10 percent or more is not unusual in United States auto plants," the Ambrake Corporation, where workers are given more discretion about how they do their jobs (and where there are no time clocks), "enjoys an absentee rate of less than five-tenths of 1 percent" (Levin, 1992, p. D8).
35. See Kanter, 1977, pp. 189–90.
36. Hackman and Oldham, 1980, pp. 138–39.
37. On this point, see Deci and Ryan, 1985, esp. p. 308.
38. McGregor, 1960, p. 103.
39. Companies with no-layoff policies do everything possible to avoid throwing people out of work. They freeze hiring, transfer workers within the organization, offer attractive retirement packages to senior employees, and consider such options as leaves of absence and job sharing. More to the point, they work with employees to decide among these options (see Levine and Tyson, 1990, pp. 215, 226; Gabor, 1992, p. F6).
40. "Contrast the situation in which a subordinate is evaluating his own performance relative to specific targets which he set a few months ago with the situation in which he is listening to his superior evaluate his performance against the superior's standards and objectives. In the latter case, the stage is set for rationalization, defensiveness, inability to understand, reactions

that the superior is being unfair or arbitrary. These are not conditions conducive to effective motivation" (McGregor, 1960, p. 87).

41. "Any effort to redesign work in a technology that permits little employee discretion is probably doomed to failure from the outset" (Hackman and Oldham, 1980, p. 122).

42. "Breakdowns occur because the new pattern of cooperative activity at the top level has not been accompanied by the development of a more participatory style of managerial leadership" (Whyte, 1983, p. 404).

43. For descriptions of various approaches to participative management, the rationales offered in its behalf, and a list of the characteristics that maximize the probability of success, see Margulies and Black, 1987; Levine and Tyson, 1990, esp. pp. 205–14.

44. Five successful, if somewhat dated, examples can be found in Bosquet, 1973, pp. 25–26. A more recent and compelling case study involving a telephone equipment manufacturer called Tellabs appears in Holusha, 1991. Still more illustrations have been collected in Simmons and Mares, 1985. Finally, any number of organizations currently working toward Total Quality Management are, in effect, putting into place a version of participative management.

45. See Levine and Tyson, 1990, pp. 222–35 for a recent description of participative management in Japanese and Swedish companies. William Foote Whyte, describing W. Edwards Deming's mission to bring statistical methods of quality control to Japan in the early 1950s, comments that "Deming thought he was teaching methods to be used by engineers and other professionals in management. The Japanese apparently reasoned that, if these methods were good for management, they should also be good for workers. This represented a quantum jump from the system Deming presented to them and enabled them to involve workers in participation in decision making to a far greater extent than has occurred in the U.S., even though we originated some of the basic ideas" (Whyte, 1983, p. 403).

46. Blinder, 1990, p. 13. See, for example, the contribution to this symposium by Levine and Tyson, 1990, esp. pp. 183–204.

47. Miller and Monge, 1986. One interesting set of studies conducted with British companies found a marked and sustained improvement in performance (using various measures) when people who did a range of jobs were given more responsibility, authority, and autonomy (Paul et al., 1969). Still other research suggests that workplace participation may lead employees to become more politically active; involvement in decision-making on the job may be an antidote to apathy in other arenas, which in turn raises the possibility that undemocratic workplaces may foster such apathy (Elden, 1981).

48. On this point, see Melcher, 1976; Levine and Tyson, 1990; Deci, 1992. In particular, Quality Circles (Levine and Tyson, 1990, p. 197) and Management by Objectives (Pinder, 1977, p. 388) have been faulted for not going far enough toward enabling substantive participation — and even, in the latter case, for amounting to "systems of phony participation."

49. O'Dell, 1987, pp. 26–27; the quotation appears on p. 27. From another source: "Countless examples exist in which employees have been encouraged to solve company problems only to discover that management is not at all committed to taking their ideas seriously" (Loden, 1985, p. 130).

50. Whyte, 1983, pp. 396–97. Exactly the same point is made by McGregor (1960, p. 125) and Herzberg (1968, p. 56).

51. In a comic strip that appeared in 1991 ("Dilbert," by Scott Adams), a worker asks his boss, "What did you mean when you said all employees are empowered? Does that mean I can control my own budget, make decisions without twelve levels of approval, and take calculated risks on my own?" Replies the boss, "No, it's just a way to blame employees for not doing the things we tell them not to do." Looking chastened, the employee muses, "No wonder you needed a new word."

52. In the survey cited earlier, 29 percent of the respondents actually explained the disappointing failure of employees to play an active role in involvement programs on the grounds that they were not rewarded for doing so (O'Dell, 1987, p. 27).

53. Levering, 1988, p. 208.

54. This point has been made by Bowles and Gintis, 1976, p. 129; Bosquet, 1973, pp. 26–27. More troubling is the argument offered by some critics to the effect that the very programs recommended for enhancing worker participation may serve to legitimate and perpetuate systems of control by making them more palatable. "Pseudo-democracy . . . is currently pitched under such labels as 'employee involvement,' 'team production,' and 'jointness.' These programs have little in common with the autonomous expression of workers' hopes and aspirations. They are as much a product of management power and a manipulative ideology as the Communist unions of the Brezhnev era," one historian remarks (Lichtenstein, 1992). The "human relations" school of management and the reforms it engendered have also been criticized for "encouraging workers to identify with corporate goals" and serving to "reinforce managerial authority and confine the subordinate's role to that of highly motivated obedience and greater productivity" (Gillespie, 1991, pp. 268, 270). Such systems, along with the work of people like McGregor and Herzberg, may have the effect of deflecting attention from "the basic economic and political structure of the organizations in which individuals work"; indeed, they are sometimes recommended explicitly "as *not* changing management's authority in any way" (Nord, 1974, pp. 558–59).

55. For example, one organizational theorist, claiming that people with a "low need for independence react positively where little participation is used," contends "a nonparticipative approach would be acceptable and contribute to positive behavioral responses" (Melcher, 1976, p. 20).

11. HOOKED ON LEARNING

1. If employers help workers to acquire skills, this is generally intended as a way to build an effective organization; it isn't a goal in its own right. By contrast, helping students to acquire skills, to become good learners and good people, is the very point of school. Another difference emerges when we consider our response to a child who causes problems for others and compare that to our attitude toward an adult worker who does the same. Most concretely, the two arenas diverge in that money and grades are not analogous: people need to earn money to survive, while grades are unnecessary. The general point about differences between workplace and classroom will strike most readers as glaringly obvious, but some people working to import the methods of the Total Quality Management movement to the schools may not have considered the importance of these differences.

Helping students become self-directed learners is fundamentally dissimilar to pleasing customers. Market models and metaphors simply do not belong in an educational context; when they are imposed by force, it is at the price of undermining the purposes of schooling (see Kohn, in press).

2. Wlodkowski is quoted in Kutner, 1990.
3. Adelman and Taylor, 1983, p. 385.
4. Silberman, 1970, p. 138.
5. "Business can . . . stop emphasizing the GPA [grade point average] during recruiting; if the school has certified that the student has graduated, such information should be enough. Business leaders must consider the fact that there is slight relationship between grades and postgraduation achievements in industry" (Milton et al., 1986, pp. 147–48). On the other hand, commentators such as Albert Shanker think grades should receive even more emphasis than they do at present: businesses "should hire entry-level workers on the basis of their high-school transcripts and recommendations from teachers, and they should start the better graduates at higher salaries," he declares (1990, p. 21).
6. See the discussion, and research cited, in Kirschenbaum et al., 1971, pp. 55–57, 195–97.
7. Dressel, 1957, p. 6. I am indebted to David Langford for calling this quotation to my attention.
8. Milton et al., 1986, p. 224.
9. By the time children reach sixth grade, according to one study, grades are the criterion they cite most often for judging their own ability (Blumenfeld et al., 1986, p. 98). Other research suggests that grades continue to play a more prominent role in children's understanding of competence as they get older (Sansone and Morgan, 1992, p. 258). Ruth Butler argues that it is when children come to see ability "as a stable trait best assessed by comparison with others" — usually at about age nine or ten — that they are most susceptible to the destructive effects of grades (1988, p. 3; see also R. Butler, 1989).
10. See Butler, 1988, esp. p. 11.
11. Tests, particularly the standardized variety, are sometimes criticized on the grounds that assessing competence is not the same thing as contributing to competence. "You don't fatten a steer by weighing it" is one rustic expression to get across the idea that evaluating students is different from teaching them. In fact, this criticism understates the problem. The more emphasis is placed on testing students, the more teaching becomes a preparation for these tests, which means that potentially innovative lessons must be set aside in order that children can be coached to fill in the right bubbles with their no. 2 pencils. Tests, in short, are not irrelevant to instruction; as Heisenberg discovered in another context, measuring affects what is being measured — in this case, for the worse. Notice how, once again, most criticisms of this practice fail to get at the root of the problem. If the question is how we assess children, our efforts will be restricted to devising more meaningful kinds of evaluation (which would, I hasten to add, represent an improvement over the current standardized tests). But the more important question is *why* we want to assess children. Even the most cleverly designed assessment mechanism, the deepest and richest measure imaginable of what children know, is not a boon to learning if its purpose is to sort students or reward them.

12. Frank Smith is more blunt: "A teacher who cannot tell without a test whether a student is learning should not be in the classroom. Faces reveal when students are not learning. They are learning unless they are bored or confused, and boredom or confusion leave unmistakable traces. It is not always possible to tell whether a student is learning a particular thing at a particular time, but that should not be a significant consideration for anyone who is not a paranoid bureaucrat" (1986, p. 259).

13. "One of the most interesting features of the interview material was the absence of reference to objective evidence of school learning in contexts in which one might expect it to be discussed. Testing, when it is mentioned at all, is given little emphasis. These teachers treat it as being of minor importance in helping them understand how well they have done. The students' enthusiasm and involvement seem much more important than do their performance on tests" (Jackson, 1968/1990, p. 123).

14. In a review of research concerning the factors that lead children to ask for help in the classroom, one writer singles out "encouragement, personal warmth, and a learning (versus performance) goal orientation" (Newman, 1991, p. 153).

15. I've been able to find only one study purporting to show that grades have a "positive" effect. High school students were asked by someone they didn't know to write a paper without hearing any justification for this assignment. (The interest value and relevance of the assignment are unclear from the description of the experiment.) Sure enough, grades were related to compliance: the more the paper was said to count toward their mark for the course — and in particular, the more students were told they would lose points for not doing it — the more likely they were to hand something in (the quality of the work was not assessed) (Cullen et al., 1975).

16. Harter, 1978.

17. Milton et al., 1986, p. 149.

18. For a discussion of how "grades put children and teachers into conflict," see Smith, 1990, p. 198; Kirschenbaum et al., 1971, pp. 115, 163.

19. In one study, experimenters had college students write an essay on a controversial topic in which they were to take a position they didn't actually believe. These essays were then given grades on a random basis (although the students didn't know this). Students who received A's were more likely to express satisfaction with their essays and also more likely to change their opinions in the direction of the views they had defended on paper (Bostrom et al., 1961). More recent research has shown that grade-oriented students have a more external locus of control, which means they are more likely to see their fate as determined by luck or other people (Milton et al., 1986, p. 140). The authors of an extended essay on grading introduce a fictitious character, newly and successfully graduated from college, who addresses the students in his old high school: "When I was a child my parents patted me on the head for doing some things, but withdrew their rewards when I did other things. So I began to conform to *their* values and expectations because those pats on the head were pretty important to me. When I got to school, the teachers hit me with the importance of getting good grades. . . . I had to conform to *their* values and expectations, which I did. So again, I got more pats on the head. And the subjects in which I got the most pats on the head were the subjects I decided I liked the most. . . . [But I was] so busy getting grades that I didn't take the time to discover who I was and what I wanted to do with my life" (Kirschenbaum et al., 1971, pp. 87–88).

20. Milton et al., 1986, p. 141.
21. Deutsch, 1985, pp. 198–99.
22. I owe this suggestion to Phil and Joan Harris, who have used it in college and third-grade classes, respectively. Phil directs the Center for Professional Development at Phi Delta Kappa, an international educational organization. Carole Ames writes, "Offering students opportunities to improve their grades suggests . . . that mistakes and errors are part of the learning process and not indicative of failure to learn" (1992a, p. 341). This reflects a larger concern to make sure that classroom practices put a premium on effort rather than identifying relative (and ostensibly fixed) levels of ability.
23. For a discussion of how rewards are most destructive when given for skills still being honed, see Condry and Chambers, 1978, pp. 63, 66.
24. This lovely phrase is from Clarke et al., 1990, p. 11.
25. Milton et al., 1986, p. 225.
26. Lepper and Greene, 1978b, pp. 138–39. Indeed, the opportunity to come up with a detailed evaluation of one's own artwork has been found to promote higher scores on a measure of creative potential as compared to having one's work judged by others (White and Owen, 1970).
27. The dean of admissions at Harvard University, William R. Fitzsimmons, reports that his office "deal[s] with a wide variety of admissions candidates, some of whom have never even attended secondary school. . . . If we have no grades of any sort we will ask the candidate for as much supplementary material as possible" (personal communication, December 1992). Likewise, the associate dean of admissions at Brown University, Michael Goldberger, observes that "more and more schools are providing us with unconventional transcripts, some of which do not have grades." He says he and his colleagues "feel comfortable that we can make a good decision" if these transcripts are sufficiently informative. Moreover, students from these schools actually "receive more time of review and they may, in fact, have more opportunities [than students from more traditional schools] to impress the admission officer reviewing the file" (personal communication, April 1993).
28. Ames, 1992b, p. 263. See also Nolen, 1988.
29. See Stipek and Kowalski, 1989.
30. Ames and Archer, 1988.
31. Bruner, 1961, pp. 26, 28. Boggiano suggests that children who are intrinsically oriented are likewise able to interpret feedback as informational rather than controlling (Boggiano et al., 1992, p. 286).
32. I especially recommend Malone and Lepper, 1987; Keller, 1987; and Adelman and Taylor, 1983. (The last of these is framed as a guide for working with learning-disabled children but actually offers a useful way of thinking about motivation in general.) For a very accessible book on the subject, see Wlodkowski and Jaynes, 1990.
33. Brophy and Kher, 1986, p. 267.
34. "Children are inherently motivated to reduce the discrepancy between the stimulus and the lack of knowledge about it, and they show curiosity, exploration, or play as a result" (Gottfried and Gottfried, 1991b, p. 5). However, as with the level of difficulty, we want to avoid too much or too little incongruity or discrepancy. "Ideas too greatly at variance with existing information and beliefs will tend to be discounted or rejected; ideas too similar to existing knowledge may be assimilated or ignored" (Lepper and Hodell, 1989, p. 92).

35. On modeling an interest in learning, see Wlodkowski and Jaynes, 1990, pp. 26–29.
36. "Teachers who cheerfully acknowledge their own failures and try again to do a task better show students that high standards are not punitive but rather permit pride in genuine accomplishment. Teachers who acknowledge areas of ability and of incompetence in themselves and others show children that competence is not a single metric by which self-worth is judged" (Potter, 1985, p. 206).
37. In fact, says one expert on early child development, "teachers should create learning encounters that amplify the problems and uncertainties in children's own thinking. These encounters will capture children's interest because they correspond to the issue on which children themselves are spontaneously working at their stage of development" (Edwards, 1986, p. 9).
38. Students have very little opportunity to talk in most American classrooms; typically, the teacher outtalks the entire class about three to one (see Silberman, 1970, p. 149; Goodlad, 1984, pp. 129–30).
39. Glasser, 1990, p. 22.
40. A number of writers, including Paulo Freire, have elucidated the political implications of this model, and particularly the way the view of the student as a passive receptacle for knowledge discourages a "critical consciousness" that could be used to make social change.
41. Jackson, 1968/1990, p. 16. "Students must try to behave as if they were in solitude, when in point of fact they are not. They must keep their eyes on their paper when human faces beckon" (ibid.).
42. I discuss these issues and describe the supporting research at some length in Kohn, 1992a, esp. chap. 10; Kohn, 1992b. Since the mid-1970s, a considerable number of educators have studied, written about, and used cooperative learning. In fact, a movement of sorts has grown up around the need to restructure classrooms so children can learn together. Interested readers may want to subscribe to, and order back issues of, the major periodical on the subject: *Cooperative Learning* Magazine, P.O. Box 1582, Santa Cruz, CA 95061.
43. A number of people within the cooperative learning movement emphasize the need to help students develop social skills, both as an end in itself and as a prerequisite for effective academic interaction. These skills include such things as listening, making eye contact, resolving conflicts, and being able to disagree with others without insulting them. Beyond such discrete capacities, though, classrooms must be transformed into caring communities such that interactions are routinely informed by concern and collaboration; cooperative learning is more than a set of techniques to be hauled out for particular lessons. In the following chapter I make the case that this approach is invaluable for promoting good values. Here I want to indicate that it facilitates effective learning as well.
44. On very basic tasks, as Robert Slavin's research (e.g., 1990) has shown, cooperative learning structures that rely on rewards for successful performance *can* promote learning gains when compared with traditional structures that also rely on rewards — or with unstructured situations where students work in groups that don't really cooperate. On the other hand, rewards clearly are not necessary in order for students to learn effectively in cooperative groups (see the results of three research projects involving versions of cooperative learning deliberately structured to exclude extrinsic

motivators, described in Kohn, 1992a, pp. 225–26; see also Niehoff and Mesch, 1991; Kohn, 1991a). There is reason to think that intrinsic motivation will decline over time when rewards are used in cooperative learning arrangements, just as it does in other settings. Observational studies suggest that students often come to place "more value on the rewards given to the groups than [on] the actual process of working together" (Ayres, 1990, p. 29). Moreover, while cooperative learning often does lead students to become more excited about what they are learning (Johnson and Johnson, 1985, p. 272), the introduction of rewards may limit or erase that advantage. For example, a direct comparison of a reward-driven approach to cooperative learning with reward-driven individualized learning did not find any higher intrinsic motivation in the former on most measures (Hom et al., 1990).

45. Thoreau is quoted in Lickona, 1991, p. 227.
46. Lepper and Hodell, 1989, p. 74.
47. "Some tasks, especially those which involve understanding and higher level cognitive processes, are difficult for teachers and students to accomplish in classrooms. . . . Teachers . . . face complex management problems resulting from delays and slowdowns and from the fact that a significant portion of the students may not be able to accomplish the assigned work. As tasks move toward memory or routine algorithms, these problems are reduced substantially. The central point is that the type of tasks which cognitive psychology suggests will have the greatest long-term consequences for improving the quality of academic work are precisely those which are the most difficult to install in classrooms" (Doyle, 1983, p. 186).
48. McNeil, 1986, pp. 157–58.
49. "Because this low-quality, standardized, fragmented approach is so unsatisfying to students (and teachers), more and more students are actively resisting and this resistance is seen as a discipline problem. School administrators then fall into the trap of thinking that discipline problems, not unsatisfying education, are the cause of low levels of achievement. This explains the increased emphasis on strict rules of deportment (more coercion), which further define a good student as a passive thing rather than an involved, questioning, even at times dissenting learner" (Glasser, 1990, p. 22).
50. Brophy and Kher, 1986, p. 286.
51. "If school is not inviting, if the tasks are not clear, interesting, and at an appropriate level, how can we expect pupils to be on task? Adverse student reactions should be expected when classes are dull, teaching is uninspired, and failure is built in. Their oppositional behavior is a sign of personal health and integrity" (Morse, 1987, p. 6).
52. Lepper and Hodell, 1989, p. 91. Lilian Katz puts it this way: it is not enough for schoolwork to be vertically valid, by which she means it prepares students for what they'll have to do next week or next year. It must also be horizontally valid — "that is, it should teach them something that will be useful, perhaps, on the way home or in some familiar aspect of community life" (1988, p. 16).
53. Dewey, 1913, pp. 20, 24, 34. Similarly, he has written elsewhere, "when it is taken away from its natural purpose, it is no wonder that it becomes a complex and difficult problem to teach language. . . . Since the language taught is unnatural, not growing out of the real desire to communicate vital impressions and convictions, the freedom of children in its use gradually

disappears, until finally the high-school teacher has to invent all kinds of devices to assist in getting any spontaneous and full use of speech" (1915/ 1990, pp. 55–56). Sadly, this indictment is no less apt today than it was early in the century.

54. O'Neil, 1992, p. 4.
55. A substantial literature has accumulated on these subjects. Interested readers might look up the writings of Eleanor Duckworth, Rheta DeVries, Lilian Katz, and others.
56. See Dweck, 1986, p. 1045.
57. Danner and Lonky, 1981, p. 1046. See also the work of Mihaly Csikszent-mihalyi and, for a discussion of how a performance orientation disrupts this preference for moderate challenge, Nicholls, 1989, chap. 7.
58. For a discussion of this point in the context of cooperative learning, see Cohen, 1986.
59. Mac Iver, 1987, p. 1259. The absence of grades helps, too.
60. Cannella, 1986, p. 300.
61. Lepper and Cordova, 1992, p. 203. Part of what makes such a program "carefully designed," Lepper has argued elsewhere, is an "integral relationship between the content being presented and the motivational devices employed" (Lepper and Malone, 1987, pp. 261–62).
62. It was Dewey who warned most cogently that "when things have to be *made* interesting, it is because interest itself is wanting." On the one hand, he said, there are "those conditions which exact the simulation of attention without securing its essence"; on the other, there is the natural expression of interest and application of effort that comes from selecting subjects "in relation to the child's present experience, powers, and needs" (1913, pp. 11, 23).
63. Richard Lauricella, quoted in Lickona, 1991, p. 148. Presumably he does not mean to suggest that every aspect of a unit must be taught differently from one year to the next, but only that an element that is changed on the basis of students' suggestions within a predictable structure can be invigorating for a teacher.
64. Yackel et al., 1991, p. 401.
65. Wang and Stiles, 1976; the quotation appears on p. 167. Unfortunately, task completion was the only outcome measured in this study.
66. Rainey, 1965, pp. 290–91.
67. Amabile and Gitomer, 1984.
68. Zuckerman et al., 1978. See also Nicholls (1989, p. 169) on the relation between choice and task involvement.
69. deCharms, 1972.
70. Ryan and Grolnick, 1986; the quotation appears on p. 553.
71. For a description of the classroom structure in this year-long experiment, see Cobb et al., 1989; Yackel et al., 1991. For a discussion of the results, see Cobb et al., 1991.
72. Boggiano et al., 1992, pp. 278–80. Informal reports from other researchers suggest that a more typical result from an intervention of this sort is an enhancement of conceptual thinking skills (along with intrinsic motivation and other psychological and social benefits) but no change on standardized test scores, which usually measure relatively superficial capabilities such as students' skill at taking standardized tests. It should be sufficient to be able to show people who care about these scores that giving students more

choice about their learning has no detrimental effect on their performance on machine-scored tests while bringing about a variety of other advantages.

73. Three studies to this effect are cited in Condry, 1977, p. 466.

74. Danner and Lonky, 1981. This, according to the researchers, "suggests that at least part of the teacher's difficult problem of matching tasks to children can be solved by providing children with more choices than they are typically offered" (p. 1050).

75. For one discussion of how classrooms can be arranged to maximize students' choice, see Ingram and Worrall, 1987. Of course, a number of alternative schools and free schools, as well as the theoretical traditions that support them, have emphasized this idea for years.

76. One model of cooperative learning that takes the idea of autonomy seriously is Group Investigation. Here, students form inquiry groups based on what they want to know about a given topic and then make decisions together about how they will divide up the labor and conduct their investigation. Each group collects information and analyzes it, then prepares and shares a final report or innovative presentation that reflects what has been learned. Finally, each group contributes to the evaluation process, perhaps making up the questions on their unit that will be included in a classwide test (if there is to be one) in order to incorporate the evaluation into the learning process. At both the elementary and secondary levels, this model has been associated with a higher level of academic achievement (along with other advantages) precisely because it gives students more control over their learning, according to Shlomo and Yael Sharan, who developed the technique (see Sharan and Sharan, 1992.) At its best, cooperative learning "gives students an active role in deciding about, planning, directing and controlling the content and pace of their learning activities. It changes the students' role from recipients of information to seekers, analyzers and synthesizers of information. It transforms pupils from listeners into talkers and doers, from powerless pawns into participant citizens empowered to influence decisions about what they must do in school" (Sharan, 1986, p. 4).

77. "Nothing is more absurd than to suppose that there is no middle term between leaving a child to his own unguided fancies and likes or controlling his activities by a formal succession of dictated directions" (Dewey, 1915/1990, p. 130).

78. Ames, 1992b, p. 266. She makes the additional point that students should be given "a choice among a range of equally difficult books or a choice of equally desirable activities or assignments. The student's choice, then, is guided by his or her interest and not by efforts to protect feelings of self-worth" (Ames, 1992a, p. 336).

79. Wassermann, 1989, p. 204.

80. On the general topic of dealing with less interesting tasks, see Glasser, 1990, p. 126; and the description of Deci's research on p. 90.

81. Ware, 1978.

82. Nolen and Nicholls, in press; the quotations appear on ms. pp. 20–21.

12. GOOD KIDS WITHOUT GOODIES

1. This distinction appears in many of their writings. "Setting limits typically involves asking children to do something that conflicts with one of their

needs or feelings. By acknowledging the potential conflict, perhaps providing an alternative outlet for satisfaction of the need or expression of the
feeling, but at least affirming the legitimacy of the need or feeling, one can
generally avoid the kind of power struggle . . . that undermines the child's
self-determination and intrinsic motivation" (Deci and Ryan, 1985, p. 252).
Elsewhere they have argued that when structures are properly used, "behav-
ior-outcome contingencies are understandable, expectations are clear, and
feedback is provided" — an arrangement diametrically different from control (Deci and Ryan, 1990, p. 245). In one experiment, children did not lose
interest in painting when limits on the way they used the materials were
phrased in a noncontrolling manner (Koestner et al., 1984).

2. Hoffman, 1960, esp. pp. 138–39.
3. See, for example, the research of Marian Radke-Yarrow and Carolyn Zahn-
   Waxler, Martin Hoffman, Nancy Eisenberg, Ervin Staub, Norma Feshbach,
   and others, much of which is cited in Kohn, 1990a.
4. Ryan et al., 1992, p. 184.
5. In two separate studies, boys who were given an explanation about why
   they shouldn't touch certain toys were less likely to do so when the experimenter left the room than those who were just told not to touch them (in
   both conditions, they were warned that a buzzer would sound if they
   disobeyed) (Cheyne and Walters, 1969; Parke, 1969).
6. For example, see Hoffman and Saltzstein, 1967; as well as virtually anything else by Hoffman on the subject of discipline.
7. Nicholls and Hazzard, 1993, p. 59.
8. Kamii, 1984, p. 11.
9. A nice discussion of this misuse of the idea of choice can be found in
   Crockenberg's critique of Assertive Discipline (1982, pp. 65–70). But the
   tactic is not limited to such programs of crude control; falsely claiming that
   a child has "chosen" to receive a punitive consequence is an element of
   certain approaches to discipline that bill themselves as more enlightened
   (e.g., see Curwin and Mendler, 1988, p. 107; Albert, 1989, p. 77; Glasser,
   1990, pp. 144–45).
10. This was found in studies with nine- to twelve-month-old babies (Stayton
    et al., 1971) and six- to seven-year-old children (Parke, 1969).
11. Moreover, in an environment where students feel safe to respond, the
    teacher probably won't feel compelled to praise, according to Maryann
    Gatheral, a teacher educator (quoted in Martin, 1977, p. 51).
12. For a more detailed discussion of the relation between secure attachment in
    infancy and nurturant caretaking in childhood, on the one hand, and
    prosocial attitudes and behaviors on the part of the child, on the other, see
    Kohn, 1990a, pp. 87–88 (and the studies cited on pp. 298–99nn100–101).
13. It was, after all, John B. Watson who wrote in an infamous passage, "There
    is a sensible way of treating children. Treat them as though they were young
    adults. . . . Let your behavior always be objective and kindly firm. Never
    hug and kiss them, never let them sit in your lap. If you must, kiss them
    once on the forehead when they say good night. Shake hands with them in
    the morning. Give them a pat on the head if they have made an extraordi-
    narily good job of a difficult task. Try it out. . . . You will be utterly ashamed
    of the mawkish, sentimental way you have been handling it. . . . Remember
    when you are tempted to pet your child that mother love is a dangerous
    instrument" (1928, pp. 81–82, 87).

14. "Little children are not 'making demands' when they cry — they are engaging in communication in the only way available" (Condry, 1978, p. 182). The best thing parents can do in this situation is to respond by meeting the child's needs as best they can. A famous study at Johns Hopkins University found that babies most likely to fuss and cry were those whose mothers hadn't responded promptly to their cries earlier. Parents who held back for fear of spoiling the baby often set a vicious circle into motion: ignoring the newborn's cries led to more crying as the baby grew, which further discouraged the parent from responding, which made the baby even more desperate, and so on (Bell and Ainsworth, 1972). More recent research has confirmed the central point (e.g., Crockenberg and Smith, 1982; Barr and Elias, 1988). One researcher has shown that mothers who are most worried about spoiling their babies are least likely to provide a warm, caring, emotionally supportive environment (Luster et al., 1989).
15. Andersen and Andersen, 1987, pp. 57–58. The article proceeds to itemize some of the behaviors that are associated with caring attitudes on the part of teachers, such as bodily relaxation, smiling, eye contact, and so on.
16. See the studies cited in Kohn, 1990a, pp. 91–92.
17. See the studies cited in ibid., pp. 90–91.
18. Hoffman and Saltzstein, 1967, p. 50. "Induction in sum should be the most facilitative form of discipline for building long-term controls which are independent of external sanctions, and the findings would seem to support this view" (p. 55).
19. Third graders who were taunted and prevented from completing a task by another child were much less likely to respond aggressively when some possible explanations for the child's behavior were offered to them (Mallick and McCandless, 1966).
20. As I have argued elsewhere, it is tempting to induce a young child to share by explaining that if she offers her toy to another child he may let her play with *his* toy. But this strategy does not promote concern for others; it promotes self-regarding shrewdness.
21. This was the finding of a survey of more than 330 parents of preschool children (Clayton, 1985).
22. The phrase "the best possible motive consistent with the facts" comes, I believe, from Nel Noddings by way of Marilyn Watson. The qualification at the end indicates that it would be foolish or disingenuous to suggest to a child who has viciously kicked someone that he probably didn't mean to hurt him. In general, though, our inclination should be to make allowances and give the child the benefit of the doubt. As one preschool teacher remarked, "I used to think that children break rules mainly to be defiant. Now I realize how hard it is for them to think about rules when they are doing something else, like playing" (quoted in Edwards, 1986, p. 164).
23. The work of Ervin Staub (e.g., 1979 and some of his more recent writings) is especially relevant here, as, indeed, it is to some of the other ideas discussed in this section.
24. See Kohn, 1990a, pp. 93–95; Kohn, 1992a, chap. 10; as well as other samples from an immense literature on cooperative learning.
25. Staub, 1978.
26. I discuss these issues at length in Kohn, 1990a, chaps. 4 and 5.
27. The fact that the word *empathy* is sometimes used to denote what I (and others) call perspective taking creates some confusion about the whole

question. At best, we need to be able to "feel into" other people's emotional life (which is the meaning of the German word, *Einfühlung*) as well as to perform the cognitive act of imagining what is going on for that person. The first is something humans demonstrate from the first moments of life: newborns are more likely to cry, and to cry longer, when they are exposed to the sound of another infant's cry than when they hear other, equally loud noises, suggesting the existence of "a rudimentary empathic distress reaction at birth," a primitive precursor to what we think of as empathy. (Sagi and Hoffman, 1976, p. 176). See also Hoffman, 1981; Kohn, 1990a, pp. 65–66, 119–20, 162–63.

28. The best source of such activities I know of is Feshbach et al., 1983.
29. For more on this point and the suggestions that follow, see Kohn, 1991b.
30. This statement is taken from unpublished materials written by the staff of the Child Development Project, whose director is Eric Schaps and whose program director is Marilyn Watson. I describe the project in more detail, including interviews with children, teachers, parents, and others affected by it, in Kohn, 1990a, chap. 6; 1990c; 1991b, pp. 505–506.
31. Apart from the work of the CDP staff, discussions about class meetings can be found in Glasser, 1969, chaps. 10–12; Nelsen, 1987, chap. 7; Lickona, 1991, chap. 8.
32. Justice, 1988, p. 34.
33. Kobasa, 1979 (and subsequent research by this researcher and her colleagues) found that control, together with a deeply felt commitment to one's activities and the tendency to perceive change as a positive challenge, contributed to a profile of "hardiness" that provides significant protection against illness. See also Karasek et al., 1988.
34. Rodin and Langer, 1977. In another study, nursing home residents who were able to control (or at least predict) when a student would come visit them were not only happier and more hopeful but also physically healthier than those who received the same number of visits but on a random schedule (Schulz, 1976).
35. For example, see Hill et al., 1990. Some studies of patient-controlled analgesia have found only some of these benefits, but this picture emerges when the research is viewed collectively. Interestingly, medical researchers have attributed the beneficial effects of this form of self-treatment to physiological factors such as individual differences in patients' responses to pain (which means that standardized doses determined by physicians give most patients more or less medication than they need). But the fact that patients overwhelmingly prefer to medicate themselves and feel less anxiety when they do so — and the existence of other sorts of research on the importance of control — suggests that psychological factors probably play a role.
36. Martin Seligman's research on helplessness is central to this field of study. For a review of some of the relevant studies by him and others, see Taylor, 1989. One recent study showed that teachers' psychological distress was inversely related to their perceived influence and autonomy at work (Tuettemann and Punch, 1992).
37. Women who were told they could choose the particulars of an exercise program at a health club were more likely to continue attending over six weeks (and to declare their willingness to keep coming after that) than were women who were told their program was simply assigned to them — even though their activities too were actually assigned on the basis of the prefer-

ences they had expressed (Thompson and Wankel, 1980). A smoking cessation program that "focused attention on the individual's own efforts in smoking cessation" was more successful than one in which people followed a set of guidelines (Harackiewicz, Sansone, et al., 1987). Adolescent girls (but not boys) were more likely to continue using an anticavity fluoride rinse for nearly half a year when they were invited to make decisions about how the program was designed and monitored (Burleson et al., 1990).

38. This research is reviewed and evaluated in Thompson, 1981.

39. Gunnar-Vongnechten, 1978.

40. Ryan and Grolnick, 1986.

41. Kamii, 1991, p. 387. In fact, the lessons of conformity that Kamii finds troubling are those that concern academic activities, such as having to "learn mathematics through blind obedience," not only behavior (ibid.).

42. McCaslin and Good, 1992, p. 13. One writer has provocatively suggested that the disturbing obedience of Milgram's subjects "might be related to the fact that they were *paid* for their participation" (Lane, 1991, p. 353*n*).

43. Berman, 1990, p. 2.

44. Glasser, 1969, p. 37. On this point, see also Ryan and Stiller, 1991, p. 118.

45. Sometimes elementary school students are asked to put their heads down when they vote; in any case, this is an apt metaphor for the whole enterprise. Voting may be the closest approximation to democracy we can manage when a quarter of a billion people must try to govern themselves, but classroom teachers can do better. "Who thinks we should take our field trip to the museum? Raise your hands. Okay; and who prefers the zoo? The zoo wins, fifteen to twelve." From this exercise in adversarial majoritarianism children learn precious little about how to solve a problem, accommodate other people's preferences, or rethink their initial inclinations. Moreover, twelve children are now unlikely to feel very excited about the upcoming field trip. About the best that can be said for voting is that it doesn't take long. The political philosopher Benjamin Barber has cogently argued that voting is "the least significant act of citizenship in a democracy" (1984, p. 187); teachers interested in democracy will discourage this form of decision-making whenever possible. (For more on this perspective, Barber's book is worth a careful read; also see Mansbridge, 1983.)

46. Deci and Ryan, 1987, p. 1031. For an empirical demonstration that internal control can have some of the same undesirable effects as external control, see Ryan, 1982.

47. Bowles and Gintis, 1976, p. 39. The authors continue: "Discipline is still the theme, but the variations more often center on the 'internalization of behavioral norms,' on equipping the child with a built-in supervisor than on mere obedience to external authority and material sanctions" (ibid.).

48. Skinner offered this comment in a famous discussion with Carl Rogers (Rogers and Skinner, 1956, p. 1065). See also Kaplan, 1991, p. 21.

49. Deci and Ryan, 1987, p. 1025.

50. Deci and a colleague have defined "supporting autonomy" in terms of "using as little control as possible; encouraging children to think through their own problems rather than giving them solutions; permitting them to try out their own plans and ideas; and allowing them to work at their own speed. Pressuring them with rewards, tokens, deadlines, and prescriptions is counter to supporting autonomy" (Deci and Chandler, 1986, p. 590; see also Deci, Eghrari, et al., 1993).

51. For example, Richard deCharms, one of the first theorists to think seriously about the importance of self-determination, argues that someone working toward that objective "must help the person (a) to determine realistic goals for himself; (b) to know his own strengths and weaknesses; (c) to determine concrete action that he can take now that will help him to reach his goals; and (d) to consider how he can tell whether he is approaching his goal, that is, whether his action is having the desired effect" (deCharms, 1972, p. 97).
52. Höss is quoted in Miller, 1984, pp. 67–68.
53. Gordon, 1989, p. 9.
54. A ludicrous example of this unity-at-all-costs philosophy was offered in the following actual conversation reported in a famous study of parenting (Sears et al., 1957, p. 353):

    CHILD: Mother, why can't I go out and play? Jane and Linda are out.
    MOTHER: It's raining, dear, and I don't want you to catch cold.
    CHILD (*looking out the window*): But it *isn't* raining, Mummy. It just stopped.
    FATHER (*overhearing the interchange*): Young lady, if your mother says it's raining, it's raining.

55. Samalin, 1987, pp. 132–33.
56. Selma Wassermann, a professor of education and former teacher, recalls her own difficulties in switching to a classroom that supported children's decisions: "It was my explicit expectation that, once informed they would have to learn to take responsibility for their learning, the children should, in fact, learn to do it simply by following my orders. Now, in retrospect, it boggles my mind that I would ever have such an expectation. . . . We can't *order* it to work; we have to *make* it work. We have to teach children the skills of working thoughtfully and responsibly together. . . . Most teachers already know this, and they act on that knowledge in such skill areas as teaching children to read and write and number. But we mostly forget that the same is true for learning interpersonal and group process skills" (1989, pp. 202–203).
57. That, at any rate, is the finding of a series of surveys taken of nearly two thousand parents in Detroit from the late 1950s to the early 1980s (Alwin, 1984).
58. Kelman, 1990, p. 44.
59. Beane, 1990, p. 35.

APPENDIX A.
A CONVERSATION WITH B. F. SKINNER

1. Skinner, 1983, p. 407.

APPENDIX B. WHAT IS INTRINSIC MOTIVATION?

1. For example, based on her studies of creativity, Amabile says that people are "intrinsically motivated to engage in a particular task if they view their task engagement as motivated primarily by their own interest and involvement in the task" (1985, p. 393).

2. One theorist argues that the existence of free will prevents us from collapsing IM into reinforcement theory (Csikszentmihalyi, 1978, pp. 207–208). See also Deci and Ryan's discussion of IM as "the prototypical form of self-determination" (1990, p. 253).

3. "Intrinsic motivation may be better conceived of as an internally generated need to engage in activities that make one feel good rather than as a set of specific internal motivators" (Pretty and Seligman, 1984, p. 1251). This approach to the question is not very popular among most people who think about the subject, probably because it reduces cognitive and motivational questions to an uncomplicated desire for pleasure. Moreover, the implication is that various activities are interchangeable since what appears to be a genuine interest in one can just as easily be satisfied by something else that enhances one's mood.

4. This is offered by an educational researcher in the context of classroom motivation (Harter, 1981, p. 310; see also Butler, 1988, p. 2).

5. Deci and Ryan, 1985, p. 32. These two features are later combined in describing IM as "the innate, natural propensity to engage one's interests and exercise one's capacities, and in so doing, to seek and conquer optimal challenges" (p. 43). Even more broadly, the term is defined as "the life force or energy for the activity and for the development of the internal structure" (p. 8).

6. "An exclusive focus on mastery motivation fails to take account of the intrinsic social need that directs people's interest toward the development of relational bonds and toward a concern for interpersonally valued and culturally relevant activities" (Deci and Ryan, 1990, p. 242).

7. This point is raised by Robert Sternberg and a colleague in the context of a discussion about motivation and creativity, during which they suggest that "to engage in a task 'for its own sake' suggests the unparsimonious view that there are as many motivators as there are interesting tasks" (1991, p. 15). To this, Csikszentmihalyi replies that "what motivates are not many interesting tasks, but a single propensity to enjoy interaction with challenging tasks." Nevertheless, he points out that in creative situations it is often difficult to draw a sharp line between the goal and the task itself, a fact that raises interesting questions about the intrinsic/extrinsic distinction (1991, pp. 33–34).

8. For example, see Sansone and Morgan, 1992, p. 262.

9. For empirical confirmation of the relevance of this point, that is, the appeal of the alternative activities, see Wicker et al., 1990.

10. This problem is not unique to the issue of IM, but it certainly does appear regularly in this context. For example, see Deci, 1971, Experiment 1; Luyten and Lens, 1981 ("We doubt that the paper-and-pencil measures and the behavioral measure can still be considered operationalizations of the same underlying construct, called intrinsic motivation" [p. 33]); Pretty and Seligman, 1984, esp. pp. 1250–51; Koestner et al., 1987, esp. pp. 388–89; Koestner et al., 1989; Wicker et al., 1990. For further criticisms of both measures, see Arnold, 1976. For a theoretical account of why the two measures of IM would not be expected to be similar — an explanation rather different from the one that follows in the text — see Quattrone, 1985, esp. pp. 28–29, 33.

11. Ryan et al., 1991, p. 189.

12. Ibid.; the quotations appear on pp. 197, 202.

13. Jackson, 1968/1990, p. 28.
14. For an argument that internalized behaviors were initially controlled by extrinsic motivators, see Chandler and Connell, 1987; Ryan et al., 1992. Chandler and Connell even argue that "internalized motivation is conceptually more akin to extrinsic than to intrinsic motivation" (p. 357).
15. One of the very rare exceptions is a brief discussion of IM in the course of a longer critique of psychology's acceptance of self-interest as the premise for all investigations. In reviewing the connection drawn between IM and the need for self-determination, Michael and Lise Wallach comment that "it could hardly be made more clear that the relevance of the external environment continues to be understood as depending entirely on its relation to the needs that we have for ourselves" (1983, p. 214).
16. Csikszentmihalyi, 1990, p. 69.
17. Csikszentmihalyi, 1978, p. 215.
18. In saying this, I am questioning Deci and Ryan's apparent identification of intrinsic motivation with process: they argue that someone who cleans the house because of the pleasure of having the house clean at the end is engaging in an extrinsically motivated behavior (1987, p. 1034). In fact, Ryan believes that an altruistic individual, in seeking an improvement in the welfare of the person whom he helps, is not intrinsically motivated. To qualify as the latter, he would have to take pleasure in the process of changing the stranded motorist's tire, as opposed to focusing on the result of the rescue (personal communication, April 1993; for a different perspective, see Kunda and Schwartz's description of "the desire to do the right thing" as "a different kind of intrinsic motivation" [1983, p. 764]). This dispute returns us to the question of whether the idea of intrinsic motivation is necessarily individualistic.

APPENDIX C. THE BEHAVIORISTS TALK BACK

1. The few explicit attempts to refute criticisms of the use of rewards that I have been able to find appeared in journals for behaviorists (Dickinson, 1989), organizational psychologists (Mawhinney, 1990), consulting psychologists (O'Leary et al., 1972), and educators (Slavin, 1991; Chance, 1992); and in an early chapter in a guide to behavior modification (Kaplan, 1991) and a textbook (Kalish, 1981). The arguments that follow in the text are drawn chiefly from these sources.
2. Slavin, 1991, p. 91.
3. Dickinson, 1989, p. 4.
4. Kalish, 1981, p. 143.
5. Kaplan, 1991, p. 24. See also O'Leary et al., 1972, p. 1.
6. Chance, 1992, p. 207n10.
7. Slavin, 1991, p. 90. See also O'Leary et al., 1972, p. 3.
8. Chance, 1992, p. 206.
9. Kaplan, 1991, p. 23.
10. See Chance, 1991.
11. Chance, 1992, pp. 200–201.
12. Ibid., p. 203.
13. O'Leary et al., 1972, pp. 6–7. The research in question was one of Janet Spence's studies.
14. "Most nonbehavioral researchers have used nonreinforcing rewards" (Dickinson, 1989, p. 12). In fact, it is true that money and other common rewards

are often not as important to people as we assume. But the studies that have found a detrimental effect have generally used rewards that were clearly attractive to the subjects. The only way these rewards could be classified as nonreinforcing is to define a reinforcing reward as one that produced the desired effect, in which case the argument is tautological.

15. Slavin, 1991, p. 90. The same point is made in Chance, 1991, p. 803.
16. Dickinson, 1989, p. 13. See also Slavin, 1991, p. 90.
17. Slavin, 1991, p. 91.
18. Dollinger and Thelen, 1978.
19. See, for example, Kalish, 1981, p. 143.
20. Kalish, 1981, p. 256.
21. Dickinson, 1989, pp. 2–3. "From a behavioral perspective, then, intrinsically controlled behavior consists of behavior controlled by unprogrammed consequences" — that is, those that are "more or less inevitably produced by the structural characteristics of the physical environment and the biological organism" (Mawhinney et al., 1989, p. 111).
22. Dickinson, 1989, p. 12.
23. For various elaborate methodological criticisms, see Dickinson, 1989; Mawhinney, 1990.
24. Feingold and Mahoney, 1975; Davidson and Bucher, 1978; Vasta et al., 1978; Vasta and Stirpe, 1979. I am excluding here a study sometimes cited by others (Reiss and Sushinsky, 1975) because it did not challenge the potential of rewards to undermine interest; rather, it took exception to one widely accepted reason for this effect. Specifically, it was argued that rewards distract people from the task, a hypothesis pretty well disproved in subsequent research (Ross, 1975, Experiment 2; Smith and Pittman, 1978). For a discussion of this study, see Lepper and Greene, 1976.
25. Brennan and Glover, 1980; Mawhinney et al., 1989 ($N = 3$).
26. With a single exception (Brennan and Glover, 1980), none of the studies had a control group in which subjects engaged in the activity without being rewarded for purposes of comparison. (That exception has been criticized for other reasons; see Deci and Ryan, 1985, p. 184.) Most of the studies measured interest not by how much time the subjects spent on the target task but by how much of it they did. In the case of the most widely cited finding (Feingold and Mahoney, 1975), for instance, intrinsic motivation was measured by counting the number of connect-the-dots puzzles that were completed after the reward had been withdrawn, a number that could well have reflected the children's increased skill at the activity after having had a chance to practice. In the most recent experiment, conducted with three college students (Mawhinney et al., 1989), each subject was told at the beginning that he would receive $30 for participating, which means that the students were still being rewarded even in the "nonreward" sessions.

REFERENCES

Adelman, Howard S., and Linda Taylor. "Enhancing Motivation for Overcoming Learning and Behavior Problems." *Journal of Learning Disabilities* 16 (1983): 384–92.

Adler, Alfred. *The Individual Psychology of Alfred Adler,* edited by Heinz L. Ansbacher and Rowena R. Ansbacher. New York: Basic Books, 1956.

Adler, Jerry. "Hey, I'm Terrific." *Newsweek,* 17 February 1992: 46–51.

Albert, Linda. *A Teacher's Guide to Cooperative Discipline: How to Manage Your Classroom and Promote Self-Esteem.* Circle Pines, Minn.: American Guidance Service, 1989.

Alexander, Suzanne. "For Some Students, the Value of Learning Is Measured in Pizzas and Parking Passes." *Wall Street Journal,* 29 January 1992: B1, B12.

Alwin, Duane F. "Trends in Parental Socialization Values: Detroit, 1958–1983." *American Journal of Sociology* 90 (1984): 359–82.

Amabile, Teresa M. "Effects of External Evaluation on Artistic Creativity." *Journal of Personality and Social Psychology* 37 (1979): 221–33.

———. "Motivation and Creativity: Effects of Motivational Orientation on Creative Writers." *Journal of Personality and Social Psychology* 48 (1985): 393–99.

———. "A Model of Creativity and Innovation in Organizations." In *Research in Organizational Behavior,* vol. 10, edited by Barry M. Staw and L. L. Cummings. Greenwich, Conn.: JAI Press, 1988.

Amabile, Teresa M., William DeJong, and Mark R. Lepper. "Effects of Externally Imposed Deadlines on Subsequent Intrinsic Motivation." *Journal of Personality and Social Psychology* 34 (1976): 92–98.

Amabile, Teresa M., and Judith Gitomer. "Children's Artistic Creativity: Effects of Choice in Task Materials." *Personality and Social Psychology Bulletin* 10 (1984): 209–15.

Amabile, Teresa M., Beth Ann Hennessey, and Barbara S. Grossman. "Social Influences on Creativity: The Effects of Contracted-for Reward." *Journal of Personality and Social Psychology* 50 (1986): 14–23.

Amabile, Teresa M., Beth A. Hennessey, and Elizabeth M. Tighe. "The Work Preference Inventory: Assessing Intrinsic and Extrinsic Motivational Orientations." Unpublished paper, 1991.

American Productivity and Quality Center et al. "Putting Strategy to Work: Tools for Cost and Quality Management in the 1990s." Unpublished manuscript, 1991.

Ames, Carole. "Children's Achievement Attributions and Self-Reinforcement: Effects of Self-Concept and Competitive Reward Structure." *Journal of Educational Psychology* 70 (1978): 345–55.

————. "Competitive Versus Cooperative Reward Structures: The Influence of Individual and Group Performance Factors on Achievement Attributions and Affect." *American Educational Research Journal* 18 (1981): 273–87.

————. "Achievement Goals and the Classroom Motivational Climate." In *Student Perceptions in the Classroom,* edited by Dale H. Schunk and Judith L. Meece. Hillsdale, N.J.: Erlbaum, 1992a.

————. "Classrooms: Goals, Structures, and Student Motivation." *Journal of Educational Psychology* 84 (1992b): 261–71.

Ames, Carole, and Jennifer Archer. "Mothers' Beliefs About the Role of Ability and Effort in School Learning." *Journal of Educational Psychology* 79 (1987): 409–14.

————. "Achievement Goals in the Classroom: Students' Learning Strategies and Motivation Processes." *Journal of Educational Psychology* 80 (1988): 260–67.

Andersen, Janis F., and Peter A. Andersen. "Never Smile Until Christmas? Casting Doubt on an Old Myth." *Journal of Thought* 22 (1987): 57–61.

Anderson, Richard C., Larry L. Shirey, Paul T. Wilson, and Linda G. Fielding. "Interestingness of Children's Reading Material." In *Aptitude, Learning, and Instruction,* vol. 3: *Conative and Affective Process Analyses,* edited by Richard E. Snow and Marshall J. Farr. Hillsdale, N.J.: Erlbaum, 1987.

Anderson, Rosemarie, Sam Thomas Manoogian, and J. Steven Reznick. "The Undermining and Enhancing of Intrinsic Motivation in Preschool Children." *Journal of Personality and Social Psychology* 34 (1976): 915–22.

Andrews, Lewis M., and Marvin Karlins. "Living with the Faustian Power." In *Man Controlled: Readings in the Psychology of Behavior Control,* edited by Marvin Karlins and Lewis M. Andrews. New York: Free Press, 1972.

Arkes, Hal R. "Competence and the Overjustification Effect." *Motivation and Emotion* 3 (1979): 143–50.

Arnold, Hugh J. "Effects of Performance Feedback and Extrinsic Reward upon High Intrinsic Motivation." *Organizational Behavior and Human Performance* 17 (1976): 275–88.

Asher, Steven R. "Topic Interest and Children's Reading Comprehension." In *Theoretical Issues in Reading Comprehension: Perspectives from Cognitive Psychology, Linguistics, Artificial Intelligence, and Education,* edited by Rand J. Spiro, Bertram C. Bruce, and William F. Brewer. Hillsdale, N.J.: Erlbaum, 1980.

Austin, William. "Friendship and Fairness: Effects of Type of Relationship and Task Performance on Choice of Distribution Rules." *Personality and Social Psychology Bulletin* 6 (1980): 402–408.

Ayres, Barbara. "'Three Brains Are Better Than One': Students' Perspectives on Cooperative Learning." Unpublished paper, Syracuse University, 1990.

Bachrach, Samuel B., David B. Lipsky, and Joseph B. Shedd. *Paying for Better Teachers: Merit Pay and Its Alternatives.* Ithaca, N.Y.: Organizational Analysis and Practice, 1984.

Balsam, Peter D., and Andrew S. Bondy. "The Negative Side Effects of Reward." *Journal of Applied Behavior Analysis* 16 (1983): 283–96.

Barber, Benjamin. *Strong Democracy: Participatory Politics for a New Age.* Berkeley: University of California Press, 1984.

Barker, George P., and Sandra Graham. "Developmental Study of Praise and Blame as Attributional Cues." *Journal of Educational Psychology* 79 (1987): 62–66.

Baron, Jonathan. "Utility, Exchange, and Commensurability." *Journal of Thought* 23 (1988): 111–31.

Barr, Ronald G., and Marjorie F. Elias. "Nursing Interval and Maternal Responsivity: Effect on Early Infant Crying." *Pediatrics* 81 (1988): 529–36.

Barrett, Marty, and Ann K. Boggiano. "Fostering Extrinsic Orientations: Use of Reward Strategies to Motivate Children." *Journal of Social and Clinical Psychology* 6 (1988): 293–309.

Bartis, Scott, Kate Szymanski, and Stephen G. Harkins. "Evaluation and Performance: A Two-Edged Knife." *Personality and Social Psychology Bulletin* 14 (1988): 242–51.

Batson, C. Daniel, Jay S. Coke, M. L. Jasnoski, and Michael Hanson. "Buying Kindness: Effect of an Extrinsic Incentive for Helping on Perceived Altruism." *Personality and Social Psychology Bulletin* 4 (1978): 86–91.

Baumeister, Roy F., Debra G. Hutton, and Kenneth J. Cairns. "Negative Effects of Praise on Skilled Performance." *Basic and Applied Social Psychology* 11 (1990): 131–48.

Baumrind, Diana. "Current Patterns of Parental Authority." *Developmental Psychology Monographs* 4 (1971): 1–103.

Beane, James A. *Affect in the Curriculum: Toward Democracy, Dignity, and Diversity.* New York: Teachers College Press, 1990.

Belasco, James A. *Teaching the Elephant to Dance: Empowering Change in Your Organization.* New York: Crown, 1990.

Bell, Silvia M., and Mary D. Salter Ainsworth. "Infant Crying and Maternal Responsiveness." *Child Development* 43 (1972): 1171–90.

Bennett, Peggy. "The Perils and Profits of Praise." *Music Educators Journal*, September 1988: 23–24.

Benware, Carl A., and Edward L. Deci. "Quality of Learning with an Active Versus Passive Motivational Set." *American Educational Research Journal* 21 (1984): 755–65.

Berman, Shelley. "The Real Ropes Course: The Development of Social Consciousness." *ESR Journal* (Educators for Social Responsibility), 1990: 1–18.

Bernstein, Jeremy. "The Secrets of the Old One — [Part] I." *The New Yorker*, 10 March 1973: 44–101.

Besharov, Douglas J. "Beware of Unintended Consequences." *Public Welfare*, Spring 1992: 18–19.

Biklen, Douglas P. "Behavior Modification in a State Mental Hospital." *American Journal of Orthopsychiatry* 46 (1976): 53–61.

Birch, Leann Lipps, Diane Wolfe Marlin, and Julie Rotter. "Eating as the 'Means' Activity in a Contingency: Effects on Young Children's Food Preference." *Child Development* 55 (1984): 431–39.

Blinder, Alan S. Introduction to *Paying for Productivity: A Look at the Evidence,* edited by Alan S. Blinder. Washington, D.C.: Brookings Institution, 1990.

Blumenfeld, Phyllis C., Paul R. Pintrich, and V. Lee Hamilton. "Children's Concepts of Ability, Effort, and Conduct." *American Educational Research Journal* 23 (1986): 95–104.

Boggiano, Ann K., and Marty Barrett. "Gender Differences in Depression in Children as a Function of Motivational Orientation." *Sex Roles* 26 (1992): 11–17.

———. "Maladaptive Achievement Patterns: The Role of Motivational Orientation." Unpublished paper, 1991.

Boggiano, Ann K., Marty Barrett, Anne W. Weiher, Gary H. McClelland, and Cynthia M. Lusk. "Use of the Maximal-Operant Principle to Motivate Children's Intrinsic Interest." *Journal of Personality and Social Psychology* 53 (1987): 866–79.

Boggiano, Ann K., Judith M. Harackiewicz, Janella M. Bessette, and Deborah S. Main. "Increasing Children's Interest Through Performance-Contingent Reward." *Social Cognition* 3 (1985): 400–11.

Boggiano, Ann K., Cheryl A. Klinger, and Deborah S. Main. "Enhancing Interest in Peer Interaction: A Developmental Analysis." *Child Development* 57 (1986): 852–61.

Boggiano, Ann K., and Deborah S. Main. "Enhancing Children's Interest in Activities Used as Rewards: The Bonus Effect." *Journal of Personality and Social Psychology* 51 (1986): 1116–26.

Boggiano, Ann K., Deborah S. Main, Cheryl Flink, Marty Barrett, Louise Silvern, and Phyllis Katz. "A Model of Achievement in Children: The Role of Controlling Strategies in Helplessness and Affect." In *Advances in Test Anxiety Research*, vol. 6, edited by Ralf Schwarzer, Henk M. Van Der Ploeg, and Charles D. Spielberger. Amsterdam: Swets & Zeitlinger, 1989.

Boggiano, Ann K., Deborah S. Main, and Phyllis A. Katz. "Children's Preference for Challenge: The Role of Perceived Competence and Control." *Journal of Personality and Social Psychology* 54 (1988): 134–41.

———. "Mastery Motivation in Boys and Girls: The Role of Intrinsic Versus Extrinsic Motivation." *Sex Roles* 25 (1991): 511–20.

Boggiano, Ann K., and Diane N. Ruble. "Competence and the Overjustification Effect: A Developmental Study." *Journal of Personality and Social Psychology* 37 (1979): 1462–68.

Boggiano, Ann K., Diane N. Ruble, and Thane S. Pittman. "The Mastery Hypothesis and the Overjustification Effect." *Social Cognition* 1 (1982): 38–49.

Boggiano, Ann K., Ann Shields, Marty Barrett, Teddy Kellam, Erik Thompson, Jeffrey Simons, and Phyllis Katz. "Helplessness Deficits in Students: The Role of Motivational Orientation." *Motivation and Emotion* 16 (1992): 271–96.

Bond, Michael H., Kwok Leung, and Kwok Choi Wan. "How Does Cultural Collectivism Operate? The Impact of Task and Maintenance Contributions on Reward Distribution." *Journal of Cross-Cultural Psychology* 13 (1982): 186–200.

Bosquet, Michel. "The Prison Factory." Reprinted from *Le Nouvel Observateur* in *Working Papers for a New Society,* Spring 1973: 20–27.

"Bosses' Pay." *The Economist,* 1 February 1992: 19–22.

Bostrom, Robert N., John W. Vlandis, and Milton E. Rosenbaum. "Grades as Reinforcing Contingencies and Attitude Change." *Journal of Educational Psychology* 52 (1961): 112–15.

Bowles, Samuel, and Herbert Gintis. *Schooling in Capitalist America: Educational Reform and the Contradictions of Economic Life.* New York: Basic Books, 1976.

Braham, Jim. "A Rewarding Place to Work." *Industry Week,* 18 September 1989: 15–19.

Breger, Louis, and James L. McGaugh. "Critique and Reformulation of 'Learning Theory' Approaches to Psychotherapy and Neurosis." *Psychological Bulletin* 63 (1965): 338–58.

Brennan, E. James. "Compensation: The Myth and the Reality of Pay for Performance." *Personnel Journal,* March 1985: 73–75.

Brennan, Thomas P., and John A. Glover. "An Examination of the Effect of Extrinsic Reinforcers on Intrinsically Motivated Behavior: Experimental and Theoretical." *Social Behavior and Personality* 8 (1980): 27–32.

Brophy, Jere. "Teacher Praise: A Functional Analysis." *Review of Educational Research* 51 (1981): 5–32.

———. "Conceptualizing Student Motivation." *Educational Psychologist* 18 (1983): 200–15.

Brophy, Jere, and Neelam Kher. "Teacher Socialization as a Mechanism for Developing Student Motivation to Learn." In *The Social Psychology of Education: Current Research and Theory*, edited by Robert S. Feldman. Cambridge: Cambridge University Press, 1986.

Brown, Lyn Mikel, and Carol Gilligan. *Meeting at the Crossroads: Women's Psychology and Girls' Development*. Cambridge: Harvard University Press, 1992.

Bruner, Jerome S. "The Act of Discovery." *Harvard Educational Review* 31 (1961): 21–32.

Burland, Roger. "Behaviourism in the Closed Community: The Token Economy and Performance Contracting." In *Behaviourism and Learning Theory in Education*, edited by David Fontana. Edinburgh: Scottish Academic Press, 1984.

Burleson, Joseph A., S. Stephen Kegeles, and Adrian K. Lund. "Effects of Decisional Control and Work Orientation on Persistence in Preventive Health Behavior." *Health Psychology* 9 (1990): 1–17.

Butler, Owen B. "Why We're at Risk." Speech given at the second Fortune Education Summit, Washington, D.C., October 1989. Published in pamphlet form by the Edwin Gould Foundation for Children, n.d.

Butler, Ruth. "Task-Involving and Ego-Involving Properties of Evaluation: Effects of Different Feedback Conditions on Motivational Perceptions, Interest, and Performance." *Journal of Educational Psychology* 79 (1987): 474–82.

———. "Enhancing and Undermining Intrinsic Motivation: The Effects of Task-Involving and Ego-Involving Evaluation on Interest and Performance." *British Journal of Educational Psychology* 58 (1988): 1–14.

———. "Interest in the Task and Interest in Peers' Work in Competitive and Noncompetitive Conditions: A Developmental Study." *Child Development* 60 (1989): 562–70.

———. "What Young People Want to Know When: Effects of Mastery and Ability Goals on Interest in Different Kinds of Social Comparisons." *Journal of Personality and Social Psychology* 62 (1992): 934–43.

Butler, Ruth, and Mordecai Nisan. "Effects of No Feedback, Task-Related Comments, and Grades on Intrinsic Motivation and Performance." *Journal of Educational Psychology* 78 (1986): 210–16.

Cannella, Gaile S. "Praise and Concrete Rewards: Concerns for Childhood Education." *Childhood Education* 62 (1986): 297–301.

Carlson, Carl G., Michel Hersen, and Richard M. Eisler. "Token Economy Programs in the Treatment of Hospitalized Adult Psychiatric Patients." *Journal of Nervous and Mental Disease* 155 (1972): 192–204.

Chance, Paul. "A Gross Injustice." *Phi Delta Kappan*, June 1991: 803.

———. "The Rewards of Learning." *Phi Delta Kappan*, November 1992: 200–207.

Chandler, Cristine L., and James P. Connell. "Children's Intrinsic, Extrinsic, and Internalized Motivation: A Developmental Study of Children's Reasons for Liked and Disliked Behaviours." *British Journal of Developmental Psychology* 5 (1987): 357–65.

Chandler, Theodore A. "What's Wrong with Success and Praise?" *Arithmetic Teacher*, December 1981: 10–12.

Cheyne, J. Allan, and Richard H. Walters. "Intensity of Punishment, Timing of Punishment, and Cognitive Structure as Determinants of Response Inhibition." *Journal of Experimental Child Psychology* 7 (1969): 231–44.

Chomsky, Noam. "The Case Against B. F. Skinner." *New York Review of Books,* 30 December 1971: 18–24.

Clarke, Judy, Ron Wideman, and Susan Eadie. *Together We Learn.* Scarborough, Ont.: Prentice-Hall Canada, 1990.

Clayton, Lawrence O. "The Impact upon Child-Rearing Attitudes, of Parental Views of the Nature of Humankind." *Journal of Psychology and Christianity* 4, 3 (1985): 49–55.

Clymer, Adam. "House Revolutionary." *New York Times Magazine,* 23 August 1992: 41, 47–48.

Cobb, Paul, Terry Wood, Erna Yackel, John Nicholls, Grayson Wheatley, Beatriz Trigatti, and Marcella Perlwitz. "Assessment of a Problem-Centered Second-Grade Mathematics Project." *Journal for Research in Mathematics Education* 22 (1991): 3–29.

Cobb, Paul, Erna Yackel, and Terry Wood. "Young Children's Emotional Acts While Engaged in Mathematical Problem Solving." In *Affect and Mathematical Problem Solving: A New Perspective,* edited by D. B. McLeod and V. M. Adams. New York: Springer-Verlag, 1989.

Cohen, David K., and Richard J. Murnane. "The Merits of Merit Pay." *The Public Interest,* Summer 1985: 3–30.

Cohen, Elizabeth G. *Designing Groupwork: Strategies for the Heterogeneous Classroom.* New York: Teachers College Press, 1986.

Coles, Gerald. *The Learning Mystique: A Critical Look at "Learning Disabilities."* New York: Pantheon, 1987.

Colvin, Robert H. "Imposed Extrinsic Reward in an Elementary School Setting: Effects on Free-Operant Rates and Choices." *Dissertation Abstracts International* 32, 9 (1972): 5034-A.

Condry, John. "Enemies of Exploration: Self-Initiated Versus Other-Initiated Learning." *Journal of Personality and Social Psychology* 35 (1977): 459–77.

———. "The Role of Incentives in Socialization." In *The Hidden Costs of Rewards: New Perspectives on the Psychology of Human Motivation,* edited by Mark R. Lepper and David Greene. Hillsdale, N.J.: Erlbaum, 1978.

Condry, John, and James Chambers. "Intrinsic Motivation and the Process of Learning." In *The Hidden Costs of Rewards: New Perspectives on the Psychology of Human Motivation,* edited by Mark R. Lepper and David Greene. Hillsdale, N.J.: Erlbaum, 1978.

Condry, John, and Barbara Koslowski. "Can Education Be Made 'Intrinsically Interesting' to Children?" In *Current Topics in Early Childhood Education,* vol. 11, edited by Lilian G. Katz. Norwood, N.J.: Ablex, 1979.

Covaleskie, John F. "Discipline and Morality: Beyond Rules and Consequences." *Educational Forum* 56 (1992): 173–83.

Cowan, Alison Leigh. "Executives Are Fuming over Data on Their Pay." *New York Times,* 25 August 1992: D1.

Crino, Michael D., and Michael C. White. "Feedback Effects in Intrinsic/Extrinsic Reward Paradigms." *Journal of Management* 8 (1982): 95–108.

Crockenberg, Susan, and Cindy Litman. "Autonomy as Competence in Two-Year-Olds: Maternal Correlates of Child Defiance, Compliance, and Self-Assertion." *Developmental Psychology* 26 (1990): 961–71.

Crockenberg, Susan, and Perrin Smith. "Antecedents of Mother-Infant Interaction and Infant Irritability in the First Three Months of Life." *Infant Behavior and Development* 5 (1982): 105–19.

Crockenberg, Vincent. "Assertive Discipline: A Dissent." *California Journal of Teacher Education* 9 (1982): 59–74.

Csikszentmihalyi, Mihaly. "Intrinsic Rewards and Emergent Motivation." In *The Hidden Costs of Rewards: New Perspectives on the Psychology of Human Motivation,* edited by Mark R. Lepper and David Greene. Hillsdale, N.J.: Erlbaum, 1978.

———. *Flow: The Psychology of Optimal Experience.* New York: Harper-Collins, 1990.

———. "Commentary." *Human Development* 34 (1991): 32–34.

Csikszentmihalyi, Mihaly, and Judith LeFevre. "Optimal Experience in Work and Leisure." *Journal of Personality and Social Psychology* 56 (1989): 815–22.

Cullen, Francis T., Jr., John B. Cullen, Van L. Hayhow, and John T. Plouffe. "The Effects of the Use of Grades as an Incentive." *Journal of Educational Research* 68 (1975): 277–79.

Curry, Susan J., Edward H. Wagner, and Louis C. Grothaus. "Intrinsic and Extrinsic Motivation for Smoking Cessation." *Journal of Consulting and Clinical Psychology* 58 (1990): 310–16.

———. "Evaluation of Intrinsic and Extrinsic Motivation Interventions With a Self-Help Smoking Cessation Program." *Journal of Consulting and Clinical Psychology* 59 (1991): 318–24.

Curwin, Richard L., and Allen N. Mendler. *Discipline with Dignity.* [Alexandria, Va.]: Association for Supervision and Curriculum Development, 1988.

Daley, Suzanne. "Pendulum Is Swinging Back to the Teaching of Values in U.S. Schools." *New York Times,* 12 December 1990: B14.

Danner, Fred W., and Edward Lonky. "A Cognitive-Developmental Approach to the Effects of Rewards on Intrinsic Motivation." *Child Development* 52 (1981): 1043–52.

Das, J. P., K. Schokman-Gates, and D. Murphy. "The Development of Intrinsic and Extrinsic Motivational Orientation in Normal and Disabled Readers." *Journal of Psychoeducational Assessment* 4 (1985): 297–312.

deCharms, Richard. *Personal Causation: The Internal Affective Determinants of Behavior.* New York: Academic Press, 1968.

———. "Personal Causation Training in the Schools." *Journal of Applied Social Psychology* 2 (1972): 95–113.

———. "Intrinsic Motivation, Peer Tutoring, and Cooperative Learning: Practical Maxims." In *Teacher and Student Perceptions: Implications for Learning,* edited by John M. Levine and Margaret C. Wang. Hillsdale, N.J.: Erlbaum, 1983.

Deci, Edward L. "Effects of Externally Mediated Rewards on Intrinsic Motivation." *Journal of Personality and Social Psychology* 18 (1971): 105–15.

———. "Applications of Research on the Effects of Rewards." In *The Hidden Costs of Rewards: New Perspectives on the Psychology of Human Motivation,* edited by Mark R. Lepper and David Greene. Hillsdale, N.J.: Erlbaum, 1978.

———. "The Well-Tempered Classroom." *Psychology Today,* March 1985: 52–53.

———. "The History of Motivation in Psychology and Its Relevance for Management." In *Management and Motivation: Selected Readings,* edited by Victor H. Vroom and Edward L. Deci, 2d ed. London: Penguin, 1992.

Deci, Edward L., Gregory Betley, James Kahle, Linda Abrams, and Joseph Porac.

"When Trying to Win: Competition and Intrinsic Motivation." *Personality and Social Psychology Bulletin* 7 (1981): 79–83.

Deci, Edward L., Wayne F. Cascio, and Judith Krusell. "Cognitive Evaluation Theory and Some Comments on the Calder and Staw Critique." *Journal of Personality and Social Psychology* 31 (1975): 81–85.

Deci, Edward L., and Cristine L. Chandler. "The Importance of Motivation for the Future of the LD Field." *Journal of Learning Disabilities* 19 (1986): 587–94.

Deci, Edward L., Robert E. Driver, Lucinda Hotchkiss, Robert J. Robbins, and Ilona McDougal Wilson. "The Relation of Mothers' Controlling Vocalizations to Children's Intrinsic Motivation." *Journal of Experimental Child Psychology* 55 (1993): 151–62.

Deci, Edward L., Haleh Eghrari, Brian C. Patrick, and Dean R. Leone. "Facilitating Internalization: The Self-Determination Theory Perspective." *Journal of Personality.* 55(1993): 151–62.

Deci, Edward L., Rosemary Hodges, Louisa Pierson, and Joseph Tomassone. "Autonomy and Competence as Motivational Factors in Students with Learning Disabilities and Emotional Handicaps." *Journal of Learning Disabilities* 25 (1992): 457–71.

Deci, Edward L., John Nezlek, and Louise Sheinman. "Characteristics of the Rewarder and Intrinsic Motivation of the Rewardee." *Journal of Personality and Social Psychology* 40 (1981): 1–10.

Deci, Edward L., and Joseph Porac. "Cognitive Evaluation Theory and the Study of Human Motivation." In *The Hidden Costs of Rewards: New Perspectives on the Psychology of Human Motivation,* edited by Mark R. Lepper and David Greene. Hillsdale, N.J.: Erlbaum, 1978.

Deci, Edward L., and Richard M. Ryan. *Intrinsic Motivation and Self-Determination in Human Behavior.* New York: Plenum, 1985.

———. "The Support of Autonomy and the Control of Behavior." *Journal of Personality and Social Psychology* 53 (1987): 1024–37.

———. "A Motivational Approach to Self: Integration in Personality." In *Nebraska Symposium on Motivation,* vol. 38, edited by Richard Dienstbier. Lincoln: University of Nebraska Press, 1990.

Deci, Edward L., Allan J. Schwartz, Louise Sheinman, and Richard M. Ryan. "An Instrument to Assess Adults' Orientations Toward Control Versus Autonomy with Children: Reflections on Intrinsic Motivation and Perceived Competence." *Journal of Educational Psychology* 73 (1981): 642–50.

Deci, Edward L., Nancy H. Spiegel, Richard M. Ryan, Richard Koestner, and Manette Kauffman. "Effects of Performance Standards on Teaching Styles: Behavior of Controlling Teachers." *Journal of Educational Psychology* 74 (1982): 852–59.

Deming, W. Edwards. *Out of the Crisis.* Cambridge: MIT Center for Advanced Engineering Study, 1986.

———. "Foundation for Management of Quality in the Western World." Paper delivered in Osaka, Japan, 1989; revised, 1991. Reprinted in American Association of School Administrators, ed., *An Introduction to Total Quality for Schools.* Arlington, Va.: AASA, 1991.

Deutsch, Morton. *Distributive Justice: A Social-Psychological Perspective.* New Haven: Yale University Press, 1985.

DeVries, Rheta, with Lawrence Kohlberg. *Programs of Early Education: The Constructivist View.* New York: Longman, 1987.

Dewey, John. *Interest and Effort in Education.* Boston: Houghton Mifflin, 1913.

————. *The School and Society*. Rev. ed. 1915. Reprint. Chicago: University of Chicago Press, 1990.

Dickinson, Alyce M. "The Detrimental Effects of Extrinsic Reinforcement on 'Intrinsic Motivation.'" *The Behavior Analyst* 12 (1989): 1–15.

Dienstbier, Richard A., and Gary K. Leak. "Overjustification and Weight Loss: The Effects of Monetary Reward." Paper presented at the annual convention of the American Psychological Association, Washington, D.C., September 1976.

Dinkmeyer, Don, and Gary D. McKay. *The Parent's Handbook*. 3d ed. Circle Pines, Minn.: American Guidance Service, 1989.

Dollinger, Stephen J., and Mark H. Thelen. "Overjustification and Children's Intrinsic Motivation: Comparative Effects of Four Rewards." *Journal of Personality and Social Psychology* 36 (1978): 1259–69.

Douglas, Virginia I., and Penny A. Parry. "Effects of Reward on Delayed Reaction Time Task Performance of Hyperactive Children." *Journal of Abnormal Child Psychology* 11 (1983): 313–26.

Doyle, Walter. "Academic Work." *Review of Educational Research* 53 (1983): 159–99.

Drabman, Ronald S., and Richard D. Tucker. "Why Classroom Token Economies Fail." *Journal of School Psychology* 12 (1974): 178–88.

Dreikurs, Rudolf. *Psychology in the Classroom*. New York: Harper, 1957.

Dreikurs, Rudolf, Bernice Bronia Grunwald, and Floy C. Pepper. *Maintaining Sanity in the Classroom: Classroom Management Techniques*. 2d ed. New York: Harper & Row, 1982.

Dressel, Paul. "Facts and Fancy in Assigning Grades." *Basic College Quarterly* 2 (1957): 6–12.

"Dumping the Gold Card." *Teacher Magazine*, January 1991: 15.

Dweck, Carol S. "Motivational Processes Affecting Learning." *American Psychologist* 41 (1986): 1040–48.

Dweck, Carol S., and Ellen L. Leggett. "A Social-Cognitive Approach to Motivation and Personality." *Psychological Review* 95 (1988): 256–73.

Edwards, Carolyn Pope. *Promoting Social and Moral Development in Young Children: Creative Approaches for the Classroom*. New York: Teachers College Press, 1986.

Ehrenfeld, Tom. "The Case of the Unpopular Pay Plan." *Harvard Business Review*, January–February 1992: 14–23.

Ehrenreich, Barbara. *Fear of Falling: The Inner Life of the Middle Class*. New York: HarperCollins, 1989.

Eimers, Robert C., George W. Blomgren, and Edward Gubman. "How Awards and Incentives Can Help Speed Learning." *Training*, July 1979: A3–6.

Elden, J. Maxwell. "Political Efficacy at Work: The Connection Between More Autonomous Forms of Workplace Organization and a More Participatory Politics." *American Political Science Review* 75 (1981): 43–58.

Ellig, Bruce R. *Executive Compensation — A Total Pay Perspective*. New York: McGraw-Hill, 1982.

Elliott, Elaine S., and Carol S. Dweck. "Goals: An Approach to Motivation and Achievement." *Journal of Personality and Social Psychology* 54 (1988): 5–12.

Emmer, Edmund T., and Amy Aussiker. "School and Classroom Discipline Programs: How Well Do They Work?" In *Student Discipline Strategies: Research and Practice*, edited by Oliver C. Moles. Albany: State University of New York Press, 1990.

Enzle, Michael E., and Sharon C. Anderson. "Surveillant Intentions and Intrinsic Motivation." *Journal of Personality and Social Psychology* 64 (1993): 257–66.

Enzle, Michael E., John P. Roggeveen, and Sharon C. Look. "Self- Versus Other-Reward Administration and Intrinsic Motivation." *Journal of Experimental Social Psychology* 27 (1991): 468–79.

Enzle, Michael E., and Edward F. Wright. "The Origin-Pawn Distinction and Intrinsic Motivation." Unpublished paper, 1992.

Eron, Leonard D., L. Rowell Huesmann, Eric Dubow, Richard Romanoff, and Patty Warnick Yarmel. "Aggression and Its Correlates over 22 Years." In *Childhood Aggression and Violence*, edited by David H. Crowell, Ian M. Evans, and Clifford R. O'Donnell. New York: Plenum, 1987.

Fabes, Richard A. "Effects of Reward Contexts on Young Children's Task Interest." *Journal of Psychology* 121 (1987): 5–19.

Fabes, Richard A., Nancy Eisenberg, Jim Fultz, and Paul Miller. "Reward, Affect, and Young Children's Motivational Orientation." *Motivation and Emotion* 12 (1988): 155–69.

Fabes, Richard A., Jim Fultz, Nancy Eisenberg, Traci May-Plumlee, and F. Scott Christopher. "Effects of Rewards on Children's Prosocial Motivation: A Socialization Study." *Developmental Psychology* 25 (1989): 509–15.

Fabes, Richard A., John C. McCullers, and Harry L. Hom, Jr. "Children's Task Interest and Performance: Immediate Versus Subsequent Effects of Rewards." *Personality and Social Psychology Bulletin* 12 (1986): 17–30.

Fabes, Richard A., James D. Moran III, and John C. McCullers. "The Hidden Costs of Reward and WAIS Subscale Performance." *American Journal of Psychology* 94 (1981): 387–98.

Fantuzzo, John W., Cynthia A. Rohrbeck, A. Dirk Hightower, and William C. Work. "Teachers' Use and Children's Preferences of Rewards in Elementary School." *Psychology in the Schools* 28 (1991): 175–81.

Farson, Richard E. "Praise Reappraised." 1963. Reprinted as "Praise as a Motivational Tool." In *Human Dynamics in Psychology and Education*, edited by Don E. Hamachek. 3d ed. Boston: Allyn & Bacon, 1977.

Fazio, Russell H. "On the Self-Perception Explanation of the Overjustification Effect: The Role of the Salience of Initial Attitude." *Journal of Experimental Social Psychology* 17 (1981): 417–26.

Fein, Mitchell. "Motivation for Work." In *Handbook of Work, Organization and Society,* edited by Robert Dubin. Chicago: Rand McNally, 1976.

Feshbach, Norma Deitch, Seymour Feshbach, Mary Fauvre, and Michael Ballard-Campbell. *Learning to Care: Classroom Activities for Social and Affective Development.* Glenview, Ill.: Scott, Foresman, 1983.

Firestone, Philip, and Virginia Douglas. "The Effects of Reward and Punishment on Reaction Times and Autonomic Activity in Hyperactive and Normal Children." *Journal of Abnormal Child Psychology* 3 (1975): 201–15.

Fisher, Cynthia D. "The Effects of Personal Control, Competence, and Extrinsic Reward Systems on Intrinsic Motivation." *Organizational Behavior and Human Performance* 21 (1978): 273–88.

Fiske, Edward B. "Finding Fault with the Testers." *New York Times Magazine,* 18 November 1979: 152–62.

Flink, Cheryl, Ann K. Boggiano, and Marty Barrett. "Controlling Teaching Strategies: Undermining Children's Self-Determination and Performance." *Journal of Personality and Social Psychology* 59 (1990): 916–24.

Francella, Kevin. "If Employees Perform, Then Reward 'Em." *Data Management,* August 1983: 53.

Freedman, Jonathan L., John A. Cunningham, and Kirsten Krismer. "Inferred Values and the Reverse-Incentive Effect in Induced Compliance." *Journal of Personality and Social Psychology* 62 (1992): 357–68.

Fresko, Barbara. "Reward Salience, Assessment of Success, and Critical Attitudes Among Tutors." *Journal of Educational Research* 81 (1988): 341–46.

Gabor, Andrea. "Take This Job and Love It." *New York Times,* 26 January 1992: F1, F6.

Gabor, Carol. "What Is So Frightening About 'Driving Out Fear'?" In *Performance Appraisal: Perspectives on a Quality Management Approach,* edited by Gary N. McLean, Susan R. Damme, and Richard A. Swanson. Alexandria, Va.: American Society for Training and Development, 1990.

Garbarino, James. "The Impact of Anticipated Reward upon Cross-Age Tutoring." *Journal of Personality and Social Psychology* 32 (1975): 421–28.

Gartrell, Dan. "Assertive Discipline: Unhealthy for Children and Other Living Things." *Young Children,* January 1987: 10–11.

Geller, E. Scott, Michael J. Kalsher, James R. Rudd, and Galen R. Lehman. "Promoting Safety Belt Use on a University Campus: An Integration of Commitment and Incentive Strategies." *Journal of Applied Social Psychology* 19 (1989): 3–19.

Geller, E. Scott, James R. Rudd, Michael J. Kalsher, Frederick M. Streff, and Galen R. Lehman. "Employer-Based Programs to Motivate Safety Belt Use: A Review of Short-Term and Long-Term Effects." *Journal of Safety Research* 18 (1987): 1–17.

Gillespie, Richard. *Manufacturing Knowledge: A History of the Hawthorne Experiments.* Cambridge: Cambridge University Press, 1991.

Glasser, William. *Schools Without Failure.* New York: Harper & Row, 1969.

———. *The Quality School: Managing Students Without Coercion.* New York: Harper Perennial, 1990.

Glover, John, and A. L. Gary. "Procedures to Increase Some Aspects of Creativity." *Journal of Applied Behavior Analysis* 9 (1976): 79–84.

Glucksberg, Sam. "The Influence of Strength of Drive on Functional Fixedness and Perceptual Recognition." *Journal of Experimental Psychology* 63 (1962): 36–41.

———. "Problem Solving: Response Competition and the Influence of Drive." *Psychological Reports* 15 (1964): 939–42.

Glynn, Shirley M. "Token Economy Approaches for Psychiatric Patients: Progress and Pitfalls Over 25 Years." *Behavior Modification* 14 (1990): 383–407.

Goetz, Elizabeth M., and Donald M. Baer. "Social Control of Form Diversity and the Emergence of New Forms in Children's Blockbuilding." *Journal of Applied Behavior Analysis* 6 (1973): 209–17.

Goldstein, Jeffrey H. "Beliefs About Human Aggression." In *Aggression and War: Their Social and Biological Bases,* edited by Jo Groebel and Robert A. Hinde. Cambridge: Cambridge University Press, 1988.

Goodlad, John I. *A Place Called School: Prospects for the Future.* New York: McGraw-Hill, 1984.

Gordon, Thomas. *Leader Effectiveness Training (L.E.T.): The Foundation for Participative Management and Employee Involvement.* New York: Putnam's, 1977.

———. *Teaching Children Self-Discipline . . . at Home and at School.* New York: Times Books, 1989.

Gottfried, Adele Eskeles. "Academic Intrinsic Motivation in Elementary and Junior High School Students." *Journal of Educational Psychology* 77 (1985): 631–45.

———. "Intrinsic Motivational Aspects of Play Experiences and Materials." In *Play Interactions: The Contribution of Play Materials and Parental Involvement to Children's Development*, edited by Allen W. Gottfried and Catherine Caldwell Brown. Lexington, Mass.: Lexington Books, 1986.

———. "Academic Intrinsic Motivation in Young Elementary School Children." *Journal of Educational Psychology* 82 (1990): 525–38.

Gottfried, Adele E., and Allen W. Gottfried. "Parents' Reward Strategies and Children's Academic Intrinsic Motivation and School Performance." Paper presented at the biennial conference of the Society for Research in Child Development, Seattle, April 1991a.

———. "Home Environment and Children's Academic Intrinsic Motivation: A Longitudinal Study." Paper presented at a conference on longitudinal research, Palm Springs, Calif., November 1991b.

Gowens, Pat. "Welfare, Learnfare — Unfair! A Letter to My Governor." *Ms.*, September–October 1991: 90–91.

Graham, Sandra, and Shari Golan. "Motivational Influences on Cognition: Task Involvement, Ego Involvement, and Depth of Information Processing." *Journal of Educational Psychology* 83 (1991): 187–94.

Graziano, Anthony M., and Karen A. Namaste. "Parental Use of Physical Force in Child Discipline: A Survey of 679 College Students." *Journal of Interpersonal Violence* 5 (1990): 449–63.

Green, Lawrence W., Alisa L. Wilson, and Chris Y. Lovato. "What Changes Can Health Promotion Achieve and How Long Do These Changes Last?" *Preventive Medicine* 15 (1986): 508–21.

Greenberg, Jeanne, and Herb Greenberg. "Money Isn't Everything." *Sales and Marketing Management*, May 1991: 10–14.

Greene, David, and Mark R. Lepper. "Effects of Extrinsic Rewards on Children's Subsequent Intrinsic Interest." *Child Development* 45 (1974): 1141–45.

Greene, David, Betty Sternberg, and Mark R. Lepper. "Overjustification in a Token Economy." *Journal of Personality and Social Psychology* 34 (1976): 1219–34.

Greven, Philip. *Spare the Child: The Religious Roots of Punishment and the Psychological Impact of Physical Abuse*. New York: Vintage, 1992.

Grolnick, Wendy S., and Richard M. Ryan. "Autonomy in Children's Learning: An Experimental and Individual Difference Investigation." *Journal of Personality and Social Psychology* 52 (1987): 890–98.

———. "Parent Styles Associated with Children's Self-Regulation and Competence in School." *Journal of Educational Psychology* 81 (1989): 143–54.

———. "Self-Perceptions, Motivation, and Adjustment in Children with Learning Disabilities: A Multiple Group Comparison Study." *Journal of Learning Disabilities* 23 (1990): 177–84.

Grolnick, Wendy S., Richard M. Ryan, and Edward L. Deci. "Inner Resources for School Achievement: Motivational Mediators of Children's Perceptions of Their Parents." *Journal of Educational Psychology* 83 (1991): 508–17.

Gruenberg, Barry. "The Happy Worker: An Analysis of Educational and Occupational Differences in Determinants of Job Satisfaction." *American Journal of Sociology* 86 (1980): 247–71.

Grusec, Joan E. "Socializing Concern for Others in the Home." *Developmental Psychology* 27 (1991): 338–42.

Grusec, Joan E., and Theodore Dix. "The Socialization of Prosocial Behavior: Theory and Reality." In *Altruism and Aggression: Biological and Social Origins,* edited by Carolyn Zahn-Waxler, E. Mark Cummings, and Ronald Iannotti. Cambridge: Cambridge University Press, 1986.

Grusec, Joan E., and Erica Redler. "Attribution, Reinforcement, and Altruism: A Developmental Analysis." *Developmental Psychology* 16 (1980): 525–34.

Guess, Doug, and Ellin Siegel-Causey. "Behavioral Control and Education of Severely Handicapped Students: Who's Doing What to Whom? And Why?" In *Severe Mental Retardation: From Theory to Practice,* edited by Diane Bricker and John Filler. [Reston, Va.]: Council for Exceptional Children, [1985].

Gunnar-Vongnechten, Megan R. "Changing a Frightening Toy into a Pleasant Toy by Allowing the Infant to Control Its Actions." *Developmental Psychology* 14 (1978): 157–62.

Guzzo, Richard A., Richard D. Jette, and Raymond A. Katzell. "The Effects of Psychologically Based Intervention Programs on Worker Productivity: A Meta-Analysis." *Personnel Psychology* 38 (1985): 275–91.

Guzzo, Richard A., and Raymond A. Katzell. "Effects of Economic Incentives on Productivity: A Psychological View." In *Incentives, Cooperation, and Risk Sharing: Economic and Psychological Perspectives on Employment Contracts,* edited by Haig R. Nalbantian. Totowa, N.J.: Rowman & Littlefield, 1987.

Hackman, J. Richard, and Greg R. Oldham. *Work Redesign.* Reading, Mass.: Addison-Wesley, 1980.

Haegele, Monroe J. "The New Performance Measures." In *The Compensation Handbook: A State-of-the-Art Guide to Compensation Strategy and Design,* edited by Milton L. Rock and Lance A. Berger. 3d ed., New York: McGraw-Hill, 1991.

Hagood, Rebecca. "Make Rewards Count." *Instructor,* October 1989: 12.

Haines, Donald Bruce, and W. J. McKeachie. "Cooperative Versus Competitive Discussion Methods in Teaching Introductory Psychology." *Journal of Educational Psychology* 58 (1967): 386–90.

Halachmi, Arie, and Marc Holtzer. "Merit Pay, Performance Targeting, and Productivity." *Review of Public Personnel Administration* 7 (1987): 80–91.

Haller, Harold S., and Bradley J. Whittaker. "Barriers to Change: Does the Performance Appraisal System Serve a Logical Purpose?" In *Performance Appraisal: Perspectives on a Quality Management Approach,* edited by Gary N. McLean, Susan R. Damme, and Richard A. Swanson. Alexandria, Va.: American Society for Training and Development, 1990.

Halpin, Gerald, and Glennelle Halpin. "The Effect of Motivation on Creative Thinking Abilities." *Journal of Creative Behavior* 7 (1973): 51–53.

Harackiewicz, Judith M. "The Effects of Reward Contingency and Performance Feedback on Intrinsic Motivation." *Journal of Personality and Social Psychology* 37 (1979): 1352–63.

Harackiewicz, Judith M., Steven Abrahams, and Ruth Wageman. "Performance Evaluation and Intrinsic Motivation: The Effects of Evaluative Focus, Rewards, and Achievement Orientation." *Journal of Personality and Social Psychology* 53 (1987): 1015–23.

Harackiewicz, Judith M., and George Manderlink. "A Process Analysis of the Effects of Performance-Contingent Rewards on Intrinsic Motivation." *Journal of Experimental Social Psychology* 20 (1984): 531–51.

Harackiewicz, Judith M., George Manderlink, and Carol Sansone. "Rewarding

Pinball Wizardry: Effects of Evaluation and Cue Value on Intrinsic Interest." *Journal of Personality and Social Psychology* 47 (1984): 287–300.

Harackiewicz, Judith M., Carol Sansone, Lester W. Blair, Jennifer A. Epstein, and George Manderlink. "Attributional Processes in Behavior Change and Maintenance: Smoking Cessation and Continued Abstinence." *Journal of Consulting and Clinical Psychology* 55 (1987): 372–78.

Hart, Craig H., Michele DeWolf, Patricia Wozniak, and Diane C. Burts. "Maternal and Paternal Disciplinary Styles: Relations with Preschoolers' Playground Behavioral Orientations and Peer Status." *Child Development* 63 (1992): 879–92.

Harter, Susan. "Pleasure Derived from Challenge and the Effects of Receiving Grades on Children's Difficulty Level Choices." *Child Development* 49 (1978): 788–99.

———. "A New Self-Report Scale of Intrinsic Versus Extrinsic Orientation in the Classroom: Motivational and Informational Components." *Developmental Psychology* 17 (1981): 300–12.

Harter, Susan, and Bradley K. Jackson. "Trait vs. Nontrait Conceptualizations of Intrinsic/Extrinsic Motivational Orientation." *Motivation and Emotion* 16 (1992): 209–30.

Hatry, Harry P., and John M. Greiner. *Issues and Case Studies in Teacher Incentive Plans.* Washington, D.C.: Urban Institute Press, 1985.

Haywood, H. Carl, and Harvey N. Switzky. "Work Response of Mildly Mentally Retarded Adults to Self- Versus External Regulation as a Function of Motivational Orientation." *American Journal of Mental Deficiency* 90 (1985): 151–59.

Hembree, Diana. "Breaking the Spell." *Parenting,* September 1990: 68–77, 134–35.

Hemp, Paul. "Shake-up at the Harvard Business Review." *Boston Globe,* 2 June 1992: 37, 41.

Hennessey, Beth A., Teresa M. Amabile, and Margaret Martinage. "Immunizing Children Against the Negative Effects of Reward." *Contemporary Educational Psychology* 14 (1989): 212–27.

Hennessey, Beth A., and Susan M. Zbikowski. "Immunizing Children Against the Negative Effects of Reward: A Further Examination of Intrinsic Motivation Training Techniques." *Creativity Research Journal.* In press.

Hersen, Michel. "Token Economies in Institutional Settings." *Journal of Nervous and Mental Disease* 162 (1976): 206–11.

Herzberg, Frederick. *Work and the Nature of Man.* Cleveland: World Publishing, 1966.

———. "One More Time: How Do You Motivate Employees?" *Harvard Business Review,* January–February 1968: 53–62.

———. "Workers' Needs: The Same Around the World." *Industry Week,* 21 September 1987: 29–32.

Heyman, Gail D., and Carol S. Dweck. "Achievement Goals and Intrinsic Motivation: Their Relation and Their Role in Adaptive Motivation." *Motivation and Emotion* 16 (1992): 231–47.

Hill, Harlan F., C. Richard Chapman, Judy A. Kornell, Keith M. Sullivan, Louis C. Saeger, and Costantino Benedetti. "Self-Administration of Morphine in Bone Marrow Transplant Patients Reduces Drug Requirement." *Pain* 40 (1990): 121–29.

Hitz, Randy, and Amy Driscoll. "Praise or Encouragement? New Insights into Praise: Implications for Early Childhood Teachers." *Young Children,* July 1988: 6–13.

Hoffman, Martin L. "Power Assertion by the Parent and Its Impact on the Child." *Child Development* 31 (1960): 129–43.

———. "Is Altruism Part of Human Nature?" *Journal of Personality and Social Psychology* 40 (1981): 121–37.

Hoffman, Martin L., and Herbert D. Saltzstein. "Parent Discipline and the Child's Moral Development." *Journal of Personality and Social Psychology* 5 (1967): 45–57.

Holmes, Sandra J., and Lee N. Robins. "The Role of Parental Disciplinary Practices in the Development of Depression and Alcoholism." *Psychiatry* 51 (1988): 24–35.

Holusha, John. "Grace Pastiak's 'Web of Inclusion.'" *New York Times,* 5 May 1991: F1, F6.

Hom, Harry L., Jr. "Can You Predict the Overjustification Effect?" *Teaching of Psychology.* In press.

Hom, Harry L., Jr., and Jan M. Riche. "Failure of Individuals to Predict the Detrimental Reward Effect." Paper presented at the annual convention of the American Psychological Association, Atlanta, August 1988.

Hom, Harry L., Jr., Mark Berger, Melissa K. Duncan, Arden Miller, and Aleta Blevin. "The Influence of Cooperative Reward Structures on Intrinsic Motivation." Unpublished paper, Southwest Missouri State University, 1990.

Houghton, Joan, G. J. Buzz Bronicki, and Doug Guess. "Opportunities to Express Preferences and Make Choices Among Students with Severe Disabilities in Classroom Settings." *Journal of the Association for Persons with Severe Handicaps* 12 (1987): 18–27.

Iaffaldano, Michelle T., and Paul M. Muchinsky. "Job Satisfaction and Job Performance: A Meta-Analysis." *Psychological Bulletin* 97 (1985): 251–73.

Ingram, John, and Norman Worrall. "The Negotiating Classroom: Child Self-Determination in British Primary Schools." *Early Child Development and Care* 28 (1987): 401–15.

Jackson, Philip W. *Life in Classrooms.* 1968. Reprint. New York: Teachers College Press, 1990.

Jagacinski, Carolyn M., and John G. Nicholls. "Competence and Affect in Task Involvement and Ego Involvement: The Impact of Social Comparison Information." *Journal of Educational Psychology* 79 (1987): 107–14.

Jenkins, G. Douglas, Jr. "Financial Incentives." In *Generalizing from Laboratory to Field Settings,* edited by Edwin A. Locke. Lexington, Mass.: Lexington Books, 1986.

Johnson, David W., and Roger T. Johnson. "Motivational Processes in Cooperative, Competitive, and Individualistic Learning Situations." In *Research on Motivation in Education,* vol. 2, edited by Carole and Russell Ames. Orlando, Fla.: Academic Press, 1985.

Johnson, Roger A. "Differential Effects of Reward Versus No-Reward Instructions on the Creative Thinking of Two Economic Levels of Elementary School Children." *Journal of Educational Psychology* 66 (1974): 530–33.

Johnson, Stephen M., Orin D. Bolstad, and Gretchen K. Lobitz. "Generalization and Contrast Phenomena in Behavior Modification with Children." In *Behavior Modification and Families,* edited by Eric J. Marsh, Leo A. Hamerlynck, and Lee C. Handy. New York: Brunner/Mazel, 1976.

Jordan, Paul C. "Effects of an Extrinsic Reward on Intrinsic Motivation: A Field Experiment." *Academy of Management Journal* 29 (1986): 405–12.

Jurgensen, Clifford E. "Job Preferences (What Makes a Job Good or Bad?)." *Journal of Applied Psychology* 63 (1978): 267–76.

Juster, F. Thomas. "Preferences for Work and Leisure." In *Time, Goods, and Well-Being*, edited by F. Thomas Juster and Frank P. Stafford. Ann Arbor: University of Michigan Institute for Social Research, 1985.

Justice, Blair. "The Will to Stay Well." *New York Times Good Health Magazine,* 17 April 1988: 20–21, 34–35.

Kagan, Jerome. *The Nature of the Child.* New York: Basic Books, 1984.

Kage, Masaharu. "The Effects of Evaluation on Intrinsic Motivation." Paper presented at the meeting of the Japan Association of Educational Psychology, Joetsu, Japan, 1991.

Kalish, Harry I. *From Behavioral Science to Behavior Modification.* New York: McGraw-Hill, 1981.

Kamii, Constance. "Obedience Is Not Enough." *Young Children,* May 1984: 11–14.

———. "Toward Autonomy: The Importance of Critical Thinking and Choice Making." *School Psychology Review* 20 (1991): 382–88.

Kanouse, David E., Peter Gumpert, and Donnah Canavan-Gumpert. "The Semantics of Praise." In *New Directions in Attribution Research,* vol. 3, edited by John H. Harvey, William Ickes, and Robert F. Kidd. Hillsdale, N.J.: Erlbaum, 1981.

Kanter, Rosabeth Moss. *Men and Women of the Corporation.* New York: Basic Books, 1977.

———. "The Attack on Pay." *Harvard Business Review,* March–April 1987: 60–67.

Kaplan, H. Roy. "Lottery Winners and Work Commitment." *Journal of the Institute for Socioeconomic Studies* 10 (1985): 82–94.

Kaplan, Joseph S. *Beyond Behavior Modification: A Cognitive-Behavioral Approach to Behavior Management in the School.* 2d ed. Austin, Texas: Pro-Ed, 1991.

Karasek, Robert A., Tores Theorell, Joseph E. Schwartz, Peter L. Schnall, Carl F. Pieper, and John L. Michela. "Job Characteristics in Relation to the Prevalence of Myocardial Infarction in the US Health Examination Survey (HES) and the Health and Nutrition Examination Survey (HANES)." *American Journal of Public Health* 78 (1988): 910–16.

Karen, Robert. "Shame." *Atlantic Monthly,* February 1992: 40–70.

Karniol, Rachel, and Michael Ross. "The Effect of Performance-Relevant and Performance-Irrelevant Rewards on Children's Intrinsic Motivation." *Child Development* 48 (1977): 482–87.

Kasser, Tim, and Richard M. Ryan. "A Dark Side of the American Dream: Correlates of Financial Success as a Central Life Aspiration." *Journal of Personality and Social Psychology* 65 (1993): 410–22.

Kast, Audrey, and Kathleen Connor. "Sex and Age Differences in Response to Informational and Controlling Feedback." *Personality and Social Psychology Bulletin* 14 (1988): 514–23.

Katz, Lilian G. "Mothering and Teaching — Some Significant Distinctions." In *Current Topics in Early Childhood Education,* vol. 3, edited by Lilian G. Katz. Norwood, N.J.: Ablex, 1980.

———. "The Disposition to Learn." *Principal,* May 1988: 14–17.

Kazdin, Alan E. "The Rich Rewards of Rewards." *Psychology Today,* November 1976: 98, 101–102, 105, 114.

————. "The Token Economy: A Decade Later." *Journal of Applied Behavior Analysis* 15 (1982): 431–45.

Kazdin, Alan E., and Richard R. Bootzin. "The Token Economy: An Evaluative Review." *Journal of Applied Behavior Analysis* 5 (1972): 343–72.

Kearney, William J. "Pay for Performance? Not Always." *MSU Business Topics* (Michigan State University) 27 (1979): 5–16.

Keller, John M. "Development and Use of the ARCS Model of Instructional Design." *Journal of Instructional Development* 10 (1987): 2–10.

Kelman, Anna. "Choices for Children." *Young Children,* March 1990: 42–45.

Kirsch, Irving. "The Politics of Reinforcement." *Psychotherapy: Theory, Research, and Practice* 11 (1974): 311–16.

Kirschenbaum, Howard, Rodney W. Napier, and Sidney B. Simon. *Wad-Ja-Get? The Grading Game in American Education.* New York: Hart, 1971.

Kistner, Janet A. "Attentional Deficits of Learning-Disabled Children: Effects of Rewards and Practice." *Journal of Abnormal Child Psychology* 13 (1985): 19–31.

Knitzer, Jane, Zina Steinberg, and Brahm Fleisch. *At the Schoolhouse Door: An Examination of Programs and Policies for Children with Behavioral and Emotional Problems.* New York: Bank Street College of Education, 1990.

Kobasa, Suzanne C. "Stressful Life Events, Personality, and Health: An Inquiry into Hardiness." *Journal of Personality and Social Psychology* 37 (1979): 1–10.

Koestler, Arthur. *The Act of Creation.* New York: Dell, 1967.

Koestner, Richard, Richard M. Ryan, Frank Bernieri, and Kathleen Holt. "Setting Limits on Children's Behavior: The Differential Effects of Controlling vs. Informational Styles on Intrinsic Motivation and Creativity." *Journal of Personality* 52 (1984): 233–48.

Koestner, Richard, Miron Zuckerman, and Julia Koestner. "Praise, Involvement, and Intrinsic Motivation." *Journal of Personality and Social Psychology* 53 (1987): 383–90.

————. "Attributional Focus of Praise and Children's Intrinsic Motivation: The Moderating Role of Gender." *Personality and Social Psychology Bulletin* 15 (1989): 61–72.

Koestner, Richard, Miron Zuckerman, and Jennifer Olsson. "Attributional Style, Comparison Focus of Praise, and Intrinsic Motivation." *Journal of Research in Personality* 24 (1990): 87–100.

Kohn, Alfie. *The Brighter Side of Human Nature: Altruism and Empathy in Everyday Life.* New York: Basic Books, 1990a.

————. *You Know What They Say . . . : The Truth About Popular Beliefs.* New York: HarperCollins, 1990b.

————. "The ABC's of Caring." *Teacher Magazine,* January 1990c: 52–58.

————. "Group Grade Grubbing Versus Cooperative *Learning.*" *Educational Leadership,* February 1991a: 83–87.

————. "Caring Kids: The Role of the Schools." *Phi Delta Kappan,* March 1991b: 496–506.

————. *No Contest: The Case Against Competition.* Rev. ed. Boston: Houghton Mifflin, 1992a.

————. "Resistance to Cooperative Learning: Making Sense of Its Deletion and Dilution." *Journal of Education* 174 (1992b): 34–52.

————. "Turning Learning into a Business: Concerns About 'Quality Management' at School." *Educational Leadership.* In press.

Kovach, Kenneth A. "What Motivates Employees? Workers and Supervisors Give Different Answers." *Business Horizons,* September–October 1987: 58–65.

Kramer, F. Matthew, Robert W. Jeffery, Mary Kaye Snell, and Jean L. Forster. "Maintenance of Successful Weight Loss over One Year: Effects of Financial Contracts for Weight Maintenance or Participation in Skills Training." *Behavior Therapy* 17 (1986): 295–301.

Kruglanski, Arie W. "Endogenous Attribution and Intrinsic Motivation." In *The Hidden Costs of Rewards: New Perspectives on the Psychology of Human Motivation,* edited by Mark R. Lepper and David Greene. Hillsdale, N.J.: Erlbaum, 1978.

Kruglanski, Arie W., Sarah Alon, and Tirtzah Lewis. "Retrospective Misattribution and Task Enjoyment." *Journal of Experimental Social Psychology* 8 (1972): 493–501.

Kruglanski, Arie W., Irith Friedman, and Gabriella Zeevi. "The Effects of Extrinsic Incentive on Some Qualitative Aspects of Task Performance." *Journal of Personality* 39 (1971): 606–17.

Kunda, Ziva, and Shalom H. Schwartz. "Undermining Intrinsic Moral Motivation: External Reward and Self-Presentation." *Journal of Personality and Social Psychology* 45 (1983): 763–71.

Kutner, Lawrence. "As Motivator, the Carrot May Be as Bad as the Stick." *New York Times,* 29 November 1990: C8.

———. "A Little Bribery Can Help, but Don't Make It a Habit." *New York Times,* 26 December 1991: C11.

———. "For Good Behavior, Show Good Behavior." *New York Times,* 26 November 1992: C11.

Labich, Kenneth, and Kate Ballen. "Was Breaking Up AT&T a Good Idea?" *Fortune,* 2 January 1989: 82–87.

Lacey, Hugh M. "Control, Perceived Control, and the Methodological Role of Cognitive Constructs." In *Choice and Perceived Control,* edited by Lawrence C. Perlmuter and Richard A. Monty. Hillsdale, N.J.: Erlbaum, 1979.

Lacey, Hugh, and Barry Schwartz. "The Explanatory Power of Radical Behaviorism." In *B. F. Skinner: Consensus and Controversy,* edited by Sohan Modgil and Celia Modgil. Philadelphia: Falmer, 1987.

Laird, Martha. "Goodies for Good Work — Giveaways Have Gone Too Far!" *Instructor,* March 1986: 19.

Lane, Robert E. *The Market Experience.* Cambridge: Cambridge University Press, 1991.

Lawson, Donna. "Applause! Applause! How to Handle Your Kids with Praise." *Redbook,* June 1984: 86–87, 156.

LeCompte, Margaret. "Learning to Work: The Hidden Curriculum of the Classroom." *Anthropology and Education Quarterly* 9 (1978): 22–37.

Lehman, Betsy A. "Spanking Teaches the Wrong Lesson." *Boston Globe,* 13 March 1989: 27, 29.

Lepper, Mark R. "Dissonance, Self-Perception, and Honesty in Children." *Journal of Personality and Social Psychology* 25 (1973): 65–74.

———. "Extrinsic Reward and Intrinsic Motivation." In *Teacher and Student Perceptions: Implications for Learning,* edited by John M. Levine and Margaret C. Wang. Hillsdale, N.J.: Erlbaum, 1983.

———. "Microcomputers in Education: Motivational and Social Issues." *American Psychologist* 40 (1985): 1–18.

———. "Motivational Considerations in the Study of Instruction." *Cognition and Instruction* 5 (1988): 289–309.

Lepper, Mark R., Lisa G. Aspinwall, Donna L. Mumme, and Ruth W. Chabay. "Self-Perception and Social-Perception Processes in Tutoring: Subtle Social Control Strategies of Expert Tutors." In *Self-Inference Processes: The Ontario Symposium*, vol. 6, edited by J. M. Olson and M. P. Zanna. Hillsdale, N.J.: Erlbaum, 1990.

Lepper, Mark R., and Diana I. Cordova. "A Desire to Be Taught: Instructional Consequences of Intrinsic Motivation." *Motivation and Emotion* 16 (1992): 187–208.

Lepper, Mark R., and David Greene. "Turning Play into Work: Effects of Adult Surveillance and Extrinsic Rewards on Children's Intrinsic Motivation." *Journal of Personality and Social Psychology* 31 (1975): 479–86.

———. "On Understanding Overjustification: A Reply to Reiss and Sushinsky." *Journal of Personality and Social Psychology* 33 (1976): 25–35.

———. "Divergent Approaches to the Study of Rewards." In *The Hidden Costs of Rewards: New Perspectives on the Psychology of Human Motivation*, edited by Mark R. Lepper and David Greene. Hillsdale, N.J.: Erlbaum, 1978a.

———. "Overjustification Research and Beyond: Toward a Means-Ends Analysis of Intrinsic and Extrinsic Motivation." In *The Hidden Costs of Rewards: New Perspectives on the Psychology of Human Motivation*, edited by Mark R. Lepper and David Greene. Hillsdale, N.J.: Erlbaum, 1978b.

Lepper, Mark R., David Greene, and Richard E. Nisbett. "Undermining Children's Intrinsic Interest with Extrinsic Reward: A Test of the 'Overjustification' Hypothesis." *Journal of Personality and Social Psychology* 28 (1973): 129–37.

Lepper, Mark R., and Melinda Hodell. "Intrinsic Motivation in the Classroom." In *Research on Motivation in Education*, vol. 3: *Goals and Cognitions*, edited by Carol Ames and Russell Ames. New York: Academic Press, 1989.

Lepper, Mark R., and Thomas W. Malone. "Intrinsic Motivation and Instructional Effectiveness in Computer-Based Education." In *Aptitude, Learning, and Instruction*, vol. 3: *Conative and Affective Process Analyses*, edited by Richard E. Snow and Marshall J. Farr. Hillsdale, N.J.: Erlbaum, 1987.

Lepper, Mark R., Gerald Sagotsky, Janet L. Dafoe, and David Greene. "Consequences of Superfluous Social Constraints: Effects on Young Children's Social Inferences and Subsequent Intrinsic Interest." *Journal of Personality and Social Psychology* 42 (1982): 51–65.

Lerner, Melvin J. "The Desire for Justice and Reactions to Victims." In *Altruism and Helping Behavior*, edited by J. Macaulay and L. Berkowitz. New York: Academic Press, 1970.

———. "The Justice Motive: 'Equity' and 'Parity' Among Children." *Journal of Personality and Social Psychology* 29 (1974): 539–50.

———. "The Justice Motive in Human Relations and the Economic Model of Man: A Radical Analysis of Facts and Fictions." In *Cooperation and Helping Behavior: Theories and Research*, edited by Valerian J. Derlega and Janusz Grzelak. New York: Academic Press, 1982.

"Let's Do Lunch, Billy." *People Magazine*, 24 June 1991: 103.

Leung, Kwok, and Michael H. Bond. "The Impact of Cultural Collectivism on Reward Allocation." *Journal of Personality and Social Psychology* 47 (1984): 793–804.

Levering, Robert. *A Great Place to Work.* New York: Avon, 1988.

Levin, Doron P. "Toyota Plant in Kentucky Is Font of Ideas for U.S." *New York Times*, 5 May 1992: A1, D8.

Levine, David I., and Laura D'Andrea Tyson. "Participation, Productivity, and the Firms' Environment." In *Paying for Productivity: A Look at the Evidence,* edited by Alan S. Blinder. Washington, D.C.: Brookings Institution, 1990.

LeVine, Robert A. "Cultural Environments in Child Development." In *Child Development Today and Tomorrow,* edited by William Damon. San Francisco: Jossey-Bass, 1989.

Levinson, Harry. *The Great Jackass Fallacy.* Boston: Harvard Graduate School of Business Administration, 1973.

Lewin, Kurt. *A Dynamic Theory of Personality: Selected Papers.* Translated by Donald K. Adams and Karl E. Zener. New York: McGraw-Hill, 1935.

Lewin, Kurt, Ronald Lippitt, and Ralph K. White. "Patterns of Aggressive Behavior in Experimentally Created 'Social Climates.'" *Journal of Social Psychology* 10 (1939): 271–99.

Lewis, Catherine C. "The Effects of Parental Firm Control: A Reinterpretation of Findings." *Psychological Bulletin* 90 (1981): 547–63.

Lichtenstein, Nelson. "What Happened to the Working Class?" *New York Times,* 7 September 1992: 19.

Lickona, Thomas. *Educating for Character: How Our Schools Can Teach Respect and Responsibility.* New York: Bantam, 1991.

Light, Richard J. *The Harvard Assessment Seminars: Explorations with Students and Faculty About Teaching, Learning, and Student Life.* 2d report. Cambridge: Harvard University, 1992.

Lincoln, Ann, and Saralea Chazan. "Perceived Competence and Intrinsic Motivation in Learning Disability Children." *Journal of Clinical Child Psychology* 8 (1979): 213–16.

Linden, Dana Wechsler. "Incentivize Me, Please." *Forbes,* 27 May 1991: 208–12.

Lipsey, Richard G., Peter O. Steiner, and Douglas D. Purvis. *Economics.* 8th ed. New York: Harper & Row, 1987.

Lloyd, Jean, and Lloyd Barenblatt. "Intrinsic Intellectuality: Its Relations to Social Class, Intelligence, and Achievement." *Journal of Personality and Social Psychology* 46 (1984): 646–54.

Locke, Edwin A. "Toward a Theory of Task Motivation and Incentives." *Organizational Behavior and Human Performance* 3 (1968): 157–89.

Loden, Marilyn. *Feminine Leadership; or How to Succeed in Business Without Being One of the Boys.* New York: Times Books, 1985.

Loveland, Kathryn Kernodle, and J. Gregory Olley. "The Effect of External Reward on Interest and Quality of Task Performance in Children of High and Low Intrinsic Motivation." *Child Development* 50 (1979): 1207–10.

Lovett, Herbert. *Cognitive Counseling and Persons with Special Needs: Adapting Behavioral Approaches to the Social Context.* New York: Praeger, 1985.

Luce, Sally R. "Paying for Performance." *Canadian Business Review* 10 (1983): 19–22.

Luster, Tom, Kelly Rhoades, and Bruce Haas. "The Relation Between Parental Values and Parenting Behavior." *Journal of Marriage and the Family* 51 (1989): 139–47.

Luyten, Herman, and Willy Lens. "The Effect of Earlier Experience and Reward Contingencies on Intrinsic Motivation." *Motivation and Emotion* 5 (1981): 25–36.

Mac Iver, Douglas. "Classroom Factors and Student Characteristics Predicting Students' Use of Achievement Standards During Ability Self-Assessment." *Child Development* 58 (1987): 1258–71.

Madden, Lowell. "Do Teachers Communicate with Their Students as if They Were Dogs?" *Language Arts* 65 (1988): 142–46.

Maehr, Martin L., and William M. Stallings. "Freedom from External Evaluation." *Child Development* 43 (1972): 177–85.

"Main Fault of Parents in Raising Children." *Gallup Report* no. 229, October 1984: 28.

Mallick, Shahbaz Khan, and Boyd R. McCandless. "A Study of Catharsis of Aggression." *Journal of Personality and Social Psychology* 4 (1966): 591–96.

Malone, Thomas W., and Mark R. Lepper. "Making Learning Fun: A Taxonomy of Intrinsic Motivations for Learning." In *Aptitude, Learning, and Instruction*, vol. 3: *Conative and Affective Process Analyses*, edited by Richard E. Snow and Marshall J. Farr. Hillsdale, N.J.: Erlbaum, 1987.

Mansbridge, Jane J. *Beyond Adversary Democracy.* Chicago: University of Chicago Press, 1983.

———, ed. *Beyond Self-Interest.* Chicago: University of Chicago Press, 1990.

Margulies, Newton, and Stewart Black. "Perspectives on the Implementation of Participative Approaches." *Human Resource Management* 26 (1987): 385–412.

Marlow, Edward, and Richard Schilhavy. "Expectation Issues in Management by Objectives Programs." *Industrial Management* 33 (1991): 29–32.

Marshall, Hermine H. "Motivational Strategies of Three Fifth-Grade Teachers." *Elementary School Journal* 88 (1987): 135–50.

Martin, David L. "Your Praise Can Smother Learning." *Learning,* February 1977: 43–51.

Mawhinney, T. C. "Decreasing Intrinsic 'Motivation' with Extrinsic Rewards: Easier Said than Done." *Journal of Organizational Behavior Management* 11 (1990): 175–91.

Mawhinney, Thomas C., Alyce M. Dickinson, and Lewis A. Taylor III. "The Use of Concurrent Schedules to Evaluate the Effects of Extrinsic Rewards on 'Intrinsic Motivation.'" *Journal of Organizational Behavior Management* 10 (1989): 109–29.

McCaslin, Mary, and Thomas L. Good. "Compliant Cognition: The Misalliance of Management and Instructional Goals in Current School Reform." *Educational Researcher,* April 1992: 4–17.

McCormick, Kenelm F. "Attitudes of Primary Care Physicians Toward Corporal Punishment." *Journal of the American Medical Association* 267 (1992): 3161–65.

McCullers, John C. "Issues in Learning and Motivation." In *The Hidden Costs of Rewards: New Perspectives on the Psychology of Human Motivation,* edited by Mark R. Lepper and David Greene. Hillsdale, N.J.: Erlbaum, 1978.

McCullers, John C., Richard A. Fabes, and James D. Moran III. "Does Intrinsic Motivation Theory Explain the Adverse Effects of Rewards on Immediate Task Performance?" *Journal of Personality and Social Psychology* 52 (1987): 1027–33.

McCullers, John C., and Judith A. Gardiner Martin. "A Reexamination of the Role of Incentive in Children's Discrimination Learning." *Child Development* 42 (1971): 827–37.

McGraw, Kenneth O. "The Detrimental Effects of Reward on Performance: A Literature Review and a Prediction Model." In *The Hidden Costs of Rewards: New Perspectives on the Psychology of Human Motivation,* edited by Mark R. Lepper and David Greene. Hillsdale, N.J.: Erlbaum, 1978.

McGraw, Kenneth O., and Jirina Fiala. "Undermining the Zeigarnik Effect: Another Hidden Cost of Reward." *Journal of Personality* 50 (1982): 58–66.

McGraw, Kenneth O., and John C. McCullers. "Evidence of a Detrimental Effect of Extrinsic Incentives on Breaking a Mental Set." *Journal of Experimental Social Psychology* 15 (1979): 285–94.

McGregor, Douglas. *The Human Side of Enterprise.* New York: McGraw-Hill, 1960.

———. *Leadership and Motivation: Essays of Douglas McGregor,* edited by Warren G. Bennis and Edgar H. Schein. Cambridge: MIT Press, 1966.

McLaughlin, David J. "Does Compensation Motivate Executives?" In *Executive Compensation: A Strategic Guide for the 1990s,* edited by Fred K. Foulkes. Boston: Harvard Business School Press, 1991.

McNeil, Linda. *Contradictions of Control: School Structure and School Knowledge.* New York: Routledge and Kegan Paul, 1986.

Melcher, Arlyn J. "Participation: A Critical Review of Research Findings." *Human Resource Management* 15 (1976): 12–21.

Meyer, Herbert H. "The Pay-for-Performance Dilemma." *Organizational Dynamics* 3 (1975): 39–50.

Meyer, Herbert H., Emanuel Kay, and John R. P. French, Jr. "Split Roles in Performance Appraisal." 1965. Excerpts reprinted in "HBR Retrospect." *Harvard Business Review,* January–February 1989: 26.

Meyer, Wulf-Uwe, Meinolf Bachmann, Ursula Biermann, Marianne Hempelmann, Fritz-Otto Ploeger, and Helga Spiller. "The Informational Value of Evaluative Behavior: Influences of Praise and Blame on Perceptions of Ability." *Journal of Educational Psychology* 71 (1979): 259–68.

Miller, Alice. *For Your Own Good: Hidden Cruelty in Child-Rearing and the Roots of Violence.* New York: Farrar, Straus & Giroux, 1984.

Miller, Arden, Harry L. Hom, Jr., Julie Williams McDowell, and Shauna Gionfriddo. "Influence of Developmental Conceptions of Ability, Praise, Blame, and Material Rewards on Judgments of Ability and Affect." Unpublished paper, 1992.

Miller, Katherine I., and Peter R. Monge. "Participation, Satisfaction, and Productivity: A Meta-Analytic Review." *Academy of Management Journal* 29 (1986): 727–53.

Miller, Louise Brightwell, and Betsy Worth Estes. "Monetary Reward and Motivation in Discrimination Learning." *Journal of Experimental Psychology* 61 (1961): 501–504.

Mills, Rosemary S. L., and Joan E. Grusec. "Cognitive, Affective, and Behavioral Consequences of Praising Altruism." *Merrill-Palmer Quarterly* 35 (1989): 299–326.

Milton, Ohmer, Howard R. Pollio, and James A. Eison. *Making Sense of College Grades.* San Francisco: Jossey-Bass, 1986.

Mohrman, Allan M. "Deming Versus Performance Appraisal: Is There a Resolution?" In *Performance Appraisal: Perspectives on a Quality Management Approach,* edited by Gary N. McLean, Susan R. Damme, and Richard A. Swanson. Alexandria, Va.: American Society for Training and Development, 1990.

Morgan, Mark. "Decrements in Intrinsic Motivation Among Rewarded and Observer Subjects." *Child Development* 54 (1983): 636–44.

———. "Reward-Induced Decrements and Increments in Intrinsic Motivation." *Review of Educational Research* 54 (1984): 5–30.

Morse, William C. Introduction to *Teaching Exceptional Children*, Summer 1987: 4–6.

Mossholder, Kevin W. "Effects of Externally Mediated Goal Setting on Intrinsic Motivation: A Laboratory Experiment." *Journal of Applied Psychology* 65 (1980): 202–10.

Mower, Judith C., and David Wilemon. "Rewarding Technical Teamwork." *Research–Technology Management*, September–October 1989: 24–29.

Mullen, Patricia I. "Getting to the New Paradigm." In *Performance Appraisal: Perspectives on a Quality Management Approach*, edited by Gary N. McLean, Susan R. Damme, and Richard A. Swanson. Alexandria, Va.: American Society for Training and Development, 1990.

Nash, Michael. *Making People Productive*. San Francisco: Jossey-Bass, 1985.

Naylor, Thomas H. "Redefining Corporate Motivation, Swedish Style." *Christian Century*, 30 May–6 June 1990: 566–70.

Nelsen, Jane. *Positive Discipline*. New York: Ballantine, 1987.

Newby, Timothy J. "Classroom Motivation: Strategies of First-Year Teachers." *Journal of Educational Psychology* 83 (1991): 195–200.

Newby, Timothy J., and Pamela A. Alter. "Task Motivation: Learner Selection of Intrinsic Versus Extrinsic Orientations." *Educational Technology Research and Development* 37 (1989): 77–89.

Newman, Joan, and Alan Taylor. "Effect of a Means-End Contingency on Young Children's Food Preferences." *Journal of Experimental Child Psychology* 64 (1992): 200–16.

Newman, Richard S. "Goals and Self-Regulated Learning: What Motivates Children to Seek Academic Help?" In *Advances in Motivation and Achievement*, vol. 7, edited by Martin L. Maehr and Paul R. Pintrich. Greenwich, Conn.: JAI Press, 1991.

Nicholls, John G. *The Competitive Ethos and Democratic Education*. Cambridge: Harvard University Press, 1989.

Nicholls, John G., and Susan P. Hazzard. *Education as Adventure: Lessons from the Second Grade*. New York: Teachers College Press, 1993.

Niehoff, Brian P., and Debra J. Mesch. "Effects of Reward Structures on Academic Performance and Group Processes in a Classroom Setting." *Journal of Psychology* 125 (1991): 457–67.

Nolen, Susan Bobbitt. "Reasons for Studying: Motivational Orientations and Study Strategies." *Cognition and Instruction* 5 (1988): 269–87.

Nolen, Susan Bobbitt, and John G. Nicholls. "A Place to Begin (Again) in Research on Student Motivation: Teachers' Beliefs." *Teaching and Teacher Education*. In press.

Nord, Walter R. "The Failure of Current Applied Behavioral Science — A Marxian Perspective." *Journal of Applied Behavioral Science* 10 (1974): 557–78.

O'Brien, Shirley J. "Praising Children: Five Myths." *Childhood Education*, Summer 1990: 248–49.

O'Dell, Carla. *People, Performance, and Pay*. Houston: American Productivity Center, 1987.

Ohanian, Susan. "There's Only One True Technique for Good Discipline." *Learning*, August 1982: 16–19.

O'Leary, K. Daniel, Rita W. Poulos, and Vernon T. Devine. "Tangible Reinforcers: Bonuses or Bribes?" *Journal of Consulting and Clinical Psychology* 38 (1972): 1–8.

Olson, Lynn. "Quality-Management Movement Spurs Interest in New Awards for Education." *Education Week*, 18 March 1992: 8.

O'Neil, John. "Wanted: Deep Understanding." *ASCD Update,* March 1992: 1–8.

O'Reilly, Charles A. III, and Sheila M. Puffer. "The Impact of Rewards and Punishments in a Social Context: A Laboratory and Field Experiment." *Journal of Occupational Psychology* 62 (1989): 41–53.

Orlick, Terry D., and Richard Mosher. "Extrinsic Awards and Participant Motivation in a Sport Related Task." *International Journal of Sport Psychology* 9 (1978): 27–39.

Ostroff, Cheri. "The Relationship Between Satisfaction, Attitudes, and Performance: An Organizational Level Analysis." *Journal of Applied Psychology* 77 (1992): 963–74.

Ouchi, William G. *Theory Z.* New York: Avon, 1982.

Pallak, Suzanne R., Steven Costomiris, Susan Sroka, and Thane S. Pittman. "School Experience, Reward Characteristics, and Intrinsic Motivation." *Child Development* 53 (1982): 1382–91.

Palmer, Thomas C. "Will Legislature Expand School Choice?" *Boston Globe,* 6 December 1992: A36.

Parke, Ross D. "Effectiveness of Punishment as an Interaction of Intensity, Timing, Agent Nurturance, and Cognitive Structuring." *Child Development* 40 (1969): 201–12.

Patton, Arch. "Why Incentive Plans Fail." *Harvard Business Review,* May–June 1972: 58–66.

Paul, William J., Jr., Keith B. Robertson, and Frederick Herzberg. "Job Enrichment Pays Off." *Harvard Business Review,* March–April 1969: 61–78.

Pearce, Jone L. "Why Merit Pay Doesn't Work: Implications from Organization Theory." In *New Perspectives on Compensation,* edited by David B. Balkin and Luis R. Gomez-Mejia. Englewood Cliffs, N.J.: Prentice-Hall, 1987.

Pearce, Jone L., and James L. Perry. "Federal Merit Pay: A Longitudinal Analysis." *Public Administration Review* 43 (1983): 315–25.

Pearce, Jone L., and Lyman W. Porter. "Employee Responses to Formal Performance Appraisal Feedback." *Journal of Applied Psychology* 71 (1986): 211–18.

Pearce, Jone L., William B. Stevenson, and James L. Perry. "Managerial Compensation Based on Organizational Performance: A Time Series Analysis of the Effects of Merit Pay." *Academy of Management Journal* 28 (1985): 261–78.

Pearlman, Charles. "The Effects of Level of Effectance Motivation, IQ, and a Penalty/Reward Contingency on the Choice of Problem Difficulty." *Child Development* 55 (1984): 537–42.

Peck, Charles A. "Increasing Opportunities for Social Control by Children with Autism and Severe Handicaps: Effects on Student Behavior and Perceived Classroom Climate." *Journal of the Association for Persons with Severe Handicaps* 10 (1985): 183–93.

Pelletier, Luc G., and R. J. Vallerand. "Behavioral Confirmation in Social Interaction: Effects of Teachers' Expectancies on Students' Intrinsic Motivation." Paper presented at the annual convention of the Canadian Psychological Association, Halifax, June 1989. Summarized in *Canadian Psychology* 30 (1989): 404.

Perlmuter, Lawrence C., and Richard A. Monty. "The Importance of Perceived Control: Fact or Fantasy?" *American Scientist,* November–December 1977: 759–65.

Perry, Stewart E. *San Francisco Scavengers: Dirty Work and the Pride of Owner-ship*. Berkeley: University of California Press, 1978.

Peters, Thomas J., and Robert H. Waterman, Jr. *In Search of Excellence: Lessons from America's Best-Run Companies*. New York: Harper & Row, 1982.

Peters, Tom. *Thriving on Chaos*. New York: Knopf, 1987.

———. Letter to the Editor. *Inc.*, April 1988:80–82.

Peterson, Robert F. "Power, Programming, and Punishment: Could We Be Over-controlling Our Children?" In *Behavior Modification and Families*, edited by Eric J. Mash, Leo A. Hamerlynck, and Lee C. Handy. New York: Brunner/Mazel, 1976.

Petty, M. M., Gail W. McGee, and Jerry W. Cavender. "A Meta-Analysis of the Relationships Between Individual Job Satisfaction and Individual Perfor-mance." *Academy of Management Review* 9 (1984): 712–21.

Petty, M. M., Bart Singleton, and David W. Connell. "An Experimental Evalua-tion of an Organizational Incentive Plan in the Electric Utility Industry." *Journal of Applied Psychology* 77 (1992): 427–36.

Phillips, James S., and Sara M. Freedman. "Contingent Pay and Intrinsic Task Interest: Moderating Effects of Work Values." *Journal of Applied Psychology* 70 (1985): 306–13.

Piaget, Jean. *The Moral Judgment of the Child*. Translated by Marjorie Gabain. New York: Free Press, 1965.

Pinder, Craig C. "Additivity Versus Nonadditivity of Intrinsic and Extrinsic In-centives: Implications for Work Motivation, Performance, and Attitudes." *Journal of Applied Psychology* 61 (1976): 693–700.

———. "Concerning the Application of Human Motivation Theories in Organi-zational Settings." *Academy of Management Review* 2 (1977): 384–97.

Pittman, Thane S., Ann K. Boggiano, and Deborah S. Main. "Intrinsic and Extrinsic Motivational Orientations in Peer Interactions." In *Achievement and Motivation: A Social-Developmental Perspective*, edited by Ann K. Boggiano and Thane S. Pittman. Cambridge: Cambridge University Press, 1992.

Pittman, Thane S., Ann K. Boggiano, and Diane N. Ruble. "Intrinsic and Extrinsic Motivational Orientations: Limiting Conditions on the Undermining and Enhancing Effects of Reward on Intrinsic Motivation." In *Teacher and Stu-dent Perceptions: Implications for Learning*, edited by John M. Levine and Margaret C. Wang. Hillsdale, N.J.: Erlbaum, 1983.

Pittman, Thane S., Eugenia E. Cooper, and Timothy W. Smith. "Attribution of Causality and the Overjustification Effect." *Personality and Social Psychol-ogy Bulletin* 3 (1977): 280–83.

Pittman, Thane S., Margaret E. Davey, Kimberly A. Alafat, Kathryn V. Wetherill, and Nancy A. Kramer. "Informational Versus Controlling Verbal Rewards." *Personality and Social Psychology Bulletin* 6 (1980): 228–33.

Pittman, Thane S., Jolee Emery, and Ann K. Boggiano. "Intrinsic and Extrinsic Motivational Orientations: Reward-Induced Changes in Preference for Com-plexity." *Journal of Personality and Social Psychology* 42 (1982): 789–97.

Plant, Robert W., and Richard M. Ryan. "Intrinsic Motivation and the Effects of Self-Consciousness, Self-Awareness, and Ego-Involvement: An Investigation of Internally Controlling Styles." *Journal of Personality* 53 (1985): 435–49.

Posner, Bruce G. "Pay for Profits." *Inc.*, September 1986: 57–60.

Potter, Ellen F. "'Good Job!': How We Evaluate Children's Work." *Childhood Education* 61 (1985): 203–206.

Power, Thomas G., and M. Lynn Chapieski. "Childrearing and Impulse Control in Toddlers: A Naturalistic Investigation." *Developmental Psychology* 22 (1986): 271–75.

Premack, David. "Toward Empirical Behavioral Laws: I. Positive Reinforcement." *Psychological Review* 66 (1959): 219–33.

Pretty, Grace H., and Clive Seligman. "Affect and the Overjustification Effect." *Journal of Personality and Social Psychology* 46 (1984): 1241–53.

Pritchard, Robert D., Kathleen M. Campbell, and Donald J. Campbell. "Effects of Extrinsic Financial Rewards on Intrinsic Motivation." *Journal of Applied Psychology* 62 (1977): 9–15.

Quattrone, George A. "On the Congruity Between Internal States and Action." *Psychological Bulletin* 98 (1985): 3–40.

Quick, Sue Smith. "Good as Gold." *Clearing House,* February 1990: 264.

Rachlin, Howard. *Introduction to Modern Behaviorism.* 3d ed. New York: Freeman, 1991.

Raina, M. K. "A Study into the Effect of Competition on Creativity." *Gifted Child Quarterly* 12 (1968): 217–20.

Rainey, Robert G. "The Effects of Directed Versus Non-Directed Laboratory Work on High School Chemistry Achievement." *Journal of Research in Science Teaching* 3 (1965): 286–92.

Raspberry, William. "Chump Change." *Washington Post,* 18 May 1990: A19.

Ravitch, Diane. *The Great School Wars: New York City, 1805–1973.* New York: Basic Books, 1974.

Reader, Mark J., and Stephen J. Dollinger. "Deadlines, Self-Perceptions, and Intrinsic Motivation." *Personality and Social Psychology Bulletin* 8 (1982): 742–47.

Redling, Edward T. "Myth vs. Reality: The Relationship Between Top Executive Pay and Corporate Performance." *Compensation Review* 13 (1981): 16–24.

Reiss, Steven, and Leonard W. Sushinsky. "Overjustification, Competing Responses, and the Acquisition of Intrinsic Interest." *Journal of Personality and Social Psychology* 31 (1975): 1116–25.

Render, Gary F., Je Nell M. Padilla, and H. Mark Krank. "What Research Really Shows About Assertive Discipline." *Educational Leadership,* March 1989: 72–75.

Rich, Jude T., and John A. Larson. "Why Some Long-Term Incentives Fail." In *Incentives, Cooperation, and Risk Sharing,* edited by Haig R. Nalbantian. Totowa, N.J.: Rowman & Littlefield, 1987.

Rodin, Judith, and Ellen J. Langer. "Long-Term Effects of a Control-Relevant Intervention with the Institutionalized Aged." *Journal of Personality and Social Psychology* 35 (1977): 897–902.

Roemer, Joan. "Stars and Bribes Forever." *Parenting,* October 1992: 58, 61.

Rogers, Brenda T. "Cognitive Evaluation Theory: The Effects of External Rewards on Intrinsic Motivation of Gifted Students." *Roeper Review* 7 (1985): 257–60.

Rogers, Carl R., and B. F. Skinner. "Some Issues Concerning the Control of Human Behavior: A Symposium." *Science* 124 (1956): 1057–66.

Rollins, Thomas. "Pay for Performance: The Pros and Cons." *Personnel Journal,* June 1987: 104–11.

Rosemond, John. "When Good Praise Is Bad." *Better Homes and Gardens,* August 1990: 39.

Rosen, Ned. *Teamwork and the Bottom Line: Groups Make a Difference.* Hillsdale, N.J.: Erlbaum, 1989.

Rosenfield, David, Robert Folger, and Harold F. Adelman. "When Rewards Reflect Competence: A Qualification of the Overjustification Effect." *Journal of Personality and Social Psychology* 39 (1980): 368–76.

Rosenholtz, Susan J., and Carl Simpson. "The Formation of Ability Conceptions: Developmental Trend or Social Construction?" *Review of Educational Research* 54 (1984): 31–63.

Ross, Ian Campbell. "Role Specialization in Supervision." *Dissertation Abstracts* 17, 11 (1957): 2701–2.

Ross, Michael. "Salience of Reward and Intrinsic Motivation." *Journal of Personality and Social Psychology* 32 (1975): 245–54.

Rothe, Harold F. "Output Rates Among Welders: Productivity and Consistency Following Removal of a Financial Incentive System." *Journal of Applied Psychology* 54 (1970): 549–51.

Rotter, Julie Ann. "The Effects of Contingency Usage in a Familiar Food Setting on Young Children's Subsequent Food Preferences." M.S. thesis, University of Illinois, Urbana-Champaign, 1982.

Rowe, Mary Budd. "Relation of Wait-Time and Rewards to the Development of Language, Logic, and Fate Control: Part II — Rewards." *Journal of Research in Science Teaching* 11 (1974): 291–308.

Rubin, Zick, and Anne Peplau. "Belief in a Just World and Reactions to Another's Lot: A Study of Participants in the National Draft Lottery." *Journal of Social Issues* 29 (1973): 73–93.

———. "Who Believes in a Just World?" *Journal of Social Issues* 31 (1975): 65–89.

Ryan, Richard M. "Control and Information in the Intrapersonal Sphere: An Extension of Cognitive Evaluation Theory." *Journal of Personality and Social Psychology* 43 (1982): 450–61.

Ryan, Richard M., James P. Connell, and Edward L. Deci. "A Motivational Analysis of Self-Determination and Self-Regulation in Education." In *Research on Motivation in Education*, vol. 2: *The Classroom Milieu*, edited by Carole Ames and Russell Ames. Orlando, Fla.: Academic Press, 1985.

Ryan, Richard M., James P. Connell, and Wendy S. Grolnick. "When Achievement is *Not* Intrinsically Motivated: A Theory of Internalization and Self-Regulation in School." In *Achievement and Motivation: A Social-Developmental Perspective*, edited by Ann K. Boggiano and Thane S. Pittman. Cambridge: Cambridge University Press, 1992.

Ryan, Richard M., and Wendy S. Grolnick. "Origins and Pawns in the Classroom: Self-Report and Projective Assessments of Individual Differences in Children's Perceptions." *Journal of Personality and Social Psychology* 50 (1986): 550–58.

Ryan, Richard M., Richard Koestner, and Edward L. Deci. "Ego-Involved Persistence: When Free-Choice Behavior Is Not Intrinsically Motivated." *Motivation and Emotion* 15 (1991): 185–205.

Ryan, Richard M., Valerie Mims, and Richard Koestner. "Relation of Reward Contingency and Interpersonal Context to Intrinsic Motivation: A Review and Test Using Cognitive Evaluation Theory." *Journal of Personality and Social Psychology* 45 (1983): 736–50.

Ryan, Richard M., and Cynthia L. Powelson. "Autonomy and Relatedness as Fundamental to Motivation and Education." *Journal of Experimental Education* 60 (1991): 49–66.

Ryan, Richard M., and Jerome Stiller. "The Social Contexts of Internalization: Parent and Teacher Influences on Autonomy, Motivation, and Learning." *Advances in Motivation and Achievement* 7 (1991): 115–49.

Sagi, Abraham, and Martin L. Hoffman. "Empathic Distress in the Newborn." *Developmental Psychology* 12 (1976): 175–76.

Samalin, Nancy. *Loving Your Child Is Not Enough: Positive Discipline That Works*. New York: Penguin, 1987.

Sampson, Edward E. "On Justice as Equality." *Journal of Social Issues* 31 (1975): 45–64.

Sansone, Carol, and Carolyn Morgan. "Intrinsic Motivation and Education: Competence in Context." *Motivation and Emotion* 16 (1992): 249–70.

Sansone, Carol, Charlene Weir, Lora Harpster, and Carolyn Morgan. "Once a Boring Task Always a Boring Task? Interest as a Self-Regulatory Mechanism." *Journal of Personality and Social Psychology* 63 (1992): 379–90.

Scholtes, Peter R. *The Team Handbook: How to Use Teams to Improve Quality*. Madison, Wis.: Joiner Associates, 1988.

———. "An Elaboration of Deming's Teachings on Performance Appraisal." In *Performance Appraisal: Perspectives on a Quality Management Approach*, edited by Gary N. McLean, Susan R. Damme, and Richard A. Swanson. Alexandria, Va.: American Society for Training and Development, 1990.

"School Haze." *The New Republic*, 16 December 1991: 7–8.

Schultz, Louis E. "Compensation in a Collaborative Society." In *Performance Appraisal: Perspectives on a Quality Management Approach*, edited by Gary N. McLean, Susan R. Damme, and Richard A. Swanson. Alexandria, Va.: American Society for Training and Development, 1990.

Schulz, Richard. "Effects of Control and Predictability on the Physical and Psychological Well-Being of the Institutionalized Aged." *Journal of Personality and Social Psychology* 33 (1976): 563–73.

Schwartz, Barry. "Failure to Produce Response Variability with Reinforcement." *Journal of the Experimental Analysis of Behavior* 37 (1982a): 171–81.

———. "Reinforcement-Induced Behavioral Stereotypy: How Not to Teach People to Discover Rules." *Journal of Experimental Psychology: General* 111 (1982b): 23–59.

———. *The Battle for Human Nature: Science, Morality, and Modern Life*. New York: Norton, 1986.

———. "The Experimental Synthesis of Behavior: Reinforcement, Behavioral Stereotypy, and Problem Solving." In *The Psychology of Learning and Motivation*, vol. 22, ed. Gordon H. Bower. San Diego: Academic Press, 1988.

———. "The Creation and Destruction of Value." *American Psychologist* 45 (1990a): 7–15.

———. "King Midas in America: Science, Morality, and Modern Life." In *Enriching Business Ethics*, edited by Clarence C. Walton. New York: Plenum, 1990b.

Schwartz, Barry, and Hugh Lacey. *Behaviorism, Science, and Human Nature*. New York: Norton, 1982.

———. "What Applied Studies of Human Operant Conditioning Tell Us About Humans and About Operant Conditioning." In *Human Operant Conditioning and Behavior Modification*, edited by Graham Davey and Chris Cullen. Chichester, England: Wiley, 1988.

Schwartz, Barry, Richard Schuldenfrei, and Hugh Lacey. "Operant Psychology as Factory Psychology." *Behaviorism* 6 (1978): 229–54.

Sears, Robert R., Eleanor E. Maccoby, and Harry Levin. *Patterns of Child Rearing*. Evanston, Ill.: Row, Peterson, 1957.

Seligman, Clive, Russell H. Fazio, and Mark P. Zanna. "Effects of Salience of Extrinsic Rewards on Liking and Loving." *Journal of Personality and Social Psychology* 38 (1980): 453–60.

Sewell, Trevor E., and Roberta H. Walker. "The Effects of Material and Symbolic Incentives on the Learning Ability of Low SES Black Children." *Journal of General Psychology* 106 (1982): 93–99.

Shanker, Albert. "Perestroika for the Classroom." *New Perspectives Quarterly*, Fall 1990: 20–22.

Shapira, Zur. "Expectancy Determinants of Intrinsically Motivated Behavior." *Journal of Personality and Social Psychology* 34 (1976): 1235–44.

Shapiro, E. Gary. "Racial Differences in the Value of Job Rewards." *Social Forces* 56 (1977): 21–30.

Sharan, Shlomo. "Cooperative Learning: Problems and Promise." *The International Association for the Study of Cooperation in Education Newsletter*, December 1986: 3–4.

Sharan, Yael, and Shlomo Sharan. *Expanding Cooperative Learning Through Group Investigation*. New York: Teachers College Press, 1992.

Shevin, Mayer, and Nancy K. Klein. "The Importance of Choice-Making Skills for Students with Severe Disabilities." *Journal of the Association for Persons with Severe Handicaps* 9 (1984): 159–66.

Silberman, Charles E. *Crisis in the Classroom: The Remaking of American Education*. New York: Random House, 1970.

Silverman, Buddy Robert S. "Why the Merit Pay System Failed in the Federal Government." *Personnel Journal*, April 1983: 294–302.

Simmons, John, and William Mares. *Working Together: Employee Participation in Action*. New York: New York University Press, 1985.

Skinner, B. F. *Walden Two*. 1948. Reprint. New York: Macmillan, 1962.

———. *Beyond Freedom and Dignity*. 1971. Reprint. New York: Bantam/Vintage, 1972.

———. *About Behaviorism*. New York: Knopf, 1974.

———. *A Matter of Consequences*. New York: Knopf, 1983.

———. "Can Psychology Be a Science of Mind?" *American Psychologist* 45 (1990): 1206–10.

Slater, Philip. *Wealth Addiction*. New York: Dutton, 1980.

Slavin, Robert E. *Cooperative Learning: Theory, Research, and Practice*. Englewood Cliffs, N.J.: Prentice-Hall, 1990.

———. "Group Rewards Make Groupwork Work: Response to Kohn." *Educational Leadership*, February 1991: 89–91.

Smith, Cathleen L., Donna M. Gelfand, Donald P. Hartmann, and Marjorie E. Y. Partlow. "Children's Causal Attributions Regarding Help Giving." *Child Development* 50 (1979): 203–10.

Smith, Frank. *Insult to Intelligence: The Bureaucratic Invasion of Our Classrooms*. Portsmouth, N.H.: Heinemann, 1986.

Smith, Timothy W., and Thane S. Pittman. "Reward, Distraction, and the Overjustification Effect." *Journal of Personality and Social Psychology* 36 (1978): 565–72.

Smith, Wilson Emerson. "The Effects of Anticipated vs. Unanticipated Social Reward on Subsequent Intrinsic Motivation." *Dissertation Abstracts International* 37B, 2 (1976): 1043–44.

Solomon, Burt. "Power to the People?" *National Journal*, 26 January 1991: 204–9.

Spence, Janet Taylor. "The Distracting Effects of Material Reinforcers in the Discrimination Learning of Lower- and Middle-Class Children." *Child Development* 41 (1970): 95–102.

———. "Do Material Rewards Enhance the Performance of Lower-Class Children?" *Child Development* 42 (1971): 1461–70.

Staub, Ervin. *Positive Social Behavior and Morality*, vol. 1: *Social and Personal Influences*. New York: Academic Press, 1978.

———. *Positive Social Behavior and Morality*, vol. 2: *Socialization and Development*. New York: Academic Press, 1979.

Stayton, Donelda J., Robert Hogan, and Mary D. Salter Ainsworth. "Infant Obedience and Maternal Behavior: The Origins of Socialization Reconsidered." *Child Development* 42 (1971): 1057–69.

Sternberg, Robert J., and Todd I. Lubart. "An Investment Theory of Creativity and Its Development." *Human Development* 34 (1991): 1–31.

Stipek, Deborah J., and Patricia S. Kowalski. "Learned Helplessness in Task-Orienting Versus Performance-Orienting Testing Conditions." *Journal of Educational Psychology* 81 (1989): 384–91.

Strickland, Lloyd H. "Surveillance and Trust." *Journal of Personality* 26 (1958): 200–15.

Stuart, Peggy. "Fresh Ideas Energize Reward Programs." *Personnel Journal*, January 1992: 102–3.

Swann, William B., Jr., and Thane S. Pittman. "Initiating Play Activity of Children: The Moderating Influence of Verbal Cues on Intrinsic Motivation." *Child Development* 48 (1977): 1128–32.

Switzky, Harvey N., and Geoffrey F. Schultz. "Intrinsic Motivation and Learning Performance: Implications for Individual Educational Programming for Learners with Mild Handicaps." *Remedial and Special Education* 9 (1988): 7–14.

Taylor, Frederick Winslow. *The Principles of Scientific Management*. 1911. Reprinted in *Scientific Management*. New York: Harper, 1947.

Taylor, Shelley E. *Positive Illusions: Creative Self-Deception and the Healthy Mind*. New York: Basic Books, 1989.

Terrell, Glenn, Jr., Kathryn Durkin, and Melvin Wiesley. "Social Class and the Nature of the Incentive in Discrimination Learning." *Journal of Abnormal and Social Psychology* 59 (1959): 270–72.

Thomas, John W. "Agency and Achievement: Self-Management and Self-Regard." *Review of Educational Research* 50 (1980): 213–40.

Thompson, Carol E., and Leonard M. Wankel. "The Effects of Perceived Activity Choice upon Frequency of Exercise Behavior." *Journal of Applied Social Psychology* 10 (1980): 436–43.

Thompson, Paul H., and Gene W. Dalton. "Performance Appraisal: Managers Beware." *Harvard Business Review*, January–February 1970: 149–57.

Thompson, Suzanne C. "Will It Hurt Less if I Can Control It? A Complex Answer to a Simple Question." *Psychological Bulletin* 90 (1981): 89–101.

Thorndike, Edward L. *Animal Intelligence: Experimental Studies*. New York: Macmillan, 1911.

———. *The Psychology of Wants, Interests and Attitudes*. New York: Appleton-Century, 1935.

Thorne, Paul. "Fitting Rewards." *International Management*, December 1990: 88.

Tjosvold, Dean. *Working Together to Get Things Done: Managing for Organizational Productivity.* Lexington, Mass.: Lexington Books, 1986.

Toner, Ignatius J. "Punitive and Non-Punitive Discipline and Subsequent Rule-Following in Young Children." *Child Care Quarterly* 15 (1986): 27–37.

Tousignant, Marylou. "Good Grades Yield a Bonus." *Washington Post,* 16 March 1992: A1, A8.

Tuettemann, Elizabeth, and Keith F. Punch. "Teachers' Psychological Distress: The Ameliorating Effects of Control over the Work Environment." *Educational Review* 44 (1992): 181–94.

Uchitelle, Louis. "Bonuses Replace Wage Rises and Workers Are the Losers." *New York Times,* 26 June 1987: A1, D3.

Ullmann, Leonard P., and Leonard Krasner, eds. Introduction to *Case Studies in Behavior Modification.* New York: Holt, Rinehart & Winston, 1965.

Upton, William Edward III. "Altruism, Attribution, and Intrinsic Motivation in the Recruitment of Blood Donors." *Dissertation Abstracts International* 34B, 12 (1974): 6260.

Vallerand, Robert J., and Robert Bissonnette. "Intrinsic, Extrinsic, and Amotivational Styles as Predictors of Behavior: A Prospective Study." *Journal of Personality* 60 (1992): 599–620.

Vasta, Ross, Donna E. Andrews, Ann Marie McLaughlin, Louise A. Stirpe, and Connie Comfort. "Reinforcement Effects on Intrinsic Interest: A Classroom Analog." *Journal of School Psychology* 16 (1978): 161–66.

Vasta, Ross, and Louise A. Stirpe. "Reinforcement Effects on Three Measures of Children's Interest in Math." *Behavior Modification* 3 (1979): 223–44.

Viesti, Carl R., Jr. "Effect of Monetary Rewards on an Insight Learning Task." *Psychonomic Science* 23 (1971): 181–83.

Wachtel, Paul L. *The Poverty of Affluence: A Psychological Portrait of the American Way of Life.* New York: Free Press, 1983.

Wallach, Michael A., and Lise Wallach. *Psychology's Sanction for Selfishness: The Error of Egoism in Theory and Therapy.* San Francisco: Freeman, 1983.

Wallack, Todd. "'Take Me Out to the Library.'" *USA Today,* 15 July 1992: 5D.

Walters, Roy. "Is Giving Incentives a Good Idea? Walters Says No." *Training,* July 1979: A4–5.

Wang, Margaret C., and Billie Stiles. "An Investigation of Children's Concept of Self-Responsibility for Their School Learning." *American Educational Research Journal* 13 (1976): 159–79.

Ward, William C., Nathan Kogan, and Ethel Pankove. "Incentive Effects in Children's Creativity." *Child Development* 43 (1972): 669–76.

Ware, Barbara Ann. "What Rewards Do Students Want?" *Phi Delta Kappan,* January 1978: 355–56.

Wassermann, Selma. "Children Working in Groups? It Doesn't Work!" *Childhood Education,* Summer 1989: 201–205.

Watson, Goodwin. "Work Satisfaction." In *Industrial Conflict: A Psychological Interpretation,* edited by George W. Hartmann and Theodore Newcomb. New York: Cordon, 1939.

Watson, John B. *Psychological Care of Infant and Child.* New York: Norton, 1928.

———. *Behaviorism.* Rev. ed. Chicago: University of Chicago Press, 1930.

Watson, Malcolm W., and Ying Peng. "The Relation Between Toy Gun Play and Children's Aggressive Behavior." *Early Education and Development.* In press.

Watson, Marilyn. "Classroom Control: To What Ends? At What Price?" *California Journal of Teacher Education* 9 (1982): 75–95.

Weick, Karl E. "Reduction of Cognitive Dissonance Through Task Enhancement and Effort Expenditure." *Journal of Abnormal and Social Psychology* 68 (1964): 533–39.

Weiner, Michael Jay, and Anthony M. Mander. "The Effects of Reward and Perception of Competency upon Intrinsic Motivation." *Motivation and Emotion* 2 (1978): 67–73.

Weissman, Rozanne. "Merit Pay — What Merit?" *Education Digest,* May 1969: 16–19.

Whitaker, Kathryn S., and Monte C. Moses. "Does Learning Theory Influence Teaching Practices?" *European Journal of Teacher Education* 11 (1989): 143–46.

White, Geoffry D., Gary Nielsen, and Stephen M. Johnson. "Timeout Duration and the Suppression of Deviant Behavior in Children." *Journal of Applied Behavior Analysis* 5 (1972): 111–20.

White, Kinnard, and David Owen. "Locus of Evaluation for Classroom Work and the Development of Creative Potential." *Psychology in the Schools* 7 (1970): 292–95.

White, Ralph, and Ronald Lippitt. "Leader Behavior and Member Reaction in Three 'Social Climates.'" In *Group Dynamics: Research and Theory,* edited by Dorwin Cartwright and Alvin Zander. Evanston, Ill.: Row, Peterson, 1960.

Whyte, William Foote. *Money and Motivation: An Analysis of Incentives in Industry.* New York: Harper, 1955.

————. "Worker Participation: International and Historical Perspectives." *Journal of Applied Behavioral Science* 19 (1983): 395–407.

Wicker, Frank W., Gail Brown, and Vicente Paredes. "Competing Activities and Measures of Intrinsic Motivation." *Journal of Social Psychology* 130 (1990): 813–19.

Wild, T. Cameron, Michael E. Enzle, and Wendy L. Hawkins. "Effects of Perceived Extrinsic Versus Intrinsic Teacher Motivation on Student Reactions to Skill Acquisition." *Personality and Social Psychology Bulletin* 18 (1992): 245–51.

Winett, Richard A., and Robin C. Winkler. "Current Behavior Modification in the Classroom: Be Still, Be Quiet, Be Docile." *Journal of Applied Behavior Analysis* 5 (1972): 499–504.

Winstanley, Nathan B. "Are Merit Increases Really Effective?" *Personnel Administrator,* April 1982: 37–41.

Wlodkowski, Raymond J., and Judith H. Jaynes. *Eager to Learn.* San Francisco: Jossey-Bass, 1990.

Wolfgang, Charles H., and Gerry Brudenell. "The Many Faces of Praise." *Early Child Development and Care* 9 (1982): 237–43.

"Wyeth Feared Public Reaction." *Boston Globe* (Associated Press), 11 August 1986: 19.

Yackel, Erna, Paul Cobb, and Terry Wood. "Small-Group Interactions as a Source of Learning Opportunities in Second-Grade Mathematics." *Journal for Research in Mathematics Education* 22 (1991): 390–408.

Zaslowsky, Dyan. "Denver Program Curbs Teen-Agers' Pregnancy." *New York Times,* 16 January 1989: A8.

Zeldow, Peter B. "Some Antitherapeutic Effects of the Token Economy: A Case in Point." *Psychiatry* 39 (1976): 318–24.

Zimmerman, Barry J. "The Development of 'Intrinsic' Motivation: A Social Learning Analysis." In *Annals of Child Development,* vol. 2, edited by Grover J. Whitehurst. Greenwich, Conn.: JAI Press, 1985.

Zubin, Joseph. *Some Effects of Incentives.* New York: Teachers College, 1932.

Zuckerman, Miron, Joseph Porac, Drew Lathin, Raymond Smith, and Edward L. Deci. "On the Importance of Self-Determination for Intrinsically-Motivated Behavior." *Personality and Social Psychology Bulletin* 4 (1978): 443–46.

NAME INDEX

SUBJECT INDEX

justifications for, 201–3, 210
minimizing harms of, 206–10,
337n5
perceived significance of, 158, 200,
202, 204–6
and performance orientation, 202–3
rewards for, 11, 138, 207
student involvement in determining,
209
uninformative nature of, 201–2
as unnecessary for college admission, 210, 339n27
used to sort students, 201–2
Group Investigation, 343n76

Head Start, 70
Hierarchy in organizations, 184, 196,
202, 336n54
Hyperactivity, effect of rewards on,
154

Ignoring behavior, 329n20
Immunization against effects of
rewards, 94
Incentives. *See also* Rewards
to businesses, 123n
to employees. *See* Pay for performance
to welfare recipients, 61
Incidental learning, 62–63, 64
Informational feedback
and performance orientation, 156–
57, 211
vs. praise, 96, 107–8, 109n, 110,
310n52
productive response to, 211,
321n12
from rewards, 78–79
usefulness of, 107–8, 187, 211
without rewards, 86, 185–86, 202,
211, 275
Interest. *See also* Intrinsic motivation
effect of rewards on, 69–95
effect of various controlling strategies on, 79–81, 86
Internalization of rules and values,
250–52, 273–74, 327n5,
333n26
Intrinsic motivation
behaviorists' denial of, 270, 283
definitions of, 68, 270–72, 276

as goal in itself, 147
as individualistic concept, 274–75
as irrelevant to certain goals, 273–
74
lack of desire to promote, by managers, 333n26
to learn, 144–48, 217–21
limits of contrast between extrinsic
motivation and, 274–75,
300n19, 349n7
and meaningfulness of work, 189,
275
measurement of, 272–73
vs. persistence at task, 101, 273,
281
as positive affect, 300–301n25,
349n3
and process-product distinction,
275–76, 350n18
promotion of, 90–92, 94, 138, 200,
207, 211, 213
relation to achievement, 68–69,
144–47, 321n12
relation to informational feedback,
107–8, 339n31
relation to self-determination, 79,
90, 91, 192–93, 271, 306n102
vs. reported satisfaction, 298n1
social context of, 189, 192, 275
as undermined by:
controlling strategies, 150–51
performance orientation, 157–59
praise, 99–101, 107
rewards, 69–95, 148, 175, 281–
84

"Just world" phenomenon, 20

Kefir study, 72, 77

Law of Effect, 4, 311n5
Learnfare, 296n27
Learning
active, 211–12
behaviorist model of, 213–14, 279–
80
constructivist model of, 219, 222,
223, 279–80, 297n45
cooperative, 54, 214–16, 223, 246,
340n42
as discovery, 211–13

Rewards *(cont.)*
    to improve performance at work, 12–13, 120–22
    to promote learning at school, 11, 143, 153
    as punitive or similar to punishment, 26, 50–54, 58, 59, 135–36, 173, 174–76
    qualitative vs. quantitative criteria for, 85
    qualitative vs. quantitative effects of, 44, 46, 124
    reasons for ineffectiveness of, 49–76, 126–41
    reasons for negative effect on interest, 76–79, 140, 148, 300–301n25
    reasons for popularity of, 13–18, 60, 162–64
    vs. reinforcements, 5, 280, 285n4
    and risk-taking, 62–67, 99, 139–40, 174n
    salience of, 92
    self-administered, 84–85
    as self-perpetuating, 17, 26n, 83–84, 141, 150–51
    in special education programs, 153–55, 325n64
    as substitutes for analysis and problem-solving, 59–62, 138–39, 175
    success of, at producing compliance, 15–16, 41, 160, 162, 179–80
    symbolic vs. tangible, 282–83
    temporary use of, 82–83
    use of, to promote choice, 196
    withdrawn or withheld, 52–53, 136, 174–75
    as worse than doing nothing, 39, 40, 162, 175, 180
Risk-taking, rewards and, 62–67, 99, 139–40, 174n
Rules for children
    creation of, by adults alone vs. with children, 33, 165, 236, 247, 250, 252–53
    disadvantages of listing, 164, 171
    expectation of blind conformity to, 162, 165, 249
    explaining justification for, 236
    internalization of, 250–52, 273–74, 327n5

punishment for breaking, 167–68, 231
questioning reasonableness of, 229–30, 234–35
relationship between child and adult who enforces, 57–59, 167

Safety. *See* Fear: vs. safety for children
Salience of rewards or praise, 92, 100–101
School. *See also* Control: in education; Curriculum, quality of; Grades; Learning; Teaching
    "back to basics" movement in, 115n, 326n82, 327–28n14
    business goals and models in, 322n20, 322–23n29, 336–37n1
    caring communities in, 245–47, 340n43
    competition in, 93, 151, 157, 209, 214, 220, 226
    cooperation in, 54, 214–16, 243
    emphasis on control vs. choice in, 163–65, 250, 253
    incentives for attendance, 61
    influence of behaviorism in, 213–14, 327–28n14
    punishment in, 165–66, 232n
    rewards in, 11, 65–66, 74, 82, 83–84, 89–91, 143, 151n, 153–54, 173–76
    strategies for promotion of positive values in, 239–48
Scientism, 9–10
Seat belt use, use of rewards to promote, 40–41
Self-centeredness. *See also* Generosity
    as outcome of punitive consequences, 172–73
Self-determination. *See also* Choice; Control
    denial of, by behaviorists, 84, 289n19
    effect of rewards on, 78–79, 90, 154–55, 162
    effect of various controlling practices on, 79–81, 91, 150, 169, 170n
    and evaluation, 194, 209
    illusory sense of, 195, 254–55

and interest level of task, 305*n*82, 306*n*96

lack of, by managers, 333*n*26

need for, 78, 191, 192–93, 248–50, 274

and praise vs. encouragement, 96, 106–7

promotion of, 90, 96, 193–97, 223–24, 250–52

resistance to, 253–54

trend toward emphasis on, in parenting, 254*n*

Self-esteem, 102, 115

Self-fulfilling prophecy

assumptions about children's motives as, 242–43

use of rewards as, 17, 26*n*, 83–84, 141

Self-interest, 15, 242, 287*n*26

Sex differences. *See* Gender differences

Smoking cessation

importance of self-determination in, 347*n*37

use of rewards to promote, 40

Social class

effects of praise and, 308*n*33

effects of rewards and, 75–76, 331*n*44

Special education, 153–55, 325*n*64

Spoiling, fear of, 114–16, 240

Surveillance, 79, 81

Symptom substitution, 60

Teaching. *See also* Learning; School

and beliefs about students' motives, 324*n*52

and choices for students, 221–26, 250, 253

constructivist model of, 219, 223, 279–80, 297*n*45

and creation of caring communities, 245–47

and demand for quiet, 213–15, 327*n*8

effects of controlling strategies on, 153, 159, 163, 221, 346*n*36

and emphasis on grades, 200, 205–10

high-quality, effect of extrinsic discipline system on, 328*n*14

motivation for, students' beliefs about, 153

vs. parenting, 163

of perspective taking, 245

use of controlling strategies in, 163–65, 221, 328*n*14

use of cooperation vs. competition in, 214–16, 243

use of feedback in, 309*n*42

use of rewards to improve, 44, 126, 143

and value of what is taught, 215–21, 225–26

"Team player," meaning of, 188*n*

Teamwork. *See* Cooperation

Tests. *See also* Evaluation

lack of need for in school, 203

relation to learning, 157, 200

standardized:

effects of, on curriculum, 217, 337*n*11

pressures associated with, 159

scores on, of extrinsically oriented students, 45

scores on, of students given choices, 223, 342–43*n*72

use of, as reflection of behaviorism, 213–14

timing of, 208

use of, to coerce student effort, 83–84, 149, 208

Theories X and Y, 121, 333*n*17

Threats, 79, 170–71. *See also* Punishment

"Time out" tactic with children, 328*n*17

Token economies, 5*n*, 27, 38–39, 138

Total Quality Management (TQM)

and abolition of pay for performance, 183

and difference between workplace and school, 336–37*n*1

and participatory management, 335*n*44

use of rewards to promote, 122

Values. *See* Children: values of

Violence. *See* Aggression

Voting, reasons to avoid, 249, 347*n*45